English Language Education

Volume 49

Series Editor

Xuesong Gao, School of Education, The University of New South Wales, Sydney, Australia

This series publishes research on the development, implementation and evaluation of educational programs for school-aged and adult learners for whom English is a second or additional language, including those who are learning academic content through the medium of English. The series has a dual focus on learners' language development and broader societal and policy-related issues, including the implications for teachers' professional development and policy support at the institutional and system level. The series seeks to engage with current issues in English language teaching (ELT) in educational institutions from a highly situated standpoint, examining theories, practices and policies with a conscious regard for historical lineages of development and local (re)contextualisation. By focusing on multiple educational contexts and adopting a comparative perspective, the series will transcend traditional geographical boundaries, thus will be relevant to both English-speaking countries and countries where English is a very much an additional, but important language for learning other content. This series will also cross disciplinary and methodological boundaries by integrating sociocultural and critical approaches with second language acquisition perspectives and drawing on both applied linguistics and educational research. In drawing together basic and applied policy-related research concerns, the series will contribute towards developing a more comprehensive, innovative and contextualized view of English language education internationally. Authors are invited to approach the Series Editor with ideas and plans for books.

Ferdi Çelik · Ceylan Yangın Ersanlı
Editors

Metaverse-Based Language Learning and Teaching

Innovative, Immersive Approaches and Future Directions

Springer

Editors
Ferdi Çelik
Eğitim Fakültesi
Ondokuz Mayıs Üniversitesi
Atakum, Samsun, Türkiye

Ceylan Yangın Ersanlı
Eğitim Fakültesi
Ondokuz Mayıs Üniversitesi
Atakum, Samsun, Türkiye

ISSN 2213-6967 ISSN 2213-6975 (electronic)
English Language Education
ISBN 978-3-032-31365-2 ISBN 978-3-032-31366-9 (eBook)
https://doi.org/10.1007/978-3-032-31366-9

This Springer imprint is published by the registered company Springer Nature Switzerland AG
The registered company address is: Gewerbestrasse 11, 6330 Cham, Switzerland

This book is dedicated to language educators, researchers, and learners who continue to reimagine the boundaries of teaching and learning in an era of rapid technological developments. It honors those who approach emerging immersive environments not as ends in themselves, but as spaces for critical inquiry, reflection, and meaningful social interaction. We also dedicate this work to future generations of teachers and scholars whose curiosity, creativity, and responsibility will shape more effective, inclusive and reflective metaverse-based language learning ecologies.

Foreword

Opportunities and challenges of the metaverse in language teaching and learning

Education is entering a new milestone due to the advances of immersive technologies, advanced digital platforms, and pedagogical innovation. This emerging era is opening new possibilities for redesigning language teaching and learning. At this important moment, this book offers a comprehensive examination of metaverse-based language teaching and learning while also providing a careful critique of its educational promise, assumptions, and constraints.

The metaverse is more than a technological novelty or a passing trend in educational technology. Properly understood, it signals a shift in how learners may engage with language, culture, and communication through embodied, interactive, and socially situated experiences. Immersive virtual worlds can afford forms of contextualized practice that are difficult to realize in traditional classrooms or earlier models of computer-assisted language learning, such as simulating communicative settings, adopting roles and identities, collaborating with geographically distributed peers in real time, and rehearsing language use in complex, dynamic contexts. Yet the central insight of this book is refreshingly clear: technology does not transform education by itself. The educational value of metaverse environments depends on how thoughtfully they are aligned with pedagogical goals, how responsibly they are implemented, and how critically they are evaluated.

Accordingly, this book challenges readers to confront questions that are as consequential as they are timely. How might established theories of second language acquisition (e.g., interactionist, cognitive, and sociocultural) be extended or reinterpreted in immersive environments characterized by presence, embodiment, and real-time social exchange? What ethical issues emerge when learning becomes increasingly immersive and data-intensive, and when platform design shapes participation, visibility, and agency? How can educators and institutions ensure that innovation expands opportunity rather than reinforcing inequity through unequal access, differential digital readiness, or hidden costs? These questions do not lend themselves to simple answers, and the strength of this book lies in its commitment to addressing them with intellectual rigor and practical wisdom.

The organization of the book supports that ambition. The foundational chapters clarify key concepts and map the technological landscape, offering readers a grounded understanding of platforms, tools, and the conditions that shape their educational use. The chapters on theory bring metaverse environments into dialogue with established second language acquisition (SLA) frameworks, helping the field avoid technological determinism while still recognizing that immersive contexts may introduce new variables and affordances worth theorizing. The practical section then translates these ideas into actionable guidance, including "how to design immersive learning environments," "how to support speaking, listening, reading, and writing development through metaverse-based activities," and "how to rethink assessment in ways that capture performance, interaction, and growth over time." Especially valuable is the attention to concrete design principles, evidence-informed interventions, and evaluation approaches that are plausible in real classrooms rather than idealized demonstrations.

Just as importantly, the book foregrounds dimensions that are sometimes treated as secondary in technology-driven discussions but are central to responsible implementation: socio-emotional dynamics, ethics, privacy, accessibility, and sustainability. Immersive environments can support engagement, belonging, and identity exploration; they can also intensify anxiety, isolation, or exclusion when participation norms, representation, or interactional pressures are poorly managed. Likewise, data governance, surveillance risks, algorithmic opacity, and accessibility barriers raise urgent questions for educators and policymakers. By treating these concerns as integral rather than peripheral, the book models a stance that is both forward-looking and ethically grounded. The final section extends this orientation by examining emerging trends, including developments in AI, augmented and mixed reality, and adaptive learning. It also articulates a research agenda that identifies gaps, methodological needs, and promising directions for the next phase of scholarship.

As readers engage with this volume, they are invited to approach it not only as a guide to implementing new technologies, but also as a prompt to reconsider what language education can become in immersive environments. The chapters illustrate how virtual-world experiences can enable learning designs that are authentic, interactive, and responsive to learners' diverse goals and contexts. At the same time, sustained attention is needed for the moral and institutional dimensions of decision-making, including questions of inclusion, privacy, transparency, sustainability, and the long-term implications of delegating pedagogical functions to platforms. The metaverse may expand what is possible for language teaching and learning, but it also demands renewed clarity about what matters most educationally.

This book is valuable to multiple audiences. Classroom teachers exploring immersive approaches will find design guidance and pedagogical strategies that can be adapted to local realities. Researchers will find conceptual frameworks and lines of inquiry that connect metaverse affordances with SLA theory, learning sciences, and educational psychology. Administrators and policymakers will find discussions that can inform responsible investment, infrastructure planning, and governance. Graduate students and emerging scholars will find a structured introduction to the field and a roadmap of critical issues that merit sustained investigation.

Language education has always evolved through debate, adaptation, and a commitment to helping learners bridge language and culture. Metaverse-based language teaching is the latest chapter in that ongoing history, one with genuine promise, significant risks, and many unanswered questions. This volume makes a timely and substantive contribution to the conversation by balancing innovation with critique, and possibility with responsibility. In doing so, it offers readers not only practical tools, but also a principled orientation for navigating the future of language teaching wisely, purposefully, and with care.

Gwo-Jen Hwang, Ph.D.,
Chair Professor/Vice President,
Graduate Institute of Education
Measurement and Statistics,
National Taichung University of Education,
Taichung City, Taiwan,

Chair Professor,
Graduate Institute of Digital Learning
and Education,
National Taiwan University of Science
and Technology,
Taipei city, Taiwan

Preface

Metaverse and immersive technologies are increasingly being promoted as the next frontier of education; however, most language teachers still view them primarily in promotional videos, conference keynotes, or isolated pilot projects. Between the hype and the hesitation lies a simple problem: we do not have a coherent account of what exactly it means to teach and learn a language in metaverse environments, and what is at stake in pedagogical, social, and ethical aspects when we try. This book has been written to address this gap.

Rather than celebrating immersive technologies for their own sake, or opposing them on principle, the volume poses a more demanding set of questions: How do these immersive, persistent, and social spaces alter what it means to practice a language? What new opportunities for learner interaction do these environments make possible, and at what cost? How can metaverse platforms genuinely unpack new prospects for teaching languages? We believe that language education cannot afford to overlook these questions, as metaverse environments, especially game-based ones, are already influencing the way young people play and communicate. If language teachers and researchers do not get involved in the design and critique of these environments, others will make these decisions for us, guided more by engagement and business models than by learning, equity, and human development. This volume is, therefore, not a promotion of metaverse-based learning, but an invitation to take it seriously—conceptually, empirically, and practically.

The chapters collected in this book were written with two purposes in mind. The first is that of conceptual clarity. The metaverse has become one of the most overused and underspecified terms in educational technology discourse in a remarkably short amount of time. The book makes no attempt to assign a single, discrete meaning. Instead, it charts the convergence and divergence of different strands of research and practice, with a specific focus on language learning and teaching. Readers will find a careful examination of affordances and constraints. The second goal is pedagogical depth. Many accounts of metaverse technologies in education stop at the level of tools, platforms, and demonstrations. This book focuses on the integration of immersive environments into language classrooms and their relationship to existing theories of second language acquisition.

It is important to acknowledge that metaverse-based language teaching and learning is still an emerging field. Rather than presenting definitive answers, the book aims to encourage rigorous, evidence-based implementation grounded in sound pedagogical principles. Thus, readers will notice that chapters explicitly acknowledge the developing empirical base for metaverse-based language learning and identify important areas for future research. The volume also draws on established theories of second language acquisition and pedagogical research to inform future research while discussing both the promise and the limitations of current metaverse applications for language learning.

This book is written for several overlapping audiences. It is intended firstly for language teachers who are curious, cautious, or conflicted about the metaverse technologies and who want more than marketing claims. They will discover concrete pedagogical implications, classroom practices, and design principles which can be adapted to different levels and contexts, from primary education to higher education and adult learning. Teacher educators will find resources to help pre-service and in-service educators think critically and creatively about immersive technologies. The volume is also intended for researchers specializing in applied linguistics and educational technology who are interested in investigating language learning in immersive environments, as the chapters provide suggestions, research agendas, and examples of empirical work that can serve as starting points for further investigation. For graduate students, the book can serve as a starting point for entry into a fast-growing field of immersive technologies, raising interesting questions, theoretical tensions, and unexplored areas. Finally, the book has a message for those involved in the design, development, and policy of immersive learning environments.

We are greatly indebted to the authors who generously shared their time, expertise, and, in many cases, the hard-won lessons from classroom experimentation and research design. We also express our gratitude to the reviewers who gave critical comments on earlier drafts of the chapters, which helped to sharpen the arguments. Finally, we owe the greatest debt to the learners and teachers who agreed to step into unfamiliar immersive environments and allow their experiences to be observed, recorded, and analyzed. Their curiosity and creativity are the real source of this book.

Atakum, Türkiye

Ferdi Çelik
Ceylan Yangın Ersanlı

Acknowledgments

The editors would like to express their sincere gratitude to all those whose intellectual, professional, and institutional contributions made this volume possible. First and foremost, we thank the contributing authors for their scholarly commitment, rigor, and willingness to engage critically with the pedagogical, psychological, and ethical implications of metaverse-based language teaching and learning. Their chapters demonstrate both theoretical depth and methodological diversity, significantly advancing current debates at the intersection of immersive technologies and language education.

We are also grateful to the reviewers whose careful, constructive, and timely feedback strengthened the academic quality, coherence, and clarity of the chapters. Their insights were instrumental in refining arguments, enhancing methodological transparency, and ensuring that the volume meets high scholarly standards.

We extend our appreciation to the editorial and production teams for their professionalism, responsiveness, and support throughout the development of the book. Their guidance at each stage, from proposal to final manuscript, was invaluable in bringing this project to completion.

Finally, we acknowledge the scholarly community of language education researchers, teacher educators, and practitioners whose ongoing work on immersive learning environments provided the intellectual context and motivation for this volume. It is our hope that this book will make a meaningful contribution to this evolving field and inspire further research, dialogue, and pedagogical practice in metaverse-based language teaching and learning.

Contents

Contributors

Hassan Abuhassna Faculty of Social Sciences and Liberal Arts, UCSI University, Kuala Lumpur, Malaysia

Nur Aeni Universitas Negeri Makassar, Makassar, Indonesia

Zuraina Ali Department of English, Universiti Malaysia Pahang Al-Sultan Abdullah (UMPSA), Pekan, Malaysia

Mehrasa Alizadeh Otemon Gakuin University, Ibaraki, Osaka, Japan

Hayriye Avara Amasya University, Amasya, Türkiye

Hamed Barjesteh Department of English Language, Am.C., Islamic Azad University, Amol, Iran

Yaşar Barut Ondokuz Mayıs University, Samsun, Türkiye

Fidel Çakmak Department of Foreign Language Education, Alanya Alaaddin Keykubat University, Antalya, Türkiye

Ferdi Çelik Ondokuz Mayıs University, Samsun, Türkiye

Neil Cowie English Language Academy, University of Auckland, Auckland, New Zealand

Besse Darmawati Badan Riset dan Inovasi Nasional, Jakarta, Indonesia

Volkan Duran Psychology Department, Turkey: Iğdır University, Iğdır, Turkey

Gonca Yangın Ekşi Gazi University, Ankara, Türkiye

Ceylan Yangın Ersanlı Ondokuz Mayıs University, Samsun, Türkiye

Roberto Figueroa Jr. University of the Philippines—Open University, Laguna, Philippines

R. Adline Freeda KCG College of Technology, Karapakam, Chennai, India

Nikan Fujii Bukkyo University, Kyoto, Japan

Aya Fukuda Tokyo University of Foreign Studies, Tokyo, Japan

Seçil Büyükbay İpekçi Social Sciences University of Ankara, Ankara, Türkiye

Nur Izzati Khairuddin INTI International University, Nilai, Malaysia

Muthmainnah Muthmainnah Universitas Al Asyariah Mandar, Sulawesi, Indonesia

Ehsan Namaziandost Department of English, Islamic Azad University of Ahvaz, Ahvaz, Iran

Selvi Panggua Universitas Kristen Indonesia, Toraja, Indonesia

Pan Qi School of Foreign Languages, Zao Zhuang University, Zao Zhuang, China

Kumutha Raman INTI International University, Nilai, Malaysia

Neda Fatehi Rad Department of English Language, Ke.C., Islamic Azad University, Kerman, Iran

Shaghayegh Shirzad Eiman Narimani Marketing Management Co. L. L.C., Dubai, UAE

Ayfer Su-Bergil Amasya University, Amasya, Türkiye

V. S. Krithikaa Venket KCG College of Technology, Karapakam, Chennai, India

Wei Lun Wong Faculty of Education, Universiti Kebangsaan Malaysia, Bangi, Malaysia

Muhammad Yunus Universitas Muslim Indonesia, Makassar, Indonesia

Abbreviations

AI	Artificial Intelligence
AR	Augmented Reality
CALL	Computer-Assisted Language Learning
COIL	Collaborative Online International Learning
CSs	Communication Strategies
EFL	English as a Foreign Language
ELT	English Language Teaching
ESL	English as a Second Language
XR	Extended Reality
4th IR	Fourth Industrial Revolution
ICT	Information and Communication Technology
IoT	Internet of Things
L2	Second Language
LMS	Learning-Management Systems
MALL	Mobile-Assisted Language Learning
MBLL	Metaverse-Based Language Learning
MBLT	Metaverse-Based Language Teaching
MBLTL	Metaverse-Based Language Teaching and Learning
MUVEs	Multi-User Virtual Environments
PRISMA	Preferred Reporting Items for Systematic Reviews and Meta-Analyses
SDG	Sustainable Development Goal
SDT	Self-Determination Theory
SLA	Second Language Acquisition
TBLT	Task-Based Language Teaching
3DoF	Three Degrees of Freedom
6DoF	Six Degrees of Freedom
VEs	Virtual Environments
VR	Virtual Reality

Foundations of Metaverse-Based Language Teaching and Learning

Introduction to Metaverse-Based Language Teaching and Learning

Ferdi Çelik and Ceylan Yangın Ersanlı

Abstract The chapter theoretically introduces metaverse-based language teaching and learning as a dynamic constellation of environments and practices that expands the trajectory of computer-based learning from text-based networked interaction into graphically rich, embodied, and socially mediated virtual worlds, while also indicating a shift in the way presence, place, and participation are orchestrated pedagogically. Based on sociocultural theory, communities of practice, interactionist approaches to second language acquisition, and ecological approaches to affordances, the chapter argues that the educational value of learning and teaching in the metaverse is contingent and relational in nature, and it varies with the alignment of environmental affordances, task design, facilitation, and capabilities and purposes of learners. The chapter also describes the important promises and limitations of the metaverse for language learning, such as authenticity through situated action, extended interactional resources, global connectivity, and new forms of personalization, as well as risks, including inequitable access, cognitive overload, platform volatility, privacy issues, and the non-automaticity of interaction. The chapter concludes by positioning theory-based, ethics-based, and institutionally supported design-oriented pragmatism as a justifiable approach to promoting metaverse-based language pedagogy as a rigorous subfield of computer-assisted language learning.

Keywords Metaverse-based language teaching and learning · Computer-assisted language learning · Virtual worlds · Social presence · Interaction and negotiation of meaning · Ecological affordances

F. Çelik (✉) · C. Yangın Ersanlı
Ondokuz Mayıs University, Samsun, Türkiye
e-mail: Ferdicelik99@gmail.com

F. Çelik and C. Yangın Ersanlı (eds.), *Metaverse-Based Language Learning and Teaching*, English Language Education 49,
https://doi.org/10.1007/978-3-032-31366-9_1

1 Introduction

The fast emergence of digital technologies has transformed the ecology of language education by increasing the possibilities of where, when, and with whom learning can take place, as well as anticipating designs of pedagogy that are not tied to the physical classroom. Among the wider context of digitally mediated language learning, a new paradigm of language teaching and learning, which can be referred to as metaverse-based language teaching and learning (MBLTL), has become a phenomenon that integrates immersive technologies for socially situated interaction to provide learning conditions that, at least theoretically, are closer to the communicative, contextual, and identity-mediated nature of language use in and outside the classroom (Tlili et al., 2022; Wang et al., 2022). MBLTL is not discussed in this chapter as a platform or tool, but as a dynamic constellation of environments and practices that allow learners to interact in real-time in three-dimensional digital spaces, communicate in pairs and groups, and make meaning in a culturally oriented manner (Lee et al., 2024; Mystakidis, 2022). In this perspective, the pedagogical value of MBLTL should not be reduced to novelty or technological spectacle, yet it should be seen as an opportunity to redesign participation, presence, and situated action in such a way that a new theorization of the organization, support, and evaluation of language learning becomes possible in technologically dense digital learning ecologies (van Lier, 2004; Wang & Vasquez, 2012).

Despite its origins in the 1992 science fiction novel Snow Crash by Stephenson, the term is used by scholars to describe the metaverse as an ecosystem, which is interoperable, and synchronously interacting and facilitated by converging technologies, including virtual reality, augmented reality, and artificial intelligence (Lee et al., 2024; Park & Kim, 2022). The metaverse can be conceptualized as an educational metaverse, a convergent and hyper-spatiotemporal digital ecosystem that enables multiple learners to experience immersive learning through the use of avatars in persistent virtual worlds (Mystakidis, 2022), therefore, predicting immersion, persistence, and social interaction as key defining dimensions (Park & Kim, 2022). These features of the metaverse are especially relevant to language education since they are consistent with long-term objectives of language pedagogy, such as the sustained exposure to meaningful input, the possibility of interaction and negotiation of meaning, and the establishment of social spaces in which learners can perform identities and build repertoires through participation (Long, 1996; Wenger, 1999). Meanwhile, the increasing policy and research interest in metaverse-in-education is a sign of both excitement regarding new affordances of learning and anxiety about the practical and ethical challenges of implementation that require scholarship that examines opportunities, challenges, and future research directions as opposed to assuming that they all work equally (Lin et al., 2022; Tlili et al., 2022). This definition distinguishes metaverse-based learning from other immersive technologies such as single-player VR simulations or desktop 3D environments by emphasizing the persistent, multi-user, and spatially organized nature of communication.

In language education, specifically, it is essential to recognize that the term 'metaverse' does not refer solely to fully immersive headset-based VR experiences. It also encompasses multi-user virtual environments (MUVEs) and 3D social platforms that can be accessed through desktop computers or mobile devices, such as Second Life, Mozilla Hubs, Spatial, as well as HMD-based VR platforms and purpose-built educational solutions (Jovanović & Milosavljević, 2022). From a pedagogical perspective, the defining feature is not the device but the emergence of socially shared spaces in which communication becomes spatially and materially organized. For instance, in the metaverse, learners do not just exchange messages, but communicate while moving through places, manipulating digital objects, and coordinating attention in contexts designed to simulate, stylize, or reimagine real-world settings (Lan, 2020; Sykes et al., 2019). This is also where the idea of third places becomes relevant. Building on the notion that informal social spaces can foster community building and low-stakes participation, metaverse environments can function as third places for language learners, providing contexts in which communication feels less evaluative and more exploratory, and in which learners can experiment with linguistic identities and interactional styles without the full weight of classroom pressure (Bonner & Reinders, 2018; Wehner et al., 2011). Such spaces are not automatically emancipatory, and they can reproduce exclusion if access is unequal or norms are poorly managed. However, the pedagogical appeal of metaverse environments rests on the possibility of designing social architectures that make participation more frequent, more distributed, and more meaningful than what many classrooms can sustain within limited time and institutional constraints (Stockwell, 2013). While recognizing that the metaverse as a concept is still evolving and contested across disciplines, the following operational definition is used in this volume: MBLTL is a pedagogical approach situated within the field of computer-assisted language learning that utilizes persistent, multi-user, spatially organized digital environments—accessible via desktop, mobile, and devices with immersive interfaces connected to the internet—in which learners, represented through avatars, engage in real-time, socially situated communication and collaborative activities. MBLTL is characterized by the integration of co-presence, embodied interaction, and environmental affordances that mediate meaning-making, and is realized through the principled alignment of task design, facilitation, and learner participation. In this respect, MBLTL is analytically differentiated from other immersive technologies by its emphasis on sustained social interaction within shared digital spaces.

A helpful way to understand MBLTL is to situate it historically within the longer trajectory of computer-assisted language learning (CALL), particularly the evolution from text-based interaction to graphically rich, embodied, and socially mediated environments (Warschauer, 2000). Early forms of virtual-environment language learning can be traced back to text-based multi-user dungeons (MUDs) and object-oriented MUDs (MOOs), which gained pedagogical visibility in the 1990s within the Communicative CALL era. These systems were text-based, yet they enabled learners to inhabit virtual rooms, interact with objects, and communicate with others through typed commands and messages, thereby providing a sense of place and co-presence through language itself (Schwienhorst, 2002). Projects such as schMOOze

University, developed with the explicit purpose of supporting English language learning, demonstrated that even text-only environments could support authentic communication and intercultural exchange among geographically dispersed learners (von der Emde et al., 2001). Importantly, early research suggested that computer-mediated communication could redistribute participation patterns. For example, Warschauer (1995) compared face-to-face and electronic discussions, arguing that online interaction could facilitate more equitable participation, with quieter students contributing more frequently than in conventional classroom discourse. In retrospect, this participation effect can be seen as an early articulation of a principle that continues to animate MBLTL: digital spaces can reconfigure interactional norms and lower specific social barriers, even as they introduce new forms of constraint and stratification.

The second significant change was the emergence of graphical virtual worlds, most notably Second Life, which was released in 2003 within the Integrative CALL era. Second Life presented a three-dimensional environment that was visually immersive, allowing users to create avatars, develop environments, and interact through both text and voice. These features enabled learning institutions to create virtual campuses and language learning centers (Deutschmann et al., 2009). It was important to language educators, as the setting could be created to facilitate situated, role-based communication, such as simulated cafes for informal conversation practice or structured situational communication to practice professional and academic discourse. These environments reinforced a core insight of integrative CALL: pedagogical effectiveness depends less on technological sophistication than on the alignment between environmental affordances, task design, and instructional mediation. Empirical research has indicated that these environments may facilitate interactional competence by promoting synchronous and communication activities, as well as providing visual and contextual information that aids in understanding and maintaining interaction (Peterson, 2010). Moreover, the fact that one could build or explore culturally suggestive spaces implied introducing new avenues of placing linguistic forms in cultural activities and communicative habitualization (Molka-Danielsen & Deutschmann, 2009). However, the Second Life phase also revealed long-standing limitations that remain at the core of the MBLTL discourse: technical problems related to bandwidth and hardware, steep learning curves for both instructors and learners, and high time requirements for creating a successful activity (Wang & Vasquez, 2012). The instructional message here is not that graphical virtual worlds are necessarily effective, but that it is a matter of conformity between the environmental affordances, assignment design, and facilitation practices, a lesson repeatedly reiterated in CALL scholarship more generally (Hubbard, 2023).

Since the 2010s, the landscape has diversified due to the introduction of mobile technologies, social media logics, and consumer-grade VR, which has led to both increased accessibility and new forms of immersion. The development of mobile applications and VR language-learning products, along with social VR platforms, enabled learners to engage with them without requiring the same technical expertise as previous virtual worlds (Parmaxi, 2023). Meanwhile, dedicated educational applications emerged with capabilities such as teacher controls, lesson recording, and integration with a learning management system, which can be seen as an attempt to render immersive experiences within institutional forms of teaching and responsibility. The COVID-19 pandemic heightened the desire to seek alternatives to face-to-face instruction and further explored platforms that could simulate presence and social connection by utilizing spatial audio, virtual meeting spaces, and collaborative tools (Harron & Mason, 2020; Trust & Whalen, 2020). This more general change overlapped with prior research on telecollaboration and virtual exchange, which has consistently demonstrated that intercultural communication can facilitate language acquisition and cultural awareness when properly scaffolded and reflexive (Canto et al., 2013; O'Dowd, 2018). The metaverse would, at least conceptually, add a richer sense of place, embodiment, and shared activity, which can enhance the interactional resources accessible to learners and be easily offered through text chat or video conferencing (Guichon & Cohen, 2016; Sykes et al., 2008). Within this longer CALL trajectory, metaverse-based language teaching and learning can therefore be conceptualized as an ecological elaboration of integrative CALL (Blin, 2016), one that foregrounds embodiment, place-making, and sustained participation in digitally mediated discourse communities rather than treating immersive technologies as pedagogical ends in themselves.

Accordingly, MBLTL should be conceptualized as a pedagogical discipline that emerges from the historical trajectory of computer-assisted language learning and integrates multiple theoretical traditions informing SLA, rather than being reduced to a set of technological tools or platforms (Fig. 1). A consistent description requires systems that address the social structure of learning, the conditions of interaction in language acquisition, and the affective and motivational processes that influence participation in learning. One of these theoretical perspectives is sociocultural and social-constructivist theories, which conceptualize learning as a mediated practice where knowledge is constructed through interaction with others and through cultural means (Vygotsky, 1978). A metaverse space itself is an instrument of semiotics and culture, determining what learners can see, do, and say. To the extent that learners have access to scaffolding from peers or teachers through collaborative work, and to the extent that designed environments and prompts can be used as sources of distributed support through action, Vygotsky's zone of proximal development becomes applicable (Lan, 2020). Research on virtual worlds has focused on the role of shared visual reference points, task structure, and collaborative action in supporting meaning-making and language use, where learners collaboratively construct discourse around objects and goals of shared interest (Liou, 2012; Zheng et al., 2009). This, in turn, aligns with the communities of practice viewpoint, in which learning is perceived as a shift from peripheral to whole participation through long-term involvement in the practices and repertoires of communities of practice (Lave & Wenger, 1991; Wenger, 1999). Such communities can be hosted in virtual worlds through repeated interaction, shared projects, and social norms that are carried and modified over time, as well as through multimodal interactional practices that become part of the shared community repertoire (Wigham & Chanier, 2013).

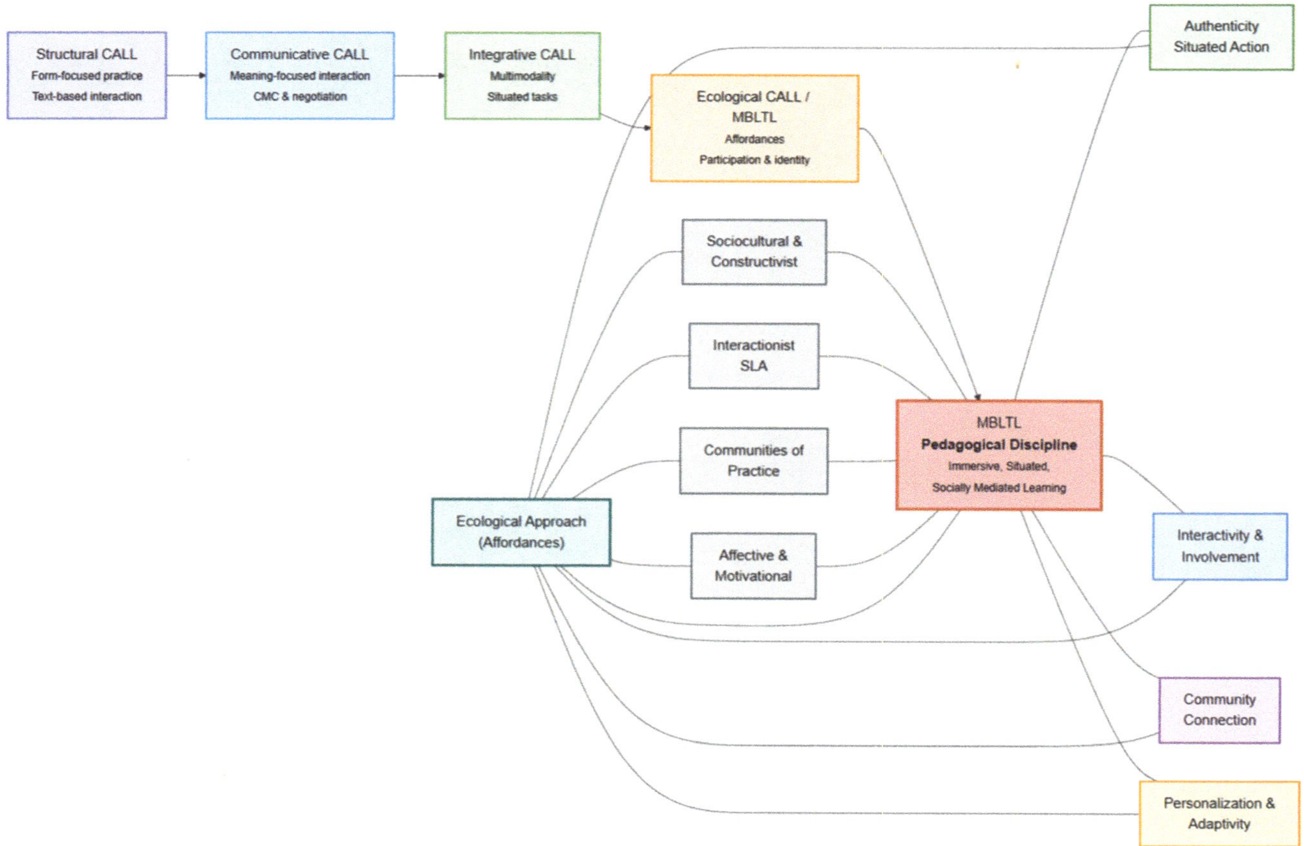

Fig. 1 MBLTL within the CALL trajectory

One of the complementary lenses is the Community of Inquiry (CoI) framework, which theorizes meaningful online learning as an outcome created at the intersection of teaching presence, social presence, and cognitive presence (Garrison et al., 1999). In this regard, the metaverse is of particular interest to language learning, as it provides a stronger sense of being with other people than most traditional online tools, as avatars, spatial audio, and co-presence can facilitate relational work, identity enactment, and conversational flow in metaverse spaces, which are the primary factors in the development of communicative competence (Çelik & Baturay, 2024; Guichon & Cohen, 2016; Uhl et al., 2023). Teaching presence as design and facilitation, which CoI also anticipates in immersive environments, is significant in situations where openness and novelty can result in distraction or disorientation without clearly entrenching instructional objectives within task structures and interactional patterns (Henderson et al., 2017). In its turn, cognitive presence is brought into the light when the metaverse activities are structured in a way that presupposes inquiry, reflection, and discourse beyond shallow participation to the long-term meaning making, which is also in line with the general focus on active learning and the significance of structured interaction for learning outcomes (Freeman et al., 2014; Garrison et al., 1999). Although CoI is not a product of SLA, it offers a set of vocabulary to discuss how immersive platforms can be pedagogically structured in a way that facilitates social interaction, thereby enhancing cognitive and linguistic development, rather than merely being social for its own sake.

Interactionist approaches in SLA are an additional explanatory factor that helps explain why certain types of communication are important in language acquisition. The interaction hypothesis, as proposed by Long (1996), places greater emphasis on the negotiation of meaning as the process by which learners receive modified input, produce modified output, and identify gaps in their linguistic knowledge. Such negotiation can be frequently used in metaverse environments, as learners can organize actions in shared spaces, work jointly, and engage in spontaneous interactions, which include breakdowns, repairs, clarifications, and confirmations (Peterson, 2012). As an example, Kastoudi (2012) showed that learners involved in a quest-based activity in Second Life were engaged in the continuous negotiation of meaning, lexical clarification, and repair as they worked together to solve problems, which led to vocabulary gains and perceived effects. In the same way, Zheng et al. (2009) and Wigham and Chanier (2013) noticed that object and avatar-based coordination through joint manipulation of objects led to deeper negotiation sequences compared to text-based communication. In addition, the multimodal nature of communication in virtual worlds where learners engage with gesture, movement and manipulation of objects in addition to linguistic resources enlarges the semiotic resources that can be used to sustain intersubjectivity when there are limitations in linguistic resources, a trend that has been observed with the accounts of situated cognition which view knowledge as inseparable from action in context (Brown et al., 1989; Sykes et al., 2019). Practically, learners can identify objects, model actions, and use the environment as an external frame of reference, which makes negotiation more concrete than it would be in decontextualized conversation tasks. The studies concerning immersive environments in language education have long maintained that the said environment can facilitate new kinds of interactions and meaning making, but also need to be designed in such a manner that the interaction richness can be converted into a learning opportunity instead of diffuse activity (Shih & Yang, 2008; Sykes et al., 2008).

There are also affective and motivational aspects that should also be considered, especially since willingness to communicate, anxiety, and long-term engagement tend to have a significant impact on the extent to which learners engage, which, consequently, influences exposure and interaction. The affective filter hypothesis proposed by Krashen (1982) remains useful in drawing attention to the possibility that anxiety and low self-confidence may constrain learners' capacity to make effective use of available input, even when that input is potentially accessible and meaningful. Virtual worlds can reduce some of the affective barriers by offering both psychological distance on the part of avatars and a situation where error is less a publicly significant consequence, thus promoting risk-taking in speaking and experimentation with new forms (Wehner et al., 2011). The inspirational theory is further theoretically established when the argument is developed within the context of self-determination theory, which argues that autonomy, competence, and relatedness contribute to fostering intrinsic motivation (Deci & Ryan, 2000). Under suitable design circumstances, metaverse environments have the potential to promote autonomy through exploratory routes, competence through instantaneous feedback, and the opportunity to practice and gain relevance through socially rich interactional environments. Empirical evidence supports these motivational and competence-related affordances of the metaverse. In a quasi-experimental study, Çelik and Baturay (2024) found that metaverse-based vocabulary learning significantly improved learner engagement, presence, and sense of community compared to a control group using a traditional platform. Çelik and Ersanlı (2025) further reported that integrating metaverse-based listening activities grounded in self-determination theory increased learners' autonomy and reduced anxiety, suggesting that the sense of control and feedback immediacy in immersive settings supports competence development. In addition, Im (2022) observed that students using the metaverse platform Gather for English classes expressed increased satisfaction and reduced anxiety over four weeks, attributing this to the freedom to explore and interact as avatars in non-threatening, socially rich contexts. It has been proposed that motivation and engagement are at least influenced by the degree of immersion and the frequency of repeated sessions, even though these effects are not automatic and require that learning activities be designed to challenge and support learners (Huang et al., 2021). Likewise, the broader research on technology and motivation in language learning highlights that motivational gains are achieved when technologies significantly increase communicative opportunities and learner agency, rather than merely providing novelty (Stockwell, 2013). In this respect, metaverse platforms can enhance motivation when learning goals are integrated into gameful experiences, as claimed in the body of research on language learning in these environments (Çelik, 2025; Çelik & Ersanlı, 2025; Reinhardt, 2019); however, they can also be counterproductive when learning logics are superseded by entertainment logics.

An ecological approach also helps connect these theoretical strands by understanding learning as a product of interactions between learners and their environments, and by paying attention to affordances as opportunities to act that are perceived and appropriated in specific situations (Gibson, 1979; van Lier, 2004). In this perspective, metaverse spaces cannot be regarded as mere delivery systems but rather as organised spaces that not only support specific types of mobility, co-presence, manipulation, and persistence, but also influence the way learners language, work on identity, and participate in social life. Notably, ecological descriptions also emphasize that affordances are not universal; they rely on the past experiences of learners, their capabilities, and purposes, which implies that the same virtual environment can facilitate expansive learning for one learner but cause cognitive overload or disengagement in others. This aligns with a long-standing assumption that design should help learners see and utilize technological possibilities to serve educational purposes, rather than assuming that affordances will be self-realizing (Sadler, 2012; Schwienhorst, 2008). It also contributes to understanding why metaverse-based learning cannot be evaluated solely based on the features of platforms, but rather on the combination of features, tasks, norms, and learner participation, which is what is truly important. The studies of the possibilities and constraints of learning languages in the metaverse emphasize that although the immersive environment may provide unparalleled opportunities in the pedagogical process, the advantages of this approach are extremely conditional. Research indicates that affordances, like co-presence, embodied interaction, and authentic task engagement, are more motivating when organized around social and communicative activities through collaboration or problem-solving (Kastoudi, 2012; Lan, 2020). On the same note, identity and spatial affordances mediated by avatars have been discovered to alleviate anxiety and promote intercultural communication in ESL settings (Im, 2022). Nevertheless, the process of learning and participation is usually limited by cognitive overload due to multimodal input, technical instability, unequal access, and lack of scaffolding (Elizondo-García & Espínola-Carballo, 2023). Taken together, these results indicate that metaverse affordances can only be converted into long-term linguistic and affective advantages in the case of their pedagogical design, contextual support, and ethical implementation, where immersion and interactivity are used to support learning.

It is within this theoretical framework that the potential of MBLTL can be further refined. Among the important promises is that of real and grounded learning experiences. Classroom teaching can be weak in offering rich communicative contexts in which language is utilized to do consequential action instead of display, yet the immersion can recreate the setting of a restaurant, office, public service, or a culturally significant site, and offer contextualized practice which can facilitate transfer by putting language into situated action (Brown et al., 1989; Mystakidis, 2022). Research on the metaverse in the English language learning process indicates that involvement and success may be facilitated when virtual worlds are constructed to align with linguistic objectives and provide meaningful activities and contextual clues (Çelik & Baturay, 2024). Likewise, research on platforms like Google Expeditions suggests that immersive experiences can lead to language learning outcomes if they are embedded in a series of pedagogical actions, as opposed to being a one-off novelty effect (Ebadijalal & Yousofi, 2024). The most important fact is that authenticity in MBLTL must be created pedagogically: this is achieved through the process of balancing scenario design, task requirements, and interactional possibilities, rather than relying on visual realism.

The second dimension of possible transformation is interactivity and involvement. The ability to manipulate objects, navigate space, and engage in dynamic scenarios that respond to the actions of the learners is also in line with the principles of active learning that highlight that learning is enhanced when learners are not merely presented with information, but rather, actively engage (Freeman et al., 2014). This may take the form of collaborative problem-solving that involves negotiated communication, project-based construction of virtual artifacts, or role-play situations that demand adaptive language use in varying conditions, facilitated by the flexibility of virtual environment design (Liou, 2012; Shih & Yang, 2008). The level of engagement can be further increased with gameful elements, and the pedagogical issue is to make gameplay support rather than distract from communicative and linguistic goals (Reinhardt, 2019). The existing background in web-based language learning and Web 2.0 tools already demonstrates that engagement itself is not enough; instead, interactional participation should be organized towards learning outcomes, and learners should be assisted in transitioning between participation, reflection, and refinement (Hubbard, 2023; Wang & Vasquez, 2012).

A third assertion is that there may be a connection between the world's communities of learners and speakers. Synchronous interaction of geographically dispersed participants can be hosted on metaverse platforms and may offer them diverse interlocutors, more than most classrooms could provide. This is closely related to the virtual exchange literature, which reports the positive effects of linguistic development and intercultural competence when learners are guided to engage in systematic cross-cultural interaction (O'Dowd, 2018; Canto et al., 2013). Global collaboration in immersive environments can be grounded in shared activities and place-based situations that support more relational work and a sense of co-presence compared to text chat and video conferencing alone (Guichon & Cohen, 2016; Uhl et al., 2023). However, according to studies on ICT in higher education, digital competence, institutional norms, and access conditions, which differ significantly across contexts, determine participation in such environments (Chen & Chen, 2025; Kozlova & Pikhart, 2021). Global connectivity is therefore a possibility, and not an inevitability; it must be constructed, enabled, and concerned with equity.

Fourth is personalization and adaptivity, which is becoming more important as immersive spaces are added with AI and analytics. The work on AI and education by UNESCO focuses on personalization and adaptive support as promising directions, but also warns that these developments raise questions related to governance, privacy, and responsible use (Miao et al., 2021). Personalization may involve differentiated pathways, adaptive task difficulty, or AI-supported conversation practice, or it can be carried out through learners' ability to regulate themselves and the presence of scaffolds to avoid overwhelming learners in open-ended environments (Jacobson et al., 2010; Schwienhorst, 2008). In this case, research evidence on motivation and engagement suggests that personalization may facilitate long-term participation when it enables learners to feel competent and in control; however, it may disrupt learning if not accompanied by a coherent curriculum progression and meaningful assessment (Deci & Ryan, 2000; Huang et al., 2021). The pedagogical question then turns to the issue of whether personalization is possible, and how it may be instructionally principled and socially supportive.

The balanced account of MBLTL should also consider the relationship between metaverse-based approaches and traditional language teaching, rather than introducing them as substitutes. Physical classroom teaching has long-term advantages, such as depth of nonverbal interaction, direct responsiveness to the slightest learner cues, and the social responsibility systems that enable many learners to continue engaging (Stockwell, 2013). The CALL research has long held the view that emerging technologies are more effective when they complement, rather than displace, pedagogically applicable practices, and when they are not used in ways that undermine the coherence, progression, and assessment validity of curricular designs (Hubbard, 2023; Wang & Vasquez, 2012). In this sense, MBLTL can be viewed as the expansion of the repertoire of potential learning events, and it can offer immersive experiences, distributed learning, and the possibilities of interaction on a global scale, without necessarily sacrificing the use of teacher pedagogical expertise to design tasks, scaffold interaction, and relate immersive experience to linguistic analysis, reflection and transfer (Garrison et al., 1999; Schwienhorst, 2008). The question of whether metaverse learning is better is not the right question to ask, but the question of under what conditions, to whom, and what outcomes a metaverse learning can provide a unique value can be a better question so that we can place a greater demand for evidence-based and context-sensitive use of educational technologies for both learners and educators to benefit (Lin et al., 2022; Tlili et al., 2022).

The problems related to implementation thus come to the fore. First-order constraints are technical infrastructure and access. High-quality immersive experiences can require specialized equipment, consistent high-speed interconnection, and technical maintenance, which is an equity issue that has been extensively documented in the literature on immersive simulations and technology integration (Castrillo et al., 2014; Dawley & Dede, 2014). Technical issues, platform instability, and high onboarding requirements may interfere with the instruction process and affect the level of confidence in the ethical dimension, which implies that pedagogical planning should incorporate orientation, general and platform-specific troubleshooting guidelines, and contingency plans that maintain the learning objectives in the case of technology failures (Harron & Mason, 2020; Schwienhorst, 2008). The other risk is cognitive overload as the combination of 3D worlds, controlling an avatar, processing language input, and output may be overwhelming for learners to handle in real-time, especially novice learners or those not accustomed to gaming and metaverse interaction conventions (Jacobson et al., 2010). Design effectiveness should thus be able to control complexity, task partitioning, and scaffold interactional routines to ensure that attention remains focused on communicative intentions and not solely on environmental exploration.

The design and facilitation of pedagogy in the metaverse imply the reconsideration of classroom control, coordination of interaction, and the relationship between structure and openness. A comparison of interaction patterns in virtual and face-to-face role-playing reveals that the dynamics of interaction differ in both contexts, and teachers must devise facilitation strategies that align with the medium's affordances and constraints (Gao et al., 2008). This extends to assessment. The interactional competence, strategic communication, and intercultural learning that arise during an immersive task may not be detected by traditional tests, which leads to the development of alternative tests (portfolios, performance-based assessments, and analysis of interactional processes) (Sykes et al., 2008). However, data-rich environments are also associated with ethical and practical challenges. In such environments, feedback can be supported by recording, analytics, and behavioral tracking; however, this method also raises concerns about privacy and places the burden on the teacher, unless the institution provides policy guidance and tools for use (Miao et al., 2021; Trust & Whalen, 2020). The process of community building is also nontrivial. Even though social presence may be simpler and more convenient to attain through avatars and co-presence, effective learning communities need norms, inclusion practices, and a focus on intercultural communication, particularly in globally networked environments of the metaverse, where a lack of understanding may emerge based on varying discourse conventions and expectations (Canto et al., 2013; Guichon & Cohen, 2016).

Finally, the implementation should be sustainable, which is only possible with institutional support rather than the personal enthusiasm of teachers. Emergency remote teaching and the adoption of technology during the pandemic have urged the need to invest in professional development, innovation recognition, and infrastructural investment in case new pedagogies can be transferred not only to pilot projects but also to sustainable practice (Harron & Mason, 2020; Trust & Whalen, 2020). The volatility of platforms is also a concern, as such virtual worlds are capable of altering policies, redesigning interfaces, or vanishing, and this makes it challenging to plan curricula over time and necessitates institutional strategies focused on portability of pedagogical designs and documentation of practices that are not limited to any particular platform (Schwienhorst, 2008; Wang & Vasquez, 2012). In this regard, MBLTL represents both technological and socio-institutional changes, which necessitate addressing issues of training, governance, ethics, and equity, in addition to innovation.

These considerations, taken together, make MBLTL a developmental step in the field of language teaching that prompts both hope and methodological distrust. It has been promising, based on realistic theoretical alignments: socially situated learning, high conditions of interaction, extended semiotic resources to make meaning, and motivational affordances of autonomy, competence, and relatedness (Deci & Ryan, 2000; Long, 1996; Vygotsky, 1978). The nature of its risks and limitations is also based on proven results regarding technology integration, unequal access, cognitive overload, non-automaticity of engagement, and the focus of pedagogical design and institutional support (Dawley & Dede, 2014; Hubbard, 2023; Jacobson et al., 2010). Thus, the chapter can position MBLTL as an emerging area characterized by design issues as well as platform opportunities, and it inquires about how metaverse environments can be organized to support language learning, how such learning can be responsibly evaluated, and how teachers and institutions can establish sustainable practices that serve language learning (Tlili et al., 2022; Wang et al., 2022). The rest of the book is founded on this, and further aspects of the book explore implementation models, activity and task designs, assessment structures, and research directions that can bring the field to a more rigorous, equitable, and pedagogically congruent practice. While the research presented in this chapter draws on a growing body of empirical studies, it is important to acknowledge that the field of MBLTL is still emerging. The empirical evidence base, though promising, consists primarily of small-scale or medium-scale studies conducted in specific institutional contexts. Larger-scale, longitudinal studies and comparative analyses across diverse educational settings would strengthen the empirical foundation for MBLTL.

2 Conclusion

The present chapter positions MBLTL as a logical extension of the CALL trajectory, and, at the same time, it identifies it as a qualitatively different pedagogical space where immersion, persistence, and socially situated participation can be actively designed by the teacher to reconfigure the experience of encountering, practicing, and appropriating language over time. The main argument that is derived from this framing is not that metaverse spaces are necessarily better than classroom teaching, but instead that they bring about unique arrangements of presence, interaction, and context that can broaden the range of possible language-learning situations, so long as design choices are based on theory and implementation is backed by strong institutional and ethical infrastructures. The pedagogical promise of MBLTL, in this sense, can be seen as conditional and relational as it is based on the social interactions between learners and other participants, interactions with environmental affordances and task demands, participation norms and their creation and maintenance, and the varied backgrounds and abilities of learners to define what can be perceived and appropriated as a meaningful learning opportunity (Schwienhorst, 2008; van Lier, 2004).

Through the theoretical lenses discussed, a consistent overlap emerges, highlighting the primacy of interaction and mediation in language development. The sociocultural account posits the distribution of learning among people, tools, and semiotic resources, making the metaverse not a neutral container but an agent of what learners can observe, act, and become in communicative practice. Interactionist views explain the importance of the communicative density of such spaces, that is, it is due to the opportunity to negotiate meaning and manage breakdowns and repair that modified input and output and noticing, which are still key processes in most SLA accounts of development, can be promoted. The CoI framework helps to supplement these perspectives by explaining how social presence and teaching presence should be strategically coordinated to make immersive sociability pedagogically consequential, and not just engaging or novel. When these views are juxtaposed with ecological explanations of affordances, the discipline is forced to consider MBLTL as a continuing design challenge: the very features that facilitate the rich interaction and authenticity may cause overload, exclusion, or diffuse activity when the learners are not guided to perceive and act on affordances in a manner that is useful in linguistic terms.

At the practice level, our discussion suggests that the further development of MBLTL will not be based on the sophistication of platforms, but rather on the maturation of pedagogical models that can reconcile immersive experiences with learning paths. This involves creating work that incorporates both communicative needs and reflective possibilities, establishing community standards that foster fair participation and intercultural awareness, and developing evaluation methods that assess interactional competence and situated performance without compromising privacy or creating an unsustainable workload. It also involves addressing the limitations facing the field, especially the inequity of access, digital competence disparities, and the instability of platforms. To this end, uncritical enthusiasm and categorical skepticism are the two least defensible positions; however, design-oriented pragmatism, where statements about the impact are grounded in evidence, context, and implementation conditions, is the most defensible.

Overall, MBLTL may be interpreted as a new pedagogical field in SLA that challenges language educators and researchers to rethink the underlying questions regarding the place of language learning, the types of participation considered learning, and the intersection of identity, affect, and community with learning in technologically mediated spaces. The chapter has laid down an introduction to the foundations of MBLTL on which the further chapters are able to discuss more operational issues, such as models of implementation, principles of task design, and research agendas that are well suited to the capture of both learning outcomes and the interactional processes in which those outcomes are plausibly created. To become a valuable subfield of CALL, the next step of MBLTL will be focusing on the methodological rigor, the ethical clarity, and the long-term focus on learning and equity, so that the metaverse could be not merely a new place to practice the old, but a well-thought-out ecology, where the language learning could be extended in a way that would be pedagogically principled.

References

Blin, F. (2016). Towards an 'ecological' CALL theory: Theoretical perspectives and their instantiation in CALL research and practice. In *The Routledge handbook of language learning and technology* (pp. 39–54). Routledge.

Bonner, E., & Reinders, H. (2018). Augmented and virtual reality in the language classroom: Practical ideas. *Teaching English with Technology, 18*(3), 33–53. https://www.ceeol.com/search/article-detail?id=683374

Brown, J. S., Collins, A., & Duguid, P. (1989). Situated cognition and the culture of learning. *Educational Researcher, 18*(1), 32–42. https://doi.org/10.3102/0013189X018001032

Canto, S., Jauregi, K., & van den Bergh, H. (2013). Integrating cross-cultural interaction through video-communication and virtual worlds in foreign language teaching programs: Is there an added value? *ReCALL, 25*(1), 105–121. https://doi.org/10.1017/S0958344012000274

Castrillo, M. D., Martín-Monje, E., & Bárcena, E. (2014). New forms of negotiating meaning on the move: The use of mobile-based chatting for foreign language distance learning. *IADIS International Journal on WWW/Internet, 12*(2), 51–67.

Çelik, F. (2025). The impact of game-based metaverse on language learning motivation, anxiety, and vocabulary. *International Journal of Applied Linguistics*, ijal.12858. https://doi.org/10.1111/ijal.12858

Çelik, F., & Baturay, M. H. (2024). The effect of metaverse on L2 vocabulary learning, retention, student engagement, presence, and community feeling. *BMC Psychology, 12*(1), 58. https://doi.org/10.1186/s40359-024-01549-4

Çelik, F., & Ersanlı, C. Y. (2025). Developing and integrating metaverse into EFL listening skills to increase learners' self-determination based on social constructivist theory. *Journal of Computer Assisted Learning, 41*(6), Article e70151. https://doi.org/10.1111/jcal.70151

Chen, F., & Chen, G. (2025). Technology-enhanced collaborative inquiry in k–12 classrooms: A systematic review of empirical studies. *Science & Education, 34*(3), 1731–1773. https://doi.org/10.1007/s11191-024-00538-8

Dawley, L., & Dede, C. (2014). Situated learning in virtual worlds and immersive simulations. In J. M. Spector, M. D. Merrill, J. Elen, & M. J. Bishop (Eds.), *Handbook of research on educational communications and technology* (pp. 723–734). Springer New York. https://doi.org/10.1007/978-1-4614-3185-5_58

Deci, E. L., & Ryan, R. M. (2000). The "what" and "why" of goal pursuits: Human needs and the self-determination of behavior. *Psychological Inquiry, 11*(4), 227–268. https://doi.org/10.1207/S15327965PLI1104_01

Deutschmann, M., Panichi, L., & Molka-Danielsen, J. (2009). Designing oral participation in Second Life: A comparative study of two language proficiency courses. *ReCALL, 21*(2), 206–226. https://doi.org/10.1017/S0958344009000196

Ebadijalal, M., & Yousofi, N. (2024). 'Take me to a virtual trip if you want me to write better!': The impact of Google Expeditions on EFL learners' writing motivation and performance. *Computer Assisted Language Learning, 37*(7), 1806–1828. https://doi.org/10.1080/09588221.2022.2123001

Elizondo-García, M. E., & Espínola-Carballo, G. (2023). Breaking boundaries: Exploring the metaverse for innovative education. In T. Cochrane, V. Narayan, C. Brown, K. MacCallum, E. Bone, C. Deneen, R. Vanderburg, & B. Hurren (Eds.), *People, partnerships and pedagogies: Proceedings of ASCILITE 2023*. https://doi.org/10.14742/apubs.2023.526

Freeman, S., Eddy, S. L., McDonough, M., Smith, M. K., Okoroafor, N., Jordt, H., & Wenderoth, M. P. (2014). Active learning increases student performance in science, engineering, and mathematics. *Proceedings of the National Academy of Sciences, 111*(23), 8410–8415. https://doi.org/10.1073/pnas.1319030111

Gao, F., Noh, J. M., & Koehler, M. J. (2008). Comparing student interactions in second life and face-to-face role-playing activities. In K. McFerrin, R. Weber, R. Carlsen, & D. Willis (Eds.), *Proceedings of SITE 2008--Society for Information Technology & Teacher Education International Conference* (pp. 2033–2035). Association for the Advancement of Computing in Education (AACE). Retrieved December 23, 2025 from https://www.learntechlib.org/primary/p/27499/

Garrison, D. R., Anderson, T., & Archer, W. (1999). Critical inquiry in a text-based environment: Computer conferencing in higher education. *The Internet and Higher Education, 2*(2–3), 87–105. https://doi.org/10.1016/S1096-7516(00)00016-6

Gibson, J. J. (1979). *The ecological approach to visual perception*. Psychology Press.

Guichon, N., & Cohen, C. (2016). Multimodality and CALL. In F. Farr & L. Murray (Eds.), *The Routledge handbook of language learning and technology* (pp. 509–521). Routledge.

Harron, J. R., & Mason, L. (2020). Creating virtual spaces: Using extended reality and transformative technologies to prepare teachers to thrive in an ever-changing world. In R. E. Ferdig & K. E. Pytash (Eds.), *What teacher educators should have learned from 2020* (pp. 213–228). Association for the Advancement of Computing in Education (AACE).

Henderson, M., Selwyn, N., & Aston, R. (2017). What works and why? Student perceptions of "useful" digital technology in university teaching and learning. *Studies in Higher Education, 42*(8), 1567–1579. https://doi.org/10.1080/03075079.2015.1007946

Huang, W., Roscoe, R. D., Johnson-Glenberg, M. C., & Craig, S. D. (2021). Motivation, engagement, and performance across multiple virtual reality sessions and levels of immersion. *Journal of Computer Assisted Learning, 37*(3), 745–758. https://doi.org/10.1111/jcal.12520

Hubbard, P. (2023). Emerging technologies and language learning: Mining the past to transform the future. *Journal of China Computer-Assisted Language Learning, 3*(2), 239–257. https://doi.org/10.1515/jccall-2023-0003

Im, H.-J. (2022). College students' perspectives and attitudes toward the use of gather in online classes. *Journal of English Teaching through Movies and Media, 23*(3), 53–63. https://doi.org/10.16875/stem.2022.23.3.53

Jacobson, M. J., Kim, B., Miao, C., Shen, Z., & Chavez, M. (2010). Design perspectives for learning in virtual worlds. In M. J. Jacobson & P. Reimann (Eds), *Designs for learning environments of the future* (pp. 111–141). Springer. https://doi.org/10.1007/978-0-387-88279-6_5

Jovanović, A., & Milosavljević, A. (2022). Vortex metaverse platform for gamified collaborative learning. *Electronics, 11*(3), 317. https://doi.org/10.3390/electronics11030317

Kastoudi, D. (2012). Using a quest in a 3D virtual environment for student interaction and vocabulary acquisition in foreign language learning. *The EuroCALL Review, 20*(1), 97. https://doi.org/10.4995/eurocall.2012.16189

Kozlova, D., & Pikhart, M. (2021). The use of ICT in higher education from the perspective of the university students. *Procedia Computer Science, 192*, 2309–2317. https://doi.org/10.1016/j.procs.2021.08.221

Krashen, S. D. (1982). *Principles and practice in second language acquisition.* Pergamon.

Lan, Y.-J. (2020). Immersion, interaction, and experience-oriented learning: Bringing virtual reality into FL learning. *Language Learning & Technology, 24*(1), 1–15. https://doi.org/10.64152/10125/44704

Lave, J., & Wenger, E. (1991). *Situated learning: Legitimate peripheral participation.* Cambridge University Press.

Lee, L.-H., Braud, T., Zhou, P. Y., Wang, L., Xu, D., Lin, Z., Kumar, A., Bermejo, C., & Hui, P. (2024). All one needs to know about metaverse: A complete survey on technological singularity, virtual ecosystem, and research agenda. *Foundations and Trends® in Human-Computer Interaction, 18*(2–3), 100–337. https://doi.org/10.1561/1100000095

Lin, H., Wan, S., Gan, W., Chen, J., & Chao, H. C. (2022). Metaverse in education: Vision, opportunities, and challenges. In *2022 IEEE International Conference on Big Data* (pp. 2857–2866). IEEE. https://doi.org/10.1109/BigData55660.2022.10021004

Liou, H. C. (2012). The roles of Second Life in a college computer-assisted language learning (CALL) course in Taiwan, ROC. *Computer Assisted Language Learning, 25*(4), 365–382. https://doi.org/10.1080/09588221.2011.597766

Long, M. H. (1996). The role of the linguistic environment in second language acquisition. In W. C. Ritchie & T. K. Bhatia (Eds.), *Handbook of second language acquisition* (pp. 413–468). Academic Press.

Miao, F., Holmes, W., Huang, R., & Zhang, H. (2021). *AI and education: A guidance for policymakers.* UNESCO Publishing.

Molka-Danielsen, J., & Deutschmann, M. (Eds.). (2009). *Learning and teaching in the virtual world of Second Life.* Tapir Academic Press.

Mystakidis, S. (2022). Metaverse. *Encyclopedia, 2*(1), 486–497. https://doi.org/10.3390/encyclopedia2010031

O'Dowd, R. (2018). From telecollaboration to virtual exchange: State-of-the-art and the role of UNICollaboration in moving forward. *Journal of Virtual Exchange, 1*, 1–23. https://doi.org/10.14705/rpnet.2018.jve.1

Park, S. M., & Kim, Y. G. (2022). A metaverse: Taxonomy, components, applications, and open challenges. *IEEE Access, 10*, 4209–4251. https://doi.org/10.1109/ACCESS.2021.3140175

Parmaxi, A. (2023). Virtual reality in language learning: A systematic review and implications for research and practice. *Interactive Learning Environments, 31*(1), 172–184. https://doi.org/10.1080/10494820.2020.1765392

Peterson, M. (2010). Massively multiplayer online role-playing games as arenas for second language learning. *Computer Assisted Language Learning, 23*(5), 429–439. https://doi.org/10.1080/09588221.2010.520673

Peterson, M. (2012). Learner interaction in a massively multiplayer online role playing game (MMORPG): A sociocultural discourse analysis. *ReCALL, 24*(3), 361–380. https://doi.org/10.1017/S0958344012000195

Reinhardt, J. (2019). *Gameful second and foreign language teaching and learning: Theory, research, and practice.* Palgrave Macmillan. https://doi.org/10.1007/978-3-030-04729-0

Sadler, R. (2012). *Virtual worlds for language learning: From theory to practice.* Peter Lang AG.

Schwienhorst, K. (2002). Why virtual, why environments? Implementing virtual reality concepts in computer-assisted language learning. *Simulation & Gaming, 33*(2), 196–209. https://doi.org/10.1177/1046878102332008

Schwienhorst, K. (2008). *Learner autonomy and CALL environments.* Routledge. https://doi.org/10.4324/9780203012208

Shih, Y. C., & Yang, M. T. (2008). A collaborative virtual environment for situated language learning using VEC3D. *Educational Technology & Society, 11*(1), 56–68. https://www.jstor.org/stable/10.2307/jeductechsoci.11.1.56

Stockwell, G. (2013). Technology and motivation in English-language teaching and learning. In E. Ushioda (Ed.), *International perspectives on motivation: Language learning and professional challenges* (pp. 156–175). Palgrave Macmillan.

Sykes, J. M., Holden, C., & Knight, S. (2019). Communities: Exploring digital games and social networking (2nd Edition). In L. Ducate & N. Arnold (Eds.), *Engaging language learners through CALL: From theory and research to informed practice* (pp. 353–389). Equinox/CALICO.

Sykes, J. M., Oskoz, A., & Thorne, S. L. (2008). Web 2.0, synthetic immersive environments, and mobile resources for language education. *CALICO Journal, 25*(3), 528–546. https://doi.org/10.1558/cj.v25i3.528-546

Tlili, A., Huang, R., Shehata, B., Liu, D., Zhao, J., Metwally, A. H. S., Wang, H., Denden, M., Bozkurt, A., Lee, L.-H., Beyoglu, D., Altinay, F., Sharma, R. C., Altinay, Z., Li, Z., Liu, J., Ahmad, F., Hu, Y., Salha, S., & Burgos, D. (2022). Is Metaverse in education a blessing or a curse: A combined content and bibliometric analysis. *Smart Learning Environments, 9*(1), 24. https://doi.org/10.1186/s40561-022-00205-x

Trust, T., & Whalen, J. (2020). Should teachers be trained in emergency remote teaching? Lessons learned from the COVID-19 pandemic. *Journal of Technology and Teacher Education, 28*(2), 189–199. https://doi.org/10.70725/307718pkpjuu

Uhl, J. C., Neundlinger, K., & Regal, G. (2023). Social presence as a training resource: Comparing VR and traditional training simulations. *Research in Learning Technology, 31.* https://doi.org/10.25304/rlt.v31.2827

Van Lier, L. (Ed.). (2004). Theories of language. In L. Van Lier, M. C. Cavalcanti, H. Janks, C. Kramsch, & A. Pennycook (Eds.), *The ecology and semiotics of language learning* (Vol. 3, pp. 23–53). Springer Netherlands. https://doi.org/10.1007/1-4020-7912-5_2

Von Der Emde, S., Schneider, J., & Kötter, M. (2001). Technically speaking: Transforming language learning through virtual learning environments (MOOs). *The Modern Language Journal, 85*(2), 210–225. https://doi.org/10.1111/0026-7902.00105

Vygotsky, L. S. (1978). *Mind in society: The development of higher psychological processes.* Harvard University Press.

Wang, M., Yu, H., Bell, Z., & Chu, X. (2022). Constructing an edu-metaverse ecosystem: A new and innovative framework. *IEEE Transactions on Learning Technologies, 15*(6), 685–696. https://doi.org/10.1109/TLT.2022.3210828

Wang, S., & Vasquez, C. (2012). Web 2.0 and second language learning: What does the research tell us? *CALICO Journal, 29*(3), 412–430. https://doi.org/10.11139/cj.29.3.412-430

Warschauer, M. (1995). Comparing face-to-face and electronic discussion in the second language classroom. *CALICO Journal, 13*(2), 7–26. https://doi.org/10.1558/cj.v13i2-3.7-26

Warschauer, M. (2000). The death of cyberspace and the rebirth of CALL. *English Teachers' Journal, 53*(1), 61–67.

Wehner, A. K., Gump, A. W., & Downey, S. (2011). The effects of Second Life on the motivation of undergraduate students learning a foreign language. *Computer Assisted Language Learning, 24*(3), 277–289. https://doi.org/10.1080/09588221.2010.551757

Wenger, E. (1999). *Communities of practice: Learning, meaning, and identity.* Cambridge University Press.

Wigham, C. R., & Chanier, T. (2013). A study of verbal and nonverbal communication in Second Life – the ARCHI21 experience. *ReCALL, 25*(1), 63–84. https://doi.org/10.1017/S0958344012000250

Zheng, D., Young, M. F., Wagner, M. M., & Brewer, R. A. (2009). Negotiation for action: English language learning in game-based virtual worlds. *The Modern Language Journal, 93*(4), 489–511. https://doi.org/10.1111/j.1540-4781.2009.00927.x

Ferdi Çelik holds a Ph.D. in English Langauge Education at Ondokuz Mayıs University, Samsun, Türkiye. His work centers on metaverse-based language teaching and learning as an extension of computer-assisted language learning. He emphasizes sociocultural theory, communities of practice, and ecological affordances in virtual worlds. Çelik explores the promises and limitations of immersive environments for authentic interaction and global connectivity. His contributions provide a foundational framework for understanding MBLTL as a dynamic pedagogical paradigm.

Ceylan Yangın Ersanlı is a professor at Ondokuz Mayıs University, Samsun, Türkiye. She collaborates on projects examining the shift from traditional to immersive digital language pedagogies. Her research highlights interactionist approaches to second language acquisition in virtual settings. Ersanlı addresses issues of presence, participation, and personalization in metaverse environments.

Exploring the Metaverse Based Language Teaching Technology Landscape

Ehsan Namaziandost and Fidel Çakmak

Abstract This chapter reviews the theoretical foundations of Metaverse-Based Language Learning and Teaching (MBLLT) and provides a technological framework for the educational Metaverse for immersive language learning. It analyzes immersive language learning environments, presenting the typology and design principles of the MBLLT environment with a focus on language learning. Some case studies and empirical evidence are presented to demonstrate how metaverse-driven environments can support learner-centered, multimodal language learning experiences. The chapter also explores the ethical, psychological, and societal dimensions of MBLLT and concludes by considering implications and next phases of research directions, along with future technological trends in metaverse-based language learning and teaching.

Keywords Metaverse-based language learning · Immersive learning · Extended reality (XR) · Multimodal communication · Ethical pedagogy · Digital equity

1 Introduction

With technological advancement, computer-assisted language learning (CALL) has created an ecosystem characterized by using its potential for ubiquity, interactivity, and contextual adaptability (Godwin-Jones, 2021). This shift has transformed mobile-assisted language learning (MALL) from a level where the portability of mobile devices and the ubiquity of internet connectivity were novel features (Çakmak, 2019) in the first two decades of the 21st century to one where the extended reality (XR) technologies such as virtual reality (VR) and augmented reality

E. Namaziandost
Department of English, Islamic Azad University of Ahvaz, Ahvaz, Iran

F. Çakmak (✉)
Department of Foreign Language Education, Alanya Alaaddin Keykubat University, Antalya, Türkiye
e-mail: fidel.cakmak@alanya.edu.tr

F. Çelik and C. Yangın Ersanlı (eds.), *Metaverse-Based Language Learning and Teaching*, English Language Education 49,
https://doi.org/10.1007/978-3-032-31366-9_2

(AR) have emerged as immersive context to promote dynamic, learner-centered experiences (Guo et al., 2021; Lan, 2025).

In recent years, Metaverse-based language learning and teaching (MBLLT) has become a pedagogical model capable of supporting autonomous, collaborative, and immersive learning environments (Asrifan et al., 2025; Çelik & Baturay, 2024). The growing interest in MBLTL is therefore associated with radical changes in instruction delivery models. Pandemic lockdowns and the rapid shift to remote learning increased the use of digital tools, mobile applications, and immersive platforms, creating both opportunities and challenges for language educators (Ahmed & Opoku, 2022; Alhawsawi & Alzaid, 2025; Reinders et al., 2022). As a result of that and with many technological advancements and products on the market, the world of education began to realize potential of smart technologies beyond emergency solutions in times of global crisis and acknowledged them as an effective component of blended and hybrid learning frameworks (Singh et al., 2021). Mobile devices and, more recently, AI technologies have enabled learners to independently engage with instructional materials, freeing them from the spatiotemporal constraints of conventional classrooms (Alam & Mohanty, 2023; Zhong & Zhao, 2025). Similarly, XR technologies have allowed learners to experience language in simulated real-world contexts and to learn through engagement with multi-modal metaverse experiences (Alsamh et al, 2024; Huang & Tseng, 2025; Xu et al., 2025).

Despite these advancements, integrating MBLTL technologies into pedagogical practice requires structured criteria and an integrative framework that connects learning theories and design paradigms to pedagogical applications (Lan, 2025; Tong et al., 2025). The field of foreign language learning has been expanded by the introduction of gamification applications such as Duolingo and Xeropan, as well as more immersive VR platforms such as Immerse and Mondly VR (Tariq, 2026).

Accordingly, the aim of this chapter is to provide a review of the technological side of MBLLT by evaluating how metaverse platforms and tools impact the effectiveness of foreign language learning. The analysis of studies presents the state of the art in meta-analyses. It provides insights into the pedagogical affordances and challenges encountered when integrating emerging innovations in language learning and teaching.

The chapter is structured in a set of thematic domains as follows:

- platforms and learning-management systems (LMS) supporting mobile and immersive content
- mobile and gamified applications for practicing language skills
- communication with metaverse platforms for authentic interaction
- XR-based environments simulating real-world use
- AI-driven adaptive systems providing data-informed feedback

Additionally, the chapter also conceptualizes MBLLT holistically as a dynamic, immersive ecosystem. This review provides language educators and researchers on MBLLT insights to enable them to design and implement the tools and platforms in their local contexts.

2 Theoretical Foundations of MBLLT

The theoretical foundations of MBLTLT are based on a mix of key theories such as constructivist (Dewey, 1938; Piaget, 1972), sociocultural, and experiential learning theories (Kolb, 1984), the cognitive theory of multimedia learning (Mayer, 2021), interaction hypothesis (Long, 1996), output hypothesis (Swain, 1995), embodied cognition (Barsalou, 2008), situated learning theory (Brown et al., 1989) and social presence (Biocca et al., 2003) These theories enable us to have an understanding of how learners can construct meaning through collaboration, and internalize knowledge created or co-created within immersive language learning environments. They are important to plan pedagogical implementations that connect the metaverse's technological designs with foreign language learning and teaching.

To start with, the constructivist approach proposes that learners can construct meaning through meaningful interaction with their environment (Dewey, 1938; Piaget, 1972). The metaverse, through its immersive, multisensory, and interactive qualities, can foster meaning-making processes by valuing language learners as active agents who co-construct understanding of language inputs through active engagement and collaboration. Kolb's (1984) experiential learning cycle in metaverse designs marks the importance of four stages of learning: concrete experience, reflective observation, abstract conceptualization, and active experimentation. In MBLLT environments, learners take part in engaging and immersive experiences (e.g., a learner can take part in role-playing, such as an encounter with a friend as an avatar in a virtual cinema), reflect on such experiences, observe his or her learning processes and outcomes, internalize language inputs, and apply them in other contexts of communicative interactions. These processes can be enhanced by immediate feedback mechanisms and the sense of presence that the metaverse-based environment can afford (Lan, 2025). Such experiential learning in a metaverse context can support deeper retention and transfer of language knowledge into a new context of language learning. This is one way the benefit of metaverse use is manifested by engaging learners actively and engaged in dynamic learning contexts informed by constructivist and experiential learning principles.

Long's (1996) Interaction and Swain's (1995) Output Hypotheses highlight interaction and production as mechanisms for language learning. In a metaverse context, real-time exchanges with peers (including feedback from AI tutors) or non-player characters afford language learners opportunities for active meaning creation through negotiation with AI agents.

Embodied cognition provides a framework for understanding cognitive processes in the body when a person is in interaction with the environment (Barsalou, 2008). In the metaverse context, language learners can exploit avatars through navigational patterns, physical movement, and emotional reactions. Such experiences can foster comprehension and incidental vocabulary learning in metaverse platforms (Çelik & Baturay, 2024; Godwin-Jones, 2025).

Situated learning theory (Brown et al., 1989) supports learning by noting that input and its implications for future use are obtained more effectively in authentic contexts. Metaverse platforms with immersive 3D simulations, adaptive agents, and tutoring can help language learners to practice functions (e.g., ordering food, asking for directions, and booking a room) in realistic virtual contexts. Such authenticity in context can close the gap between language use in classrooms and real-world contexts (Godwin-Jones, 2025). Additionally, presence marks cognitive engagement and emotional connection (Biocca et al., 2003). When learners feel present in the virtual world with others, their cognitive and affective engagement might increase their desire to communicate (Fathi et al., 2025). The situated and realistic nature of the metaverse, therefore, creates language learning experiences that foster a sense of connection with others (Çelik & Baturay, 2024).

Mayer's (2021) cognitive explanation of multimedia learning theory explains how language learners make meaning from input received through visual and nonvisual channels. The metaverse is designed for multimedia-enriched instruction and integrates visuals, audio, text, and interactivity. When multimedia instruction is effectively designed on the principles of multimedia learning, it can be processed smoothly through dual-channel processing, which can lessen extraneous cognitive load and facilitate contributing to improved comprehension and retention (Mayer, 2021). However, it is also noted that the abundance of input channels in the metaverse might increase the risk of cognitive overload, especially for novice learners (Makransky & Petersen, 2021). Effective instructional design in MBLLT exploits input that is engaging and sensory-rich, along with a structured pedagogical focus and learning objectives, which can foster immersive language learning experiences.

Social presence (Biocca et al., 2003) in MBLLT recognizes the importance of social behavior and the perception of others as real in immersive and mediated contexts. The level of social presence is of importance in digital learning environments (Kreijns et al., 2022), especially in language learning, as it influences learning outcomes (Ko, 2012). In MBLLT contexts, visual and spatial affordances can provoke our sensory system and create an embodied sense of coexistence (Zhang et al., 2022a, 2022b), which, in turn, might increase the frequency of interaction and feedback.

Taking these theoretical perspectives into account is essential to an integrated understanding of MBLLT as a multilayered pedagogical construct. By understanding the construct, language educators can create a pedagogically and theoretically solid, and socially inclusive MBLLT environment through the construction of knowledge and collaboration in immersive contexts.

3 Technological Framework of the Metaverse in Education

To understand the Metaverse' potential and promises, it is essential to understand the core technological infrastructure that provides the pedagogical focus on how it can be applied to learn a foreign language.

3.1 Core Technological Infrastructure

The educational Metaverse has been premised on a technological infrastructure that establishes immersive, interactive and sensory-enriched experiences through high-quality visuals and audios as learning aids. Technological layers are essential for supporting the complexity inherent to immersive language practice, which heavily relies on optimized latency and sensory-rich input (Zhang et al., 2022a, 2022b) (Table 1).

In summary, the technological infrastructure of the educational Metaverse fosters immersive, interactive, and personalized language learning experiences. From high-speed communication networks and XR modeling tools to AI-driven analytical technologies and blockchain-based authentication and ownership, each layer addresses concern to provide a secure, adaptive, and contextually meaningful language learning environment.

Table 1 Technological infrastructure in educational Metaverse

Technological layer	Key components	Function in language learning
Networking and Communication	5G/6G, Distributed Systems	Provides optimized latency and high bandwidth for real-time interaction, multi-user audios, and non-verbal communication for conversations and task engagement.
Modeling	Extended Reality (XR), 3D Engines (Unity, Unreal Engine, WebXR frameworks), Digital Twin Platforms	Creates virtually authentic and context-specific learning contexts (e.g., a Turkish restaurant) and affords personalized avatars for conversation
Interaction Technologies	Virtual Reality (VR), Augmented Reality (AR), Tactile Feedback	Increases the sense of social presence and create embodied natural communication. Utilizes multimodal input (e.g., sound, text, gaze) and multi-sensory feedback.
Analytical Technologies	Artificial Intelligence (AI), Big Data, Natural Language Processing (NLP)	Provides performance evaluation (e.g. error correction, and adaptive feedback)
Authentication and Ownership	Cryptographic tokens, bitcoin	Provides digital identity verification, manages learning records (e.g., skill certificates and badges), and affords secure tracking.

3.2 Domain-specific Components for Immersive Language Practice

Domain-specific components within the Metaverse can create immersive language learning experiences. Through immersive language learning experiences, learning environments might transform the virtual space from an idle space into an active, communicative, and social learning space.

The primary components for the MBLLT are through Extended Reality (XR), which encompasses VR, AR, and Mixed Reality (MR). VR headsets (e.g., Meta Quest 3) having high-resolution LCD panels, afford high immersion and fully embodied experiences, allowing full interactivity through haptic navigations placing the learner in an effectively mediated language learning environment, which has been shown to positively impact comprehension and vocabulary retention (Akyıldız, 2025; Kaplan-Rakowski & Gruber, 2023; Kaplan-Rakowski & Thrasher, 2025). AR and MR-based environments can be accessed via smart glasses or other mobile devices, and can also afford learners with immersive, context-aware language practice by bringing digital language elements into the real physical world. Despite the similar realities between AR and MR, the differences lie in the interaction between users and reality. In AR, the design is limited to manipulation and interaction with virtual items; however, in MR, users can interact with real objects in real-time, augmented by MR-specific features. In the review studies on AR implementation in foreign language learning by Schorr et al. (2024), it was found that learning with AR could create positive affective learning through increased motivation, enjoyment, and satisfaction through learner-centered instructional designs and real-time practice and feedback. It can also improve the development of social skills and collaboration. The review also mentions the human-oriented, technical, and physical limitations of an AR context. When these limitations are taken into consideration and implemented in alignment with the curriculum, it is feasible to create different ARs that promote learning. Likewise, MR technologies can bring the virtual item into reality (in front of their eyes) through smart glasses, which is in alignment with the spatial contiguity principle by Mayer (2021), enabling learners to focus their attention on elements in their visual field while avoiding external physical distractions.

Within the diverse realities MBLLT provides, avatars function as the digital representation of the learner or agent in the context through which the learner's sense of presence, solidarity, and collaboration for task completion can be augmented. This embodiment of presence can reduce the psychological limitations associated with productive and social skills in a foreign language, such as speaking anxiety or feeling shy to cooperate with others and enhance language practice by means of unprompted interaction with personalized representations (Islam & Wang, 2025; Wang & Zou, 2025) and pragmatic feedback (Richards, 2025).

Another technological component is the integration of AI-assisted non-Player Characters (AIANPCs) in MBLLT contexts. Unlike static NPCs, AIANPCs run on advanced AI systems, natural language processing, and large language models to enable learners to engage in realistic, contextually relevant dialogues in a virtual environment (Campitiello et al., 2024).

The AIANPCs can help enable real-time, dynamic feedback on language input shared between language learners and AIANPCs. They can stimulate immersive role-playing scenarios that imitate real-life interactions (e.g., asking for directions or visiting a museum) in an interface where the role-plays can be repeated as many times as needed for practice. Storytelling could be another example of implementation, as AIANPCs can enable foreign language learners to practice productive skills such as speaking and writing. As a pioneering study in the Chinese EFL context, Xiao et al.'s (2025) study found that Students' engagement with AIANPCs facilitated higher-order cognitive skills, such as conceptualization, reasoning, and evaluative contemplation, resulting in a better-structured, coherent, evidence-based organization in argumentative writing. Integrating AIANPCs in an EFL context can grant an immersive, independent, and meaningful learning experience without depending on the affordances of traditional teaching contexts. Overall, the technological sophistication of these AIANPCs is reflected in language education through their potential to maintain context, adapt their response patterns, and mimic humanlike behaviors that are aligned with promoting authenticity and the effectiveness of the interaction (Gonzales et al., 2025). Because its technological components are highly immersive, the Metaverse enables the creation of authentic learning environments. 3D Modeling technologies can afford users to reproduce historical sites, artifacts, or representations of foreign cities, providing visually and sensorially rich contexts that facilitate semantic memory activation, enhance vocabulary acquisition, and support effective language learning (Cantone et al., 2023; Lee, 2023; Shu & Gu, 2023).

The technological layers address three key pedagogical principles in foreign language learning:

1. Authenticity and Immersion: High-fidelity XR and 5G/6G networking provide immersive learning experiences, connecting the authentic and contextualized communicative purposes to the target language being learnt.
2. Embodied Cognition: Interaction technologies such as VR, AR and avatars make physical movement and gesture tangible, strengthen the connection between sensory input and action outputs, and facilitate memory by making the learning more meaningful and easily retrieved.
3. Adaptive and Personalized Feedback: AIANPCs empower language learners with personalized learning experiences and real-time feedback for skill practice.

In conclusion, the technological framework of the educational Metaverse goes beyond the limitations of traditional classroom-based or screen-based language instruction. By integrating key principles, Metaverse prioritizes language learning and turns it into an authentic, immersive, personalized, and technologically mediated experience.

4 Metaverse-Based Language Learning and Teaching Environments

Aligning with the learning theories and technological framework, the Metaverse is realized through the design and deployment of specific MBLLT environments. These environments are advanced technology-mediated virtual learning spaces created to employ the pedagogical affordances of immersive technology for language learning.

4.1 Typology of the MBLLT environment

MBLLT environments can be categorized based on their degree of immersion, aim, and the primary technology mediated. Table 2 shows the categorization of the MBLLT environment.

As shown in Table 2, MBLLT environments are distinguished by the nature and extent of learner engagement they afford. Fully immersive VR environments afford

Table 2 Typology of the MBLLT environment

Environment type	Primary technology	Key characteristics	Language learning focus	Example platforms
Fully Immersive Virtual Worlds	VR	High sense of presence; 3D avatars; complete isolation from the physical world.	Conversational practice; cultural immersion; alleviated affective filter.	*Immerse*, *VRChat* (custom worlds)
Augmented/ Mixed Reality (AR/MR) Spaces	AR/MR (Mobile or Headset)	Reflection of digital content onto real-world environments; context-sensitive interaction.	Vocabulary learning; situated learning; translation; real-world task completion practice.	*Mondly AR*, custom mobile AR apps
Desktop-Based 3D Virtual Worlds	Desktop/ Web-based 3D Graphics	Lower immersion but high accessibility; highly immersive virtual spaces with avatar interaction.	Collaborative tasks; virtual site visits; blended-learning integration.	*Second Life*, *Roblox* (educational experiences)
AI-Driven Conversational Agents	AI, NLP	Adaptive, one-on-one dialogue practice with AIANPCs	Grammar drills; pronunciation practice, collaborative task completion.	*Mondly VR* (NPC scenarios)

high sensory presence and emotional engagement, whereas AR/MR applications extend learning into authentic real-world contexts through context-sensitive systems. Desktop-based 3D worlds bridge the gap between accessibility and interactivity, which enables collaborative, task-based activities across more contexts. Meanwhile, AI-driven conversational agents individualize learning through interactional loops, adaptive feedback, and correction. Collectively, the modalities display a range of immersion and mediation, and each needs to be considered along with personalized, pedagogical, and technical design parameters. The diversity of platforms highlights the importance of designating learning experiences and integrating them with cognitive, affective, and social dimensions for interaction, feedback, and presence in the MBLLT environments.

4.2 Design Principles of the MBLLT Environment

The design of highly effective MBLLT environments is based on pedagogical frameworks that connect language learning theory with virtual reality assets. The Design of Immersive Virtual Environments for Language Learning (DIVE-L) guideline, offered by Durmaz (2025), outlines six principles for creating or selecting these spaces for language learning practice.

4.3 Situated Meaning

The situated meaning principle emphasizes creating environments where the language outcome is real and contextually meaningful. In an MBLLT environment, this means creating real-world scenarios, such as checking in at a hotel or buying a movie ticket, where the language input has real-time, practical outcomes. The environment in its design provides the relevant visual and auditory affordances to support language comprehension and production.

4.4 Multi-modality

The multimodality principle supports that effective MBLLT environments employ the potential of Metaverse to present input through multiple sensory channels simultaneously (visual, auditory, textual, haptic). For instance, an AIANPC may utter an expression during a daily-life task. When it is uttered, the textual correspondence is displayed at the very time, which reinforces the Input Hypothesis (Krashen, 1982) by making the language input comprehensible in a multi-modal environment. Multimodality in the MBLLT environment, such as leaflets, tags, menus, or interactive objects labeled in a foreign language, fosters incidental vocabulary learning and improves translation competence.

4.5 Technical Interactions

The technical interaction principle points out accessibility and interactivity of the environment, and has three subsections:

a. User-Interface (UI) Interaction: The smoothness through which learners navigate menus, tasks, or objects in the environment.
b. User-Environment Interaction: The potential to deploy virtual objects (e.g., holding a virtual item, turning on a light) to complete a given task, which facilitates embodied cognition.
c. User-User Interaction: The potential for real-time dialogue and collaboration between language learners and instructors, which is mediated by real-like avatar gestures and temporospatial audio.

4.6 Pedagogical Interactions

The pedagogical interaction principle addresses instructional design elements that entail language-focused tasks, such as language learning tasks to complete, peer collaboration, avatar interactions, AINPC interactions, and feedback. MBLLT environments must include communicative tasks that language learners can practice negotiating or clarifying meaning (Interaction Hypothesis) and collaborating with peers or AI agents. The environment must also provide real-time, structured, and dynamic feedback provided by AI-assisted agents.

4.7 Autonomy

The autonomy principle highlights that MBLLT environments should promote learner autonomy by allowing learners to regulate their own learning progress and explore the learning assets in the virtual world at their own pace. This principle corresponds to game-based learning principles, where learners' self-regulation and autonomy are key drivers of effective language learning. Resources such as in-world glosses, task-specific tips, or guides must be available to support independent and self-regulated learning.

4.8 Affordability

The affordability principle is a socioeconomic consideration that accessibility and the cost of hardware (e.g., VR headsets) and platform subscriptions do not pose a barrier to its availability in a learning space. Considerate MBLLT environments must make use of platforms that offer free or low-cost access, such as web-based 3D worlds or accessible consumer VR hardware, to make access feasible for language learners.

4.9 Case Studies in Metaverse-Based Language Learning

Implementations of MBLLT environments demonstrate the practical application of these design principles. Case studies can provide more information about their implementation in the language learning space.

4.10 Immerse: The Highly Immersive Language Classroom

Immerse is a highly immersive commercial VR platform particularly designed for language instruction. It is designed on the principles of Situated Meaning and Technical Interactions by affording live, instructor-regulated classes in realistic 3D environments. Learners can customize avatars and interact with them, and the instructor can use voice, gestures, and emotional reactions, which, in turn, can create a strong sense of presence and embodiment (Zhang et al., 2022a, 2022b). The environment is designed to lessen the affective filter by providing a safe, stress-free learning space for language practice, leading to increased comprehension and retention (Kaplan-Rakowski & Gruber, 2023; Kaplan-Rakowski & Thrasher, 2025; Thrasher et al., 2024).

4.11 Mondly VR: AI-Driven Scenario Practice

Mondly VR works with AI-driven conversational agents. The platform places the language learner in diverse real-world scenarios and employs advanced NLP to provide interactive dialogue with AIANPCs. This approach employs the Pedagogical Interactions principle (Waring, 2016) by providing numerous, rapid, and personalized feedback on fluency and grammar use for communicative purposes. The scenarios can also be designed to be entirely contextual and stress free, employing situated meaning without necessitating a human instructor for each learning session.

4.12 VRChat: The Social Immersion Context

Language instructors can exploit platforms like VRChat and RecRoom for their social and collaborative features. They represent the Full Immersive Virtual Worlds type, where the primary learning mechanism is User-to-User Interaction in a social context in VRChat. Case studies have demonstrated that using VRChat in the EFL context significantly enhances students' speaking ability, especially in terms of accuracy and fluency, by enabling them to use English for real, social, intercultural, and communicative purposes (Cahyadi et al., 2022; Knutzen et al., 2025).

Some case studies were conducted to test MBLLT tools. To start with, Çelik (2025) in his recent research, investigated the impact of Fortnite, MBLLT environment, with a group of pupils on learning vocabulary in an EFL context and found that after two week intervention of shopping context created in Fortnite and practice of 80 words with exploration, peer collaboration and role-plays, students whom were placed in the experimental group outperformed control group who did not have this practice significantly. Additionally, there was a significant improvement in motivation and decrease of anxiety in the experimental group. Another case study is from Japan and was carried out by Dizon and Tang (2024). With a qualitative research design, they explored four Japanese EFL learners' perceptions of immersive VR language learning through VRChat and found that the intervention encouraged their use of multiple interactional acts to express themselves better, and they found the experience authentic while interacting with the avatar within the VRChat. Interestingly, Shin et al. (2025) used it for assessment purposes rather than teaching and randomly placed 60 Korean young pupils in three conditions (face-to-face, Zoom, and Metaverse platform, Zepeto) for the assessment of their oral communication skills in English and found that students who were in the Metaverse group significantly did better than their counterparts in the Zoom and face-to-face groups. These recent case studies from different EFL contexts show that when implemented in a foreign language learning context with affordances for intervention in alignment with teaching objectives and content, application of the Metaverse can yield improvement in language learning.

In conclusion, MBLLT environments require a carefully planned design and a deep understanding of how people learn with technology. By using principles and thinking about what AR and VR can do, these environments can enable language learning more interesting and tailored to each student than traditional environments can. The metaverse is a smart educational ecosystem, of which success hinges on the design of learning experiences that blend immersion, accessibility, and cognitive engagement in instructional design.

5 Ethical, Psychological, and Societal Dimensions of Metaverse-Based Language Learning

While the technological framework and pedagogical environments of the Metaverse open up ample and immersive opportunities for foreign language learning, language educators must undergo a thorough evaluation of the ethical, psychological, and societal dimensions before they teach within the MBLLT environments. In other words, the shift to immersive, engaging, and real-time language learning environments with the Metaverse requires a proactive approach to data governance, learners' mental state and well-being, and inclusive access for quality language education.

Ethical MBLLT environments, particularly those utilizing VR and AR generate highly sensitive personal data, referred to as "biometric data". It is defined as "…personal data resulting from specific technical processing relating to the physical, physiological or behavioral characteristics of a natural person, which allow or confirm the unique identification of that person." (European Parliamentary Research Service, 2021, p. 10). They are specified as a special category of data under EU law because they can overtly reveal personal identity and therefore require the highest level of protection. In metaverse-based environments, such biometric data can be obtained from haptic motion, head-mounted displays, heart rate monitors, or AI-assisted emotion recognition systems. Such unprecedented biometric tracking can undoubtedly pose risks to privacy and data protection and threaten freedom of expression, personal rights, and human dignity.

While such biodata is considered as user profile input for adaptive customized language learning, it can create ethical risks. Learners' biometric information and interaction logs can reveal identity and user profiles beyond what is justifiable for pedagogical gains, potentially degrading privacy norms and creating moral intricacies (Dwivedi et al., 2022). When planning for the implementation of MBLLT, it is important to put first things like clear consent protocols, limited data retention, and safe cloud storage. Laiz-Ibáñez et al. (2025) stated these concerns and regarded biometric data misuse as a significant privacy issue. To reduce the chances of hidden surveillance and misuse, they suggested privacy-by-design models with encrypted interactions and governance by more than one agency. Chamola et al. (2025) emphasized that data protection focuses on other important issues, including transparency, fairness, and accountability. By thoroughly analyzing the ethical issues surrounding biodata, it is possible to create effective and safe governance for the educational metaverse. Ethical design must be cognizant of the potential misuse of biodata and uphold learners' right to anonymity in virtual environments through secure software development practices such as DevSecOps. This has consequences for human-centered, responsible innovation in MBLLT settings, where immersive technologies must be reconciled with human dignity, data minimization, and equitable access (Dincelli & Yayla, 2024).

The use of avatars has brought up questions about digital identity and behavior in virtual spaces. Avatars can help people get over their emotional barriers and make it easier to do public speaking in front of a group, yet having anonymous entity, they can also make it easier for people to harass others online, cross boundaries, and act inappropriately (Abhinaya et al., 2024). To ensure that language learners have a safe, fair, and respectful place to learn, MBLLT platforms need to have codes of conduct, a moderation mode (for both learners and instructors, as well as automated systems), and easy ways to track misconducts and avoid them. Additionally, the risk of deepfakes and identity manipulation in the Metaverse presents a significant threat to authenticity, learner dignity, and safety in educational environments, necessitating novel methods of authentication and digital literacy for both language learners and educators (Roe et al., 2024; Wu et al., 2023).

The psychological dimensions of MBLLT are multilayered, encompassing both significant benefits, such as increased motivation, mindfulness, concurrent with reduced anxiety and distractions (Arpaia et al., 2022), and the potential detrimental effect of abuse on mental well-being (Aboul-Yazeed et al., 2025) as well as the potential for cognitive load caused by over-immersion (Mancone et al., 2024; Sari et al., 2024). When sensitively designed, metaverse environments can increase engagement, motivation, and communicative confidence (Aydın, 2022). However, excessive immersion and unequal access to immersive technologies can also create new psychological and social challenges.

One of the psychological affordances of MBLLT setting resides in its capacity to lower learners' affective filter. Virtual environments provide a psychologically safe setting where learners can practice communication without being assessed; this can provide greater willingness to communicate (WTC) and language output (Fathi et al., 2025). Empirical research reveals that learners in MBLLT contexts give heightened motivation, engagement, and emotional resilience compared to traditional classrooms (Çelik & Baturay, 2024; Chang, 2025; Dandona & Bhatt, 2025).

While immersion occurs in MBLLT situations, it brings psychological and physiological concerns when exposure is excessive. Prolonged usage of head-mounted displays and high-sensory XR environments can generate cybersickness, confusion, and weariness (Gale et al., 2024). Moreover, fully immersive technologies may obliterate boundaries between virtual and physical environments. This can worsen addictive tendencies. To overcome these risks, educators should establish pedagogical frameworks that relate immersive activities to real-world applications. Structured session limitations, regular breaks between employment, and changing duties between virtual and real locations can assist language learners to preserve mental well-being (Damaševičius & Sidekerskienė, 2024). Additionally, educators should be well-trained to be aware of students' over-immersion through the use of reflective tools such as learning journals or logs for emotional reflection. These methods increase learners' resilience against the risks.

The societal ramifications of MBLLT extend beyond education to include matters of cultural representation, digital equity, and accessibility. Immersive technologies entail the potential to enhance intercultural communicative competence among language learners when they engage in culturally situated situations with AIANPCs and participate in virtual exchanges that emulate authentic discourse and pragmatic functions. However, these benefits might be linked to the ethical and culturally sensitive design of the virtual world. Ensuring that MBLLT environments, avatars, and

NPC discussions reflect the linguistic and cultural diversity of target populations helps promote inclusivity and equitable cultural representation. It should be recognized that ethnocentric preconceptions can be both harmful and insidious, particularly in models that rely on large language models. Contextual authenticity requires deliberate and rapt attention.

As far as equity concerns, accessibility and affordability of hardware, wearable technologies, network infrastructure, and internet connectivity are not evenly distributed among socioeconomic and geographical contexts. Generally, devices and infrastructure are costly, and this causes disadvantages for the language learner if they live in rural or suburban areas. These patterns of digital gap are similar to those previously observed in the CALL or MALL context. In addition to assets, the digital literacy necessary to navigate through MBLLT environments is not commonly observed among language instructors or researchers. To address the inequalities, corporate and educational institutions should work together on inclusive design and capacity-building among users and educators. Developing MBLLT applications that run on mobile and browser-based platforms can lower the hardware barrier to access, while teacher-training initiatives can increase digital readiness (Amiri, 2025; Gürkan, 2025; Lee & Hwang, 2023).

Given the fact that the revolutionary potential of XR and AI can be impressive and transforming, it is equally crucial to recognize the opposing restrictions that often dictate the scalability and sustainability of these technologies over time. First, institutional preparation can be different from one context to another. Without defined governance structures and standards, and leadership commitment, XR/AI projects might remain in the pilot stage and may fail to become part of everyday life. Secondly, the costs related to infrastructure and total ownership may be high since they include purchase of hardware and software, connectivity, maintainance, licensing, updates, cybersecurity, and technical support. These expenditures could intensify inequalities among educational institutions and geographical areas. Third, teacher training is a necessary step. To ensure effective integration, language teachers must have technological affordances and be open to redesign their lessons, align their assessments, and have professional development (Haobsh & Kardaş, 2025). Finally, language learners may not want to use XR/AI due to privacy concerns, motion discomfort, or doubts about personalized feedback. Recognizing these limitations can highlight the fact that the impact of education depends on the context, the ability to implement changes, and the ability to manage change, rather than the technology itself.

The next phase of MBLLT can be defined by the integration of AI, multimodal sensing, and 6G infrastructure. According to Alsamh et al. (2024), in near future, multisensory and low 6G networks will enable hyper-realistic, haptic, and affective communication, providing unprecedented immersion and responsiveness. Future research should, therefore, explore AI-enhanced adaptive systems capable of analyzing learners' cognitive and emotional states in real time, while language learning (Godwin-Jones, 2025; Yadav et al., 2025).

Studies on ethics of virtual learning (Abhinaya et al., 2024; Dincelli & Yayla, 2024) address the call for privacy-by-design frameworks, data consent processes, and the responsible use of AI-driven analytics. Future research can be designed to investigate possible models for ethical implementation for secure data governance across platforms while maintaining user privacy and accountability. Additionally, since the current paper has not been premised on an empirical research design due to the lack of technology in the local context of the researcher, future research can explore the psychological impacts of identity representation and avatar embodiment on oral and written communication, empirically investigating whether digital identity and interaction with avatars have a significant impact on learner motivation, self-efficacy, and task completion in EFL contexts.

References

Abhinaya, S. B., Sabir, A., & Das, A. (2024). Enabling developers, protecting users: Investigating harassment and safety in VR. *Proceedings of the 33rd USENIX Security Symposium (USENIX Security '24).* USENIX Association. https://doi.org/10.48550/arXiv.2403.05499

Aboul-Yazeed, R. S., Darwish, A., & Hassanien, A. E. (2025). Flourish the mood: A systematic review on the impacts of metaverse on psychological and mental health. *Frontiers in Virtual Reality, 6*, 1429038. https://doi.org/10.3389/frvir.2025.1429038

Ahmed, V., & Opoku, A. (2022). Technology-supported learning and pedagogy in times of crisis: The case of the COVID-19 pandemic. *Education and Information Technologies, 27*, 365–405. https://doi.org/10.1007/s10639-021-10706-w

Akyıldız, Y. (2025). The impact of virtual reality on vocabulary learning and cognitive efficiency. *Journal of Educational Technology and Online Learning, 8*(2), 152–163. https://doi.org/10.31681/jetol.1613357

Alam, A., & Mohanty, A. (2023). Educational technology: Exploring the convergence of technology and pedagogy through mobility, interactivity, AI, and learning tools. *Cogent Engineering, 10*(2). https://doi.org/10.1080/23311916.2023.2283282

Alhawsawi, S., & Alzaid, F. (2025). Systematic review of virtual reality's uses on vocabulary learning in higher education. *Smart Learning Environment, 12*(60). https://doi.org/10.1186/s40561-025-00414-0

Alsamh, M. H., Hawbani, A., Kumar, S., & Alsamhi, S. H. (2024). Multisensory metaverse-6G: A new paradigm of commerce and education. *IEEE Access, 12*, 75657–75677. https://doi.org/10.1109/ACCESS.2024.3392838

Amiri, S. M. H. (2025, March 26). Digital transformations in education: Research insights for 21st-century learning. *International Journal of Innovative Science, Engineering & Technology (IJISET), 12*(3), 1–15. https://doi.org/10.2139/ssrn.5194886

Arpaia, P., D'Errico, G., & De Paolis, L. T. (2022). A narrative review of mindfulness-based interventions using virtual reality. *Mindfulness, 13*, 556–571. https://doi.org/10.1007/s12671-021-01783-6

Asrifan, A., Aini, N., & Khristianto. (2025). The Future of education in the metaverse: Immersive, interactive, and collaborative learning. In R. González Vallejo (Ed.), *Harnessing chatbots for effective language teaching* (pp. 75–116). IGI Global Scientific Publishing. https://doi.org/10.4018/979-8-3693-9974-3.ch004

Aydın, S. (2022). The Metaverse in foreign language learning: A theoretical framework. *Innovational Research in ELT, 3*(2), 12–19. https://doi.org/10.29329/irelt.2022.505.2

Barsalou, L. W. (2008). Grounded cognition. *Annual Review of Psychology, 59*, 617–645. https://doi.org/10.1146/annurev.psych.59.103006.093639

Biocca, F., Harms, C., & Burgoon, J. K. (2003). Toward a more robust theory and measure of social presence: Review and suggested criteria. *Presence: Teleoperators and Virtual Environments, 12*(5), 456–480. https://doi.org/10.1162/105474603322761270

Brown, J. S., Collins, A., & Duguid, P. (1989). Situated cognition and the culture of learning. *Educational Researcher, 18*(1), 32–42. https://doi.org/10.3102/0013189X018001032

Cahyadi, P., Wardhana, D. I. A., Ansori, W. I., & Farah, R. R. (2022). Enhancing students' English speaking ability through VRChat game as learning media. *Journal of Research on Language Education, 3*(2), 54–61. https://doi.org/10.33365/jorle.v3i2.2135

Çakmak, F. (2019). Mobile learning and mobile-assisted language learning in focus. *Language and Technology, 1*(1), 30–48. https://dergipark.org.tr/tr/download/article-file/665969

Campitiello, L., Beatini, V., & Di Tore, S. (2024). Non-player character smart in virtual learning environment: Empowering education through artificial intelligence. In F. Palomba & C. Gravino (Eds.), *Artificial intelligence with and for learning sciences: Past, present, and future horizons* (Lecture Notes in Computer Science), 14545. Springer. https://doi.org/10.1007/978-3-031-57402-3_14

Cantone, A. A., Francese, R., Sais, R., Santosuosso, O. P., Sepe, A., Spera, S., Tortora, G., & Vitiello, G. (2023). Contextualized experiential language learning in the metaverse. In *Proceedings of the 15th Biannual Conference of the Italian SIGCHI* (pp. 1–7). ACM. https://doi.org/10.1145/3605390.3605395

Çelik, F. (2025). The impact of game-based metaverse on language learning motivation, anxiety, and vocabulary. *International Journal of Applied Linguistics*. https://doi.org/10.1111/ijal.12858

Çelik, F., & Baturay, M. H. (2024). The effect of metaverse on L2 vocabulary learning, retention, student engagement, presence, and community feeling. *BMC Psychology, 12*, 58. https://doi.org/10.1186/s40359-024-01549-4

Chamola, V., Peelam, M. S., Mittal, U., Hassija, V., Singh, A., Pareek, R., Mangal, P., Sangwan, D., de Albuquerque, V. H. C., Mahmud, M., & Brown, D. J. (2025). Metaverse for education: Developments, challenges, and future direction. *Computer Applications in Engineering Education, 33*, Article e70018. https://doi.org/10.1002/cae.70018

Chang, Y.-S. (2025). Engagement, academic emotions, and artificial intelligence application creativity in the metaverse: A study of facial expressions. *Journal of Computer Assisted Learning, 41*(3). https://doi.org/10.1111/jcal.70030

Damaševičius, R., & Sidekerskienė, T. (2024). Virtual worlds for learning in metaverse: A narrative review. *Sustainability, 16*(5), 2032. https://doi.org/10.3390/su16052032

Dandona, A., & Bhatt, S. (2025). Cognitive and emotional dimensions of sustainability: Building business resilience in the virtual world. In W. Leal Filho, S. Kautish, & V. P. Gupta (Eds.), *Metaverse and sustainability: Business resilience towards sustainable development goals* (*World Sustainability Series*). Springer. https://doi.org/10.1007/978-3-031-89545-6_5

Dewey, J. (1938). *Experience and education*. Kappa Delta Pi.

Dincelli, E., & Yayla, A. (2024). Teaching case: Security and privacy implications of virtual reality applications in the metaverse: A case of development, security, and operations (DevSecOps). *Journal of Information Systems Education, 35*(3), 261–270. https://doi.org/10.62273/JMZA1065

Dizon, G., & Tang, D. (2024). Explorations in the proto-metaverse: EFL learners' experiences and perceptions of immersive virtual reality for language learning. *The EuroCALL Review, 31*(2), 4–16. https://doi.org/10.4995/eurocall.2024.18946

Durmaz, O. (2025, June 28). DIVE-L: Design of immersive virtual environments for language learning – Guidelines for thoughtful integration for instructors. *The FLTMAG*. https://fltmag.com/design-of-immersive-virtual-environments-for-language-learning/

Dwivedi, Y. K., Hughes, L., Baabdullah, A. M., Ribeiro-Navarrete, S., Giannakis, M., Al-Debei, M. M., Dennehy, D., Metri, B., Buhalis, D., Cheung, C. M. K., Conboy, K., Doyle, R., Dubey, R., Dutot, V., Felix, R., Goyal, D. P., Gustafsson, A., Hinsch, C., Jebabli, I., & Wamba, S. F. (2022). Metaverse beyond the hype: Multidisciplinary perspectives on emerging challenges, opportunities, and agenda for research, practice and policy. *International Journal of Information Management, 66*, Article 102542. https://doi.org/10.1016/j.ijinfomgt.2022.102542

Fathi, J., Zou, D., & Zhaleh, K. (2025). Promoting intercultural communicative competence and willingness to communicate in EFL learners through virtual reality: A mixed-methods examination. *Computer Assisted Language Learning, 1–44,*. https://doi.org/10.1080/09588221.2025.2496827

Gale, E., O'Sullivan, A., Matthews, O., Dunn, J., Uchaeva, D., & McCarthy-Torrens, A. (2024). Glassware heroes: Using a virtual reality game to teach glassware assembly reduces mistakes made by laboratory novices. *ChemRxiv.*https://doi.org/10.26434/chemrxiv-2024-66p8h

Godwin-Jones, R. (2021). Evolving technologies for language learning. *Language Learning & Technology, 25*(3), 6–26. http://hdl.handle.net/10125/73443

Godwin-Jones, R. (2025). AI and VR converge: The future of language learning in an emerging metaverse. In Y. J. Lan, G. Y. Qi, & D. Chun (Eds.), *AI-mediated language education in the metaverse era* (*Chinese Language Learning Sciences*). Springer. https://doi.org/10.1007/978-981-95-0245-5_11

Gonzales, W. D. W., Shen, D. J., Yan, A., Xie, N., Francisco, M. L., & Wong, P. P. Y. (2025). AI NPCs in an educational metaverse: Evaluating the effectiveness of prompt templates for contextual interactions. In E. C. K. Cheng (Ed.), *Innovating education with AI. AETS 2024. Lecture notes in educational technology.* Springer. https://doi.org/10.1007/978-981-96-4952-5_4

Guo, X., Guo, Y., & Liu, Y. (2021). The development of extended reality in education: Inspiration from the research literature. *Sustainability, 13*(24), 13776. https://doi.org/10.3390/su132413776

Gürkan, A. M. (2025). Enhancing education through the Metaverse: Perspectives from Türkiye. *Digital Society, 4*(31). https://doi.org/10.1007/s44206-025-00183-w

Haobsh, T., & Kardaş, D. (2025). Yabancılara Türkçe öğretiminde dijital platformların informal öğrenmeye etkisi. In B. Bağcı Ayrancı & T. G. Şahin (Eds.), *Türkçe eğitimi araştırmaları* (pp. 31–50). Akademisyen Yayınevi. https://doi.org/10.37609/akya.3640.c6990

Huang, T.-C., & Tseng, H.-P. (2025). Extended reality in applied sciences education: A systematic review. *Applied Sciences, 15*(7), 4038. https://doi.org/10.3390/app15074038

Islam, M. Z., & Wang, G. (2025). Avatars in the educational metaverse. *Visual Computing for Industry, Biomedicine, and Art, 8*, 15. https://doi.org/10.1186/s42492-025-00196-9

Kaplan-Rakowski, R., & Gruber, A. (2023). An experimental study on reading in high-immersion virtual reality. *British Journal of Educational Technology, 55*(2), 541–559. https://doi.org/10.1111/bjet.13392

Kaplan-Rakowski, R., & Thrasher, T. (2025). The impact of high-immersion virtual reality and interactivity on vocabulary learning. *British Journal of Educational Technology, 56*(6), 2647–2670. https://doi.org/10.1111/bjet.13603

Knutzen, K., Rothenberger, L., Tribusean, I., & Xu, Y. (2025). Using social virtual reality in teaching intercultural communication. *Technology, Knowledge and Learning, 30*, 1167–1187. https://doi.org/10.1007/s10758-025-09822-0

Ko, C.-J. (2012). A case study of language learners' social presence in synchronous CMC. *ReCALL, 24*(1), 66–84. https://doi.org/10.1017/S0958344011000292

Kolb, D. A. (1984). *Experiential learning: Experience as the source of learning and development.* Prentice Hall.

Krashen, S. (1982). *Principles and practice in second language acquisition.* Pergamon Press.

Kreijns, K., Xu, K., & Weidlich, J. (2022). Social presence: Conceptualization and measurement. *Educational Psychology Review, 34*(1), 139–170. https://doi.org/10.1007/s10648-021-09623-8

Laiz-Ibáñez, H., Mendaña-Cuervo, C., & Carus Candas, J. L. (2025). The metaverse: Privacy and information security risks. *International Journal of Information Management Data Insights, 5*(2), Article 100373. https://doi.org/10.1016/j.jjimei.2025.100373

Lan, Y. J. (2025). Language learning in the metaverse. In Y. J. Lan, G. Y. Qi, & D. Chun (Eds.), *AI-mediated language education in the metaverse era* (pp. 11–30). Springer.

Lee, H., & Hwang, Y. (2023). Training with, about, for metaverse: Mixed-methods research on training pre-service teachers as metaverse-certified practitioners. *Journal of English Teaching through Movies and Media, 24*(4), 73–93. https://doi.org/10.16875/stem.2023.24.4.73

Lee, S. M. (2023). Second language learning through an emergent narrative in a narrative-rich customizable metaverse platform. *IEEE Transactions on Learning Technologies, 16*(6), 1071–1081. https://doi.org/10.1109/TLT.2023.3267563

Long, M. H. (1996). The role of linguistic environment in second language acquisition. In W. C. Ritchie, & T. K. Bhatia (Eds). *Handbook of second language acquisition* (pp. 413–468).

Makransky, G., & Petersen, G. B. (2021). The cognitive affective model of immersive learning (CAMIL): A theoretical research-based model of learning in immersive virtual reality. *Educational Psychology Review, 33*, 937–958. https://doi.org/10.1007/s10648-020-09586-2

Mancone, S., Tosti, B., Corrado, S., & Diotaiuti, P. (2024). Effects of video game immersion and task interference on cognitive performance: A study on immediate and delayed recall and recognition accuracy. *PeerJ, 12*, Article e18195. https://doi.org/10.7717/peerj.18195

Mayer, R. E. (2021). *Multimedia learning* (3rd ed). Cambridge University Press.

European Parliamentary Research Service. (2021). *Person identification, human rights and ethical principles: Rethinking biometrics in the era of AI* (STU 697191). European Parliament. https://www.europarl.europa.eu/thinktank/en/document/EPRS_STU(2021)697191

Piaget, J. (1972). *The psychology of the child*. Basic Books.

Reinders, H., Lai, C., & Sundqvist, P. (2022). Language learning and teaching beyond the classroom. In H. Reinders, C. Lai, & P. Sundqvist (Eds.), *The Routledge handbook of language teaching and learning beyond the classroom* (pp. 1–6). Routledge.

Richards, P. (2025). Computer simulations for (im)politeness instruction: Avatar versus interface feedback. In M. González-Lloret, J. M. Sykes, & J. K. Yoshioka (Eds.), *Pragmatics & language learning* (pp. 1–20). National Foreign Language Resource Center, University of Hawai'i. http://hdl.handle.net/10125/75345

Roe, J., Perkins, M., & Furze, L. (2024). Deepfakes and higher education: A research agenda and scoping review of synthetic media. *Journal of University Teaching & Learning Practice, 21*(10), 1–22. https://doi.org/10.53761/2y2np178

Sari, R. C., Pranesti, A., Solikhatun, I., et al. (2024). Cognitive overload in immersive virtual reality in education: More presence but less learnt? *Education and Information Technologies, 29*, 12887–12909. https://doi.org/10.1007/s10639-023-12379-z

Schorr, I., Plecher, D. A., Eichhorn, C., & Klinker, G. (2024). Foreign language learning using augmented reality environments: A systematic review. *Frontiers in Virtual Realities, 5*, 1288824. https://doi.org/10.3389/frvir.2024.1288824

Shin, D., Kwon, S. K., Noh, W. I., & Hwang, Y. (2025). Exploring the role of the metaverse in english speaking proficiency tests. *Journal of Computer Assisted Learning, 41*(1), Article e13108. https://doi.org/10.1111/jcal.13108

Shu, X., & Gu, X. (2023). An empirical study of a smart education model enabled by the edu-metaverse to enhance better learning outcomes for students. *Systems, 11*(2), 75. https://doi.org/10.3390/systems11020075

Singh, J., Steele, K., & Singh, L. (2021). Combining the best of online and face-to-face learning: Hybrid and blended learning approach for COVID-19, post-vaccine, and post-pandemic world. *Journal of Educational Technology Systems, 50*(2), 140–171. https://doi.org/10.1177/00472395211047865

Swain, M. (1995). Three functions of output in second language learning. In G. Cook & B. Seidlhofer (Eds.), *Principle and practice in applied linguistics* (pp. 125–144). Oxford University Press.

Tariq, M. U. (2026). The role of AI in personalized English language learning. In A. Shukla, B. Meeprom, K. Khunasathitchai, & N. Yadav (Eds.), *AI-powered English teaching* (pp. 93–124). IGI Global Scientific Publishing. https://doi.org/10.4018/979-8-3373-1952-0.ch003

Thrasher, T., Kaplan-Rakowski, R., Chun, D., & Sadler, R. (2024). Virtual reality: "Awesome", "OK", or "not so good" for language learning? *Editorial Universitat Politècnica de València*. https://doi.org/10.4995/EuroCALL2023.2023.16948

Tong, P., Yang, H., & Ji, H. (2025). Metaverse applications in language education: A critical narrative review and integrative framework for pedagogical innovation. *Educational Research Review, 100733*. https://doi.org/10.1016/j.edurev.2025.100733

Wang, C., & Zou, B. (2025). D-ID Studio: Empowering language teaching with AI avatars. *TESOL Journal, 16*(2), Article e70034. https://doi.org/10.1002/tesj.70034

Waring, Z. H. (2016). *Theorizing pedagogical interaction.* Routledge.

Wu, X., Hui, P., & Zhou, H. (2023). Deepfake in the metaverse: An outlook survey. *arXiv*, 2306.07011. https://doi.org/10.48550/arXiv.2306.07011

Xiao, Y., Li, D., & Guo, K. (2025). Generative AI-powered non-player characters in digital storyline-based learning: An innovative approach to EFL writing. *Innovation in Language Learning and Teaching.* https://doi.org/10.1080/17501229.2025.2545397

Xu, J., Zhai, X., Chen, N.-S., Ghani, U., Istenic, A., & Xin, J. (2025). Integrating AI-driven wearable metaverse technologies into ubiquitous blended learning: A framework based on embodied interaction and multi-agent collaboration. *Education Sciences, 15*(7), 900. https://doi.org/10.3390/educsci15070900

Yadav, R., Nghiem, X., & Yadav, M. (2025). Adaptive AI in metaverse language education. In R. González Vallejo (Ed.), *Harnessing chatbots for effective language teaching* (pp. 49–74). IGI Global Scientific Publishing. https://doi.org/10.4018/979-8-3693-9974-3.ch003

Zhang, G., Cao, J., Liu, D., & Qi, J. (2022a). Popularity of the metaverse: Embodied social presence theory perspective. *Frontiers in Psychology, 13*, Article 997751. https://doi.org/10.3389/fpsyg.2022.997751

Zhang, X., Chen, Y., Hu, L., & Wang, Y. (2022b). The metaverse in education: Definition, framework, features, potential applications, challenges, and future research topics. *Frontiers in Psychology, 13*, 1016300. https://doi.org/10.3389/fpsyg.2022.1016300

Zhong, R., & Zhao, Y. (2025). Education paradigm shifts in the age of AI: A spatiotemporal analysis of learning. *ECNU Review of Education, 8*(2), 319–342. https://doi.org/10.1177/20965311251315204

Ehsan Namaziandost is affiliated with the Department of English at Islamic Azad University of Ahvaz, Iran. His research focuses on metaverse-based language learning and teaching, particularly immersive and multimodal environments. Namaziandost examines extended reality technologies and their pedagogical applications. He contributes to frameworks that connect learning theories with technological design in educational metaverses. His work addresses ethical, psychological, and societal dimensions of immersive language instruction.

Fidel Çakmak is an assistant professor in the Department of Foreign Language Education at Alanya Alaaddin Keykubat University, Antalya, Türkiye. His expertise spans computer-assisted and mobile-assisted language learning, with a strong emphasis on extended reality. Çakmak explores the evolution from traditional CALL to metaverse-based approaches. He analyzes platforms, case studies, and empirical evidence for learner-centered immersive experiences. His contributions provide a comprehensive technological framework for future trends in language pedagogy.

Theoretical Foundations of Second Language Acquisition in Metaverse-Based Language Teaching and Learning

Seçil Büyükbay İpekçi and Gonca Yangın Ekşi

Abstract The first section of this chapter establishes Metaverse-Based Language Teaching and Learning (MBLTL) by integrating five essential second language acquisition (SLA) theories: the Input Hypothesis, Interaction Hypothesis, Sociocultural Theory, Output Hypothesis, and Embodied Cognition. The theoretical foundations underpinning the use of metaverse environments for language learning have received limited scholarly attention despite the growing use of virtual reality applications in language education. The proposed framework explains how metaverse features, including real-time multimodal communication, spatial presence, contextualized learning, and embodied interaction, operationalize established SLA principles. The chapter demonstrates, through systematic analysis of recent evidence from 2020 to 2025, that immersive environments improve comprehensible input through multimodal redundancy, enable meaning negotiation through collaborative tasks, support extended output production, sociocultural learning through digital scaffolding, and enhance conceptual understanding through movement-meaning connections. The framework presents visual representations of these integrations, together with virtual environment assessment methods and implementation instructions for differentiating between student proficiency levels.

Keywords Computer-assisted language learning (CALL) · Metaverse-based language teaching and learning (MBLTL) · Second language acquisition (SLA) · Embodied cognition · Virtual immersive environments · English language teaching (ELT)

S. B. İpekçi (✉)
Social Sciences University of Ankara, Ankara, Türkiye
e-mail: secil.buyukbayipekci@asbu.edu.tr

G. Y. Ekşi
Gazi University, Ankara, Türkiye
e-mail: ygonca@gazi.edu.tr

F. Çelik and C. Yangın Ersanlı (eds.), *Metaverse-Based Language Learning and Teaching*, English Language Education 49,
https://doi.org/10.1007/978-3-032-31366-9_3

1 Introduction

The metaverse has transitioned from science fiction to real-world virtual platforms that support permanent three-dimensional multi-user interactions over the past few years. Educational institutions now view these virtual environments as new learning platforms that unite student immersion with social interaction and interactive features. The current scholarly consensus defines the metaverse as a space for user participation in virtual worlds where people use avatars to interact with one another and create shared spaces in real time. The capabilities of these environments led to the creation of new teaching methods that offered alternative virtual active spaces to enrich traditional educational content and linked language education to collaborative activities and physical exercises (Godwin-Jones, 2023; Mystakidis, 2022).

The educational environment has undergone a major transformation because students in the twenty-first century need to handle new types of communication tasks. Modern students require educational experiences that combine interactive elements with contextual learning and identity-based, goal-oriented content rather than traditional drill-based or mechanical practice methods.

The main advantage of metaverse-based language teaching and learning (MBLTL) lies in transforming the learning environment where students interact with language rather than substituting for existing technologies. Students in three-dimensional spaces explore virtual streets, shops, and museums, using gestures to manipulate virtual objects and collaborating with peers and artificial intelligence agents on complex tasks. The immersive learning experiences in virtual environments support Second Language Acquisition (SLA) by aligning with and expanding upon established SLA theoretical mechanisms. The emerging research literature emphasizes four main affordances of MBLTL: real-time multimodal communication, spatial immersion, contextualized learning, and embodied interaction (Chun et al., 2022; Godwin-Jones, 2023; Lin & Lan, 2015).

Theoretical frameworks of SLA serve as fundamental tools for explaining language acquisition in virtual learning spaces. Virtual environments deliver comprehensible input through spoken words, written text, visual cues, and auditory signals, while reinforcing the same message across modes, helping students better understand and remember the input. MBLTL students use verbal exchanges and joint object handling to generate clarification requests, recasts, and confirmation checks through meaning negotiation. Immersive settings enable students to produce output through spoken and written communication as well as through coordinated bodily actions accompanied by speech. Avatars, shared building interfaces, and structured collaborative tasks function as mediational tools for scaffolded participation. The sensorimotor experiences in MBLTL enable learners to develop deeper conceptual understanding because they involve physical gestures, object manipulation, and spatial navigation (Godwin-Jones, 2023).

As the research base for MBLTL is still developing, research conducted in the early stages supports the proposed theories. Meta-analytic evidence from 21 quantitative studies involving 1,144 participants demonstrates significant positive effects of

VR on both the linguistic and affective dimensions of language learning (Chen et al., 2022), although heterogeneity in study designs and the need for more rigorous empirical investigations are noted. More specifically, a quasi-experimental study conducted in Türkiye demonstrated that metaverse-based teaching using the Spatial.io platform led to improved L2 vocabulary acquisition and retention, increased student engagement, and stronger feelings of community (Çelik & Baturay, 2024). Research on metaverse applications in language education shows positive results, but experts agree that stronger theoretical models and more experimental evidence are needed for further development (Fan & Chiang, 2023; Li & Yu, 2023). There are some studies that demonstrate the correlation between virtual reality immersion and increasing student motivation and show positive learning effects in specific situations. On the other hand, researchers also emphasize some methodological challenges and theoretical foundation requirements, as well as the above-mentioned benefits (Dhimolea et al., 2022; Kaplan-Rakowski et al., 2023; Peixoto et al., 2021). The research indicates promising results but demonstrates the need for better theoretical connections between findings. Research findings that lack theoretical foundations will stay disconnected from tools and become impractical for educational context application and pedagogical development. This chapter takes as its point of departure the identified theoretical gap, with the aim of establishing a connection between SLA theories and metaverse tools by examining their specific affordances.

The framework provides teachers with evidence-based teaching methods, which include role-plays and design tasks for pushed output and peer mentoring for sociocultural mediation and gesture-based tasks for meaning construction. Scientists must follow the research framework to study specific mechanisms through their examination of presence effects on noticing abilities, embodied interaction effects on retention, and avatar identity effects on communication willingness (Chun et al., 2022; Godwin-Jones, 2023).

Implementation faces challenges, including variable hardware access, avatar-mediated social dynamics, and multimodal interaction assessment. Robust theoretical frameworks must address these barriers to improve rather than hinder practice.

It is important to note that while this framework integrates well-established SLA theories with emerging metaverse affordances, the empirical validation of these specific connections remains an important area for future research.

The chapter fulfills two essential goals. The chapter demonstrates how to use traditional SLA theories in immersive learning spaces through the development of teaching and research methods based on their fundamental operations. The proposed model combines metaverse functionality with educational design principles, research methods, and assessment techniques into a single framework instead of following a predetermined structure. The research supports language education technological advancement through theoretical foundations that leverage immersive platforms' distinctive features. (Çelik & Baturay, 2024; Lin & Lan, 2015).

2 Theoretical Background

Research on technology in second language acquisition (SLA) has advanced through successive technological developments, which created new inquiries about language perception and processing and usage by learners. The development of technology in language learning began with computer-assisted language learning (CALL), which analyzed screen-based input and feedback and assessment (Chapelle, 2001) before transitioning to mobile-assisted language learning (MALL), which enabled learners to practice languages through portable devices with context-sensitive features (Kukulska-Hulme & Shield, 2008). The present metaverse research on immersive avatar environments follows this trend by providing social presence, embodied experiences, and detailed contextual information to large numbers of users. The interpretation of these possibilities requires a theoretical foundation based on fundamental SLA frameworks.

3 Input, Noticing, and Comprehension

The Input Hypothesis developed by Krashen (1982, 1985) serves as a fundamental concept in SLA because learners acquire language through exposure to comprehensible input that slightly exceeds their current understanding level (i + 1). Schmidt (1990, 2001) developed the Noticing Hypothesis, which states that learners need to focus on linguistic elements during exposure to language acquisition. The research in CALL focused on text enhancement methods, glosses, and captions, and multimodal input to make language noticeable while preventing learner confusion (Chapelle, 2001).

The metaverse enhances these research inquiries because it enables students to encounter different input forms, which include written signs, environmental noises, body gestures, eye movements, and audio signals that accompany text and speech. Students achieve a better understanding through redundant communication channels because these channels distribute mental workload and enable them to identify meaning by matching signals. The environment's interactive elements, which include hotspots and object affordances, enable students to detect crucial information without requiring distracting highlighting methods. Interactive elements, including hotspots and object affordances, enable students to detect crucial information without distracting highlighting. The research findings also support the theoretical framework established by the study. To exemplify, Wang et al. investigated AR and VR environments that produced superior vocabulary learning and retention outcomes with positive student feedback. Xie et al. (2025) proved that IVR environments built through input processing theory produced better long-term vocabulary retention than PowerPoint-based instruction, especially when students took the test after a delay. The research indicates that metaverse environments that use multimodal redundancy and immersive contextualization help students better detect information and understand it.

4 Interaction, Negotiation, and Feedback

The Interaction Hypothesis developed by Long (1996) demonstrates that students learn language through conversational meaning while receiving form-function feedback through recasts, which help them understand language structures. The core emphasis of CALL negotiation is that it connects learners' needs with appropriate input. Through negotiation, students can request clarification and verify their comprehension. Research focuses on technology-based communication systems, which support both immediate and postponed computer-mediated communication (CMC) to help students get feedback, practice speaking turns, and learn from diverse cultural perspectives.

The shared artifact manipulation capabilities of metaverse platforms generate negotiation sequences that extend past basic verbal communication because users can work together on shared tasks. The process of creating virtual objects and solving spatial puzzles with others requires learners to ask for clarification and verify their understanding while teachers and peers provide immediate, relevant feedback that matches the current activity. The platform features support task-based language teaching principles because tasks function as the core design elements, and students focus on meaningful language exchange (Ellis, 2003; Long, 2015). Research studies from recent times show that VR environments create spaces for complex meaning sequence negotiations through immersive experiences. Chen and Sevilla-Pavón (2023) studied Taiwan-Spain virtual exchange participants who used English-as-a-lingua-franca (ELF) to negotiate meaning through embodied semiotic resources, including head movements and gestures, facial expressions, body posture, and spatial arrangements in their immersive VR platform. The researchers used multimodal interaction analysis to show that avatar-based representations helped users indicate, understand, and explain their meaning to resolve misunderstandings through non-verbal communication channels. The research confirms Long's (1996) form-function feedback theory by showing that immersive environments create advanced multimodal negotiation processes, which standard CMC systems lack.

5 Output, Pushed Production, and Metalinguistic Reflection

The Output Hypothesis developed by Swain (1985, 1995, 2005) states that language production activities that exceed learners' current abilities lead to enhanced processing depth, hypothesis evaluation, and metalinguistic thinking. The use of writing tools, chat functions, and recording platforms in CALL research has been studied to examine output, while MALL expanded speaking and writing opportunities through voice notes, short videos, and mobile presentations.

The metaverse enables users to generate output through spoken words and written messages, non-verbal signals, and physical movements. The design of presentation spaces, collaborative design studios, and role-play scenarios enables creators to establish specific requirements that extend the duration of discussions. The shared environment allows learners to link objects with gestures while speaking, which strengthens their discourse connections and enables advanced explanatory methods. The dual-channel production system of output theory faces new challenges because researchers need to study how verbal and physical communication streams work together to develop interlanguage skills. The features of immersive environments affect students' desire to communicate, which stands as a vital emotional factor that affects their output creation. The research by Fathi et al. (2025) used the ImmerseMe platform for VR-based intervention to show that EFL students developed better intercultural competence and communication skills through VR training than traditional classroom methods. The research by Wu and Hung (2022) showed that VR-based learning improved students' English-speaking abilities while simultaneously boosting their willingness to communicate and their ability to learn independently. The anonymous nature of VR avatars helps users feel less anxious when speaking foreign languages, which leads to an environment where they feel secure enough to take risks and produce more extended responses, according to Swain's Output Hypothesis.

6 Sociocultural Theory: Mediation, ZPD, and Communities of Practice

SCT defines learning as a social activity that depends on tools and signs and participant interaction within the Zone of Proximal Development (ZPD) according to Vygotsky (1978) and Lantolf and Thorne (2006). The theory demonstrates that language acquisition happens through social activities because it requires scaffolding, guided participation, and cultural artifacts that affect mental operations. The research on CALL technology within SCT frameworks employs technology to steer learning activities while students team up to construct knowledge (Lantolf & Thorne, 2006; Warschauer, 1997).

The Metaverse environment operates under SCT principles because its virtual objects, collaborative tools, and permanent items function as mediational tools that direct participant behavior regarding attention distribution and role and responsibility management. Research evidence supports these theoretical findings through studies conducted in different virtual world environments and language learning settings. Lan (2020a, 2020b) developed a complete theoretical framework that proves virtual reality environments operate based on Vygotsky's sociocultural theory by showing students need to participate in real-world situations for learning. Lan conducted multiple SCT-based studies, which proved that virtual worlds enable foreign language learning through immersion, imagination, and interaction when students use new learning activities and mediational resources. The theoretical framework of these studies received confirmation through empirical research conducted in metaverse environments during 2024–2025. The Spatial.io platform study conducted by Çelik and Baturay (2024) with 86 Turkish high school students demonstrated that metaverse environments with immersive and interactive features enhance vocabulary learning and retention through social multisensory interactions that support knowledge development. Çelik and Ersanlı (2025) developed EFL listening lessons in the metaverse through social constructivist theory to demonstrate how virtual collaborative activities enhance student motivation and self-determination through genuine learning experiences. The metaverse operates as a mediational environment that enables students to develop collective understanding through collaborative work on assignments by using virtual tools to steer their focus according to sociocultural learning principles.

7 Embodied Cognition: Grounding Meaning in Action

The embodied cognition theory states that mental operations develop from physical body experiences instead of depending on symbolic processing (Barsalou, 2008; Lindgren & Johnson-Glenberg, 2013; Wilson, 2002). Language learning benefits from gesture and posture, spatial orientation, and object handling because these physical actions help students understand metaphors, remember information, and comprehend material better. Research indicates that students learn better when they use gestures during speech and perform actions because meaningful movement enhances their ability to remember and apply learned material (Lindgren & Johnson-Glenberg, 2013).

The metaverse provides an embodied experience because users navigate through virtual spaces while using controllers or body-tracking systems to perform gestures and virtual object manipulation for goal achievement. The physical interactions in immersive environments enable students to connect abstract language elements to their actual perceptions through tasks that involve navigation and construction activities. The fundamental design element of embodiment in immersive environments allows teachers to connect physical actions with semantic meaning, which traditional screens cannot support.

8 From CALL/MALL to Immersion: Continuities and Extensions

The metaverse extends the capabilities of CALL and MALL methods instead of eliminating their use. The development of multimodality results in situated multimodality because of connected spatial cues, which enable co-present collaboration through shared objects, and MALL's context-sensitive design transforms into virtual worlds (Dede, 2009; Godwin-Jones, 2023). Research studies through meta-analysis show that virtual reality environments generate superior affective results than traditional computer-assisted language learning systems when it comes to student motivation and anxiety reduction (Qiu et al., 2024).

9 Framework Alignment with Metaverse Affordances

The theoretical frameworks (Input Hypothesis, Interaction Hypothesis, Output Hypothesis, Sociocultural Theory, Embodied Cognition) are operationalized through metaverse affordances. The combination of multimodal redundancy with designed salience helps students notice more efficiently because it presents multiple signals that point to the same information. The process of shared task execution leads to negotiation patterns that create the most efficient link between form and meaning. Students develop their vocabulary and sentence structure through real-life communication needs that emerge from role-plays, design tasks, and presentations.

Scaffolding and scripts function as sociocultural mediational tools that guide students through sequential steps that match their current understanding level within their Zone of Proximal Development. Physical exercise allows people to connect theoretical concepts with physical movements, which leads to better memory retention and practical skill development. The platform does not achieve superiority over other platforms through this alignment. The framework establishes particular requirements for immersive environments to enhance SLA mechanisms, which generate experimental predictions about spatial language acquisition through embodied co-manipulation when compared to text-based methods, thus leading research toward mechanism-based studies instead of tool-centered investigations.

10 Caveats and Theoretical Refinements

The framework demonstrates potential but requires further theoretical expansion. The research on multimodality needs to establish whether gestures, haptics, and gaze function as individual communication channels or as part of the input process. The use of avatars creates uncertainty about personal identity because users must consider their appearance, anonymity, and social expectations when deciding to interact with others. The design elements that help understanding become overwhelming for new learners when they do not receive adequate management of their mental workload. Theoretical models must integrate socio-material barriers with cognitive factors to address equity and access challenges.

11 Conceptual Framework for MBLTL

The following section develops an integrated framework that unites essential SLA theories with the special features of metaverse-based language teaching and learning (MBLTL). The framework avoids repeating each theory from scratch by showing how its fundamental principles operate together and expand through immersive 3D environments that support multiple users.

12 Integrative Model of SLA and Metaverse Affordances

The conceptual framework of MBLTL, presented in Fig. 1, shows how established SLA theories (Input Hypothesis, Interaction Hypothesis, Output Hypothesis, Sociocultural Theory, and Embodied Cognition) function through the unique features of the metaverse. The framework illustrates this relationship through its outer ring, which displays four theoretical bases (Input/Noticing, Interaction, Embodied Cognition, and Sociocultural Theory) and its inner sections, which represent the four metaverse affordances (Real-time Multimodal Communication, Spatial Presence, Embodied Interaction, and Contextualized Learning.

The research uses Multimodal Communication and Spatial Presence, Embodied Interaction, and Contextualized Learning to operationalize these theories in immersive virtual environments. Notably, Swain's (1985, 1995, 2005) Output Hypothesis, though theoretically fundamental and discussed extensively in the theoretical background, does not appear as a discrete element in Fig. 1. The core ability to generate output in metaverse environments through pushed output production consists of various linked elements. Extended verbal output occurs through Real-time Multimodal Communication during collaborative exchanges, embodied output emerges through Embodied Interaction when learners coordinate gestures with speech, and authentic production happens via Contextualized Learning in meaningful communicative contexts. The integration of output in this system follows task-based language teaching methods because students generate output through activities rather than isolated production exercises, which differentiates metaverse-based learning from traditional CALL environments where output functions independently.

The circular design in Fig. 1 emphasizes the non-hierarchical, recursive nature of these components. The multiple theoretical principles operate through each affordance, which enables continuous bidirectional feedback loops between language learning processes rather than sequential progression.

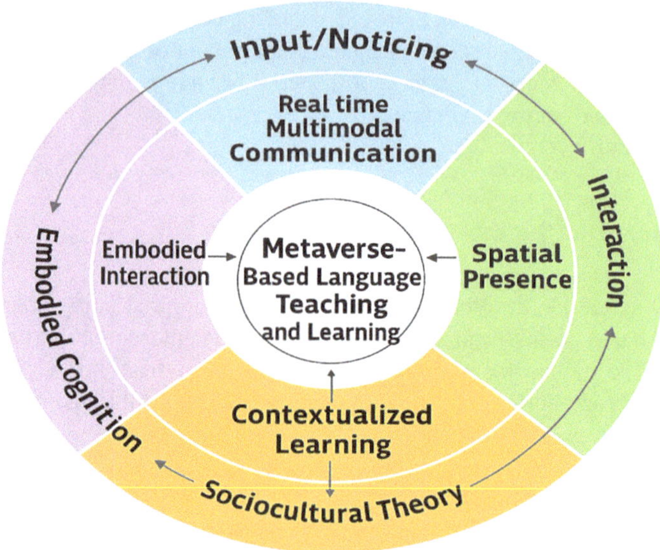

Fig. 1 Integrative conceptual framework for metaverse-based language teaching and learning (MBLTL): a non-hierarchical cyclical model

The circular model in Fig. 1 illustrates the non-linear recursive process of language learning within metaverse environments. The radial structure of this model differs from sequential models because it shows how multiple affordances become active at the same time during immersive learning experiences. The color scheme separates theoretical domains from each other while MBLTL stands at the center to show its function as a unifying framework that links all current theories together. The framework integrates four theoretical foundations (outer ring), which support four metaverse capabilities (inner segments) that form the core of MBLTL. The outer ring shows four theories, which include Input/Noticing (Krashen, 1985 and Schmidt, 1990, 2001), Interaction (Long, 1996), Embodied Cognition (Barsalou, 2008; Wilson, 2002), and Sociocultural Theory (Lantolf & Thorne, 2006; Vygotsky, 1978). The inner segments show Real-time Multimodal Communication (blue) which allows students to receive understandable input while participating in team-based activities through visual and auditory and textual communication channels and Spatial Presence (green) which supports students to practice spatial language through three-dimensional virtual environments (Dede, 2009; Lan, 2020a, 2020b) and Embodied Interaction (purple) which lets students interact physically with objects by linking their movements to specific meanings.

The system enables students to interact with objects and spaces while generating language through its interface, and provides Contextualized Learning (orange), which creates authentic digital environments with built-in support for sociocultural learning principles. The circular arrangement represents the non-hierarchical, interconnected nature of these components, where each affordance simultaneously supports multiple theories and each theory manifests through multiple affordances. The feedback loops in Fig. 1 demonstrate the continuous two-way communication process of virtual environment learning, unlike traditional instructional sequences, where activities target isolated skills.

Virtual marketplaces enable real-time multimodal communication for speech-based meaning negotiation, while users experience spatial presence through navigation of three-dimensional space, and they can use embodied interaction to point at and manipulate virtual products and learn through contextualized experiences that mimic real commercial transactions. The metaverse enables students to use multiple affordances at once, which creates learning experiences that differ from traditional language learning methods.

13 Framework Architecture and Component Integration

The integrated framework operates through three hierarchical levels, which convert basic SLA mechanisms into advanced virtual learning experiences. The first level of the framework includes basic SLA mechanisms that use multimodal redundancy to enhance input and noticing processes and co-presence and shared objects to facilitate interaction and multichannel production for output, digital tools, and scaffolding for sociocultural mediation and movement-meaning coupling for embodied cognition.

The second level contains metaverse affordances, which function as connecting elements between theoretical models and real-world implementation methods. Real-time multimodal communication enables users to interact through speech, gestures, and body movements at the same time, while spatial presence and immersion create authentic language learning environments, and contextualized learning spaces deliver relevant linguistic content, and embodied interaction systems link physical actions to mental processing.

The central MBLTL shows improved learning results, which develop when SLA theories combine with metaverse functionality. The outcomes from this integration include students who notice language features faster because of environmental cues, who maintain purposeful dialogue through collaborative tasks, who produce extended, authentic speech in real-world scenarios, who receive adaptive virtual support for self-directed learning, and who develop abstract concept understanding through physical metaphors and spatial representations.

14 Mechanism-Specific Applications Within Virtual Environments

The theoretical connection between SLA mechanisms and metaverse capabilities needs to be converted into practical educational approaches. The integrative framework (Fig. 1) shows how these mechanisms work together in MBLTL environments, but educators need to create specific applications for each mechanism to implement and evaluate. The following section analyzes how the core SLA theories operationalize through metaverse affordances to transform into observable learning results through metaverse-specific features and teaching approaches, starting from their theoretical foundations. The process model in Fig. 2 shows a systematic approach to transform theoretical principles into measurable results for each mechanism through four stages. The model shows how established SLA theories use particular metaverse features, including multimodal communication, spatial presence, and embodied interaction, to create specific teaching methods that result in particular learning effects. The simultaneous operation of these mechanisms in actual virtual learning environments produces the combined effects that researchers have identified. The following analysis explains how each theoretical principle operationalizes through metaverse affordances, which show how metaverse features enable theory-to-practice conversion and identify the best pedagogical design principles to achieve maximum mechanism effectiveness.

The model demonstrates how five fundamental SLA theories (purple, left column) become operational through metaverse capabilities (pink, second column), which lead to specific teaching methods (blue, third column) that produce quantifiable student learning results (green, right column). The horizontal arrows show the step-by-step transformation process of each theoretical mechanism, which demonstrates how metaverse-based language learning theories are applied in practice.

15 Input and Noticing Enhancement

The traditional classroom setting limits input delivery because it follows linear teaching approaches and has limited sensory access channels. The framework removes this limitation through environmental input layering, which provides contextual information through orthographic signage, ambient conversations, gesture demonstrations, and spatial arrangements in virtual environments. Students learn prepositions through hands-on activities when they explore virtual tunnels and buildings and move between virtual trees because the experience connects abstract language concepts to physical space understanding.

The adaptive noticing systems operate as interactive educational tools that present important information through environmental cues that respond to student actions and their needs. The system employs non-intrusive signals to show students important linguistic elements while maintaining their ability to communicate naturally,

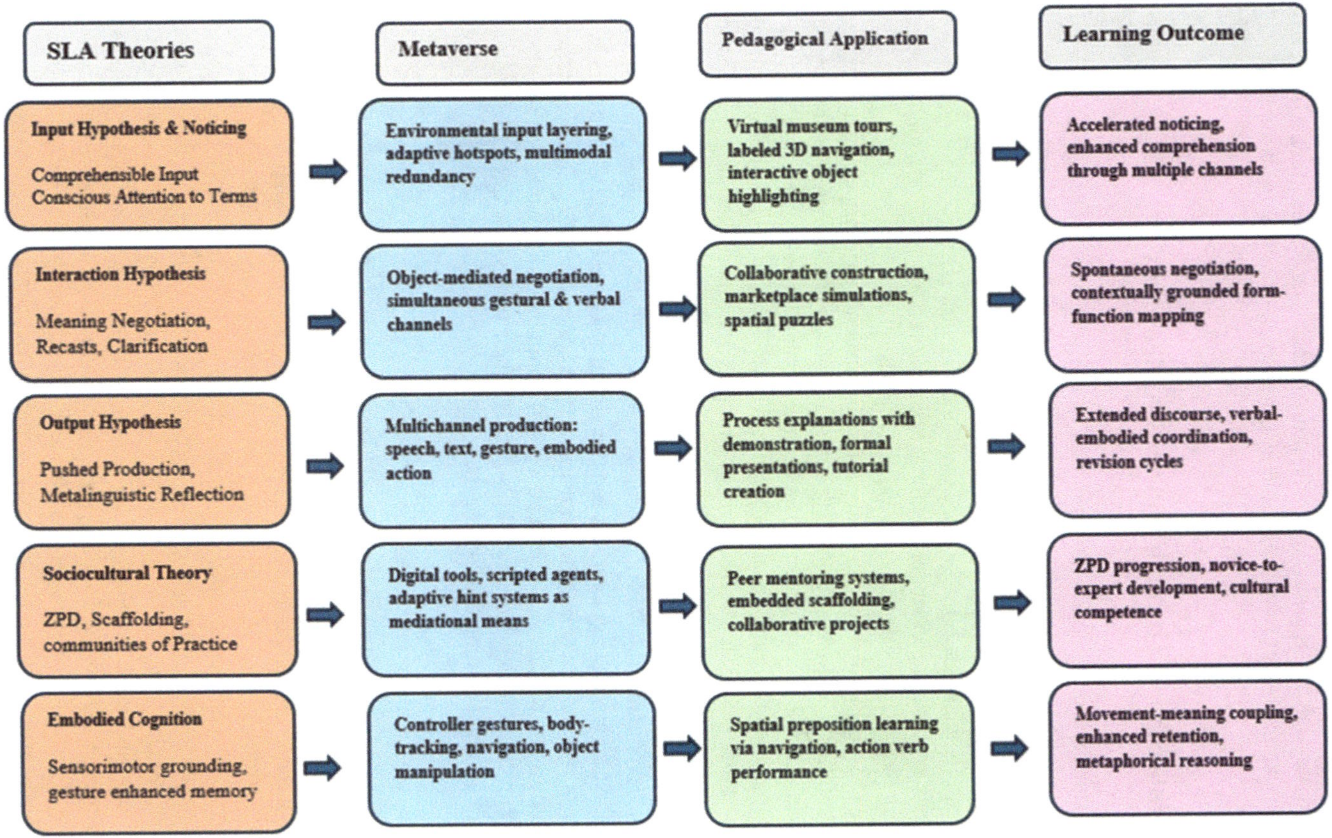

Fig. 2 Process flow model: translation of SLA mechanisms into learning outcomes in MBLTL

and presents basic language elements through multiple sensory channels to prevent students from losing important information. Students learn new multiple encoding methods through different learning paths after experiencing avatar speech with virtual surface text and body gestures and spatial arrangements in virtual environments.

16 Interaction Through Shared Problem-Solving

The framework introduces a new approach to interaction by using object-mediated negotiation sequences to expand beyond spoken words. Learners work together on virtual construction tasks, spatial puzzles, and digital artifact creation, which leads to spontaneous clarification requests and confirmation checks that stem from actual task requirements instead of pre-designed conversation starters. The collaborative activities produce the essential meaning negotiation, long identified for language learning through activities that serve specific goals.

The way people take turns in virtual three-dimensional spaces operates differently from traditional text-based communication methods. Virtual environments support multiple active communication flows at once, which allow users to use gestures, object manipulation, and speaking simultaneously. The system replicates natural human communication patterns through complex sequences that move past basic Q&A exchanges to include active demonstrations and joint meaning development and verification processes.

When communication fails, learners can use additional contextual repair methods to fix their understanding. Learners can use virtual space resources to fix misunderstandings by pointing at objects, showing actions, or making diagrams. The repair mechanisms help students achieve successful communication while helping them develop more complex language skills through their ability to express themselves through different communication channels.

17 Multichannel Output Production

The framework enables students to create new output possibilities by allowing them to use different communication methods within individual learning activities. Students need to link their verbal descriptions of laboratory procedures to their physical demonstrations, which requires them to coordinate their spoken words with their body movements. The combination of verbal and physical elements in learning activities forces students to develop accurate language skills because they need to explain complex procedures while handling physical movements and spatial awareness.

Virtual presentation areas and auditoriums let students unite academic formal speech with physical demonstrations through their presentations. Students who need to present research findings through three-dimensional model manipulation must develop advanced skills to connect formal language with technical terms and spatial references. The tasks present genuine situations that demand students to create long-term discussions that match the needs of professional communication.

Students must develop virtual tutorials for process documentation through the combination of recorded actions with step-by-step verbal explanations. Students need to manage multiple channel production while maintaining content consistency and developing language that meets requirements for clear communication and precise teaching methods. Students can enhance their metalinguistic understanding through multiple rounds of revision because virtual artifacts stay accessible for extended periods.

18 Sociocultural Mediation in Immersive Communities

The framework enables Vygotskian mediation and Zone of Proximal Development through avatars, scripted agents, and persistent digital tools that provide scaffolding for participation. Teachers can implement dynamic hint systems and peer-mentoring scripts to help students transition from peripheral to full engagement in situated communities of practice. The virtual space enables students to access sociocultural mediational tools through its built-in features and scripts and teacher-controlled scaffolding, which helps students advance through their Zone of Proximal Development.

Virtual exchange projects that span different cultures create optimal settings for sociocultural mediation activities. The research by Shadiev et al. (2020) proved that VR activities help students build intercultural competence through structured virtual environment participation, which leads to enhanced cultural understanding through avatar-based communication. The research by Gruber and Wagner (2024) confirmed that VR virtual exchange programs create opportunities for students to develop intercultural citizenship skills through collaborative work that builds common understanding between different cultural groups. The research shows how metaverse platforms enable Vygotskian mediation principles and ZPD to support digitally based practice communities. Virtual practice communities emerge naturally when students complete authentic collaborative work across multiple sessions in virtual environments. The communities assist new members to progress from beginner to expert level through essential task guidance.

The framework creates permanent learning environments through community development, which continue beyond regular classroom hours. Digital mentoring platforms in virtual spaces provide culturally sensitive support systems that adjust their assistance based on students' individual needs. The systems recognize that sociocultural mediation needs help for cognitive growth and assistance with identity development and social network integration. Users can explore different cultural approaches and communication methods through safe digital environments that virtual spaces provide.

19 Embodied Cognition and Movement-Meaning Coupling

The theoretical background establishes that embodied cognition theory shows mental operations emerge from physical body experiences instead of depending on symbolic processing (Barsalou, 2008; Wilson, 2002). The framework uses embodied cognition principles to make physical gestures, navigation, and object manipulation essential for meaning transmission in metaverse environments. The core design element of embodiment in immersive spaces allows teachers to link physical movements with semantic value, which traditional screens lack, thus enabling specific educational applications of the theoretical concepts.

Students learn to remember and apply their knowledge better by linking abstract language to physical activities through body movements. The connection between metaverse environments and embodied cognition mechanisms enables learners to achieve better conceptual understanding because virtual experiences require physical gestures and object manipulation and spatial navigation that produce enduring memory connections.

Virtual environments enable embodied experiences through controller-based interaction and body-tracking systems. These systems allow users to perform gestures and manipulate virtual objects to reach their goals. The physical activities help students to develop metaphorical thinking skills since they connect abstract linguistic concepts to tangible spatial and kinesthetic experiences. Students also learn the meaning of prepositions, aspect markers, and spatial vocabulary by navigating and manipulating tasks. The research of Chen et al. (2022) and Qiu et al. (2024) through their meta-analysis of 21 quantitative studies proved these theoretical assumptions correct by showing VR produces positive results for language learning with vocabulary improvement when students move during learning activities. The findings of the research study support the embodied cognition theory about metaverse language learning environments.

20 Implementation Guidelines Across Proficiency Levels

The first stage of learning requires students to perform basic object-handling activities, which connect essential language structures to actual physical movements. Students who participate in virtual scavenger hunts must navigate through spaces to describe their positions, which helps them understand spatial prepositions through direct physical experience. Students can develop their basic communication skills through structured social exchange activities that occur within an authentic virtual environment. Students can develop their vocabulary, spatial skills, and navigation abilities through virtual exploration activities that teach color and shape recognition. Students at this level handle complex team assignments that demand prolonged teamwork and effective conflict management. Students must synchronize their individual approaches and perspectives through problem-solving activities, which present multiple solution paths to achieve genuine meaning negotiation. The combination of environmental signals with contextual assistance in role-play scenarios enables learners to develop professional and social competencies while they learn appropriate language registers and cultural understanding. The requirement for students to connect their spoken descriptions with physical demonstrations during process explanation tasks leads to better language proficiency.

Advanced learners perform abstract concept visualization tasks, which demand sophisticated linguistic skills to present and defend their ideas. Students in professional simulation environments must connect technical vocabulary with spatial competencies and teamwork skills to make decisions.

21 Implementation Process Framework

The implementation of MBLTL needs a structured approach that includes the proper order of technology deployment, teaching methods adjustment, and evaluation methods integration. The implementation process described in Fig. 3 provides institutions and educators with a complete framework to adopt the theoretical framework in their practical teaching environments.

The flowchart presents a structured implementation process that starts with institutional readiness assessment (blue rectangles), followed by technical infrastructure evaluation, teacher preparation, and pilot testing stages. The yellow diamonds in the flowchart function as decision points, which allow the implementation process to shift direction based on pilot test results. The framework advances to performance

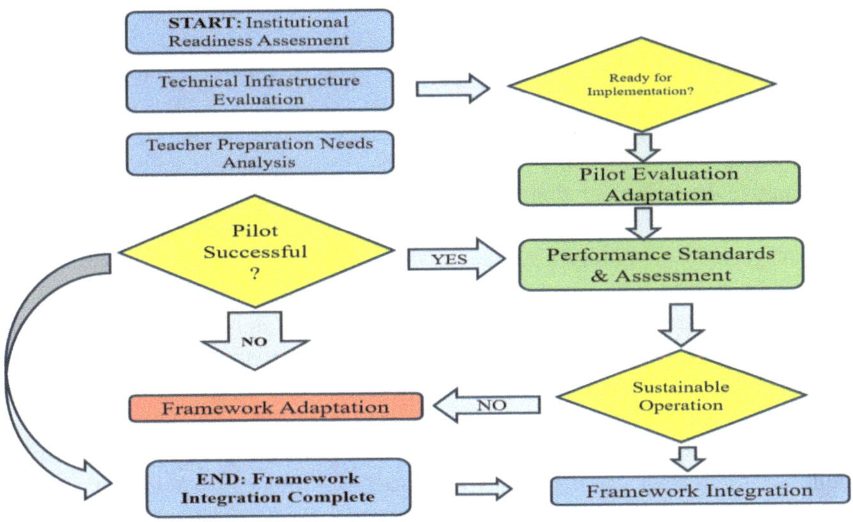

Fig. 3 Implementation process flowchart for MBLTL framework adoption

standards and sustainable operation (green rectangles) after successful pilot tests, but unsuccessful pilots require framework adaptation (pink rectangle) and multiple rounds of improvement.

The system employs dashed light blue arrows to show feedback loops, which enable continuous development, and to show the primary implementation path. The framework ends with two points, which represent that organizations can either adopt the system completely or continue developing their processes because organizations need to modify their operational procedures during implementation.

Organizations need to start their implementation process by assessing their readiness through system checks, teacher readiness assessments, and student information verification. The first assessment phase determines the best entry point for framework adoption and chooses suitable support systems to ensure successful implementation.

The framework provides flexible professional development content that organizations can adjust to meet their specific requirements and teacher competency levels. The training program begins with teaching students to use virtual environments and perform basic operations before advancing to complex framework functions and multiple assessment techniques. Institutions use pilot phases to test framework components with small student groups for building their expertise while developing site-specific implementation plans.

The pilot phases provide vital information for complete deployment planning while organizations use them to develop their capabilities and establish confidence. The pilot testing results demonstrate system functionality while showing local implementation barriers together with their corresponding solutions.

22 Assessment Integration Within the Framework

The assessment process in virtual learning environments happens through ongoing student observation during their virtual activities instead of using separate testing periods. The assessment process through process observation tracks student development by analyzing their interaction records, their spatial movements, and their collaborative work participation. Teachers can detect student learning requirements through this method, which allows them to give specific help without disrupting students' genuine communication activities.

The framework allows continuous assessment through three methods, which include learner interaction logs, spatial behavior patterns, and collaborative contribution analysis. Teachers can monitor student development in real-time without stopping the learning process to understand their problem-solving methods, teamwork abilities, and collaborative skills, which standard assessment methods fail to detect.

Assessment tasks based on authentic performance require students to use multiple communication channels for achieving actual communicative goals in real-life situations. The assessment method evaluates students' integrated competence by measuring their ability to link verbal, gestural, and spatial elements effectively in meaningful contexts. The assessment tasks of virtual marketplace negotiations and laboratory procedure explanations in laboratories and design presentation collaborations present scenarios that match real-world language requirements.

The framework allows teachers to evaluate different communication abilities, which recognize the complex nature of virtual environment interactions. Virtual environment assessment needs to measure students' abilities in spatial awareness, teamwork, and technology skills, and communication recovery methods, together with their linguistic accuracy and fluency. The full assessment approach provides teachers with precise student performance data to determine their learning needs.

23 Technology-Pedagogy Integration Principles

The framework bases its educational methods on virtual environment components, which activate specific SLA mechanisms to produce measurable learning results. The selection process for virtual environment features might need to follow established SLA principles instead of using technological complexity or visual attractiveness as selection criteria, as the method could enable students to learn virtual space navigation while developing their language skills through controlled exposure to new elements. Additionally, the virtual environment may present technological and linguistic challenges in a step-by-step sequence, which enables students to learn basic interaction skills before advancing to complex communicative tasks. Thus, the method might enable students to develop their language skills without technological barriers while establishing a step-by-step learning progression that enhances their abilities and confidence. Virtual environments also need to establish purposeful contexts through suitable linguistic environments that serve functional needs instead of providing interesting or new experiences.

The authenticity and connection of virtual contexts to learner objectives take precedence over technological complexity and visual attractiveness. Virtual learning scenarios must present authentic communication situations and cultural environments that match the needs of academic and professional or personal language use to help students develop real-world communication abilities.

24 Framework Implementation Challenges and Solutions

The management of cognitive load in virtual learning environments focuses on minimizing the overwhelming effects of multiple sensory inputs, which students experience through visual, auditory, and kinesthetic stimulation. The framework tackles this problem through a method that starts with basic interaction methods before moving to complex multimodal activities. The ability of learners to manage their environment through sensory input control helps them match their processing abilities to their preferences, which stops overwhelming situations that block learning progress. The current research studies have also documented these obstacles. The learning results in

Qiu et al.'s (2024) meta-analysis study showed inconsistent results because students experienced mental fatigue from using poorly constructed virtual reality learning spaces. The research by Wang et al. (2025) demonstrated that students' actual learning achievements did not match their perceived technology effectiveness, which indicated that feeling immersed in technology does not guarantee better learning results. The study shows that teachers might need to create learning spaces that control mental strain while using virtual reality technology for educational purposes.

The organized task structure with specific learning targets helps students stay focused on their communication and linguistic goals instead of being distracted by new environmental factors and complicated technological elements. Moreover, students can internalize the experiences through scheduled reflection sessions that help them link new language knowledge to their current abilities to prevent unprocessed input from disrupting their learning process.

The system includes technical accessibility features because students face different levels of access to advanced virtual reality equipment and reliable internet connections. The framework supports various technical settings through flexible technology standards that work between entry-level desktop computers and full virtual reality systems. Students can access virtual learning benefits through haptic controllers and mouse and keyboard interaction, which allow them to participate regardless of their hardware specifications.

Students can choose from different participation options in this system, which allows them to work independently or with others based on their technical skills and educational needs. The framework acknowledges that MBLTL implementation success depends on operational consistency between different institutional and individual technology systems to preserve both theoretical soundness and learning success.

The framework requires teachers to receive extensive professional development, which teaches them both technological competencies and innovative teaching approaches. The training for technical skills should include instruction about how to navigate virtual environments, solve typical problems, and understand the full range of platform functions and restrictions. Technical expertise alone does not fulfill the requirements because it requires teaching methods that adapt traditional classroom practices to virtual learning while maintaining SLA principles.

Virtual classroom management requires new approaches to handle student attention and behavioral guidance, and learning support in three-dimensional spaces because traditional classroom management methods fail to work in these environments.

Teachers need to develop their assessment skills through training in both theoretical assessment methods and virtual environment assessment techniques to evaluate multimodal competencies while preserving language proficiency measurement standards.

25 Systemic Dynamics and Pedagogical Applications

The central integration hub in Fig. 1 demonstrates how metaverse technology adds distinct value to language learning theory. Virtual environments establish learning environments that surpass traditional teaching methods because they enable students to experience new educational spaces that dissolve established theoretical limitations. The hub demonstrates how input transforms into interaction, which produces output that enables sociocultural involvement and deepens awareness through ongoing integrated processes.

The mechanisms in Fig. 1 function as an interconnected cycle that starts with multimodal input that triggers noticing and leads to output generation and socio-cultural mediation and embodiment that strengthen conceptual understanding. The framework shows how these mechanisms generate improved learning outcomes when teachers properly use them in virtual learning environments. Teachers need to establish complex input environments through narrative worlds with multiple multi-modal signals that deliver understandable content to students while maintaining their active involvement and motivation. Students learn negotiation skills through working together on projects and marketplace activities, which establish authentic communication needs and complex problem-solving tasks. Students develop purposeful output abilities through tasks that include design showcases, group presentations, and process documentation because these activities need detailed language usage and extensive discourse.

The scaffolding method provides support through teacher avatars and adaptive prompts and peer mentoring systems, which deliver assistance based on student needs and their current developmental range. The integration of embodied practice enables students to learn linguistic concepts through physical activities, which combine spatial abilities with gestures, navigation, and object handling as fundamental language learning elements instead of optional activities.

Educators can use these principles to create systematic teaching methods from technological progress that uphold theoretical foundations through virtual learning environment capabilities for better language learning results. The framework enables teachers to conduct controlled virtual learning space implementation based on SLA research evidence for creating new educational approaches.

26 Research Agenda and Responsible Innovation

The framework from this chapter allows researchers to concentrate on theoretical bases instead of evaluating platform-specific effectiveness claims. The research questions need to examine specific mechanisms from Fig. 1 instead of performing broad evaluations between different platforms. The research method allows researchers to create findings that work across multiple virtual platforms and technological advancements while advancing our understanding of language acquisition mechanisms.

27 Methodological Framework for MBLTL Research

Research about metaverse-based language learning continues to gain popularity, yet systematic reviews show that scientists lack essential evidence. The research by Fan and Chiang (2023) evaluated twelve empirical studies to determine that scientists need to study contemporary metaverse systems, create new theoretical models, and conduct thorough experimental research. The authors Li and Yu (2023) pointed out two main obstacles that stem from digital competence issues and the requirement for extended research to measure long-term learning outcomes. The proposed research agenda fills existing knowledge gaps by using proven SLA theory to study specific learning mechanisms while shifting from platform-focused effectiveness studies to theoretical development research.

28 Theory-Driven Experimental Design

The framework demands that researchers conduct studies about mechanisms instead of performing platform evaluation research. Researchers should study three specific topics, which include how spatial presence affects grammatical noticing, how embodied interaction impacts memory retention, and how avatar-mediated identity shapes willingness to communicate.

The design needs experimental methods to adjust particular framework elements while keeping other factors stable. Researchers need to change individual metaverse capabilities systematically while keeping all other experimental elements constant. The research design for spatial presence studies requires participants to perform identical tasks between high-immersion VR and desktop virtual worlds and traditional multimedia presentations. The design also needs to measure cognitive processing indicators through dependent variables, which include attention distribution patterns and new context learning abilities, instead of focusing on learning results. Virtual environment affordances enable researchers to study learner development through time because participants learn to use new virtual tools and master different communication methods. The research design uses quasi-experimental methods to study institutional limitations by studying natural implementation differences.

29 Measurement Approaches and Instrumentation

The assessment of virtual environment communication needs measurement tools that both track complex multimodal interactions and uphold valid assessment standards. The assessment tools for language need to transform their methods to accommodate the multiple simultaneous communication channels found in virtual environments. Virtual environment logging systems generate new opportunities to study learner behavior through recorded data of their avatar movements, object handling, eye tracking, and communication patterns.

The data streams from these systems allow researchers to study learning processes at a detailed level, but they need to create coding systems that convert behavioral data into meaningful indicators of language learning. Virtual environment learning generates cognitive process data through physiological measurements that show students' attention distribution and mental workload changes, which they cannot express through words. The assessment of language production needs to move past traditional fluency and accuracy metrics because it should evaluate how learners coordinate gestures and their ability to use space correctly, and their repair methods effectively, while understanding that verbal and non-verbal communication function as one unified system.

30 Data Collection and Validation Strategies

The virtual environment captures all data aspects through simultaneous recording of spatial positions, object handling, spoken words, and physical body reactions. The study of complex multimodal task learning processes requires stimulated recall protocols that show exact interaction patterns from multiple viewing points. Researchers can study large interaction datasets through automated tools to identify communication patterns, problem-solving methods, and language development progress. Virtual learning environments become observable through digital ethnographic methods, which reveal spontaneous social structure formation and community organization patterns. Virtual learning transfer assessment requires researchers to study it as an independent research topic when they investigate virtual learning environments. The evaluation of language usage in actual situations after virtual instruction serves as a vital checkpoint to verify that learning outcomes match real-world requirements. Researchers must develop dependable assessment methods to evaluate interactive learning platforms that produce significant student performance effects.

31 Cross-Platform and Cross-Cultural Validation

The framework requires a theoretical foundation that generates results that function across different virtual environment platforms and cultural environments. A systematic validation is also necessary through replication studies to demonstrate its predictive accuracy across different technological platforms and participant demographics. Additionally, research designs that exclude platform-dependent components should focus on basic SLA operations to develop educational principles that will endure technological advancements. Virtual environment design for language education requires cross-cultural validation because it incorporates cultural elements. The design elements in virtual worlds stem from their creators' cultural background, which leads to positive effects on particular communication methods, social relationships, and learning strategies. Research needs to study framework elements' performance across different cultural settings and educational frameworks to verify their effectiveness for students from diverse backgrounds and educational contexts.

Large-scale studies conducted through international partnerships help researchers determine framework effectiveness across different educational environments, technological frameworks, and cultural backgrounds. The research requires standardized methods that allow scientists to analyze local variations while maintaining both experimental quality and results that can be compared between study sites. The collaborative research approach generates robust evidence while building international expertise in MBLTL.

32 Ethical Considerations and Responsible Implementation

Research conducted in virtual environments requires the collection of personal data, which includes behavioral patterns, communication content, and possible physiological measurements. Researchers must create complete informed consent protocols that explain all behavioral monitoring procedures and data processing and protection methods. Standard anonymization techniques fail to protect personal identities because behavioral patterns remain identifiable.

The study needs to demonstrate how limited technology access leads to unequal student learning outcomes and prevents the implementation of research findings. The availability of advanced VR technology and dependable internet access generates varying results between different geographic locations and socioeconomic backgrounds. The research design must implement different technology levels and interaction methods to generate results that function across multiple implementation environments while identifying vital technological components for MBLTL success. The virtual learning environment through avatars creates multiple ethical concerns about how students interact with their digital spaces. The virtual environment duplicates physical space social inequalities through new digital-based social systems which operate based on users' technological capabilities. The research must study how participants choose their digital personas while protecting their freedom and creating fair opportunities for all participants.

The immersive nature of VR technology raises critical questions about protecting students from emotional harm and maintaining their psychological well-being. VR exposure for extended periods leads to cybersickness, disorientation, and emotional problems when users experience difficult social situations or public virtual mistakes. Research protocols need to perform VR susceptibility tests and establish easy exit options and psychological assistance for participants who need it. The researchers need to track participants who develop anxiety symptoms, experience social isolation, or develop negative self-perceptions through their avatar-based interactions.

The continuous recording functions of virtual environments generate surveillance threats that surpass traditional classroom monitoring methods. The combination of recorded movements, gaze directions, and interactions generates complete behavioral profiles that expose personal information that users did not intentionally share. The research team needs to create specific data storage guidelines that should only collect essential educational data while explaining all behavioral assessment purposes to participants.

Virtual learning spaces create special consent problems because students struggle to distinguish between educational activities and personal social interactions. Participants struggle to understand their consent boundaries because avatar-mediated interactions seem less realistic than traditional face-to-face communication. The informed consent process needs to include specific details about voice and movement recording, social encounter risks, anonymity restrictions, and data withdrawal options after activity completion.

The design of avatars and virtual environments needs cultural sensitivity to prevent the repetition of stereotypes and the exclusion of specific cultural groups. The creators of virtual environments base their social behavior assumptions on their cultural background when designing these spaces. The development process should include multiple stakeholders, and designers should create multiple avatar options that enable learners to express their identity naturally without Western design limitations.

33 Future Research Directions

33.1 Emerging Technologies and Expanding Possibilities

Artificial intelligence enables virtual learning environments to develop adaptive tutoring systems, intelligent feedback systems, and personalized learning paths through their integration. The research needs to study how AI-based virtual learning systems can provide sophisticated scaffolding support to language students while maintaining the social elements that make virtual learning spaces successful for language education. The research needs to track the exact connection between automated system assistance and authentic human interaction within virtual learning environments. The combination of haptic feedback systems enables students to develop embodied cognition better because touch-based information delivery strengthens their understanding of spatial and kinesthetic concepts.

Research needs to study how haptic feedback impacts language learning while determining if touch-based input creates new learning paths that enhance students' comprehension of language elements. The research requires experts in language acquisition to work with specialists who develop haptic technology systems. The research needs collaboration between experts who study language acquisition and specialists who create haptic technology systems. The future implementation of brain-computer interfaces in virtual environment language learning will enable scientists to monitor cognitive processes that behavioral assessments cannot detect, such as attention, memory, and processing patterns. The new technologies allow scientists to study learning mechanisms in unprecedented ways, but they create essential privacy issues regarding mental processes.

33.2 Interdisciplinary Collaboration Opportunities

Virtual environment language learning research needs to work more closely with cognitive science experts who study embodied cognition, spatial reasoning, and multimodal processing. Research partnerships would enable scientists to understand virtual environment learning processes better while discovering physical activities that boost cognitive development. The study of virtual learning communities needs educational psychology expertise to analyze motivation, identity, and social dynamics within these virtual spaces. Research partnerships should investigate how virtual environment elements influence student motivation, self-assurance, and learning endurance to build sustainable language skills. The research needs to combine psychological aspects of individual learners with social elements and technological factors. The creation of virtual learning environments for language education needs computer science collaboration to build dedicated platforms that perform better than gaming and general-purpose platforms. The development of purpose-built learning environments would let researchers add language learning features through evidence-based design principles. The successful execution of these partnerships requires both parties to understand how technical capabilities match educational standards.

34 Conclusion

The research examines how established Second Language Acquisition theories operate in virtual learning environments to create a metaverse-based framework for language education. The proposed framework goes beyond typical technology adoption because virtual learning spaces create new educational environments that remove theoretical barriers to establish novel connections between them.

The framework shows how SLA mechanisms work with metaverse features to create better learning experiences that follow evidence-based research. Research studies employing meta-analysis have proven that VR technology produces substantial positive effects for language education, according to Chen et al. (2022) and Qiu et al. (2024). The research supports the theoretical models of multimodal negotiation, which Chen and Sevilla-Pavón (2023) described, and vocabulary retention findings from Wang et al.(2025), Xie et al. (2025), the study by Fathi et al. (2025), and willingness to communicate (Fathi et al., 2025). The chapter presents a new conceptual framework, but Fan and Chiang (2023) and Li and Yu (2023) show through their systematic reviews that more research needs to be done to validate the effectiveness of combined theoretical frameworks.

The framework provides particular approaches to transform recreational virtual environments into educational learning spaces for teaching purposes. The framework demonstrates how theoretical principles become practical learning exercises by following its implementation steps, which begin with simple object manipulation for novices and advance to complex professional simulations for advanced learners. Virtual environments enable ongoing assessment through various evaluation methods, which generate more comprehensive learning assessments than traditional single-point testing approaches. The research agenda investigates particular mechanisms instead of platform comparisons because this method generates results that remain applicable to upcoming technological developments. Future research needs to examine specific questions about spatial presence effects on noticing, embodied interaction effects on retention, and avatar identity effects on willingness to communicate to develop cumulative theoretical knowledge instead of producing results specific to particular platforms.

The chapter shows both the positive aspects and the challenges that scientists face when they study virtual environments. Researchers can now monitor learning processes in full detail through behavioral logs and physiological data, and complete interaction records, which new data collection methods provide. The sophisticated research tools generate major ethical challenges regarding privacy safeguards, system accessibility, and digital identity representation, which scientists must address properly. The framework helps solve practical implementation problems by using structured complexity progression, adaptable technology needs, and complete teacher readiness protocols. The framework includes essential elements for successful implementation, which include cognitive load management, technical accessibility, and cultural sensitivity to avoid previous technology integration failures. The theoretical framework supports future technological progress by allowing the integration of artificial intelligence systems, haptic feedback systems, and brain-computer interfaces without compromising core language learning principles. The research opportunities for interdisciplinary collaboration between MBLTL, cognitive science, educational psychology, and computer science enable knowledge sharing that benefits all participating fields.

The chapter supports responsible innovation to direct virtual environment language learning development through accessible and ethical standards and equitable practices. The digital divide recognition, along with inclusive design principles, works to guarantee MBLTL accessibility for all learners while avoiding the creation of new educational disparities. The framework helps MBLTL transition from experimental status to evidence-based teaching methods. The framework unites established SLA theory with new technological capabilities to create a systematic development approach that strengthens proven language teaching methods. Virtual environments create new learning environments that enable students to practice embodied multimodal collaborative language use on an extensive scale. The capability enables students to experience theoretical concepts through direct practice, which lets them practice prepositions in space and build shared meaning through object collaboration and develop cultural competence by exploring identities in protected virtual spaces.

35 Limitations and Future Directions

The chapter establishes a complete theoretical structure for MBLTL, yet researchers need to address multiple essential constraints. Initially, the framework exists as a conceptual structure because researchers have not validated it through empirical testing as an integrated model. The individual SLA mechanisms receive strong empirical evidence from research (Chen & Sevilla-Pavón, 2023; Chen et al., 2022; Wang et al., 2025), yet scientists have not conducted holistic longitudinal studies to verify the proposed metaverse framework integration of all five theoretical frameworks. Thus, research needs to verify how the predicted mechanism interactions work in real classrooms and identify specific conditions that support their effectiveness.

Secondly, the framework focuses exclusively on language acquisition processes, yet it fails to measure educational results that include cultural competence development, critical thinking abilities, and learner autonomy beyond linguistic aspects. The framework offered requires expansion to include theoretical connections that address additional educational outcomes that sociocultural mediation does not fully cover (Gruber & Wagner, 2024; Shadiev et al., 2020).

The system encounters operational issues that stop it from functioning properly. The high costs of VR equipment, together with necessary technical systems and teacher training programs, function as barriers that primarily affect schools with limited financial resources. The framework detects these problems through theoretical evaluation, yet it lacks specific approaches to address the digital resource inequality between educational institutions.

The framework also bases its analysis on Western SLA theories from Krashen, Long, and Swain, and Vygotsky, which might not effectively explain learning processes in different educational and cultural settings. Research studies that might validate the framework across different educational systems and cultural approaches to language learning are necessary to establish its predictive value. Metaverse technology advancements at a fast pace will make the current platform features obsolete because new capabilities will emerge. The framework depends on SLA mechanisms as its base, instead of particular technological elements, which makes it resistant to becoming obsolete. The framework requires continuous theoretical development to stay effective with advancing technologies.

References

Barsalou, L. W. (2008). Grounded cognition. *Annual Review of Psychology, 59*(1), 617–645. https://doi.org/10.1146/annurev.psych.59.103006.093639

Chapelle, C. A. (2001). *Computer applications in second language acquisition.* Cambridge University Press. https://doi.org/10.1017/cbo9781139524681

Chen, B., Wang, Y., & Wang, L. (2022). The effects of virtual reality-assisted language learning: A meta-analysis. *Sustainability, 14*(6), 3147. https://doi.org/10.3390/su14063147

Chen, H. I., & Sevilla-Pavón, A. (2023). Negotiation of meaning via virtual exchange in immersive virtual reality environments. *Language Learning & Technology, 27*(2), 118–154. https://doi.org/10.64152/10125/73506

Chun, D. M., Karimi, H., & Sañosa, D. J. (2022). Traveling by headset: Immersive VR for language learning. *CALICO Journal, 39*(2), 129–149. https://doi.org/10.1558/cj.21306

Çelik, F., & Baturay, M. H. (2024). The effect of metaverse on L2 vocabulary learning, retention, student engagement, presence, and community feeling. *BMC Psychology, 12*, 58. https://doi.org/10.1186/s40359-024-01549-4

Çelik, F., & Ersanlı, C. Y. (2025). Developing and integrating metaverse into EFL listening skills to increase learners' self-determination based on social constructivist theory. *Journal of Computer Assisted Learning, 41*(6), Article e70151. https://doi.org/10.1111/jcal.70151

Dede, C. (2009). Immersive interfaces for engagement and learning. *Science, 323*, 66–69. https://doi.org/10.1126/science.1167311

Dhimolea, T. K., Kaplan-Rakowski, R., & Lin, L. (2022). A systematic review of research on high-immersion virtual reality for language learning. *TechTrends, 66*, 810–824. https://doi.org/10.1007/s11528-022-00717-w

Ellis, R. (2003). *Task-based language learning and teaching*. Oxford University Press.

Fan, L., & Chiang, J. (2023). A systematic review of the application of metaverse in language education: Prominent themes, research methods, impacts, and future challenges. *Journal of Language Teaching, 3*(10), 1–14. https://doi.org/10.54475/jlt.2023.026

Fathi, J., Zou, D., & Zhaleh, K. (2025). Promoting intercultural communicative competence and willingness to communicate in EFL learners through virtual reality: A mixed-methods examination. *Computer Assisted Language Learning, 1–44*,. https://doi.org/10.1080/09588221.2025.2496827

Godwin-Jones, R. (2023). Emerging spaces for language learning: AI bots, ambient intelligence, and the metaverse. *Language Learning & Technology, 27*(2), 6–27. https://doi.org/10.64152/10125/73501

Gruber, A., & Wagner, M. (2024). Fostering interdisciplinary intercultural citizenship with virtual reality in a world language virtual exchange project. *Intercultural Communication Education, 7*(1), 1304. https://doi.org/10.29140/ice.v7n1.1304

Kaplan-Rakowski, R., Grotewold, K., Hartwick, P., & Papin, K. (2023). Generative AI and teachers' perspectives on its implementation in education. *Journal of Interactive Learning Research, 34*(2), 313–338. https://www.learntechlib.org/primary/p/222363/

Krashen, S. D. (1982). *Principles and practice in second language acquisition.* Pergamon.

Krashen, S. (1985). *The input hypothesis: Issues and implications.* Longman.

Kukulska-Hulme, A., & Shield, L. (2008). An overview of mobile assisted language learning: From content delivery to supported collaboration and interaction. *ReCALL, 20*(3), 271–289. https://doi.org/10.1017/S0958344008000335

Lan, Y. J. (2020a). Immersion, interaction and experience-oriented learning: Bringing virtual reality into FL learning. *Language Learning & Technology, 24*(1), 1–15. https://doi.org/10.64152/10125/44704

Lan, Y. J. (2020b). Immersion into virtual reality for language learning. In *Psychology of learning and motivation* (Vol. 72, pp. 1–26). Academic Press. https://doi.org/10.1016/bs.plm.2020.03.001

Lantolf, J. P., & Thorne, S. L. (2006). *Sociocultural theory and the genesis of second language development.* Oxford University Press.

Li, M., & Yu, Z. (2023). A systematic review of the metaverse-based blended English learning. *Frontiers in Psychology, 13*, Article 1087508. https://doi.org/10.3389/fpsyg.2022.1087508

Lin, T. J., & Lan, Y. J. (2015). Language learning in virtual reality environments: Past, present, and future. *Educational Technology & Society, 18*(4), 486–497.

Lindgren, R., & Johnson-Glenberg, M. (2013). Emboldened by embodiment: Six precepts for research on embodied learning and mixed reality. *Educational Researcher, 42*(8), 445–452. https://doi.org/10.3102/0013189X13511661

Long, M. H. (1996). The role of the linguistic environment in second language acquisition. In W. C. Ritchie & T. K. Bhatia (Eds.), *Handbook of second language acquisition* (pp. 413–468). Academic Press.

Long, M. H. (2015). *Second language acquisition and task-based language teaching.* Wiley-Blackwell.

Mystakidis, S. (2022). Metaverse. *Encyclopedia, 2*(1), 486–497. https://doi.org/10.3390/encyclopedia2010031

Peixoto, B., Pinto, R. D., Melo, M., Cabral, L., & Bessa, M. (2021). Immersive virtual reality for foreign language education: A PRISMA systematic review. *IEEE Access, 9*, 48952–48962. https://doi.org/10.1109/ACCESS.2021.3068858

Qiu, X. B., Shan, C., Yao, J., & Fu, Q. K. (2024). The effects of virtual reality on EFL learning: A meta-analysis. *Education and Information Technologies, 29*, 1379–1405. https://doi.org/10.1007/s10639-023-11738-0

Schmidt, R. W. (1990). The role of consciousness in second language learning. *Applied Linguistics, 11*(2), 129–158. https://doi.org/10.1093/applin/11.2.129

Schmidt, R. (2001). Attention. In P. Robinson (Ed.), *Cognition and second language instruction* (pp. 3–32). Cambridge University Press. https://doi.org/10.1017/CBO9781139524780.003

Shadiev, R., Wang, X., & Huang, Y. M. (2020). Promoting intercultural competence in a learning activity supported by virtual reality technology. *International Review of Research in Open and Distributed Learning, 21*(3), 157–174. https://doi.org/10.19173/irrodl.v21i3.4752

Swain, M. (1985). Communicative competence: Some roles of comprehensible input and comprehensible output in its development. In S. Gass & C. Madden (Eds.), *Input in second language acquisition* (pp. 235–252). Newbury House.

Swain, M. (1995). Three functions of output in second language learning. In G. Cook & B. Seidlhofer (Eds.), *Principles and practice in applied linguistics* (pp. 125–144). Oxford University Press.

Swain, M. (2005). The output hypothesis: Theory and research. In E. Hinkel (Ed.), *Handbook of research in second language teaching and learning* (pp. 495–508). Routledge. https://doi.org/10.4324/9781410612700-38

Vygotsky, L. S. (1978). *Mind in society: Development of higher psychological processes.* Harvard University Press. https://doi.org/10.2307/j.ctvjf9vz4

Wang, Z., Zou, D., & Peng, P. (2025). Effects of mobile metaverse-based vocabulary learning on learners' perception and performance: A case study of Chinese EFL learners. *Journal of Computers in Education, 12*, 1333–1366. https://doi.org/10.1007/s40692-024-00348-5

Warschauer, M. (1997). Computer-mediated collaborative learning: Theory and practice. *The Modern Language Journal, 81*, 470–481. https://doi.org/10.1111/j.1540-4781.1997.tb05514.x

Wilson, M. (2002). Six views of embodied cognition. *Psychonomic Bulletin & Review, 9*, 625–636. https://doi.org/10.3758/BF03196322

Wu, Y. H., & Hung, S. T. (2022). The effects of virtual reality-infused instruction on elementary school students' English-speaking performance, willingness to communicate, and learning autonomy. *Journal of Educational Computing Research, 60*(6), 1558–1587. https://doi.org/10.1177/07356331211068207

Xie, T., Zhang, H., & Yang, Y. (2025). Effect of immersive virtual reality based upon an input processing model for second language vocabulary retention. *Education and Information Technologies, 30*, 12365–12385. https://doi.org/10.1007/s10639-025-13333-x

Seçil Büyükbay İpekçi is a researcher at the Social Sciences University of Ankara, Türkiye. Her work integrates major second language acquisition theories with metaverse environments. She examines how immersive features support input, interaction, output, sociocultural scaffolding, and embodied cognition. İpekçi proposes frameworks for evidence-based curriculum design in virtual spaces. Her research addresses cognitive load, accessibility, and ethical concerns in metaverse-based language learning and teaching (MBLTL).

Gonca Yangın Ekşi is a professor at Gazi University, Ankara, Türkiye. She specializes in applying SLA theories to digital and immersive language learning contexts. Her contributions explore multimodal communication, spatial presence, and contextualized interaction in metaverses. Ekşi advocates for theoretically grounded pedagogical innovations. She provides guidance for educators transitioning to virtual immersive environments.

Practical Applications in Metaverse-Based Language Teaching and Learning

Designing Immersive Language Learning Environments

Mehrasa Alizadeh, Nikan Fujii, and Neil Cowie

Abstract Despite the increasing use of Metaverse tools in education, research on how immersive platforms can best support language learning remains limited. In particular, little is known about how learners employ communication strategies (CSs) during avatar-mediated interaction and how these may be influenced by sociocultural factors such as gender. This study addresses these gaps by examining the design and implementation of an immersive learning environment in *Frame*, a browser-based Metaverse platform, to develop small-talk skills among 22 Japanese university-level EFL learners. The chapter outlines key design considerations to ensure accessibility and optimal learner performance in *Frame*. It also examines learners' communication strategies during avatar-mediated interactions by analyzing video-recorded interactions in *Frame* using an established coding framework. Verbal CSs were categorized systematically, while nonverbal CSs were described qualitatively. The analysis additionally explores how male and female learners navigate the affordances of avatar-based communication. The findings enhance theoretical understanding of learners' strategic competence in immersive environments and provide practical insights for designing effective Metaverse-based language-learning experiences. While this chapter provides design principles based on emerging research and best practices, it is important to note that the field of metaverse-based educational design is still developing. These principles should be viewed as informed recommendations rather than established best practices with extensive longitudinal empirical validation.

Keywords Immersive learning environments · Metaverse · Communication strategies (CSs) · Avatar-mediated interaction · Gender variation

M. Alizadeh (✉)
Otemon Gakuin University, Ibaraki, Osaka, Japan
e-mail: m-alizadeh@otemon.ac.jp

N. Fujii
Bukkyo University, Kyoto, Japan
e-mail: nsadvandfujii@gmail.com

N. Cowie
English Language Academy, University of Auckland, Auckland, New Zealand
e-mail: ncowie2012@gmail.com

F. Çelik and C. Yangın Ersanlı (eds.), *Metaverse-Based Language Learning and Teaching*, English Language Education 49,
https://doi.org/10.1007/978-3-032-31366-9_4

1 Introduction

Understanding the pedagogical and technical design that shapes an immersive learning space is a necessary foundation for examining learner behavior within it. As Dede (2009) notes, immersive technologies can provide rich and multisensory learning experiences, yet their educational value ultimately depends on thoughtful design and purposeful implementation. Without such implementation, immersive platforms risk emphasizing novelty over meaningful learning and sustained engagement (Jiang & Fryer, 2024). By analyzing the design considerations for utilizing a Metaverse platform called *Frame*, such as accessibility, cognitive load, and user interaction, this study situates learner communication within a pedagogically grounded environment. Documenting these design principles clarifies how the learning space supports adaptable and inclusive use in future contexts. Recent research suggests that Metaverse-mediated communication enhances motivation and fosters contextualized language use (Lee & Ahn, 2025; Lan et al., 2018). Learners in these environments often engage in multimodal negotiation of meaning, using gestures, spatial positioning, and environmental cues alongside speech (Chen & Sevilla-Pavón, 2023). However, few studies have systematically analyzed communication strategy (CS) use in the Metaverse through a structured framework, and even fewer have leveraged existing CS models to capture Metaverse-specific behaviors.

Research on CSs has long examined how second language (L2) learners manage linguistic gaps and sustain interactional flow. Foundational models (Dörnyei & Scott, 1997; Faerch & Kasper, 1983; Tarone, 2007) categorize strategies by function, including direct, indirect, and interactional types. While these frameworks have been widely applied to face-to-face and text-based communication (e.g., Nakatani, 2006), their use in immersive environments remains limited. Platforms such as Frame, where spatial affordances like avatar gestures, movement, and shared virtual objects reshape interactional dynamics, may require an expanded conception of strategic competence. Moreover, gender remains an underexplored dimension in immersive communication. Prior studies suggest that female learners often employ more interactional strategies and demonstrate higher willingness to negotiate meaning, whereas male learners may favor more direct or risk-taking strategies (Coates, 2015; Nakatani, 2006). However, in immersive learning contexts, avatars may blur or reconfigure gender identities, offering expressive flexibility that could alter established gendered communication patterns (Sundén, 2003).

Against this background, the present study aims to bridge pedagogical design and communicative practice by first identifying the principles that guided the creation of an inclusive, high-performing immersive space in *Frame*, and then examining how EFL learners employ CSs within that environment. More specifically, through applying Dörnyei and Scott's (1997) taxonomy, this study analyzes verbal CSs and provides a descriptive account of the use of nonverbal CSs in *Frame*. Finally, it explores how gender may influence learners' strategic preferences and interactional choices in avatar-mediated communication. To this end, the following research questions were formulated to guide the study:

1. What principles guided the design of an inclusive and high-performing immersive learning space in *Frame*?
2. What is the full range and function of CSs used by Japanese EFL learners in *Frame*?
3. Do male and female learners show different preferences for CS use in *Frame*?

2 A Review of the Related Literature

2.1 Immersive Language Learning: Environment Design

Designing an immersive language learning environment requires the same degree of pedagogical intentionality and theoretical grounding as any other learning context. As argued by Esteves et al. (2023), the process begins with identifying clear learning objectives and aligning them with appropriate content design. This step ensures that the implementation of immersive technologies is driven not by novelty or technological fascination but by pedagogical value. In other words, immersive technologies should be integrated to meaningfully enhance learning outcomes and support established theories of second language acquisition rather than merely serve as a showcase of innovation. Below are considerations for designing effective immersive learning environments.

2.1.1 Choosing and Adapting the Technology

Selecting suitable technologies, both hardware and software, is a crucial early consideration. In educational contexts, access to high-performance devices is often limited, and institutions frequently adopt a Bring Your Own Device (BYOD) approach. This approach allows learners to access the immersive environment remotely from anywhere at any time. However, it may also mean that students join the learning environment with devices of varying processing power or internet speeds. Consequently, educators must ensure that their chosen platform can operate reliably across diverse technical conditions.

Since most teachers are not software developers, they typically rely on existing Metaverse platforms rather than building custom environments from scratch. Many of these platforms, however, were initially designed for entertainment or social interaction rather than for education. Therefore, educators must adapt them creatively to align with pedagogical goals and language-learning principles, such as interaction, collaboration, and meaningful communication. This adaptation requires thoughtful design decisions regarding both the spatial layout of the virtual environment and the tasks performed within it.

2.1.2 Task and Interaction Design

An essential consideration in immersive learning design is creating meaningful tasks and opportunities for interaction. The central question for educators is how the immersive environment can support communicative experiences beyond what is possible on conventional platforms such as Zoom or Microsoft Teams. Puentedura's (2006) Substitution, Augmentation, Modification, and Redefinition (SAMR) model offers a valuable framework for reflection in this regard. It encourages educators to design transformative learning experiences using technology rather than simply replicating existing classroom activities with added technological complexity. Ideally, immersive environments allow learners to engage in situated, embodied, and collaborative communication, redefining how language is used and learned.

2.1.3 Degrees of Immersion and Interactivity of Immersive Platforms

Different immersive environments provide varying degrees of freedom and interactivity. These are typically classified as either three degrees of freedom (3DoF) or six degrees of freedom (6DoF). 3DoF environments, such as 360-degree photos or videos, allow users to look around in all directions but not to move freely within the space. Avatars may or may not be used, and interaction with others is often minimal. 6DoF environments, in contrast, enable users to move naturally in all directions and interact dynamically with other participants or digital objects. These environments can provide more engaging and realistic learning experiences, but require significantly higher processing power and more advanced hardware. Moreover, many 3DoF and 6DoF platforms are proprietary and may involve licensing or subscription fees. Therefore, when planning immersive learning projects, particularly those intended for long-term or large-scale implementation, financial sustainability must be considered alongside pedagogical and technological factors.

2.1.4 Accessibility and the Digital Divide

Accessibility remains one of the most critical considerations in immersive learning design. Although browser-based Metaverse platforms are becoming increasingly lightweight and mobile-friendly, performance and usability still vary widely depending on the device, network quality, and user location. Students who lack access to high-end hardware may experience lag, disconnection, or limited interaction capabilities. Such discrepancies can exacerbate the digital divide and affect learner equity. Consequently, when selecting a platform, educators should prioritize environments that run efficiently on average devices and can be accessed seamlessly on smartphones, tablets, and standard laptops.

2.1.5 Training and Support

Another essential factor is user readiness (Cowie & Alizadeh, 2025). Both teachers and students require orientation and ongoing support to engage effectively in immersive environments. Since most users have limited or no prior experience with Metaverse technologies, it is essential to incorporate training into the curriculum rather than treating it as an afterthought. The chosen platform should have an intuitive interface with a manageable learning curve so that users of varying digital literacy levels can participate confidently. Well-structured pre-training sessions and continuous technical support are key to minimizing anxiety and maximizing engagement.

2.1.6 Integrating Pedagogy and Technology

Ultimately, the successful design of an immersive language-learning environment depends on integrating technological, pedagogical, and content knowledge (TPACK) (Mishra & Koehler, 2006). This framework highlights the interdependence between teachers' understanding of language pedagogy, content knowledge, and technological affordances. A well-designed immersive environment not only enhances language learning but also contributes to teacher professional development by expanding educators' capacity to use emerging technologies effectively and critically (Cowie & Alizadeh, 2022).

2.2 Communication Strategies (CSs)

CSs form a core component of strategic competence, defined by Canale and Swain (1980) as "the verbal and nonverbal CSs that may be called into action to compensate for breakdowns in communication due to performance variables or to insufficient competence" (p. 30). Research over the past four decades has been dominated by two perspectives: the interactionist and the psycholinguistic. The interactionist view (Tarone, 2007) emphasizes the joint negotiation of meaning, in which learners consciously employ strategies such as approximation, circumlocution, code-switching, or appeals for help to manage gaps during interaction. The psycholinguistic view (Bialystok, 1990; Faerch & Kasper, 1983) instead focuses on cognitive problem-solving, distinguishing between reduction strategies (e.g., topic avoidance, message abandonment) and achievement strategies (e.g., restructuring, word coinage, code-switching). Despite differing emphases, both perspectives regard CSs as adaptive tools for maintaining communicative flow and compensating for limited linguistic resources.

Building on these foundations, Dörnyei (1995) proposed a widely used taxonomy of direct, indirect, and interactional strategies, expanding earlier models (e.g., Faerch & Kasper, 1983) with categories such as stalling devices and prefabricated patterns. While these frameworks provide valuable analytical lenses, they differ more in terminology than substance (Bialystok, 1990) and have been variously adapted to suit evolving communicative contexts.

A recurring debate concerns the teachability of CSs. Proponents argue that explicit strategy instruction enhances fluency and learner autonomy (Dörnyei, 1995; Maleki, 2007; Nakatani, 2006), whereas critics question its ecological validity and transferability to authentic settings (Bialystok, 1990; Ellis & Barkhuizen, 2005). This tension underscores the importance of examining CSs in naturalistic and context-rich environments afforded by computer-mediated and immersive communication platforms. In a similar vein, recent research continues to acknowledge the relevance of CSs in contemporary L2 interaction. In examining the use of CSs among L2 learners, Yang et al. (2022) highlighted the importance of strategies such as repair, paraphrase, and appeals for clarification in sustaining interaction across diverse proficiency levels. This confirms earlier findings that strategic competence remains central to communicative success, even as learning contexts evolve. For example, Nikian et al.'s (2016) work in technology-mediated environments corroborates this understanding. Studies exploring AR/VR-supported EFL learning also suggest that immersive interfaces may alter learners' opportunities for meaning negotiation by introducing new multimodal resources and constraints. Although these emerging studies do not focus specifically on CS taxonomies, they demonstrate a growing interest in how strategic behavior manifests in digitally enriched environments.

2.2.1 Computer-Mediated CSs

As language learning transitioned into digital contexts, scholars examined how CSs are employed in computer-mediated communication (CMC). In text-based environments, strategies often shift from gestures and prosody to compensatory textual devices, such as repetition, simplification, emoticons, or clarification requests (Jenks, 2009). Research has shown that even in synchronous chatrooms, learners continue to negotiate meaning through familiar mechanisms, although the form of CSs adapts to the medium (Smith, 2003; Yanguas, 2010). Yanguas (2010), for example, found that learners engaged in meaning negotiation during both audio- and video-based CMC used clarification and repair strategies similar to those in face-to-face interaction. However, the presence of visual cues in video mode led to more natural turn-taking and interactional flow, underscoring how modality shapes but does not eliminate core negotiation mechanisms.

CMC also raised new considerations: the persistence of written records and the reduced presence of nonverbal cues influence how learners manage breakdowns. For example, studies highlight learners' reliance on discourse markers, orthographic emphasis (e.g., capitalization), and the use of emoticons or symbols to supplement missing paralinguistic cues (Wigham & Chanier, 2013). This suggests that while the taxonomy of CSs remains broadly recognizable, digital mediation reshapes their manifestation and frequency.

2.2.2 Metaverse-Based CSs

The rise of immersive learning environments has opened new directions in the study of CSs, as learners interact through avatars in shared 3D environments. Research in collaborative virtual environments (Becker & Mark, 1999; Guye-Vuillème et al., 1999) has shown that avatars' gaze, gestures, and spatial positioning serve as substitutes for face-to-face nonverbal communication. In language learning contexts, the Metaverse presents both opportunities and challenges: while proxemics, pointing, and embodied gestures facilitate the negotiation of meaning, technical constraints such as audio delays or automatic speech recognition (ASR) errors introduce new sources of communication breakdown (Hasler & Friedman, 2012; Wigham & Chanier, 2013).

Studies of avatar-mediated interaction suggest that conventional CSs, such as repair, repetition, and appeals for help, continue to appear, but learners also innovate Metaverse-specific behaviors (Yee et al., 2007). For example, object manipulation, avatar repositioning, or the use of exaggerated gestures can serve as compensatory strategies when verbal communication falters. These findings necessitate extending the application of earlier CS frameworks and taxonomies to account for embodied, technology-mediated resources.

2.3 Research Gap

While existing research on the use of CSs in face-to-face and computer-mediated contexts has yielded substantial insights into learners' communication behavior (Bialystok, 1990; Faerch & Kasper, 1983; Smith, 2003; Tarone, 2007), studies carried out in immersive learning environments remain limited. Existing research on avatar-mediated interaction (e.g., Wigham & Chanier, 2013) has focused mainly on nonverbal behavior, such as gesture and gaze, and has often taken place outside EFL settings. Additionally, traditional CS taxonomies (Dörnyei, 1995; Dörnyei & Scott, 1997) developed in face-to-face or text-based contexts may insufficiently represent the embodied and spatial aspects of communication enabled by Metaverse platforms. Furthermore, as stated earlier, while the pedagogical and technical design of immersive learning environments appears to have a significant impact on learners' engagement, there is insufficient research on how various design elements, such as accessibility, spatial layout, and task arrangement, affect learners' strategic behavior. Consequently, there is a limited understanding of how EFL learners use both verbal and nonverbal strategies in structured, pedagogically effective immersive environments.

Drawing on the previously discussed theoretical and empirical foundations, the study employs an exploratory qualitative approach to examine the intersection of pedagogical design and CS within an immersive learning environment. Specifically, it documents the principles that guided the creation of an inclusive and cognitively manageable virtual space in *Frame* and examines how these design features shaped

Japanese EFL learners' use of CSs. By using Dörnyei and Scott's (1997) taxonomy as a starting point for analysis, the study adds Metaverse-specific and embodied interaction patterns to the framework, thereby developing the concept of strategic competence in avatar-mediated environments. In addition, gender differences in the use and preferences of CSs are examined to explore how identity and technological affordances jointly influence learners' strategic performance. By focusing on both design and behavior, this study aims to contribute to the theoretical framework of CS research in immersive environments and to enhance the practical application of EFL pedagogy in virtual contexts.

2.3.1 Theoretical Framework

This study employs a three-layer framework linking technology-mediated pedagogy, immersive design, and strategic competence to explain how learners use CSs in *Frame* (Fig. 1). Rather than treating CS use as an isolated skill, the framework views it as behavior shaped by pedagogical intent and digital affordances.

Grounded in TPACK (Mishra & Koehler, 2006), the immersive environment was deliberately designed so that technological features, such as spatial layout, cross-device accessibility, spatial audio zoning, and pre-immersion training, served communicative learning goals. These design principles (e.g., customization, visual clarity, private voice zones) acted as interactional conditions that organized communication by reducing crowding, preventing audio overlap, and enabling focused small-group talk.

Within these conditions, CS use emerged as a situated strategic behavior. Learners relied predominantly on verbal CSs such as repair, repetition, and clarification, consistent with strategic competence models (Canale & Swain, 1980; Dörnyei & Scott, 1997), while limited avatar embodiment reduced nonverbal options to cues such as gaze direction and spatial orientation. Strategic competence in *Frame*, therefore, involved both linguistic and technological adaptation, as learners adjusted

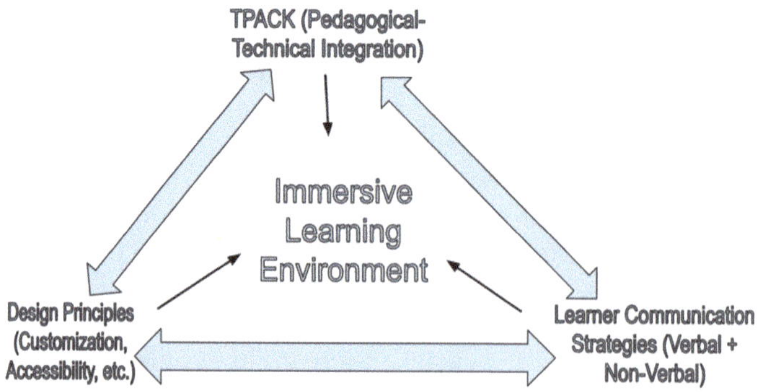

Fig. 1 Integrated model of immersive language learning design and strategic communication in *Frame*

their communicative moves to the affordances and constraints of the immersive environment.

3 Methodology

3.1 Study Design and Participants

This study adopted a qualitative case study design with two interconnected aims: (1) to document the pedagogical and technical design principles underlying the creation of an inclusive immersive learning space in *Frame*, and (2) to observe how Japanese EFL learners interacted and employed CSs within this environment. This dual focus links the design of the learning context to the analysis of learner behavior, ensuring that communication patterns are interpreted within a pedagogically meaningful framework.

For this purpose, 37 undergraduate students from various Japanese universities were recruited through purposeful sampling to participate in an eight-week course on small talk skills delivered in *Frame*. Participants were selected based on their intermediate or higher English proficiency, as determined by self-reported standardized test scores (TOEIC, Eiken, GTEC, or TOEFL). Their unfamiliarity with one another was intentional, as it increased the authenticity of spontaneous interaction. Of the 37 students who initially enrolled, 10 withdrew due to scheduling conflicts and inconsistent attendance, resulting in a final dataset of 27 participants (10 males, 17 females; ages 18–25) who completed all immersive tasks. During the course, a total of 80 pair interactions were video-recorded in *Frame*. For the present analysis, 22 interaction videos were purposively selected. Each selected video captured one dyadic interaction between two students. Overall, 22 students (13 female and nine male) participated, forming 22 distinct dyads. However, several students appeared in more than one video.

Ethical approval was obtained from the first author's institutional ethics committee. All participants of this study were at least 18 years old and, therefore, legally adults in Japan; however, informed consent protocols were still strictly followed to uphold ethical transparency. They received detailed information about the study's purpose, procedures, and their rights, including the option to participate voluntarily and to withdraw at any time without penalty. Written informed consent was obtained before data collection. Participants were assured of confidentiality, and all identifying information was anonymized during transcription and reporting.

3.2 Data Collection Procedure

Data were collected using the *Frame*[1] platform, a browser-based immersive environment accessible via PC, smartphone, or VR headset. The environment was selected for its accessibility, moderate processing demands, and capacity to accommodate up to 30 users simultaneously. To facilitate pair and group activities, private voice zones, similar to Zoom breakout rooms, were configured to isolate audio among participants within each zone. Ten "dummy avatars" acted as virtual teaching assistants, enabling recording across zones using TechSmith Snagit®[2] 2023. These avatars were controlled entirely by the researchers, and students were informed that they would not interact with them, as their only purpose was to record student-to-student interactions. Before data collection, a one-hour pilot test was conducted with a group of volunteer teachers. The session allowed the researchers to experiment with *Frame* and identify potential technical issues that actual participants might encounter. Insights from this pilot informed the design of the virtual environment used in the study. Before the main study was launched, the participants attended two orientation sessions covering platform navigation, avatar customization, and chat/mic controls. Japanese-captioned screencasts were also shared on YouTube to reinforce understanding.

3.2.1 Immersive Learning Space and Task Design

During early trials in *Frame*, a setting was selected where avatars frequently overlapped in a narrow space, making it difficult to see clearly who was speaking. This created confusion and reduced interaction quality. Based on these observations, the environment was redesigned with a wider layout that provided students with greater mobility and spatial separation. This, in turn, improved both visibility and conversational flow. Additional design features included private voice zones for small-group collaboration, a clear spatial layout to reduce confusion, and interactive objects for task-based learning to encourage engagement.

The course followed a flipped learning approach, in which students watched two videos before each weekly lesson on small talk in English and how to build successful bonds with others. The videos were created by the third author and one co-creator and hosted on YouTube (https://tinyurl.com/smalltalkframe). Links to the individual videos were shared with the students on a Google Site (https://sites.google.com/view/smalltalk-en/home) created for this study. During the one-hour synchronous online lessons, the students engaged in several rounds of group work. In addition, at the end of the lesson, they had two rounds of small-talk practice in pairs, during which they were asked to discuss any topic of their choice for five minutes.

[1] https://framevr.io/

[2] https://www.techsmith.com/snagit/

3.2.2 Observation of Pair Interactions

The selected 22 videos (approx. five minutes each) were transcribed and coded using a structured qualitative scheme. Verbal strategies included repair, repetition, clarification/confirmation, message abandonment, fillers/hesitation, code-switching/translation, approximation, and circumlocution. Moreover, Metaverse-specific nonverbal behaviors included gaze, gestures, and spatial positioning. The 22 interactions were purposely sampled from the wider dataset of 80 to capture variability in gender pairings and interactional styles, while allowing for fine-grained, line-by-line coding. Data saturation was reached by randomly sampling a diverse set of videos from each week of the intervention. Saturation was confirmed when further samples failed to reveal any additional CSs or interactional patterns. Coding reliability was ensured through iterative reviews and peer debriefing sessions between the first and second authors, which helped refine code definitions and confirm category alignment (Lincoln & Guba, 1985). A record of coding rules and decisions was maintained to ensure transparency and support replication.

4 Results and Discussion

The following section integrates results and discussion for each respective research question. It examines how design principles, CSs, and gender patterns emerged within immersive environments and what they reveal about language use in such environments.

4.1 Research Question 1: What Principles Guided the Design of an Inclusive and High-Performing Immersive Learning Space in Frame*?*

Analysis of pilot implementation and participant feedback revealed four interrelated design principles that guided the creation of an inclusive and pedagogically effective immersive space in *Frame*: customization, pilot testing, accessibility, and user training (Table 1). These principles emerged as critical for ensuring both technical feasibility and meaningful communicative engagement within the virtual environment.

These principles aimed to ensure that the space was inclusive, technically feasible, and conducive to communication and collaboration. They are explored in detail in the following sections.

Table 1 Design principles and implementation decisions in the Frame immersive learning space

Design principle	Design actions/Decisions	Pedagogical purpose/Rationale
Customization of the virtual environment	Selected a bright, open space large enough for all avatars; created private voice zones; avoided visually dense or dark environments.	Promoted ease of navigation, reduced visual overlap, and encouraged comfortable, focused interaction.
Pilot testing and iterative refinement	Conducted a pilot in *Atrium*; identified spatial and audio overlap issues; switched to a larger, open layout.	Improved spatial functionality and ensured smooth small-group communication through user feedback.
Accessibility and technical performance	Adopted BYOD policy; prioritized lightweight, cross-platform environments with stable performance on mobile and low-end devices.	Ensured equitable participation regardless of hardware or internet quality; minimized digital barriers.
User training and technical support	Provided tutorial videos, written guides, and live orientation; offered ongoing troubleshooting support.	Reduced cognitive load, built user confidence, and prevented technical issues from hindering engagement.

4.1.1 Customization of the Immersive Learning Environment

Analysis of the pilot and early-stage trials revealed that spatial configuration played a decisive role in shaping interaction quality within *Frame*. Environments that were overly compact caused avatars to visually overlap on 2D screens, reducing mutual visibility and increasing communicative hesitation. Conversely, extensive layouts led to disorientation and reduced opportunities for spontaneous engagement. Based on these observations, an open yet moderately scaled virtual space was selected and further customized to balance comfort and interactivity. Clear visual lines, bright lighting, and minimalist textures were found to enhance focus and orientation, while private voice zones effectively enabled small-group discussions without cross-talk interference. Overall, the findings underscored that visual simplicity and spatial coherence were key design elements supporting ease of communication and social presence. This aligns with research indicating that moderate realism and structured simplicity enhance presence and collaboration in shared virtual environments (Yousefdeh & Oyelere, 2024) and that subjective presence is sensitive to visual clarity and environmental coherence (Saha et al., 2025).

4.1.2 Pilot Testing and Iterative Refinement

Findings from the initial pilot phase, conducted in *Frame*'s "Atrium" environment (a two-storied hall with a glazed facade furnished with tables and stools, as shown

Fig. 2 The Atrium environment in *Frame* viewed from the third-person camera mode

in Fig. 2), provided critical feedback on spatial and auditory constraints. Participants consistently noted that confined indoor areas limited movement and led to overlapping audio streams, which disrupted conversational flow. Observational analysis confirmed these perceptions: avatars frequently clustered in narrow spaces, and turn-taking became irregular due to sound interference. In response, as displayed in Fig. 3, the research team implemented iterative adjustments, shifting to a more expansive outdoor-style environment called the "Resort" that facilitated smoother navigation and more precise audio segmentation in line with spatial-audio design principles of immersive environments (Cao et al., 2023; Cummings & Bailenson, 2016). These revisions demonstrated that early user testing served as an essential diagnostic stage, validating the role of empirical feedback in optimizing immersive language environments for pedagogical use (Alnuaimi & Awad, 2025).

4.1.3 Accessibility and Technical Performance

Technical testing across diverse devices revealed that system performance varied significantly depending on hardware and internet stability, confirming the importance of accessibility as a design principle. These results parallel findings in collaborative virtual environments, where differences in device capacities and network conditions lead to inconsistent rendering or lag (Xie et al., 2021; Yang et al., 2022). Because participants joined the sessions from multiple contexts, including home, campus, and public spaces, those using lower-spec laptops or mobile devices experienced occasional lag or delayed rendering in complex environments. By contrast, lightweight spaces loaded quickly and maintained consistent performance across platforms, aligning with accessibility challenges identified in broader reviews of Metaverse deployments (Abadía et al., 2024). These findings informed the final

Fig. 3 The Resort environment in *Frame* viewed from the third-person camera mode

selection of a streamlined environment optimized for cross-platform access, ensuring that even participants with limited technological resources could fully engage. This design outcome reflected a broader pedagogical goal: reducing the digital divide while sustaining equitable participation in immersive learning.

4.1.4 User Training and Technical Support

Collectively, these findings confirmed that scaffolding digital literacy was a prerequisite for meaningful communicative interaction within immersive environments. This is consistent with research showing that user training and technological preparedness are central to effective virtual learning engagement. For example, Makransky and Petersen (2021) highlight that immersive learning demands cognitive resources for both technological navigation and content processing; thus, adequate pre-training reduces extraneous cognitive load and facilitates deeper engagement. Furthermore, Bailenson (2018) notes that user familiarity and comfort are key determinants of social presence and participation in virtual learning environments. In this study, practical training and technical scaffolding mitigate such barriers, sustaining learner engagement and promoting a more equitable participation experience across devices and proficiency levels.

4.2 Research Question 2: What Is the Full Range and Function of CSs Used by Japanese EFL Learners in Frame*?*

4.2.1 Verbal CSs

The analysis of 22 pair interactions (each lasting an average of five minutes) revealed a variety of verbal CSs used by learners in *Frame* (Table 2). As shown, repair, clarification/confirmation, and repetition were the most frequent strategies, collectively accounting for nearly 60% of all observed cases.

These strategies were essential in maintaining conversational flow despite frequent lexical or grammatical limitations, echoing previous research that identifies strategic competence as a key factor in compensating for limited linguistic resources (Canale & Swain, 1980; Dörnyei & Scott, 1997). For example, repetition often served dual functions of self-repair and confirmation, a finding consistent with studies highlighting repetition as both a monitoring and a solidarity-building device in second-language discourse (Kormos, 2006). Fillers and hesitation markers such as "uh" and "mm" appeared across nearly every interaction, aligning with Clark and Tree's (2002) interpretation of such devices as planning tools that help speakers maintain conversational continuity while formulating utterances.

Message abandonment, though less frequent, has also been reported in prior research as a reduction strategy used when learners cannot retrieve required forms (Faerch & Kasper, 1983). Finally, instances of code-switching, typically involving the insertion of Japanese lexical items or literal translations, reflect well-documented tendencies among bilingual and EFL speakers to draw on their first language as a communicative resource in moments of lexical difficulty (Cenoz, 2003; Nakatani, 2006).

The relationship between the *Frame* environment's design and learners' CSs was evident in how spatial and auditory configurations shaped interaction. Private voice zones fostered conversational privacy and psychological safety, encouraging more

Table 2 Frequency of verbal CSs across 22 videos

CS type (Predefined)	CS frequency	% of total CSs
Repair	34	21
Clarification/confirmation	31	19
Repetition	29	18
Fillers/hesitation	27	17
Approximation	13	8
Message abandonment	12	7
Circumlocution	9	6
Code-switching/translation	7	4
Total CSs coded	162	100

frequent use of repair and clarification strategies. The open spatial layout minimized crowding and audio overlap, supporting smoother turn-taking and reducing message abandonment. At the same time, visual simplicity and a moderate scale limited the use of embodied gestures, leading learners to rely more on verbal compensation. Thus, accessibility-oriented design enhanced comfort and inclusivity. It also subtly guided learners toward sustained verbal engagement, suggesting that environmental design may actively mediate communicative behavior rather than merely framing it.

4.2.2 Nonverbal CSs

Overall, nonverbal CSs in the *Frame* environment were limited and yielded only slight variation across dyads. In most cases, participants maintained a fixed standing position and faced each other throughout the conversation (Fig. 4). Unlike real-world interactions, few gestures or changes in posture were observed, a pattern consistent with prior research noting that avatar-mediated communication often restricts embodied expressiveness due to limited tracking or gesture recognition (Wigham & Chanier, 2013). However, this relative stillness may also suggest that Japanese learners prioritized verbal exchange over embodied expression within the *Frame* immersive learning space, reflecting a tendency observed in EFL contexts where cognitive focus on accuracy can override multimodal fluency (Yanguas, 2010).

Considering that subtle spatial adjustments occasionally occurred, such as taking a small step backward when a partner initiated a turn or directly addressing them, these movements may signal attentiveness or deference rather than disengagement.

Fig. 4 An illustration of standing positions and gaze direction in *Frame*

Similar findings have been reported in studies of proxemics and politeness in Japanese interaction, where interpersonal distance and subtle shifts in body orientation convey respect and attentiveness (Nakane, 2007; Yamada, 1997). Likewise, sustained gaze, often perceived as "staring," was frequently observed when speakers paused to think or formulate responses. This behavior appears to reflect cognitive engagement rather than social discomfort, which aligns with cultural communication norms emphasizing silence and reflective listening as pragmatic resources in Japanese discourse (Harumi, 2011; Ishii & Bruneau, 1994).

These patterns may indicate that learners' nonverbal strategies in *Frame* were shaped by both the platform's technological constraints and culturally grounded expectations of appropriate behavior. The limited range of gesture and movement aligns with observations that Japanese communicative style tends to privilege verbal precision, silence as a resource, and restraint over overt expressivity (Nakane, 2007; Yamada, 1997). In this context, the controlled expressiveness of *Frame* avatars, restricted to a basic orientation or stance, may have felt familiar rather than limiting, and that, in turn, led to reinforcing norms of subtlety and interpersonal caution.

At the same time, the anonymity and reduced social cues afforded by avatar-mediated interaction appeared to soften the pressure to perform politeness, enabling learners to take greater risks through repair and clarification moves without fear of face-threatening consequences. Thus, while cultural norms of deference and controlled embodiment persisted, *Frame* may have provided a moderated communicative space in which familiar interactional habits were both preserved and carefully renegotiated.

4.3 *Research Question 3: Do Male and Female Learners Show Different Preferences for Communication Strategy Use in* Frame?

As demonstrated in Table 3, both male and female learners used a comparable overall range of CSs, although subtle preferences emerged. Male participants relied slightly more on repair (11%), repetition (9%), and clarification/confirmation (11%), reflecting a greater tendency toward direct, problem-solving behaviors. In contrast, female learners employed fillers and hesitation markers more frequently (10% compared to males' 6%), which may indicate a stronger orientation toward maintaining interpersonal flow. These results partially align with prior studies suggesting that female learners tend to favor interactional support strategies and cooperative negotiation, while males more often adopt assertive or risk-taking approaches (Coates, 2015; Nakatani, 2006).

However, the relatively small differences observed here suggest that avatar-mediated communication in *Frame* may attenuate traditional gendered patterns of language use. As Sundén (2003) argues, avatars can blur or reconfigure gender identities, allowing users to perform identity more flexibly than in face-to-face settings.

Table 3 Gender comparison of strategy use

CS type (Predefined)	Male	% of total CSs	Female	% of total CSs
Repair	19	11	15	9
Repetition	15	9	14	9
Clarification/confirmation	18	11	13	8
Message abandonment	7	4	5	3
Fillers/hesitation	10	6	17	10
Code-switching/translation	3	2	4	2
Approximation	9	5	4	2
Circumlocution	5	3	4	2
Total CSs coded:	86		76	

This aligns with Yee and Bailenson's (2007) "Proteus effect," which shows that avatar characteristics can influence users' self-perception and social behavior, often moderating gendered expectations in digital contexts. Similarly, research in virtual collaboration has found that immersive environments can reduce the visibility of social markers such as gender or status, leading to more balanced participation (Nowak & Fox, 2018). Within *Frame*, this expressive flexibility likely lessened the social pressure associated with gendered communication norms, and enabled comparable levels of strategic engagement across male and female learners. These findings imply that immersive environments offer new affordances for communication and foster greater equity in interaction, thereby supporting inclusive pedagogical goals in EFL contexts.

Moreover, learners' flexible deployment and reduced gender differences in *Frame* indicate that immersive 3D spaces can reconfigure familiar communicative norms by softening social constraints and expanding opportunities for strategic engagement. For example, observational data and post-intervention reflections indicated that *Frame*'s gamified and visually interactive environment distinguished it from text-based or conventional CMC platforms. Several participants noted that the playful affordances of avatar movement, spatial exploration, and environmental customization made the sessions feel "game-like" and less formal. This sense of immersion and novelty appeared to heighten curiosity and engagement, particularly among learners with a prior interest in gaming that may have fostered a more participatory and less evaluative atmosphere than typically experienced in classroom or video-based communication.

5 Implications for Designing Immersive Online Courses

The findings suggest that immersive learning environments should be treated as strategic communication environments where design decisions directly shape learners' interactional behavior. For English teachers, this means that building an effective Metaverse-based classroom involves more than selecting a platform; it requires purposeful choices about spatial layout, audio configuration, task sequencing, and strategic support. Teachers should consider how features such as private voice zones, open layouts, clear lines of sight, and simple environmental textures influence communication. For example, private zones can lower social pressure and encourage learners to attempt repair or clarification, while clutter-free spaces reduce cognitive load and promote attentiveness. These insights highlight that spatial design itself is a form of pedagogical support, not an aesthetic afterthought.

Furthermore, immersive tasks should intentionally target strategy development rather than expecting it to emerge naturally. To this end, teachers can introduce brief pre-task modeling of CSs (e.g., clarification requests, confirmation checks, paraphrasing). This could be performed by embedding strategy prompts into task instructions or by attaching them to virtual signs/objects in the environment. Teachers could also use video playback or post-task debriefs to help learners analyze the strategies they used or missed. These practices help students internalize strategic behaviors and transfer them beyond the virtual setting.

Because immersion can be cognitively demanding, pre-immersion training should combine technical orientation with low-stakes communicative warm-ups. Allowing learners to experiment with avatar movement, spatial audio, and turn-taking in a supportive environment can reduce anxiety and ensure more equitable participation, particularly for those with limited technological experience. Moreover, teachers can intentionally leverage the reduced visibility of the body and flexible identity representation in avatars to mitigate social hierarchies, support shy learners, and encourage balanced participation. Designing tasks that foster collaboration, not performance, can help learners focus on meaning-making rather than self-presentation.

6 Limitations

While this study provides valuable insights into EFL learners' strategic behaviors in immersive contexts, several limitations must be acknowledged. Firstly, during the course, *Frame*'s browser-based platform occasionally constrained interaction through latency, inconsistent audio quality, and limited gesture recognition. These issues were compounded by disparities in internet stability, device processing power, and digital literacy, which sometimes affected engagement and ease of navigation.

Furthermore, participants accessed *Frame* primarily via personal laptops and, in some cases, smartphones without headsets. Such factors may have reduced spatial immersion and auditory realism. The task design also privileged verbal negotiation, with limited opportunities for embodied collaboration; as a result, few gesture-based strategies emerged. Cultural communication norms may have additionally shaped interaction, as Japanese learners often employ controlled body language and silence as pragmatic resources, favoring verbal precision over overt expressivity. Finally, because the researchers were involved in both environment design and data analysis, reflexivity measures were implemented through peer debriefing and iterative coding; nevertheless, some interpretive bias may remain.

7 Conclusion

This study sheds light on how pedagogical design and learner interaction intersect within an immersive EFL environment. The findings demonstrate that effective learning in *Frame* depended on factors beyond spatial aesthetics or novelty. In other words, it required purposeful design grounded in accessibility, cognitive ease, and user preparedness. When digital literacy was scaffolded and technical barriers were minimized, learners could focus on communication rather than navigation. This, in turn, resulted in more equitable participation and sustained engagement.

Interactional data also revealed that learners strategically managed linguistic limitations through repetition, repair, and clarification, reaffirming the adaptive and collaborative nature of communication in immersive settings. Nonverbal behaviors, albeit limited, reflected culturally influenced communication styles that value attentiveness and subtle spatial cues over overt gestures. These observations suggest that immersive environments do not erase cultural norms but rather translate them into new modalities of presence and attentiveness. Interestingly, gender differences were marginal, suggesting that avatar-mediated interaction may soften traditional gendered dynamics by allowing learners to express their identities with greater fluidity and confidence. In this sense, *Frame* may also have functioned as a space for social and identity experimentation, which is a form of linguistic and interpersonal equalization rarely achieved in face-to-face classrooms.

Overall, these findings emphasize that immersive environments, when thoughtfully designed and ethically implemented, can extend the possibilities of communicative language teaching. They offer spaces where learners negotiate meaning, build confidence, and develop intercultural understanding and digital competence simultaneously. Future work should explore how sustained engagement in such environments shapes communicative identity and strategic competence over time, particularly as immersive technologies become more deeply integrated into language education.

Acknowledgements This research is funded by the Japan Society for the Promotion of Science Grants-in-Aid for Scientific Research (Project Number: 22 K13756).

References

Abadia, R., Fritsch, J., Abdelaal, S., & Jayawickrama, T. (2024). Opportunities overcome challenges in adopting immersive virtual reality in online learning. *Computers and Education Open, 7*, 100208. https://doi.org/10.1016/j.caeo.2024.100208

Alnuaimi, M. A., & Awad, M. (2025). VR environment of digital design laboratory: A usability study. *Frontiers in Virtual Reality, 6*, 1566680. https://doi.org/10.3389/frvir.2025.1566680

Bailenson, J. (2018). *Experience on demand: What virtual reality is, how it works, and what it can do*. W. W. Norton & Company.

Becker, B., & Mark, G. (1999). Constructing social systems through computer-mediated communication. *Virtual Reality, 4*(1), 60–73. https://doi.org/10.1007/bf01434995

Bialystok, E. (1990). *Communication strategies: A psychological analysis of second-language use*. Blackwell.

Canale, M., & Swain, M. (1980). Theoretical bases of communicative approaches to second language teaching and testing. *Applied Linguistics, I*(1), 1–47. https://doi.org/10.1093/applin/I.1.1

Cao, Y., Ng, G.-W., & Ye, S.-S. (2023). Design and evaluation for immersive virtual reality learning environment: A systematic literature review. *Sustainability, 15*(3), 1964. https://doi.org/10.3390/su15031964

Cenoz, J. (2003). Chapter 4. The intercultural style hypothesis: L1 and L2 interaction in requesting behaviour. In V. Cook (Ed.), *Effects of the second language on the first* (pp. 62–80). Multilingual Matters. https://doi.org/10.21832/9781853596346-006

Chen, H.-I., & Sevilla-Pavón, A. (2023). Negotiation of meaning via virtual exchange in immersive virtual reality environments. *Language Learning & Technology, 27*(2), 118–154. https://doi.org/10.64152/10125/73506

Clark, H. H., & Tree, J. E. F. (2002). Using uh and um in spontaneous speaking. *Cognition, 84*(1), 73–111. https://doi.org/10.1016/s0010-0277(02)00017-3

Coates, J. (2015). *Women, men, and language: A sociolinguistic account of gender differences in language*. Routledge. https://doi.org/10.4324/9781315645612

Cowie, N., & Alizadeh, M. (2022). The affordances and challenges of virtual reality for language teaching. *International Journal of TESOL Studies, 4*(3), 50–65. https://doi.org/10.46451/ijts.2022.03.05

Cowie, N., & Alizadeh, M. (2025). Virtual reality for language learning. *ELT Journal*, ccaf025. https://doi.org/10.1093/elt/ccaf025

Cummings, J. J., & Bailenson, J. N. (2016). How immersive is enough? A meta-analysis of the effect of immersive technology on user presence. *Media Psychology, 19*(2), 272–309. https://doi.org/10.1080/15213269.2015.1015740

Dede, C. (2009). Immersive interfaces for engagement and learning. *Science, 323*(5910), 66–69. https://doi.org/10.1126/science.1167311

Dörnyei, Z. (1995). On the teachability of communication strategies. *TESOL Quarterly, 29*(1), 55–85. https://doi.org/10.2307/3587805

Dörnyei, Z., & Scott, M. L. (1997). Communication strategies in a second language: Definitions and taxonomies. *Language Learning, 47*(1), 173–210. https://doi.org/10.1111/0023-8333.51997005

Ellis, R., & Barkhuizen, G. (2005). *Analysing learner language*. Oxford University Press.

Esteves, J. R., Cardoso, J. C. S., & Gonçalves, B. S. (2023). Design recommendations for immersive virtual reality application for English learning: A systematic review. *Computers, 12*(11), 236. https://doi.org/10.3390/computers12110236

Faerch, C., & Kasper, G. (1983). *Strategies in interlanguage communication*. Longman.

Guye-Vuilleme, A., Çapın, T., Pandzic, I. S., Magnenat-Thalmann, N., & Thalmann, D. (1999). Nonverbal communication interface for collaborative virtual environments. *Virtual Reality, 4*(1), 49–59. https://doi.org/10.1007/bf01434994

Harumi, S. (2011). Classroom silence: Voices from Japanese EFL learners. *ELT Journal, 65*(3), 260–269. https://doi.org/10.1093/elt/ccq046

Hasler, B. S., & Friedman, D. A. (2012). Sociocultural conventions in avatar-mediated nonverbal communication: A cross-cultural analysis of virtual proxemics. *Journal of Intercultural Communication Research, 41*(3), 238–259. https://doi.org/10.1080/17475759.2012.728764

Ishii, S., & Bruneau, T. (1994). Silence and silences in cross-cultural perspective: Japan and the United States. In L. A. Samovar & R. E. Porter (Eds.), *Intercultural communication: A reader* (pp. 246–251). Wadsworth.

Jenks, C. J. (2009). When is it appropriate to talk? Managing overlapping talk in multi-participant voice-based chat rooms. *Computer Assisted Language Learning, 22*(1), 19–30. https://doi.org/10.1080/09588220802613781

Jiang, J., & Fryer, L. K. (2024). The effect of virtual reality learning on students' motivation: A scoping review. *Journal of Computer Assisted Learning, 40*(1), 360–373. https://doi.org/10.1111/jcal.12885

Kormos, J. (2006). *Speech production and second language acquisition.* Lawrence Erlbaum Associates.

Lan, Y.-J., Hsiao, I. Y. T., & Shih, M.-F. (2018). Effective learning design of game-based 3D virtual language learning environments for special education students. *Educational Technology & Society, 21*(3), 213–227. http://www.jstor.org/stable/26458519

Lee, S.-M., & Ahn, T. Y. (2025). L2 learner experiences in a playful constructivist metaverse space. *ReCALL, 37*(1), 129–145. https://doi.org/10.1017/S0958344024000235

Lincoln, Y. S., & Guba, E. G. (1985). *Naturalistic inquiry.* Sage.

Makransky, G., & Petersen, G. B. (2021). The cognitive affective model of immersive learning (CAMIL): A theoretical research-based model of learning in immersive virtual reality. *Educational Psychology Review, 33*(3), 937–958. https://doi.org/10.1007/s10648-020-09586-2

Maleki, A. (2007). Teachability of communication strategies: An Iranian experience. *System, 35*(4), 583–594. https://doi.org/10.1016/j.system.2007.04.001

Mishra, P., & Koehler, M. J. (2006). Technological pedagogical content knowledge: A framework for teacher knowledge. *Teachers College Record, 108*(6), 1017–1054. https://doi.org/10.1111/j.1467-9620.2006.00684.x

Nakane, I. (2007). *Silence in intercultural communication: Perceptions and performance.* John Benjamins. https://doi.org/10.1075/pbns.166

Nakatani, Y. (2006). Developing an oral communication strategy inventory. *The Modern Language Journal, 90*(2), 151–168. https://doi.org/10.1111/j.1540-4781.2006.00390.x

Nikian, S., Nor, F. M., Rejab, A. B., Hassan, H., & Zainal, Z. (2016). The challenges in instilling communicative competence in second language learners. *Journal of Advanced Review on Scientific Research, 26*(1), 1–12. https://www.akademiabaru.com/doc/ARSRV26_N1_P1_12.pdf

Nowak, K. L., & Fox, J. (2018). Avatars and computer-mediated communication: A review of the definitions, uses, and effects of digital representations. *Review of Communication Research, 6*, 30–53. https://doi.org/10.12840/ISSN.2255-4165.2018.06.01.015

Puentedura, R. (2006). *Transformation, technology, and education.* http://hippasus.com/resources/tte/

Saha, S., Dobbins, C., Gupta, A., & Dey, A. (2025). Differentiating presence in virtual reality using physiological signals. *Pervasive and Mobile Computing, 111*, 102065. https://doi.org/10.1016/j.pmcj.2025.102065

Smith, B. (2003). Computer–mediated negotiated interaction: An expanded model. *The Modern Language Journal, 87*(1), 38–57. https://doi.org/10.1111/1540-4781.00177

Sundén, J. (2003). *Material virtualities: Approaching online textual embodiment.* Peter Lang.

Tarone, E. (2007). Sociolinguistic approaches to second language acquisition research—1997–2007. *The Modern Language Journal, 91*, 837–848. http://www.jstor.org/stable/4626135

Wigham, C. R., & Chanier, T. (2013). A study of verbal and nonverbal communication in second life—The ARCHI21 experience. *ReCALL, 25*(1), 63–84. https://doi.org/10.1017/S0958344012000250

Xie, C., Li, X., Hu, Y., Peng, H., Taylor, M., & Song, S. L. (2021). Q-VR: System-level design for future mobile collaborative virtual reality. In *Proceedings of the 26th ACM international conference on architectural support for programming languages and operating systems* (pp. 587–599). https://doi.org/10.1145/3445814.3446715

Yamada, H. (1997). *Different games, different rules: Why Americans and Japanese misunderstand each other*. Oxford University Press. https://doi.org/10.1093/oso/9780195094886.001.0001

Yang, H., Tsung, L., & Cao, L. (2022). The use of communication strategies by second language learners of Chinese in a virtual reality learning environment. *SAGE Open, 12*(4). https://doi.org/10.1177/21582440221141877

Yanguas, Í. (2010). Oral computer-mediated interaction between L2 learners: It's about time! *Language Learning & Technology, 14*(3), 72–93. https://doi.org/10.64152/10125/44227

Yee, N., & Bailenson, J. N. (2007). The proteus effect: The effect of transformed self-representation on behavior. *Human Communication Research, 33*(3), 271–290. https://doi.org/10.1111/j.1468-2958.2007.00299.x

Yee, N., Bailenson, J. N., Urbanek, M., Chang, F., & Merget, D. (2007). The unbearable likeness of being digital: The persistence of nonverbal social norms in online virtual environments. *Cyberpsychology & Behavior, 10*(1), 115–121. https://doi.org/10.1089/cpb.2006.9984

Yousefdeh, S. A. G., & Oyelere, S. S. (2024). Investigating co-presence and collaboration dynamics in realtime virtual reality user interactions. *Frontiers in Virtual Reality, 5*, 1478481. https://doi.org/10.3389/frvir.2024.1478481

Mehrasa Alizadeh is Associate Professor at Otemon Gakuin University in Ibaraki, Osaka, Japan, where she teaches English as a foreign language to Japanese students. Mehrasa's research interests include mobile learning, immersive learning, and the use of virtual reality in language education. She has published and presented extensively on immersive learning in international conferences and journals.

Nikan Fujii is a lecturer at, the Department of English and American Studies, Bukkyo University, Kyoto, Japan. Her research focuses on the effects of online platforms on language learning. Fujii's recent work also includes studies on analyzing avatar-based interactions and gender variations in virtual environments. Her research aims to enhance theoretical understanding of strategic competence in online and immersive settings.

Neil Cowie works at the English Language Academy, University of Auckland, New Zealand. He teaches English for academic purposes to international students who wish to go on to postgraduate education. As part of this role, one research avenue is to trace students through their learning journeys in order to improve teaching approaches and materials for future students. A further area of interest is the application of virtual reality to language education, and especially how it might enhance inter-cultural communication.

Developing Speaking and Listening Skills in the Metaverse

Nur Aeni, Muhammad Yunus, Besse Darmawati, Muthmainnah Muthmainnah, and Selvi Panggua

Abstract In this chapter, we examine the potential of metaverse-based instruction as an effective method for developing integrated speaking and listening skills among English as a Foreign Language (EFL) students. An eight-week mixed-method intervention study with 30 undergraduate students of Universitas Negeri Makassar engaged us in investigating how immersive virtual environments (VEs) counter stubborn existing issues in traditional EFL classrooms. The results showed that VEs made a difference in speaking (mean gain = 5.52 points, Cohen's $d = 3.08$) and listening skills (mean gain = 1.43 points, Cohen's $d = 1.68$), with the contributions of the spatial audio systems, avatar-mediated communication, and immersive virtual environments. These virtual sceneries alleviate the anxiety caused by foreign language learning within a psychologically safe space while developing contexts for authentic communication to serve naturalistic language use. This study would be the empirical evidence answering pedagogical advice for practical recommendations on EFL teachers and curriculum developers on how the metaverse technology should be implemented in ESL/EFL contexts, evidence-based directions on effective integration, and specifying situations in which virtual pedagogy complements face-to-face instruction.

N. Aeni (✉)
Universitas Negeri Makassar, Makassar, Indonesia
e-mail: nur_aeni@unm.ac.id

M. Yunus
Universitas Muslim Indonesia, Makassar, Indonesia
e-mail: muhammad.yunus@umi.ac.id

B. Darmawati
Badan Riset dan Inovasi Nasional, Jakarta, Indonesia
e-mail: bess001@brin.go.id

M. Muthmainnah
Universitas Al Asyariah Mandar, Sulawesi, Indonesia

S. Panggua
Universitas Kristen Indonesia, Toraja, Indonesia
e-mail: selvipanggua@ukitoaraja.ac.id

F. Çelik and C. Yangın Ersanlı (eds.), *Metaverse-Based Language Learning and Teaching*, English Language Education 49,
https://doi.org/10.1007/978-3-032-31366-9_5

Keywords Virtual reality · EFL instruction · Speaking skills · Technology-enhanced language learning

1 Introduction

The fast pace of digital transformation in education has greatly impacted the teaching of English as a Foreign Language (EFL), offering new possibilities for innovative practices that cannot be limited to the traditional classroom. Among these technologies, the metaverse represents a potential platform that provides immersive and interactive environments for turning language learning into authentic and engaging experiences.

This chapter highlights the prospect of metaverse-based instruction to develop the integrated skills of speaking and listening, two of the most difficult skills for EFL learners to acquire. Building on empirical evidence derived from an intervention study, this is a discussion that goes beyond theory and that integrates research findings with practical suggestions to provide teachers and curriculum developers with a roadmap to efficiently integrate a virtual learning environment within their programs.

In new research on technology-supported language learning, immersive learning environments were said to yield positive results. Yu (2021) confirmed through meta-analysis that virtual reality technology use in education produces consistently positive learning outcomes. Christou et al. (2025), found that metaverse-generated situations made learning activities more communicative and real, encouraging student engagement in more meaningful ways. Likewise, Lee and Ko (2024) asserted that virtual reality platforms help alleviate speaking anxiety, create opportunities for natural conversation, and provide a regular practice schedule for oral communication. Wu and Hung (2022) further demonstrated that virtual reality-infused instruction significantly improved students' English-speaking performance, willingness to communicate, and learning autonomy.

Learning experiences that are authentic and situated generally bring together these theoretical orientations, as they all subscribe to the theory and application of experiential learning, social constructivism, and communicative language teaching. These theoretical frameworks fit with metaverse affordances in that visual immersion, spatial audio, and sociality all converge to create a learning environment that supports the development of skills and sustains learner engagement at the same time.

2 Theoretical Framework and Literature Synthesis

2.1 *Metaverse in Language Education*

The imagineering (Benesse Corporation) of the metaverse as an educational platform transcends conventional virtual reality or computer-assisted language teaching. As Tang (2026), established in their foundational review, language learning in virtual reality environments has evolved considerably from its early applications to now encompass rich, socially interactive spaces. Zhang (2024) refers to five core elements pertaining to language learning: immersion, interactivity, continuity, social presence, and multimodality. It is the combination of these components that results in what Christou et al. (2025), call "immersive, interactive virtual environments allowing avatar-mediated communication and realistic simulations of genuine communicative situations.

Research suggests that the metaverse fuses the immersive aspect of VR and the context awareness of AR, but with social spaces that enable enduring and authentic interaction. As a result, more regular opportunities for communicative practice that typically would not flow from classroom-based language learning (such as limited time for personal practice or exposure to a variety of communicative contexts) became possible through this integration.

The notion of immersion in metaverse language learning is constituted by several factors, which result in an optimal outcome of learning. Visual immersion refers to realistic virtual environments (VEs) with believable depictions of real or imaginary locations, enabling the creation of captivating settings that capture attention and sustain learner attention for extended periods. These settings need to strike a balance between realism and playability, providing enough detail to feel present and be convincing, whilst also being performant enough on a wide range of gaming hardware configurations.

Interactivity in metaverse environments extends beyond simple menu selection or button pressing to encompass complex gestural communication, spatial movement, and object manipulation that create rich, multimodal learning experiences. This interactivity enables learners to assume active roles in their learning processes while receiving immediate feedback and an adaptive response to their actions.

2.2 *Speaking Skill Development Through Virtual Environments*

The development of speaking skills in virtual environments has been made possible through various key benefits which distinguish metaverse-directed instruction from traditional practice. Avatar-mediated interaction provides a highly significant factor in reducing speaking anxiety and increasing the motivation to use language. Kaplan-Rakowski and Gruber (2023) demonstrated that high-immersion virtual reality significantly reduced foreign language anxiety when speaking in public. Ironsi (2023) found that the use of avatar-mediated role-playing in virtual worlds produced significant improvement in fluency, accuracy, and complexity among English as a Foreign Language (EFL) learners compared to traditional classroom role-playing, attributing these achievements to reduced social pressure and increased motivation to communicate. Psychological benefits of avatar representation go beyond simple anonymity. Research evidence suggests that virtual characters allow learners a feeling of empowerment and creativity, challenging them to experiment with varied communicative styles and register use. Hua and Wang (2023) discovered that the use of avatars in narrations greatly improved creativity, narrative structuring, and linguistic sophistication, while learners were also found to be more confident in the expression of complex concepts and feelings. Hwang and Lee (2025) similarly found that EFL students integrating speaking practice into metaverse environments reported significantly increased confidence when using their avatars. The paradigms of Task-Based Language Teaching (TBLT) demonstrate a considerable level of congruence with virtual spaces, in which real-world contexts can be created to encourage spontaneous interaction. According to Kul et al. (2026), the embedding of communicative tasks in authentic virtual contexts facilitates not just linguistic accuracy and fluency but also the students' pragmatic and sociolinguistic abilities. The intrinsic dynamism of virtual worlds allows learners to respond to the social and cultural aspects of language in ways which traditional classroom environments are incapable of offering. The incorporation of gamified content across various metaverse platforms greatly reduces anxiety levels by shifting language learning from an official testing paradigm to an enjoyable experience. Reward-based achievement systems, progress meters, and co-op challenges create a positive mindset toward speaking practice, while also providing intrinsic motivation toward continued engagement. They appear to be particularly effective among younger learners, who are likely to respond positively to instructional contexts like game worlds. Cultural interaction through online worlds presents the possibility of contact with various linguistic variations and communicative behaviors, while also evading the practical challenges and expenses of travel abroad. Users can access people of varied cultural contexts, hear unfamiliar accent differences, and develop their intercultural communicative skills, which are becoming even more imperative in the globalizing age.

2.3 *Speaking Skill Development Through Virtual Environments*

The development of listening comprehension skills in metaverses is increasingly supported by using spatial audio technologies that simulate real-world acoustic environments. Unlike traditional auditory materials that are heard from one point source, spatial audio produces three-dimensional listening environments like real-world listening events. Bozorgian et al. (2025), suggest that the use of three-dimensional spatial audio has enhanced the ability of learners to distinguish voices, maintain focus in background noise, and retain attention in long listening tasks.

The educational importance of spatial audio goes beyond mere technological advancement. Studies indicate that students who were subjected to spatially enriched audio performed better compared to their peers who used standard recordings, as observed during both global and local listening comprehension tests. Tai and Chen (2021) found that immersive virtual reality had a significant positive impact on EFL learners' listening comprehension, while Lan (2020) established that immersion into virtual reality creates uniquely effective conditions for language learning by providing contextually rich environments.

Interactive listening exercises set in the metaverse environment change the dynamics of passive consumption, which becomes active involvement. Instead of just consuming pre-recorded lessons, students are involved in dynamic conversational exchanges which require instant comprehension and response. Such interactivity facilitates the integration of listening and speaking skills, thus underlining the interdependent nature of verbal communication used in real contexts.

Virtual settings enable the integration of multiple modes of input that augment listening comprehension. Further input based on visual context, gestures, environmental signals, and interactive components collectively support understanding in a way that approximates the multilevel multimodal input typical of direct interpersonal communication.

The blend of visual and audio stimuli in virtual environments seemingly generates significant benefits to beginners, who often face difficulty absorbing information communicated via purely audio modes. The use of nonverbal communicative strategies, like facial expressions, lip action, gestures, and body language, facilitates comprehension, thus enabling learners to access higher-level linguistic content than possible via audio input alone.

The built-in interactive nature of virtual listening activities allows students to ask for clarification, adjust audio settings, or re-listen to difficult passages, thus enabling them to enhance their ability to comprehend. Such features encompass scaffolding, which can be gradually reduced as students gain higher levels of proficiency in listening, thus promoting adaptive learning strategies adjusted to each learner's specific requirements and skills.

2.4 *Affective Factors and Engagement in Virtual Learning*

The psychological aspects of language learning are greatly influenced by the affordances of metaverse spaces. Immersive virtual experiences have been shown consistently in research to increase motivation, decrease anxiety, and facilitate long-term engagement. Çelik and Baturay (2024) established that students in metaverse-based courses had greater intrinsic motivation than students in face-to-face classrooms, crediting this improvement to novelty, interactivity, and learner autonomy afforded in virtual spaces. Presence, which includes spatial presence, social presence, and co-presence, is important to the success of virtual learning experiences. Presence has been shown to be related to higher levels of cognitive processing, more engaging learning experiences, and higher levels of satisfaction with the learning experience. Metaverse environments, with their immersive qualities, enable the creation of presence through realistic visualization, spatial sound, and interactive virtual worlds that respond to learning activity. Further, the motivational advantages of language learning in the metaverse seem to be due to several elements that counteract well-known sources of demotivation in conventional language education. Virtual worlds' novelty and technological advances generate initial enthusiasm and curiosity that can be followed up with well-designed learning experiences with suitable challenge levels and clear indicators of progress. Gamification features embedded in metaverse platforms utilize established motivation mechanics such as achievement acknowledgment, social comparison, and progress visualization. These features need to be carefully balanced in order to strengthen, instead of weakening, intrinsic motivation in learning languages. Syawaluddin and Aeni (2025) revealed the meaningful difficulties in line with actual learning objectives are more effective than meaningless point systems or badges that have no application to actual language learning. Avatar-based communication appears to break down social obstacles to community building in traditional classrooms. Cross-cultural community building in virtual spaces offers opportunities for genuine intercultural communication that sustains both language growth and global competency growth. Such interactions introduce learners to various viewpoints, communication styles, and cultural routines and offer real-life contexts for language practice with interlocutors from other linguistic and cultural backgrounds.

2.5 *Technological Foundations and Platform Capabilities*

The effectiveness of metaverse-based language learning depends heavily on the technological infrastructure and platform capabilities that support immersive educational experiences. Modern metaverse platforms integrate advanced graphics rendering, spatial audio processing, artificial intelligence, and networking technologies to create seamless virtual environments that can accommodate multiple simultaneous users while maintaining high-quality visual and auditory experiences.

Artificial intelligence integration enables sophisticated features, including automated assessment, personalized feedback, intelligent tutoring, and adaptive content delivery that can enhance the educational value of virtual environments. AI-powered virtual characters can serve as conversation partners, providing consistent availability for speaking practice while adapting to individual learner proficiency levels and learning preferences, (Bozorgian et al. (2025).

Networking and communication technologies enable real-time multiplayer interactions that are essential for collaborative learning activities and social presence in virtual environments. These systems must handle voice communication, text messaging, avatar movement synchronization, and environmental interactions while maintaining low latency and high reliability across geographically distributed users.

Platform accessibility considerations include compatibility with various hardware devices, operating systems, and assistive technologies that enable participation by learners with diverse technical capabilities and physical needs. Successful educational metaverse platforms must balance advanced technological features with broad accessibility to ensure equitable participation opportunities.

3 Research Context and Methodology

The empirical foundation for this chapter draws from a comprehensive intervention study conducted at Universitas Negeri Makassar, involving 30 undergraduate students in an eight-week metaverse-based EFL program. The research utilized a mixed-methods approach that combined quantitative performance measures with qualitative investigations of the learners' experiences and perceptions. It should be noted that this study employed a pre-post intervention design without a control group, which limits causal attribution of the observed improvements. The empirical foundation for this chapter draws from a comprehensive intervention study conducted at Universitas Negeri Makassar. It should be noted that this study, while contributing valuable insights, is part of an emerging research base in metaverse-based language learning. As the field develops, additional large-scale studies and longitudinal investigations across diverse educational contexts will be essential to substantiate these preliminary findings.

The intervention used the resources of the Dexlightex metaverse environment, which was equipped with spatial audio devices, avatar customization tools, and programmed virtual worlds to mimic real-world communicative environments. Two groups participated in a 16-session training schedule, each session lasting 90 minutes and containing three general groups of activities: mock interview simulations in replica environments, role-playing simulations, and spontaneous conversational exchanges.

Data were collected using a battery of objective measurements carried out pretesting and post testing on speaking (IELTS type) and listening (TOEFL type) skills, with a significant amount of semi-structured interviews about learner experiences, their perceptions, and attitudes toward virtual learning environments. Such an approach yielded both objective measures of language proficiency development and subjective insights into the mechanisms through which improvements were observed.

3.1 Participants

The study participants were selected through purposive sampling from undergraduate students enrolled in English language education programs at Universitas Negeri Makassar. Selection criteria included intermediate English proficiency levels (B1-B2 on the Common European Framework of Reference), prior experience with basic computer applications, and voluntary consent to participate in an extended virtual learning program.

The participant demographic profile revealed considerable diversity in terms of educational background, prior language learning experience, and technology familiarity. Ages ranged from 19 to 23 years, with 18 females and 12 male participants representing typical gender distributions in Indonesian English language education programs. Most participants had studied English for 6–10 years in formal educational settings but reported limited opportunities for authentic oral communication practice.

Technology experience varied significantly among participants, with some reporting extensive gaming and virtual environment familiarity while others had minimal exposure to three-dimensional virtual platforms. This diversity provided valuable insights into the accessibility and usability of metaverse-based language learning across different technology comfort levels.

3.2 Intervention Design and Implementation

The eight-week intervention was systematically designed to allow stepwise skill development through progressively increased communicative task complexity and experience within the virtual environment. The first two weeks were devoted to orienting students to the platform, building avatars, and developing basic navigation skills so all participants could effectively participate in subsequent activities.

Weeks three to six provided significant instructional activities such as virtual interview practice, role-playing exercises, and group problem-solving activities. These activities were designed to integrate speaking and listening skill development while providing authentic communicative contexts that reflected real-world language use scenarios.

The final two weeks concentrated on independent practice and peer collaboration, whereby participants assumed greater responsibility for planning and facilitating their own learning activities. This transition from instructor-led to learner-led activities enabled the development of self-regulated learning abilities while maintaining motivation through peer interaction and support.

3.3 Virtual Learning Environment

The Dexlightex platform provided multiple virtual environments designed to support diverse communicative activities and learning preferences. Professional settings included conference rooms, office spaces, and interview environments that supported business communication practice. Social environments encompassed cafés, parks, and recreational spaces that facilitated informal conversational practice.

The spatial audio implementation provided three-dimensional soundscapes that supported natural conversational dynamics including overlapping speech, background noise management, and directional audio cues that enhanced speaker identification and attention focusing. These audio features were crucial for developing listening skills that transfer effectively to real-world communicative contexts.

Simulation of job interviews, university admissions, and business networking contexts allowed students to rehearse speaking under controlled conditions during virtual practice sessions. Practice tasks incorporated real-time pressures, formal register demands, and constructive feedback so students became accustomed to high-stakes communicative environments.

Simulation role-playing immersed students in collaborative narratives, problem-solving exercises, and intercultural dialogue activities which provided opportunities to employ language creatively while building intercultural communication competencies. These exercises drew upon the potential of virtual worlds to create interactive scaffolds which would be challenging or unachievable in physical classroom settings.

3.4 Data Collection Instruments

Speaking ability was examined according to IELTS speaking tests, assessing four criteria: fluency and coherence, lexical resource, grammatical range and accuracy, and pronunciation. Each criterion is measured on a scale of 0 to 9 by trained examiners following a standard rubric. The total time allocated for conducting the speaking test was 15 minutes, during which three parts were examined: personal interview questions (Part 1), individual long turn (Part 2), and two-way discussion (Part 3).

Listening comprehension was assessed using the four sub-skills as adapted from the TOEFL listening test: understanding main ideas, identifying supporting details, understanding speakers' attitude, and inferring/pragmatic understanding. The items were in the form of multiple-choice questions related to either academic lectures or conversations, and each criterion had a possible sub score from 0 to 6. By incorporating the instructions and the time provided to complete all sections, the listening comprehension test lasted 60 minutes.

Qualitative data were collected through semi-structured interviews conducted in the participants' native language (Bahasa Indonesia) to ensure that their experiences and perceptions are fully expressed. The interview protocol focused on various aspects of technology usability, effectiveness for learning purposes, motivational aspects, and their preference for virtual or traditional learning methods. Each interview lasted between 30–45 minutes and was audio recorded with the participant's permission for later transcription and analysis.

3.5 Data Analysis Procedures

Analyses of the quantitative data involved the paired-samples t-test to find differences between the pre-test and post-test speaking and listening performance scores. Effect sizes were computed using Cohen's *d* and placed at 0.2, 0.5, and 0.8 for small, medium, and large effects, respectively. Statistical significance was set at a level of α =.05. Summary descriptive statistics, including means, standard deviations, and 95% confidence intervals, were calculated for all measures. All statistical analyses were done using SPSS Version 26.0.

Qualitative Data from semi-structured interviews were analysed by thematic analysis following Miles and Huberman (1994). Interview transcripts were independently coded by two researchers to find repeated themes connected to learner experiences, perceptions, and attitudes toward metaverse-based instruction. Initial inductive codes were generated and clustered into broader thematic categories through iterative review and refinement over time. Inter-rater reliability was established through discussion and consensus-building to resolve discrepancies through collaborative review of original data. Representative quotes were taken to show these primary themes, and participant anonymity is maintained with the use of pseudonyms.

The integration of mixed methods data occurred through converging parallel designs, where both quantitative and qualitative data were collected simultaneously, analysed independently, and subsequently compared to find convergence and divergence. Such an interpretation would allow triangulation of findings, where qualitative data elucidate the mechanisms through which the positive permits hypotheses of quantitative improvements while providing quantitative objective measures of the effectiveness of the intervention.

3.6 Ethical Considerations

The research has obtained ethical approval from the Research Ethics Committee of Universitas Negeri Makassar. All participants provided written informed consent after receiving complete information about the objectives, procedures, potential risks, and benefits of the study. Participants were expressly informed they were entitled to withdraw at any time without facing penalties or unfavorable consequences relating to their academic status.

All collected data were anonymous by participant codes (P01-P30) and were stored in secure password-enabled files that were accessed only by the research team. Audio recordings of interview transcription were devoid of identifying information and stored separately from consent forms, and all qualitative excerpts in this chapter have been transformed into pseudonyms to prevent the identification of the participant. The study complied with institutional policies on data protection and internationally established ethical guidelines on educational research, such as the principles from the Declaration of Helsinki and the Belmont Report.

Participants were made familiar with the fact that it is entirely voluntary to participate and be free from academic grades or ranks within the English language education program. Without financial or academic remuneration for taking part in the research, it could be said that no coercion took place at this point. During the whole program, technical support was available for sharing problems related to the use of the virtual learning platform to all participants, as well as alternative ways to participate for those students with continued technical difficulties.

4 Results and Analysis

4.1 Speaking Skill Development Outcomes

The quantitative analysis revealed substantial improvements in speaking performance, with participants demonstrating a mean improvement of 5.52 points on standardized assessments. The effect size analysis yielded a Cohen's d value of 3.08, indicating an exceptionally large practical impact that extends well beyond statistical significance. These improvements were consistent across all IELTS speaking criteria, with gains ranging from 8.37 to 8.99% in fluency and coherence, lexical resource, grammatical range and accuracy, and pronunciation, as detailed in Table 1.

The uniformity of improvements across multiple speaking competencies suggests that metaverse-based instruction facilitates holistic oral proficiency development rather than isolated skill enhancement. Participants' qualitative reports provided insights into the mechanisms underlying these improvements, with 97% reporting enhanced speaking confidence attributed to avatar-mediated anxiety reduction and the psychological safety provided by virtual identities.

Figure 1 provides a visual representation of these improvements, demonstrating consistent gains across all four IELTS speaking criteria. The parallel nature of improvement patterns suggests that metaverse-based instruction facilitates holistic oral proficiency development rather than isolated skill enhancement.

The qualitative data revealed that avatar representation created a sense of psychological distance from social judgment while maintaining the communicative pressure necessary for skill development. Participants described feeling empowered to experiment with different speaking styles, take communicative risks, and engage in extended discourse without the self-consciousness that often inhibits oral participation in traditional classroom settings.

Table 1 Speaking performance improvements across IELTS criteria ($N = 30$)

IELTS speaking criteria	Pre-test *M* (SD)	Post-test *M* (SD)	Mean Diff.	% Gain	*t*	*p*	Cohen's *d*	95% CI
Fluency and coherence	5.23 (0.68)	5.70 (0.62)	0.47	8.99	8.94	<.001	0.72	[0.35, 0.59]
Lexical resource	5.17 (0.71)	5.63 (0.66)	0.46	8.90	8.67	<.001	0.68	[0.34, 0.58]
Grammatical range and accuracy	5.13 (0.73)	5.60 (0.65)	0.47	9.16	8.82	<.001	0.69	[0.35, 0.59]
Pronunciation	5.27 (0.64)	5.73 (0.61)	0.46	8.73	9.12	<.001	0.74	[0.34, 0.58]
Overall speaking score	20.80 (2.54)	26.32 (2.18)	5.52	26.54	16.87	<.001	3.08	[4.86, 6.18]

Note $N = 30$. IELTS speaking scores range from 0–9 for individual criteria. Overall speaking score is the sum of four criteria (range 0–36). All paired-samples *t*-tests were statistically significant at $p < .001$. Cohen's *d* values indicate large to exceptionally large effect sizes. CI = Confidence Interval with df = 29

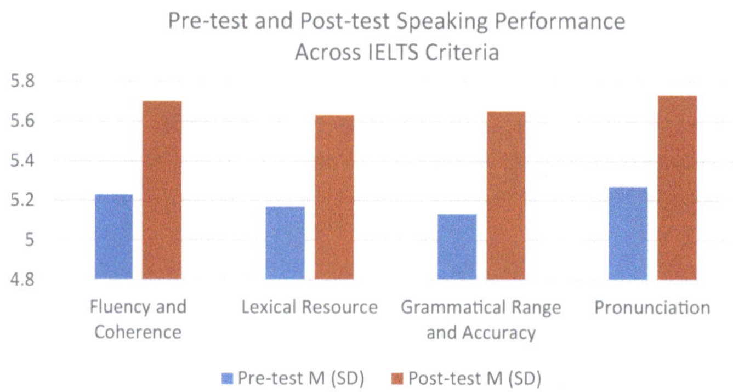

Fig. 1 Pre-test and post-test speaking performance across IELTS criteria

Representative Participant Voice:

> At first I was very nervous to speak English in class because everyone could see me and judge my mistakes. But in the metaverse with my avatar, I felt free. I could practice speaking without worrying about my face turning red or people laughing at me. (P07, female, age 20)

Fluency improvements were particularly notable in terms of speech rate, pause patterns, and discourse organization. Participants demonstrated increased speech rate with reduced hesitation phenomena, suggesting greater automaticity in language production processes. The virtual environment's immediate feedback mechanisms appeared to support real-time self-correction and fluency monitoring that transferred to improved overall speaking performance.

Coherence development manifested through improved discourse organization, topic development, and transitional language use. The conversational nature of metaverse interactions required participants to maintain coherent discourse over extended exchanges, developing skills in topic maintenance, elaboration, and logical progression that are essential for effective communication.

The narrative opportunities provided through virtual role-play and storytelling activities supported the development of temporal sequencing, causal relationships, and descriptive language that enhanced overall discourse coherence. Participants reported increased comfort with extended speaking tasks and greater confidence in organizing and expressing complex ideas.

Representative Participant Voice:

> Before this program, I rarely spoke in English class because I was afraid to make mistakes. But after practicing with my avatar in different virtual places like cafés and offices, I feel much more confident. Now I even volunteer to answer questions in my regular English class. (P18, female, age 20)

Vocabulary development occurred through contextual exposure to domain-specific terminology, colloquial expressions, and register-appropriate language use within authentic virtual environments. The immersive nature of virtual contexts provided natural vocabulary acquisition opportunities that appeared more effective than traditional decontextualized vocabulary instruction.

Participants demonstrated increased lexical diversity and appropriate word choice in post-intervention assessments. The variety of virtual environments and communicative scenarios exposed learners to diverse lexical domains while providing meaningful contexts for vocabulary application and retention.

Collocation and idiomatic expression use showed marked improvement, suggesting that the conversational nature of virtual interactions supported the acquisition of natural language patterns that are often difficult to teach through explicit instruction. The social interaction requirements of virtual environments created authentic contexts for formulaic language use and pragmatic appropriateness.

4.2 Listening Comprehension Enhancement

Listening skill development demonstrated equally impressive outcomes, with participants achieving a mean improvement of 1.43 points and a large effect size (Cohen's $d = 1.68$). The improvements were distributed across all TOEFL listening criteria, with particularly strong gains in supporting details recognition (28.88% improvement) and speaker attitude identification (27.62% improvement) as shown in Table 2.

The spatial audio technology emerged as the most significant factor in listening skill enhancement, with 100% of participants providing positive feedback about the three-dimensional audio experiences. Participants reported improved ability to distinguish between multiple speakers, enhanced focus on relevant information, and

Table 2 Listening comprehension improvements across TOEFL criteria ($N = 30$)

TOEFL listening criteria	Pre-test *M* (SD)	Post-test *M* (SD)	Mean Diff.	% Gain	*t*	*p*	Cohen's *d*	95% CI
Main ideas	3.87 (0.82)	4.73 (0.74)	0.86	22.22%	7.23	<.001	1.10	[0.62, 1.10]
Supporting details	3.63 (0.89)	4.68 (0.71)	1.05	28.93%	8.94	<.001	1.30	[0.81, 1.29]
Speaker attitude	3.70 (0.85)	4.72 (0.69)	1.02	27.57%	8.76	<.001	1.32	[0.78, 1.26]
Inference & Pragmatics	3.77 (0.79)	4.63 (0.76)	0.86	22.81%	7.45	<.001	1.11	[0.63, 1.09]
Overall listening score	15.97 (2.89)	18.76 (2.47)	2.79	25.33%	9.87	<.001	1.68	[2.21, 3.37]

Note $N = 30$. TOEFL listening subscores range from 0–6. The overall listening score is the sum of four criteria (range 0–24). All paired-samples t-tests were statistically significant at $p < .001$. Cohen's $d = 1.68$ indicates a large effect size. 100% of participants provided positive feedback about spatial audio technology. CI = Confidence Interval. df = 29

better comprehension of implicit meanings through the integration of audio and visual contextual cues.

Representative Participant Voice:

> The 3D sound was amazing. I could hear where different people were speaking from, just like real life. This helped me focus on one conversation even when others were talking nearby. I learned to listen better in noisy situations. (P23, female, age 22)

The qualitative analysis revealed that spatial audio technology addresses fundamental limitations of traditional listening instruction by providing authentic acoustic environments that mirror real-world listening challenges. Participants described developing more sophisticated listening strategies, including selective attention, speaker identification, and environmental noise filtering skills that are essential for effective communication in natural contexts.

The spatial audio features of the metaverse platform supported the development of phonological awareness, sound discrimination, and acoustic pattern recognition that form the foundation of listening comprehension. Three-dimensional soundscapes provided rich acoustic input that challenged learners' auditory processing abilities while offering contextual support through environmental audio cues.

Participants demonstrated improved ability to identify individual phonemes, word boundaries, and intonational patterns in post-intervention assessments. The conversational nature of virtual interactions required real-time processing of connected speech phenomena, including liaison, elision, and assimilation, that are often absent from traditional listening materials.

Prosodic awareness development was particularly evident in participants' improved recognition of stress patterns, rhythm, and intonational meaning. The natural conversational context of virtual interactions provided authentic exposure to prosodic variation that supported the development of more sophisticated listening strategies.

The contextually rich virtual environments supported the development of inferencing skills, background knowledge activation, and predictive processing that characterize effective listening comprehension. Visual contextual cues combined with spatial audio to provide multiple information sources that supported comprehension of challenging linguistic input.

Participants demonstrated increased ability to use contextual information to compensate for linguistic gaps, make predictions about upcoming content, and monitor comprehension effectiveness. These metacognitive strategies appeared to develop naturally through the interactive demands of virtual communication rather than through explicit strategy instruction.

Schema activation and application skills showed marked improvement, with participants demonstrating greater facility in connecting new input to existing knowledge structures and using world knowledge to support comprehension of implicit meanings and cultural references.

4.3 Engagement and Motivational Outcomes

The affective dimensions of learning in metaverse environments demonstrated remarkable positive changes. Eighty-seven percent of participants reported significantly higher engagement levels compared to traditional classroom instruction, with detailed accounts of transformation from passive recipients to active participants in the learning process.

Representative Participant Voice:

> The metaverse made learning English exciting, not boring like a usual class. I wanted to log in every session because it felt like playing a game, but I was learning. The virtual environments were so realistic that I forgot I was practicing English. (P14, male, age 21)

The gamified elements and achievement systems within the metaverse platform contributed to sustained motivation throughout the intervention period. Participants described the virtual learning environment as more enjoyable, relevant, and personally meaningful than conventional classroom activities. The sense of agency and autonomy provided by virtual environments appeared to enhance intrinsic motivation and promote self-directed learning behaviours.

Community building emerged as an unexpected but significant benefit of the metaverse-based approach. Participants reported developing stronger peer relationships and collaborative learning partnerships through shared virtual experiences. These social connections extended beyond the virtual environment, creating supportive learning communities that persisted after the formal intervention concluded.

Representative Participant Voice:

> I think combining the metaverse and traditional class is best. In the metaverse, we can practice speaking freely and have fun, but in regular class, the teacher can explain grammar rules clearly on the board. We need both ways to learn English completely. (P26, male, age 21)

The autonomous nature of virtual learning experiences appeared to enhance intrinsic motivation through increased learner control over pacing, content selection, and interaction preferences. Participants reported feeling more responsible for their learning outcomes and more invested in the learning process compared to traditional instructor-directed activities.

Creative expression opportunities provided through avatar customization, virtual world exploration, and collaborative storytelling activities supported the development of personal investment in the learning process. Participants described virtual environments as spaces for self-expression and identity exploration that extended beyond language learning to encompass broader personal development goals.

The authentic communicative contexts provided by virtual environments created meaningful purposes for language use that enhanced motivation through clear connections between learning activities and real-world communication needs. Participants reported increased confidence in their ability to use English effectively in professional and social contexts.

The social affordances of virtual environments facilitated the formation of learning communities that provided peer support, collaborative learning opportunities, and authentic communicative contexts. These communities appeared to develop organically through shared virtual experiences rather than through instructor-imposed group formations.

Peer tutoring and mutual assistance behaviors emerged naturally within virtual learning communities, with more advanced learners providing support and encouragement to struggling peers. These peer support networks continued beyond formal learning sessions, creating sustained learning communities that extended the educational impact of the intervention (Table 3).

5 Pedagogical Implications and Implementation Guidelines

5.1 Design Principles for Effective Metaverse-Based EFL Instruction

The empirical evidence suggests several key design principles that contribute to the effectiveness of metaverse-based language instruction. Avatar customization emerges as a crucial feature that enables learners to create virtual identities that reflect their preferred self-presentation while providing psychological distance from social anxiety. The ability to modify avatar appearance, clothing, and accessories allows learners to experiment with different personas and gain confidence in various communicative contexts, Shin et al. (2025).

Table 3 Summary of individual participant performance changes ($N = 30$)

Participant	Pre-Speaking	Post-Speaking	Speaking Gain	Pre-Listening	Post-Listening	Listening Gain
P01	20.5	26.0	+5.5	15.2	18.5	+3.3
P02	21.0	27.0	+6.0	16.1	19.2	+3.1
P03	19.5	25.5	+6.0	14.8	17.9	+3.1
P04	22.0	27.5	+5.5	17.2	20.1	+2.9
P05	20.0	26.5	+6.5	15.5	18.8	+3.3
P06	19.0	24.5	+5.5	14.2	17.2	+3.0
P07	21.5	27.0	+5.5	16.8	19.6	+2.8
P08	18.5	25.0	+6.5	13.9	17.5	+3.6
P09	22.5	28.0	+5.5	17.5	20.3	+2.8
P10	20.5	26.0	+5.5	15.7	18.9	+3.2
P11	19.5	25.5	+6.0	14.5	17.8	+3.3
P12	21.0	26.5	+5.5	16.3	19.1	+2.8
P13	20.0	26.0	+6.0	15.8	18.7	+2.9
P14	22.0	27.5	+5.5	17.0	19.8	+2.8
P15	18.0	24.0	+6.0	13.5	16.9	+3.4
P16	21.5	27.0	+5.5	16.6	19.4	+2.8
P17	20.5	26.5	+6.0	15.9	19.0	+3.1
P18	19.0	25.0	+6.0	14.4	17.6	+3.2
P19	23.0	28.5	+5.5	18.1	20.8	+2.7
P20	20.0	26.0	+6.0	15.6	18.8	+3.2
P21	21.5	27.5	+6.0	16.7	19.5	+2.8
P22	19.5	25.0	+5.5	14.7	17.7	+3.0
P23	22.5	28.0	+5.5	17.3	20.0	+2.7
P24	20.5	26.5	+6.0	15.8	18.9	+3.1
P25	18.5	24.5	+6.0	13.8	17.3	+3.5
P26	21.0	27.0	+6.0	16.2	19.1	+2.9
P27	20.0	25.5	+5.5	15.4	18.6	+3.2
P28	22.0	27.5	+5.5	17.1	19.9	+2.8
P29	19.0	25.0	+6.0	14.3	17.5	+3.2
P30	21.5	27.5	+6.0	16.5	19.4	+2.9
Mean	20.80	26.32	5.73	15.97	18.76	3.05
SD	2.54	2.18	0.45	2.89	2.47	0.28

Note Individual participant data demonstrating consistent improvement patterns across both speaking and listening measures. All 30 participants showed gains in both skill areas. Pseudonyms (P01-P30) protect participant identity in accordance with ethical protocols

Spatial audio technology represents another essential component that distinguishes effective metaverse-based instruction from conventional virtual learning environments. The three-dimensional audio capabilities must be sufficiently sophisticated to create realistic acoustic environments that challenge learners' listening skills while providing clear, comprehensible input. The integration of directional audio cues with visual contextual information appears to be particularly important for developing authentic listening competencies.

Virtual environment design should prioritize authenticity and cultural relevance while maintaining sufficient flexibility to accommodate diverse learning objectives and activities. The most effective virtual spaces combine realistic physical environments with interactive elements that respond to learner actions and promote meaningful communication. The variety of available environments appears to be important for maintaining engagement and providing exposure to different communicative contexts (Kumar et al., 2026).

Successful implementation of metaverse-based language instruction requires careful attention to technical infrastructure that supports high-quality virtual experiences while maintaining accessibility for diverse learner populations. Hardware requirements include sufficient processing power for three-dimensional graphics rendering, high-quality audio equipment for spatial audio processing, and reliable internet connectivity for real-time multiplayer interactions.

Software platform selection should prioritize educational features over entertainment elements while maintaining sufficient engagement value to sustain learner motivation. Essential features include robust avatar customization systems, diverse virtual environment options, integrated communication tools, and administrative capabilities for instructor monitoring and assessment.

Pedagogical training should address the unique affordances and constraints of virtual environments, including strategies for managing multiple simultaneous conversations, techniques for providing feedback in virtual contexts, and approaches for integrating virtual experiences with traditional instruction. Instructors must develop skills in virtual classroom management, including managing technical difficulties, maintaining student engagement, and ensuring productive collaborative interactions.

5.2 Integration with Traditional Pedagogical Approaches

A significant finding from the empirical research concerns learners' preference for blended approaches that combine metaverse-based instruction with traditional pedagogical methods. Eighty percent of participants expressed preference for integrated approaches that leverage the unique affordances of both virtual and conventional learning environments.

This preference suggests that metaverse-based instruction is most effective when strategically integrated with established pedagogical practices rather than implemented as a wholesale replacement for traditional methods. Virtual environments appear particularly well-suited for developing oral communication skills, providing authentic practice opportunities, and enhancing learner motivation and engagement.

Traditional classroom instruction retains important advantages for explicit grammar instruction, metalinguistic awareness development, and formal writing skills. The optimal integration appears to involve using metaverse environments for communicative practice and skill application while relying on conventional methods for explicit instruction and formal knowledge development.

The blended approach allows educators to capitalize on the strengths of each modality while mitigating their respective limitations. Traditional instruction can provide the systematic, structured presentation of linguistic forms and rules that support accuracy development, while virtual environments offer opportunities for meaningful practice that promotes fluency and communicative competence. This complementary relationship suggests that the future of language education lies not in choosing between technological and traditional approaches, but in creating synergistic combinations that enhance overall learning effectiveness.

5.3 Challenges and Mitigation Strategies

The implementation of metaverse-based EFL instruction involves several practical challenges that require careful consideration and planning. Technical infrastructure requirements represent a significant barrier for many educational institutions, including high-specification computing equipment, quality audio hardware, and reliable internet connectivity. These requirements may limit accessibility and scalability, particularly in resource-constrained educational contexts.

Instructor preparation and professional development represent another crucial consideration. Effective metaverse-based instruction requires educators to develop new technological competencies while adapting their pedagogical approaches to virtual environments. This transformation involves not only technical training but also reconceptualizing the instructor's role as a facilitator of virtual learning experiences.

Student preparation and digital literacy also influence the success of metaverse-based programs. While younger learners may adapt quickly to virtual environments, some students may experience technology-related anxiety or sensory overload. Gradual introduction to virtual environments, comprehensive orientation programs, and ongoing technical support appear essential for maximizing participation and minimizing barriers to engagement.

Cost considerations extend beyond initial hardware and software investments to include ongoing maintenance, technical support, platform subscriptions, and professional development expenses. Educational institutions must develop sustainable funding models that can support long-term implementation while demonstrating return on investment through improved learning outcomes.

Privacy and data security concerns become particularly important in virtual learning environments that collect detailed behavioral data and enable real-time interaction monitoring. Institutional policies must address data collection, storage, and usage while ensuring compliance with relevant privacy regulations and maintaining student trust.

Quality assurance and accreditation processes may require adaptation to accommodate metaverse-based instruction. Traditional evaluation criteria for educational programs may not adequately address the unique characteristics and affordances of virtual learning environments. The development of appropriate quality indicators and evaluation frameworks represents an important policy priority for educational institutions and accrediting bodies.

Strategies for addressing technical infrastructure challenges include partnering with technology providers to develop educational pricing models, implementing bring-your-own-device policies that leverage student-owned equipment, and creating shared virtual learning labs that provide access to high-specification hardware for students who lack adequate personal devices.

Professional development challenges can be addressed through comprehensive training programs that combine technical skill development with pedagogical adaptation workshops. Mentoring partnerships between technology-experienced and novice instructors can provide ongoing support while building institutional capacity for virtual learning implementation.

Student support strategies should include pre-program technology assessments, individualized technical support services, and alternative participation options for students who experience technical difficulties or accessibility barriers. Institutions should also develop clear communication protocols for addressing technical issues that arise during virtual learning sessions.

6 Future Directions and Emerging Trends

6.1 Technological Advancement and Accessibility

The continued development of metaverse technologies promises to address current limitations while expanding the pedagogical possibilities for language instruction. Advances in artificial intelligence are enabling more sophisticated virtual agents that can serve as conversational partners and provide personalized feedback on language performance. These developments may address scalability concerns by reducing the instructor workload while maintaining high-quality interactive experiences.

Improvements in hardware accessibility and cost reduction are gradually making metaverse technologies more feasible for widespread educational implementation. The development of web-based metaverse platforms that operate through standard internet browsers may eliminate many technical barriers while maintaining the essential features that contribute to learning effectiveness.

The integration of advanced analytics and learning management systems within metaverse platforms offers possibilities for detailed tracking of learner progress, automated assessment, and personalized learning pathways. These capabilities could enhance the pedagogical value of virtual environments while providing educators with comprehensive data on student performance and engagement.

Artificial intelligence integration in metaverse language learning environments is advancing rapidly, with developments in natural language processing, speech recognition, and conversational AI creating opportunities for more sophisticated virtual tutoring systems. These AI-powered systems can provide immediate feedback on pronunciation, grammar, and communicative appropriateness while adapting to individual learner needs and preferences (Aeni et al., 2025).

Machine learning algorithms are being developed to analyze learner behavior patterns within virtual environments, identifying optimal learning pathways and predicting areas where additional support may be needed. These predictive capabilities could enable proactive interventions that prevent learning difficulties before they become significant barriers to progress.

Voice recognition and natural language processing technologies are becoming increasingly sophisticated, enabling more accurate assessment of speaking performance and more natural interactions with AI-powered virtual characters. These developments may eventually enable fully automated speaking assessment and feedback systems that can provide consistent, objective evaluation of oral proficiency development.

Haptic feedback technologies are emerging that could add tactile dimensions to virtual learning experiences, providing physical sensations that enhance immersion and support kinesthetic learning preferences. These technologies might enable new types of language learning activities that incorporate physical manipulation and tactile exploration of virtual objects and environments.

6.2 Research and Development Priorities

Several research priorities emerge from the current evidence base for metaverse-based language instruction. Longitudinal studies examining the retention and transfer of skills developed through virtual environments are essential for understanding the long-term effectiveness of these approaches. Current research provides compelling evidence for short-term learning gains, but questions remain about the durability of these improvements and their application to real-world communicative contexts.

Cross-cultural research investigating the effectiveness of metaverse-based instruction across diverse cultural and linguistic contexts represents another important priority. The cultural dimensions of virtual identity, social interaction norms, and learning preferences may significantly influence the effectiveness of virtual learning environments in different educational contexts.

Comparative studies examining different metaverse platforms and technological configurations are needed to identify the most effective features and design principles for educational applications. Research should investigate the relative importance of visual fidelity, spatial audio quality, avatar customization options, and interactive features in promoting learning outcomes.

Research on assessment and evaluation methodologies for virtual learning environments is crucial for establishing reliable and valid measures of language proficiency development in metaverse contexts. Traditional assessment instruments may not adequately capture the communicative competencies developed through virtual environment experiences.

7 Implications for Curriculum Development and Educational Policy

7.1 *Curriculum Integration Frameworks*

The integration of metaverse-based instruction into formal EFL curricula requires careful consideration of learning objectives, assessment strategies, and pedagogical alignment. The evidence suggests that virtual environments are particularly effective for developing communicative competencies, including speaking fluency, listening comprehension, and pragmatic awareness. Curriculum designers should consider allocating virtual learning experiences to objectives that align with these strengths while maintaining traditional approaches for other language skills and competencies.

Assessment strategies for metaverse-based learning present both opportunities and challenges for curriculum development. The authentic communicative contexts provided by virtual environments enable performance-based assessments that reflect real-world language use more accurately than traditional testing methods. However, the development of reliable, valid assessment protocols for virtual environments requires careful consideration of technical factors, scoring procedures, and fairness considerations.

Curriculum frameworks should specify clear learning outcomes that can be achieved through metaverse-based instruction while identifying complementary objectives that are better addressed through traditional pedagogical approaches. This specification requires a detailed analysis of the affordances and limitations of virtual learning environments in relation to established language learning goals and competency frameworks.

Sequencing and scaffolding considerations become particularly important in blended curricula that combine virtual and traditional instruction. Research suggests that certain sequences may be more effective than others, with explicit instruction often providing the necessary foundation knowledge before communicative practice in virtual environments.

7.2 *Policy Considerations and Strategic Planning*

Educational institutions considering the adoption of metaverse-based instruction must address several policy and strategic considerations. Investment in technological infrastructure requires long-term commitment and strategic planning to ensure sustainability and scalability. The rapid pace of technological development in virtual reality and metaverse platforms necessitates flexible procurement strategies that can accommodate evolving technologies.

Privacy and data protection considerations become particularly important in virtual learning environments that collect detailed behavioural data and enable real-time interaction monitoring. Institutional policies must address data collection, storage, and usage while ensuring compliance with relevant privacy regulations and maintaining student trust.

Faculty development and support policies should address the professional development needs of instructors transitioning to virtual learning environments while providing ongoing support for technological and pedagogical challenges. These policies should also consider workload implications and compensation structures for faculty members who invest significant time in developing virtual learning expertise.

Intellectual property and content ownership policies become complex in virtual environments where user-generated content, collaborative creations, and platform-specific assets may raise questions about ownership rights and usage permissions. Clear policies should address these issues while protecting both institutional and individual interests.

7.3 *Methodological Limitations*

Several limitations should be acknowledged in interpreting this study's findings. First, the absence of a control or comparison group limits causal attribution. While the large effect sizes (Cohen's $d = 3.08$ for speaking; $d = 1.68$ for listening) and consistent improvements across multiple measures provide strong preliminary evidence of effectiveness, observed improvements may be partially attributable to practice effects, maturation, or increased motivation from participating in a novel intervention. The pre-post design, though appropriate for exploratory research, cannot fully isolate the unique contribution of metaverse-based instruction from confounding variables. Future research should employ randomized controlled trial designs with control groups receiving traditional instruction or alternative technology-enhanced interventions to establish stronger causal claims regarding metaverse pedagogy's distinctive effects.

Second, the purposive sampling of 30 undergraduate students from a single institution constrains generalizability. The sample was relatively homogeneous in terms of educational context (Universitas Negeri Makassar), proficiency level (B1-B2 on the

CEFR), age range (19–23 years), and cultural background (Indonesian). This homogeneity, while enabling focused investigation of the intervention's effects within a specific population, limits the extent to which findings can be extrapolated to other contexts. The effectiveness of metaverse-based instruction may vary across different proficiency ranges (beginner to advanced), age groups (children, adolescents, adults), educational systems (primary, secondary, tertiary), cultural contexts (collectivist vs. individualist societies), and linguistic backgrounds (different L1s). Potential selection bias also merits acknowledgment, as participants volunteered for an eight-week virtual learning program, potentially indicating higher motivation or technology affinity than typical EFL learners. Cross-cultural replication studies with diverse, randomly sampled populations are needed to assess the broader applicability of these findings and identify potential moderating variables that influence intervention effectiveness.

Third, technological infrastructure requirements present potential barriers to scalability and equitable implementation. All participants in this study had access to adequate computing equipment (laptops or desktop computers meeting minimum specifications) and reliable high-speed internet connectivity (minimum 10 Mbps). These prerequisites, while feasible in this university context, may not be universally available. In resource-constrained educational settings, particularly in developing countries or rural areas, technological inequities may limit accessibility and create digital divides that exclude learners without sufficient technological resources. The financial costs associated with hardware acquisition, software licenses for metaverse platforms, ongoing maintenance, technical support personnel, and instructor training may pose prohibitive challenges for widespread adoption. Educational institutions considering metaverse implementation must carefully assess infrastructure readiness, budget sustainability, and strategies for ensuring equitable access across diverse student populations.

Fourth, the eight-week intervention timeframe, while sufficient to demonstrate short-term learning gains, precludes assessment of long-term retention and transfer effects. The study documented immediate post-intervention improvements but did not include delayed post-tests to measure skill retention over subsequent months or years. Questions remain regarding whether improvements persist after the intervention concludes and the virtual learning environment is no longer available. Additionally, the study did not directly assess the transfer of skills developed in virtual contexts to real-world communicative situations outside the metaverse environment. Longitudinal studies with multiple assessment points (e.g., immediate post-test, 3-month follow-up, 6-month follow-up) and authentic real-world communication tasks are needed to determine whether metaverse-developed competencies demonstrate durability and ecological validity, Hwang (2025).

Fifth, instructor expertise and familiarity with metaverse technologies may influence implementation effectiveness. The instructor who facilitated this intervention had prior experience with virtual learning environments and received specialized training in metaverse pedagogy before the study commenced. This expertise potentially contributed to the successful navigation of technical challenges, effective activity design, and skilled virtual classroom management. Teachers without comparable technological proficiency or pedagogical preparation may encounter greater implementation difficulties. The professional development requirements for educators adopting metaverse-based instruction including technical skill development, pedagogical adaptation, and ongoing support structures warrant systematic investigation to inform scalable implementation models.

Sixth, this study focused exclusively on speaking and listening skills, leaving questions about metaverse effectiveness for other language competencies. The immersive, communicative nature of virtual environments appears particularly well-suited for oral language development, but applicability to reading comprehension, writing proficiency, grammatical accuracy, and other linguistic dimensions remains uncertain (Muthmainnah et al., 2025). Future research should investigate whether metaverse platforms can effectively support comprehensive language learning across all skill areas or whether they represent specialized tools best suited for specific competencies within blended pedagogical approaches.

Finally, the study employed standardized assessment instruments (IELTS and TOEFL formats) that may not fully capture the unique competencies developed through metaverse experiences. While these measures provide reliable proficiency indicators, they were designed for traditional language learning contexts and may not adequately assess skills such as virtual communication management, multimodal comprehension, or technology-mediated pragmatic competence. Development of assessment frameworks specifically designed for virtual learning environments represents an important methodological priority for future research.

8 Conclusion

Both the empirical findings indicated that there was considerable improvement in speaking and listening skills through metaverse-based instruction, with equally large effect sizes (Cohen's $d = 3.08$ and 1.68, respectively) pointing to their significance both in a statistical and practical manner. In driving these changes, three mechanisms happen to be instrumental: (1) anxiety reduction through avatar presence, (2) authentic listening experiences afforded by spatial audio technologies, and (3) enhanced engagement given by immersive virtual environments. These findings could also lend themselves to actionable recommendations for practitioners and designers of language curricula in order to enhance the effectiveness of language instruction.

This chapter has shown the necessity for a more thoughtful integration as opposed to outright replacement of traditional pedagogical methods. The students' preference for blended learning models indicates that the future of language education is not about finding one out of technological or traditional techniques but rather about creating combinations where both methods, with their respective strong points, would synergistically work. The conditions for this would entail carefully considering the learning objectives and relevant technological and pedagogical principles to optimize effectiveness while addressing the practical issues of implementing the solutions.

Discussion on design principles, implementation considerations, and future research directions provides a framework for educators and institutions wishing to adopt metaverse-based instruction. The evidence points to the successful implementation requiring careful consideration of the relevant technical infrastructure, instructor training and preparation, student support, and strategic integration into existing curricula and learning activities.

Looking toward the future, the continued development of metaverse technologies promises to address current limitations while expanding pedagogical possibilities. However, the realization of this potential requires sustained commitment to research, professional development, and strategic planning from educational institutions, policymakers, and technology developers. The transformation of language education through immersive virtual environments represents both an opportunity and a responsibility to enhance learning experiences while maintaining the fundamental goals of effective language instruction (Aeni et al. (2024).

The findings have paramount consequences on language education policies at institutional, regional, and national levels. To start with, the funding agencies are encouraged to give priority to grants that provide support for the building of metaverse infrastructures in schools and universities with limited resources, given the recognition that technological equity is vital to democratizing access to such high-impact learning environments. Secondly, curriculum standards should formally include tech-mediated communicative competencies alongside traditional proficiency standards since twenty-first-century language learners need both kinds of skills for intercultural communication in physical and virtual contexts. Thirdly, there should be the inclusion of pedagogy for virtual environments in teacher certification programs so that both pre-service and in-service teachers have the competence to design, implement, and assess effective metaverse-based language instruction. Finally, the accreditation framework should consider evolving to assess blended approaches, those working with a combination of traditional and virtual, and focused on learning outcomes achieved through diverse pedagogical modalities rather than on seat-time measures. This study provides statistical effect sizes ($d = 3.08$ and 1.68) to persuasively advocate for those policy changes as evidence that metaverse technology has positive returns on communicative competence for learners when investment is structured.

Broader implications, looking beyond EFL instruction, are applicable to technology-enhanced education in an increasingly digital world. Other fields will create their own virtual learning environments, drawing on principles and practices of metaverse-based language instruction, while the results will contribute to our understanding of how immersive technology supports worthwhile learning endeavors.

With further shifts in education, metaverse technologies anticipate decent avenues for heightened engagement, authenticity, and efficiency in language instruction. This chapter provided evidence that promises a significant address for language learners in an environment that fosters cross-cultural communication and international educational collaboration. To ensure the fulfillment of this promise will involve research, consideration, implementation, and the established aim for educational excellence within virtual learning environments.

Getting metaverse language learning into classrooms will be a tough road, and investments in technology, training, and curriculum development must be made. However, there are some important considerations to weigh: improved learner engagement, learning outcomes, accessibility, and proper reality-check communication.

The prospects of language education in the digital future will see more integration of virtual and traditional learning modalities, with the provision by metaverse technologies of immersive, authentic, and engaging educational experiences to ensure learners' success in an interconnected global society, gaining weight.

References

Aeni, N., Winahyu, S. K., Muthmainnah, M., Mansyur, U., Syamsidar, Izmi S. A., & Padli, F. (2025). An analysis of Jenni speak: How AI can improve speaking skills in Indonesian Higher Education? In B. Virdee, S. D. Correia, P. Bedi, & A. Swaroop (Eds.), *Proceedings of International Conference on Artificial Intelligence and Networks*. ICAIN. Lecture notes in networks and systems (Vol. 1270). Springer. https://doi.org/10.1007/978-981-96-2015-9_20.

Aeni, N., Darmawati, B., Yunus, M., Mulyanah, A., Sharma, A., & Hamka, D. W. (2024). Disclosing user views: A qualitative investigation of writing and speaking ability development via integration of Jenni AI and Jenni speak. In *International conference on advances in Information Communication Technology & Computing* (pp. 191–203). Springer. https://doi.org/10.1007/978-981-97-6103-6_13

Bozorgian, H., Muhammadpour, M., Davariyan, H., & Ezami, A. (2025). Second life app functions as a booster in second language listening comprehension. *International Journal of Listening*, 1–16. https://doi.org/10.1080/10904018.2025.2527745

Çelik, F., & Baturay, M. H. (2024). The effect of metaverse on L2 vocabulary learning, retention, student engagement, presence, and community feeling. *BMC Psychology, 12*, Article 259. https://bmcpsychology.biomedcentral.com/articles/10.1186/s40359-024-01549-4

Christou, E., Parmaxi, A., & Christoforou, M. (2025). Implementation and application of extended reality in foreign language education for specific purposes: A systematic literature review. Universal Access in the Information Society. https://link.springer.com/article/10.1007/s10209-025-01191-w

Hua, C., & Wang, J. (2023). Virtual reality-assisted language learning: A follow-up review (2018–2022). *Frontiers in Psychology, 14*, Article 1153642. https://doi.org/10.3389/fpsyg.2023.1153642.

Hwang, Y., & Lee, J. H. (2025). "Yes, I am more confident with my avatars": Integrating EFL students' speaking practice into metaverse. *RELC Journal, 56*(3), 760–771. https://doi.org/10.1177/00336882241251952

Hwang, Y. (2025). Reconceptualization of textbook with the metaverse: Pre-service English teachers' experiences and perceptions of designing TechBoox. *Computer Assisted Language Learning, 38*(8), 2170–2201. https://doi.org/10.1080/09588221.2024.2378771

Ironsi, C. S. (2023). Investigating the use of virtual reality to improve speaking skills: Insights from students and teachers. *Smart learning Environments, 10*, Article 27. https://slejournal.springeropen.com/articles/10.1186/s40561-023-00272-8

Kaplan-Rakowski, R., & Gruber, A. (2023). The impact of high-immersion virtual reality on foreign language anxiety when speaking in public. *Smart learning Environments, 10*, Article 46. https://doi.org/10.1186/s40561-023-00263-9

Kul, Ü., Besalti, M., Çelik Demirci, S., & Korkmaz, S. (2026). Examining the relationship between pre-service teachers' technological pedagogical content knowledge and generative artificial intelligence acceptance. *Discover Education, 5*, 54. https://doi.org/10.1007/s44217-026-01111-x

Kumar, B., Raj, S., Anand, M., Verma, V. K., Tripathi, P., & Jha, A. (2026). Enhancing conversational recommendations through contrastive user preference modeling. *Discover Artificial Intelligence*. https://doi.org/10.1007/s44163-026-00912-1

Lan, Y.-J. (2020). Immersion into virtual reality for language learning. *Psychology of Learning and Motivation, 72*(3), 1–26. https://doi.org/10.1016/bs.plm.2020.03.001

Lee, J., & Ko, Y. (2024). Comparing metaverse and face-to-face instruction for enhancing English skills and attitudes among EFL adolescents. *Education and Information Technologies, 29*(7), 8341–8362. https://link.springer.com/article/10.1007/s10639-024-13162-4

Tai, T., & Chen, H. H. (2021). The impact of immersive virtual reality on EFL learners' listening comprehension. *Journal of Educational Computing Research, 59*, 1272–1293. https://doi.org/10.1177/0735633121994291

Miles, M. B., & Huberman, A. M. (1994). *Qualitative data analysis: An expanded sourcebook* (2nd ed.). SAGE Publications.

Muthmainnah, M., Cardoso L., Marzuki, A. G., & Al Yakin, A. (2025). A new innovative metaverse ecosystem: VR-based human interaction enhances EFL learners' transferable skills. Discover Sustainability, 6, Article 156. https://link.springer.com/article/10.1007/s43621-025-00913-7

Shin, D., Kwon, S. K., & Noh, W. I. (2025). Exploring the role of the metaverse in English speaking proficiency tests. *Journal of Computer Assisted Learning*. https://onlinelibrary.wiley.com/doi/full/10.1111/jcal.13108

Syawaluddin, A., & Aeni, N. (2025). Play and learn: Digital traditional games for vocabulary mastery in young learners. *Discover Education, 4*(1), 103. https://doi.org/10.1007/s44217-025-00485-8

Tang, Q. (2026). Analysis of interactive efficacy in college English classroom with multimodal machine learning. Discover Artificial Intelligence. Advance online publication. https://doi.org/10.1007/s44163-026-01209-z

Wu, Y.-H., & Hung, S.-T. A. (2022). The effects of virtual reality infused instruction on elementary school students' English-speaking performance, willingness to communicate, and learning autonomy. *Journal of Educational Computing Research, 60*(6), 1558–1587. https://doi.org/10.1177/07356331211068207

Yu, Z. (2021). A meta-analysis of the effect of virtual reality technology use in education. Interactive Learning Environments. Advanced Online Publication. https://doi.org/10.1080/10494820.2021.1989466

Zhang, Q. (2024). Mediation/moderation effects of engagement, foreign language enjoyment, and ambiguity tolerance in metaverse-based foreign language learning. *International journal of educational technology in Higher Education, 21*, Article 40. https://educationaltechnologyjournal.springeropen.com/articles/10.1186/s41239-024-00484-z

Nur Aeni is an associate professor at Universitas Negeri Makassar, Indonesia. Her studies investigate immersive virtual environments for developing integrated speaking and listening skills in EFL learners. Aeni conducts mixed-methods interventions demonstrating gains in oral proficiency through spatial audio and avatar-mediated communication. She provides empirical evidence and practical recommendations for metaverse integration in ESL/EFL contexts. Her work emphasizes psychological safety and authentic interaction in virtual pedagogy.

Muhammad Yunus is a professor at Universitas Muslim Indonesia. He collaborates on projects exploring technology-enhanced speaking and listening development. Yunus contributes to empirical studies on metaverse-based instruction for EFL undergraduates. His research highlights the role of immersive simulations in alleviating language anxiety. He supports evidence-based directions for curriculum developers in virtual language learning.

Besse Darmawati is a researcher at Badan Riset dan Inovasi Nasional, Indonesia. Her work focuses on innovative applications of virtual reality in language skill development. Darmawati participates in intervention studies measuring speaking and listening gains in immersive environments. She examines the contributions of spatial audio and authentic communicative contexts. Her contributions inform practical integration of metaverse technologies in EFL instruction.

Muthmainnah Muthmainnah is an associate professor at Universitas Al Asyariah Mandar, Indonesia. She investigates immersive technologies for enhancing oral skills in foreign language learners. Muthmainnah collaborates on mixed-methods research demonstrating the effectiveness of virtual environments. Her focus includes naturalistic language use and learner engagement in metaverse settings. She provides insights for complementing traditional instruction with virtual pedagogy.

Selvi Panggua is an associate professor at Universitas Kristen Indonesia, Toraja, Indonesia. Her research explores the potential of metaverse platforms for speaking and listening proficiency. Panggua contributes to empirical studies on undergraduate EFL learners. She examines immersive simulations and personalized feedback mechanisms. Her work supports practical recommendations for technology-enhanced language classrooms.

Immersive Literacy: Enhancing Reading and Writing through Metaverse-Based Pedagogy

V. S. Krithikaa Venket and R. Adline Freeda

Abstract This chapter aims to describe how metaverse worlds can be utilized to develop higher literacy levels by integrating factors such as 3D virtual worlds, avatars, and real-time collaborative work. This chapter is unique in that it places great importance on reading, a variable that has sometimes been overlooked in immersive learning studies compared to listening and speaking. Virtual reality (VR) and game-based learning have led the charge in studies, but few empirical studies have addressed metaverse-specific literacy pedagogies. This chapter, therefore, closes an important gap by contributing theoretical remarks as well as case-based analysis of literacy development in metaverse spaces. By conducting a focused examination of how metaverse technology specifically affects text-based skills, it adds to the expanding body of immersive learning. In addition to quantitative measures, such as literacy performance tests administered before and after the intervention, qualitative techniques were employed to collect data, including observation diaries, learner reflections, and artifact analysis of production artifacts. Based on the initial findings of the case study, metaverse-guided literacy activities were observed to increase students' interest and engagement, resulting in improved writing fluency and enhanced reading comprehension. It provides researchers with suggestions for future studies on scalability, accessibility, and long-term learning. At the societal level, the chapter suggests that the metaverse offers collaborative and inclusive learning environments that foster digital literacy and support multilingual learners. The chapter ends with the presentation of the metaverse as a forward-looking tool for language teaching. The research on metaverse-based literacy development is still emerging. As this field develops, large-scale empirical studies examining literacy gains across diverse learner populations and educational contexts is essential to build a robust evidence base.

Keywords Metaverse in education · Digital narrative construction · Interactive storytelling · Collaborative writing · Virtual language learning

V. S. K. Venket (✉) · R. A. Freeda
KCG College of Technology, Karapakam, Chennai, India

F. Çelik and C. Yangın Ersanlı (eds.), *Metaverse-Based Language Learning and Teaching*, English Language Education 49,
https://doi.org/10.1007/978-3-032-31366-9_6

1 Introduction

The transformation of teaching practice by digital innovation has been perhaps most visibly seen in the field of language teaching. Over the past 20 years, learning environments have increasingly diverged from traditional classrooms toward digitally mediated spaces for engaging with content in ways previously unimaginable. Of the most promising of these new learning environments is the metaverse, which brings together virtual reality (VR), augmented reality (AR), and three-dimensional (3D) interactive spaces within a persistent, networked ecosystem (Damaševičius & Sidekerskienė, 2024; Ibrahim et al., 2017; Kaplan-Rakowski & Gruber, 2023; Lee et al., 2022). In contrast to previous online learning environments that relied on text, video conferencing, and static content, the metaverse offers a fully immersive, embodied experience where students can communicate in real-time with avatars, spatially structured classrooms, and shared tools (Çelik & Baturay, 2024). This transformation creates new possibilities for language instruction that not only provide new approaches to rehearsing oral communication but also new opportunities for developing literacy capabilities such as reading and writing. In traditional digital classrooms, reading and writing tend to be isolated text-based practices. Conversely, the metaverse transforms them into active, multimodal, and co-participatory learners, whereby they engage with linguistic content placed within narratives, games, and virtual worlds (Park & Kim, 2022). This chapter elaborates these affordances, arguing that the metaverse holds high potential to transform literacy pedagogy by situating text-based tasks in completely immersive, interactive spaces (Kaplan-Rakowski & Gruber, 2023).

1.1 Context of Immersive Learning and Metaverse in Language Education

To provide a background of immersive learning and metaverse in language instruction, we first need to begin with noting that immersive learning has traditionally been linked with methods that place students in environments that resemble real-world settings. Some of the earliest applications of immersive learning in language teaching involved the use of VR simulations and serious games as interventions to enhance listening and speaking skills, particularly in task-based or communicative language teaching paradigms (Lan, 2020). Students gained more motivation, experienced less anxiety, and showed greater participation levels, as these environments provided protected spaces for experimentation and practice. The metaverse builds upon this heritage, introducing distinctive characteristics that extend beyond VR or game-based learning (Kourtesis et al., 2024). Firstly, it supports persistent worlds, meaning students can return to the same virtual environments between sessions, thereby establishing familiarity and continuity in their educational experience. Secondly, it supports embodiment using avatars, which promotes identity exploration and social presence, essential for collaborative learning. Third, it accommodates collaborative working simultaneously, whereby students come together and create digital things, stories, and problem-solving exercises through a cooperative workspace. For language learners, these affordances mean that linguistic input no longer comes in the form of texts or pre-designed exercises. Instead, it arises spontaneously as a result of interaction with other students, digital entities, and narrative situations of the virtual world. Texts can take the form of signposts, storyboards, dialogue boxes, or collaborative writing spaces, making literacy thoroughly immersed in more general communicative activities. The metaverse not only builds on the course of immersive learning but also restructures how learners interact with and generate language (Li et al., 2023).

1.2 Rationale for Emphasizing Reading and Writing Competence

While there is an expanding literature base around immersive learning, most studies to date have focused on oral skills such as speaking and listening while literacy has been given relatively little attention. This is particularly notable when considering that reading and writing remain fundamental skills for academic achievement, professional growth, and cross-cultural communication. The omission of literacy, then, leaves current immersive learning studies with a limited perspective on the potential of technology, such as the metaverse, to support language learning in an integrative manner. Metaverse reading holds promise much beyond fundamental understanding activities (Li et al., 2022).

In virtual worlds, texts are multimodal, placed in visual, spatial, and narrative contexts that require active interpretation. Students can be presented with narratives embedded in virtual worlds, decode textual clues to complete narrative-driven puzzles, or interact with peer-created texts that change dynamically over time. These activities encourage critical reading literacies, as students need to navigate and make sense of information in multiple modalities, engaging in meaning-making in collaboration with others. Writing also evolves significantly in metaverse environments (Li et al., 2023). Rather than isolated, individual compositions, writing becomes a collaborative co-construction facilitated by collaborative software tools, such as shared whiteboards, digital narrative environments, and systems for peer-to-peer review. Students may participate in crowdsourced stories, role-play using dialogue composition, or revise drafts instantly from peer and instructor feedback.

These methods encourage iterative composition, creativity, and students' agency in the composition process. The interactive environment also situates composition within actual communication contexts—whether publishing a virtual magazine in a virtual classroom or composing in-world narratives that avatars enact. Thus, it responds to the demand for participating in reading and writing in metaverses on a double level. Pedagogically, there is a research difference in learning engagement through the exploration of neglected but necessary skills. Practically, it equates students with reading skills that are better suited to meet the needs of communication in the twenty-first century, including digital, multimodal, and cooperative. This chapter contributes to both empirical insights and theoretical understanding of the literature on learning technology-based language by examining how meta-based interventions can promote these results.

1.3 Metaverse and Literacy Learning: A Conceptual Context

The concept of literacy learning has conventionally been rooted in classroom activities and paper-based texts. However, with the technological revolution, the manner in which learning occurs has continued to change through the means of reading and writing. From early computer-aided language learning (CALL) through online platforms and game-based learning, the incorporation of new digital technologies continues to redefine what it is to be literate. The metaverse is the next iteration in this progression, with its immersive and interactive worlds opening up new literacies for pedagogy (Nguyen et al., 2025). The journey from virtual worlds to the metaverse is outlined here, along with a description of how it differs from virtual reality (VR) and game-based learning, and a positioning of the discussion within theoretical explanations of immersive literacy (Wang et al., 2025). Virtual worlds such as Second Life, Active Worlds, and OpenSim have been viewed as sites where language learning occurs since ancient times, around the early 2000s (Kojić et al., 2020). While they opened up the potential of immersive technologies for second language acquisition, their educational impact was circumscribed by technical constraints, barriers to access, and inadequate integration into the curriculum. In literacy instruction, this entails that learners are not limited to static reading and writing exercises but instead are immersed in dynamic, multimodal, and socially embedded literacy activities. The metaverse thus repositions literacy as an experiential, community-based process that responds to the learning requirements of the twenty-first century (Prabakaran et al., 2025).

1.4 Difference with VR and Game-Based Learning

It is necessary to differentiate the metaverse from surrounding technologies, such as VR simulations and game-based learning, which, although interconnected, have distinct pedagogical significance (Qiu et al., 2023). Virtual reality is generally designed to immerse learners in one-off environments that reproduce exact situations

(Yudintseva, 2023)—for instance, practicing a conversation with an avatar character or traveling in a city to practice vocabulary (Lan, 2020). Although it is beneficial for oral communication, VR's capacity for developing reading and writing skills is limited, as lessons or sounds become secondary to the input. Throughout the game, however, players benefit from the game's self-inspired nature to encourage commitment. Serious games for literacy learning can include puzzling, story-building, or deciphering textual hints (Gee, 2003). The metaverse is different in that it merges the immersive presence of VR with the interactive, motivational affordances of games, as well as continuity, collaboration, and co-creation (Tan et al., 2024). Literacy activities in metaverse spaces are not secondary to gameplay or simulations but are core activities (Wang et al., 2025). Students can collaboratively write digital stories, tag 3D objects with text, or create common artifacts that persist in the virtual environment from one session to another. In contrast to VR or games, which tend to be time-bound experiences, the metaverse accommodates persistent literacy development, in which texts and group products change over time, mirroring actual reading and writing practices in real communities (Parmaxi, 2023).

2 Theoretical Perspectives on Immersive Literacy

To understand the promise of metaverses for literature instruction, it is essential to have a grounding in theoretical frameworks that are sensitive to the ways students are engaged with multimodal texts in the digital environment (Lee, 2023). Three frameworks are relevant:

New Literacies Studies (NLS). This approach emphasizes the reality that literacy involves not only reading and writing skills, but also a set of socially situated practices, including references, tools, and communities. Literacy in the metaverse involves more than just reading and writing skills; it also encompasses multimodal reading and writing—negotiating spatial texts, untangling visual narratives, and collectively co-constructing digital artifacts. The joint and situational nature of metaverse platforms aligns best with the sociocultural orientation of NLS (Park & Kim, 2022).

Multiliteracies Framework. The New London Group (1996) states that the multiliteracies framework prioritizes students being engaged through different channels of meaning-making, such as linguistic, visual, spatial, and gestural communication. The metaverse is a good case in point, as it locates reading and writing in 3D environments where learners must interpret multimodal signs and produce texts that blend different semiotic resources (Fan & Chiang, 2023). Writing in such environments can involve the use of text and images, sound, and arranging the physical space, as complex as communication in the information age.

2.1 *Constructivist and Socio-Constructivist Learning Theories*

Constructivist, by its perspective, believes that students actively build knowledge as they engage with their world. The metaverse supports this by situating literacy tasks within authentic, problem-solving contexts. In contrast, views literacy learning as social because learners build meaning together (Peterson, 2013). Metaverse group authorship, peer review, and cooperative world-making are exemplary illustrations of these paradigms, demonstrating that immersive worlds can facilitate higher-order literacy skills, including reflective writing, imagination, and critical thinking. All in all, these models emphasize that metanity is not a solitary cognitive function, but instead a socially mediated, polynomial, and dynamic practice. By subtracting these approaches, teachers can design interventions that extend beyond print-based literature functions to embrace fluid, participatory, and reference-based practices introduced by immersive media.

2.2 *Reading and Writing in Metaverse Spaces*

The procurement of literacy skills and writing instruction should be at the heart of the consequences. However, these skills have been overshadowed by a focus on oral communication, as well as immersive and technology-based language training. Although speaking and listening fit more readily into synchronous collaboration in digital contexts, the affordances of the metaverse also position it as a rich context for developing text-based competencies. In metaverse environments, reading and writing extend beyond traditional, paper-bound practices into dynamic, multimodal, and socially mediated activities. This section discusses the importance of text-based skills in immersive environments, highlights the often-overlooked role of reading in immersive pedagogy, and examines writing as an interactive and collaborative process within metaverse spaces (Alfadil, 2024).

3 Importance of Text-Based Skills in Immersive Environments

In learning environments, text-based skills serve as the building blocks for academic achievement and long-term language development. Reading allows learners to access content knowledge across disciplines, while writing provides a means of producing, organizing, and communicating ideas effectively. In the metaverse, these abilities take on new forms. The text no longer resides in books or electronic files. However, it appears in a virtual world: contained within virtual objects, displayed on interactive panels, woven into stories, or created by fellow students in real-time. Thus, students need to employ reading processes that are not linear, but multimodal, incorporating written, visual, auditory, and spatial inputs. Similarly, writing in the metaverse transcends traditional exercises such as essays or grammar drills. It becomes situated within communicative and creative contexts, where learners may contribute to collaborative storylines, annotate shared objects, or script dialogue for avatars. These tasks reflect authentic uses of literacy in professional and social spheres, where digital writing increasingly takes the form of collaborative documents, multimodal texts, and interactive media. By situating literacy in immersive environments, educators can foster not only proficiency in language mechanics but also adaptability to evolving modes of communication (Yudintseva, 2023).

3.1 Overlooked Role of Reading in Immersive Pedagogy

Although critical, reading has been relatively overlooked in immersive learning literature. The text no longer resides in books or electronic files. However, it appears in a virtual world: contained within virtual objects, displayed on interactive panels, woven into stories, or created by fellow students in real-time. Thus, students need to employ reading processes that are not linear, but multimodal, incorporating written, visual, auditory, and spatial inputs. Yet, this perspective sells short the promise of immersive worlds to redefine reading as a higher-order, social process (Kaplan-Rakowski & Gruber, 2024). In metaverse spaces, reading does not occur in isolation but is often tied to problem-solving, exploration, and interaction. For example, learners may interpret textual clues to navigate a virtual story world, analyze peer-generated texts during group tasks, or read embedded information as part of collaborative projects. In such instances, reading is embedded with action and conversation and necessitates students to read critically and contextually. Additionally, reading in the metaverse affords the possibility of fostering higher-order literacies like inference, synthesis, and critical examination.

Learners are not merely decoding words but constructing meaning across multimodal layers, integrating textual information with visual, auditory, and spatial cues. This reflects the reality of contemporary digital literacy, where reading increasingly involves navigating multimodal environments like websites, social media platforms, and digital storytelling applications. By incorporating such practices into literacy pedagogy, the metaverse can help bridge the gap between traditional reading instruction and the demands of twenty-first-century literacy.

4 To Write as an Interactive, Collaborative Process

Writing in the metaverse environment may provide a practical understanding in teaching writing. Writing assignments in classrooms are traditionally designed for personal production, linear draft, and instructor-oriented evaluation. On the other

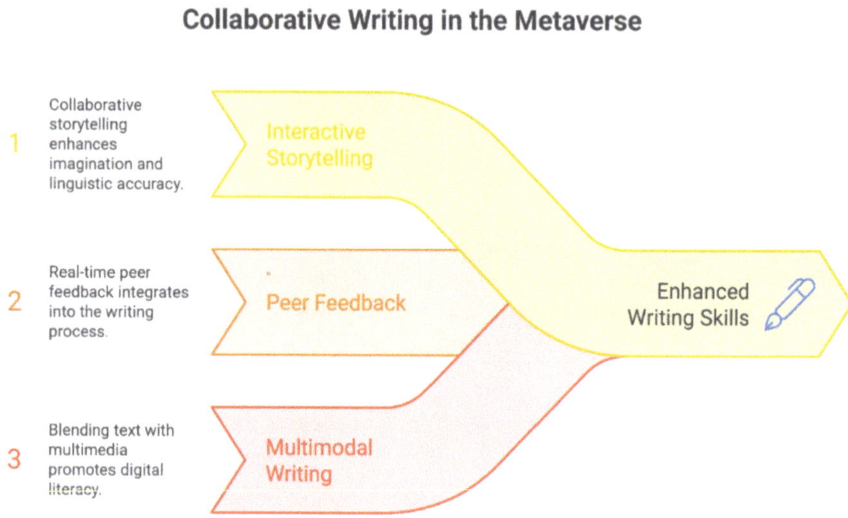

Fig. 1 Collaborative writing in metaverse

hand, metaverse provides relapse, interactivity, and cooperation. Students work in groups to create stories, essays, or reports in common virtual spaces. These activities encourage negotiation of meaning, group decision-making, and exposure to a variety of writing strategies (Fig. 1).

- *Constructive Interactive Storytelling.* Students work together to develop branching stories, whose written product determines the action of the tale. Such exercises replicate the culture of collaboration found in online storytelling, encouraging both imagination and linguistic accuracy. Students can comment on text, add comments to draft versions, and make real-time suggestions, so that feedback becomes a natural part of the writing process instead of an intervention after the fact.
- *Peer-to-Peer Feedback.* Much of writing in the metaverse involves collaborative virtual surfaces or documents that support instant peer review (Cuocci et al., 2023). Students can label texts, add comments to the draft, and provide suggestions in real-time, making their reactions an active part of the composition process, which violates a subsequent intervention (Cao, 2022).
- *Multimodal writing.* The metavense -atmosphere can integrate text with images, sound, and spatial composition. Writing assignments can thus prompt learners to blend linguistic expression with other semiotic tools, promoting digital literacy and language ability.

The co-constructional tendency of these writing activities aligns most closely with socio-constructivist theories of learning, which emphasize the role of social interaction in the acquisition of higher-order thinking skills. Metaverse writing is not just a matter of creating end products but focuses on the process of co-construction, negotiation, and revision. The cyclical process aids the development of fluency, accuracy, and confidence as well as creativity and critical engagement.

4.1 Designing Literacy Activities in the Metaverse

One of the metaverse's most remarkable affordances is that it has the potential to transform traditional literacy practices into interactive, engaging, and socially mediated activities. Unlike traditional classrooms, where reading and writing are typically single and linear events, the metaverse space offers possibilities for collaboration, creativity, and critical reading of texts. The interactive nature of 3D worlds, with avatar-based interaction and real-time feedback, allows literacy to be a live practice rather than a static exercise. This section discusses how metavars can plan literature activities in the world by examining the use of 3D virtual worlds and avatars, which promote activities, imagination, and analysis, as well as specific practices such as crowdsourcing, digital storytelling, and peer reviews. Hearing is a more natural fit for synchronous working in online environments; the affordances of the metaverse also make it a fertile context for the growth of text-related competencies. In metaverse spaces, reading and writing move beyond conventional, paper-based practices into interactive, multimodal, and socially mediated activities. This section highlights the importance of lesson-based skills in immersive rooms, emphasizing the reduced emphasis on reading in engaging teaching, and the metaverse analysis that writing is a collaborative and interactive process in space. The importance of text-based skills in the immersive environment.

In educational settings, lesson-based skills are the foundation for long-term learning success and language development. Reading allows students to acquire material knowledge of the course, and writing enables them to create, structure, and express ideas. In the metaverse, these skills are remanifested. Just as writing in the metaverse goes beyond conventional practices like essays or grammar exercises, it is placed within communicative and creative contexts, where students can contribute to collaborative narratives, comment on shared objects, or write for avatars' dialogue. These tasks represent realistic applications of literacy for professional and social contexts, where online writing is more often similar to collaborative documents, multimodal texts, and interactive media. By making students experience literacy within immersive environments, educators can develop not only language mechanics proficiency but also flexibility in changing modes of communication.

4.2 Underemphasized Role of Reading in Immersive Pedagogy

While needed, reading has been comparatively underemphasized in immersive learning literature. However, this vision overlooks the potential of immersive worlds to elevate reading to a higher level, making it a social act. In the metavense environment, reading is never alone, but is often associated with solving problems, searching, and communication. For instance, students might read clues from text in order to navigate a virtual story world, read the analyses of classmates on group assignments, or read embedded information through collaborative projects. In such instances, reading is action- and dialogue-based, calling upon students to read contextually and critically. In addition, reading in the metaverse also offers the possibility of cultivating higher-order literacies, including inference, synthesis, and critical analysis. Students are not merely decoding text but constructing meaning across multimodal levels, blending text information with spatial, auditory, and visual signals. In embedding such practices within literacy instruction, the metaverse can facilitate a reconciliation of traditional reading pedagogy with twenty-first-century literacy requirements.

5 Writing as an Interactive, Collaborative Process

Writing in the metaverse spaces provides perhaps the most revealing comprehension of literacy instruction. Classroom assignments in writing are typically focused on individual production, sequential drafts, and teacher-guided assessment (Fig. 2).

- **Multimodal Writing**: The metaverse, however, re-conceptualizes writing as iterative, interactive, and collaborative. Students can share stories, engage in peer review in real-time, and construct artifacts of work that persist across sessions, giving them a feeling of continuity and ownership of their writing practice. Several writing tasks are specifically well-adapted to metaverse environments: students can produce stories, colleagues can review live, and create digital objects that simulate sessions, allowing them to develop ownership and a sense of texture with writing behavior.

Some writing habits are particularly well-suited for the metaverse:

- **Crowdsourced writing work**: Many students collaborate on the production of stories, essays, or reports in a shared virtual environment. The tasks promote negotiation of meaning, collaborative choice-making, and acquaintance with several writing strategies.
- **Interactive Composition of Narrative**: Students are involved in branch narratives whereby their textual inputs decide the direction of the narrative. The activities mirror the interactive quality of digital narrative and promote imagination as well as linguistic accuracy.

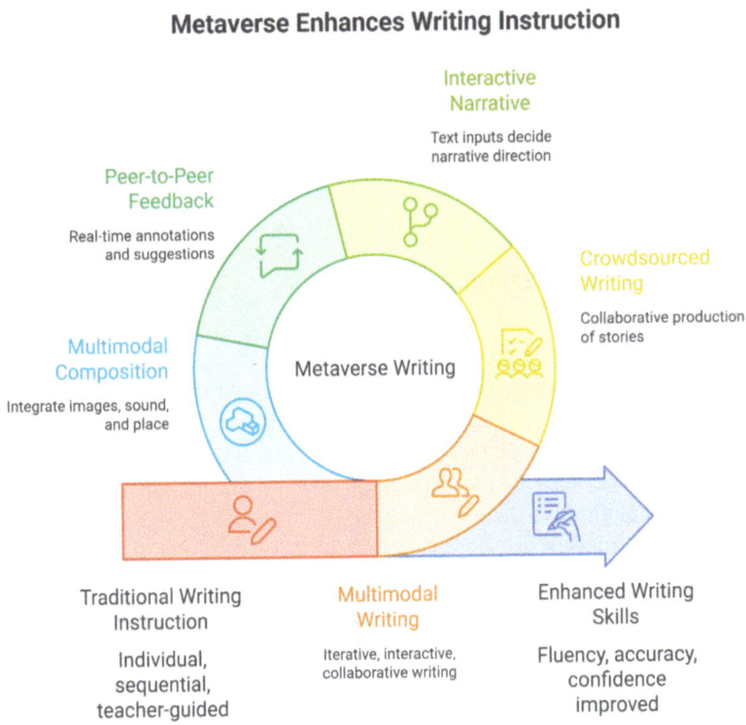

Fig. 2 Metaverse enhancing writing

- **Peer-to-Peer Feedback**: Metavense writing often involves shared digital surfaces or documents that allow colleagues to collaborate in the moment (Cuocci et al., 2023). Students can annotate the text, comment on the draft, and provide suggestions simultaneously, making the response an integral part of the writing process rather than a later activity.
- **Multimodal composition**: The metavense environment allows the images, sound, and place to be inserted into the text. Therefore, composition practices can motivate students to mix linguistic representation with other activities, which improves both digital reading skills and language capacity. The collaborative process of these writing practices aligns with socio-constructivist views on learning, which emphasize the social interaction leading to the construction of higher-order thinking processes. Metaverse writing is not just about end products but focuses on co-construction, negotiation, and revision processes. This iterative process helps learners develop fluency, accuracy, and confidence, while encouraging creativity and critical thinking.

6 Methodology

Figure 3 illustrates a mixed-methods framework that combines quantitative and qualitative methods to capture the multidimensional effects of metaverse-based literacy programs.

6.1 Mixed-Methods Research Design

Students' literacy skills are required not only to record average improvement, but also to employ mixed methodologies to capture their learning experiences and the collaborative aspects of learning in immersive rooms. The rich, through the combination of numerical data and findings, provided a comprehensive picture of how it enhances reading abilities. The study employed a convergent mixed-methods approach, where quantitative and qualitative data were gathered concurrently, analyzed individually, and subsequently merged to yield a comprehensive interpretation of the results. The quantitative strand consisted of pre- and post-intervention literacy performance assessments designed to measure reading comprehension and written fluency gains quantitatively.

This provided objective measures of the learning outcomes achieved through the intervention. The qualitative thread, on the other hand, sought to capture learners' experiences, impressions, and collaborative work habits in the metaverse. This was an especially appropriate design for investigating metaverse-literacy because the

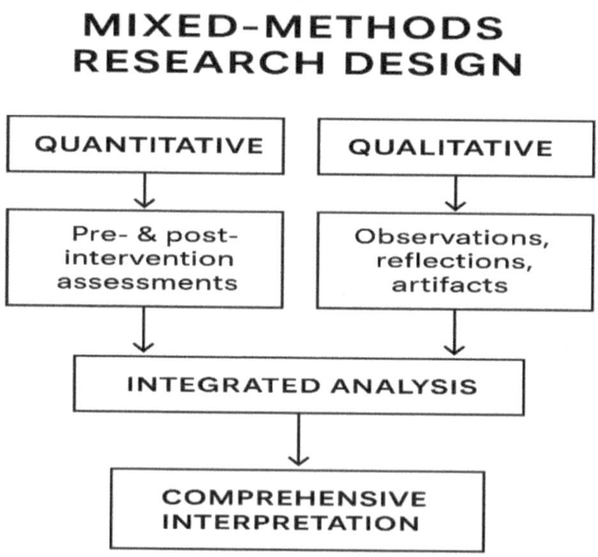

Fig. 3 Research design

immersive quality of the learning environment yields effects best accounted for by qualitative investigation. Ownership, cooperation, and creativity of students—metafoundations of literacy instruction in the metaverse—emerge best through qualitative investigation. The quantitative strand consisted of pre- and post-intervention literacy performance assessments designed to measure reading comprehension and written fluency gains quantitatively.

Observation diaries, learner reflections, and an examination of student-created artifacts enabled the study to interrogate questions related to engagement, creativity, and critical thinking. Through the combination of these views, the study was able to measure both outcomes (what happened) and processes (how learning occurred).

6.2 Case Study Context and Participants

The research's empirical component was in the form of a case study intervention with secondary school students studying English as a second language (ESL). A case study approach was selected because it can offer a detailed understanding of a bounded setting while permitting the examination of emerging practices in new settings. Participants were 42 students, aged 14 to 16 years old, recruited from two ESL classes at a metropolitan high school. The students demonstrated linguistic and cultural diversity, providing rich insights into how multilingual learners navigate literacy in interactive environments (Kaplan-Rakowski & Gruber, 2024). Voluntary participation in the study involved informed consent from both the students and their guardians.

The intervention lasted for eight weeks, during which time students participated in structured literacy activities twice a week. Sessions were approximately 60 minutes long and were integrated into the existing ESL curriculum. Activities were designed to align with curriculum goals in reading comprehension, narrative construction, and writing automaticity, making the intervention both pedagogically sound and realistically implementable.

6.3 Tools Used (Spatial.Io, FrameVR)

The two platforms used for the intervention were Spatial.io and FrameVR (Lan, 2020). The reason for choosing these two platforms is that they are accessible, easy to use, and can host collaborative activities without demanding sophisticated technical infrastructure.

- Spatial.io offered highly dynamic and customizable 3D environments in which students could engage with virtual objects, text panels, and avatars. Its multimodal capacity facilitated the embedding of texts, images, and collaborative writing tools, which made it well-suited for reading comprehension training and collaborative writing activities (Chang et al., 2023).

- FrameVR was employed to enable peer-to-peer collaboration in real-time. Its organized yet adaptive virtual rooms permitted students to co-author stories, exchange documents, and comment on co-authored whiteboards (Bailenson, 2018). The platform also enabled avatar-based interaction, which further amplified the sense of presence and identity, fundamental for participating in literacy activities (Hwang et al., 2023).

This integration enabled the study to examine how various affordances—Spatial.io's immersive visual environments and FrameVR's collaborative-focused tools—might be exploited for literacy education (Zhang et al., 2024).

6.4 Data Collection Techniques (Tests, Reflection, Diaries, Artifact Analysis)

To ensure that the conclusions were triangulated, a multi-income data collection approach was used to strengthen the validity.

Four major strategies were employed:

1. **Literacy performance test**: The students wrote understanding and fluency samples of reading and flowing before and after intervention. Reading tests evaluated the specification, synthesis, and significant interpretation of lesson skills. Writing tests evaluated flow, grammatical purity, and the capacity to present logical ideas. Comparison of the pre- and post-tests provided quantitative documentation of literacy gains.
2. **Overview diary**: Researchers and teachers led the diary, who used to register the students' interactions, participation, and behavior during the sessions (Muthmainnah et al., 2025). Entries included comments on the methods associated with student texts, the development of collaboration, and the students' reactions to difficulties. The diary provided useful, relevant information on the dynamics of classrooms within the me
3. **Learner Reflection Logs**: Learners were invited to keep reflection logs over the course of the intervention. The reflections recorded learners' views of the activities, their sense of engagement, and their understanding of literacy development. Reflection logs provided firsthand accounts in addition to external evidence from teachers and researchers.
4. **Deformation Access Analysis**: Research gathered and examined digital objects created throughout the intervention. These included the writer's stories, anecdotes, colleagues, and multimodal storytelling tasks. The analysis acknowledged the development of students' writing and creativity, as well as the importance of evidence, and the influence of colleague cooperation on reading skills results.

Through the integration of these approaches, the research was then able to tackle the core research questions from different perspectives: whether literacies increased, how students interacted with texts, and how qualitative transformations took place during the process of writing and reading. The link between the test results and reflections, diary entries, and objects ensured that the results reflect not only quantitative aspects, but also experiential aspects of reading skills in meta.

7 Literacy Performance Outcomes

Analysis of pre- and post-intervention literacy exams indicated a measurable improvement in college students' analytical comprehension and writing fluency. The standard reading comprehension score was multiplied by 14%, while writing fluency scores increased by 18 percentage points. These gains suggest that the immersive environment was no longer merely a novel platform for engagement but also contributed substantively to literacy development.

Qualitative numbers supported these results. Deformation certificate analysis confirmed that the students produced more sophisticated stories in response to the intervention, with greater consistency, richer vocabulary, and more advanced syntax. In addition, reflection logs revealed that beginners have asked to pursue the authorship; Many mentioned that the Metaverse's obligations provided more opportunities to write than traditional instructions.

The convergence of quantitative and qualitative statistics confirms the conclusion that the metanized activities undoubtedly encouraged the general performance of reading skills. It is essential that these results not only be held accountable for the outcomes of innovation, but also that the general performance surplus has been achieved through continuous involvement during the eight weeks of intervention.

7.1 Get Commitment, Inspiration, and Ownership

One of the most striking findings is observed during the respective sessions, characterized by increased commitment and heightened motivational levels. The observation diary continuously mentioned that the students showed fewer signs of distraction compared to traditional classroom hours. The use of avatars and 3D rooms created a sense of presence and identity, which increased students' desire to participate.

The students expressed that their ability to "be" in the story through their avatars read more convincingly and write more purposefully. For example, in a collaborative storytelling work, the students reported realizing that they had appeared around them instead of completing an isolated writing practice. This feeling of ownership made literature work into partnership experiences.

The reflection log highlights the loving dimension of this ownership. Students described pride in digital objects they created, especially multimodal stories that combine lessons, images, and spatial designs. It is often associated with traditional writing assignments that are limited to paper with limited pride. Ownership was also improved through a colleague's response: students felt more responsible for the quality of their contributions when they were visible to peers in shared virtual spaces.

7.2 Discussion

Together, the conclusions suggest that metaverses can play a transformative role in literacy education, combining average skill development with increased engagement and collaboration. Esmarive references can enhance understanding and writing production, leading to significant improvements in reading performance. However, the specific contribution of this study lies in demonstrating that reading and writing can be integrated into a tan immersive environment, creating a mutual cycle of interpretation and production. The intense feeling of ownership and inspiration highlights the loving dimension of learning skills in metaverses. The students were not inactive recipients of information, but were active participants in financial processes. This is important because loving commitment is often a precursor to the continuous development of literacy. In addition, the conclusions emphasize the colleague's ability to normalize relapse practice in the virtual environment. By resuming the change in the form of a collaborative and dynamic process, Metaverse supports a vision of literacy that is social, creative, and recurrent.

7.3 Implications for Teaching and Course Design

The findings from this study provide valuable insights into how teachers could benefit from metacognition technologies to promote literature skills. These platforms open up new opportunities for attractive and interactive spending commitments; they also require a good evaluation of educational integration. This section outlines the guidelines for implementing immersive readings and writing exercises and discusses how meta-cognitive activities can be effectively integrated with the course's goals.

8 Guidelines for Integrating Engaging Readings and Writing Exercises

A first step for teachers is to expand meta-based reading skills beyond innovation and entertainment. Teachers must carefully design activities that clearly target the consequences of reading and writing, and utilize immersive functions such as avatars, spatial stories, and collaboration equipment. For reading, it means entering texts in meaningful virtual contexts—for example, displaying a story on interactive panels in a simulated environment that reflects the historical context. This relevant anchoring enhances understanding by situating the text within multimodal signals and facilitating students' connections between linguistic details and sensory and spatial elements.

For writing, teachers can integrate collaborative tools that encourage students to generate, revise, and share digital texts. Annotation of crowds, interactive history labeling, and shared documents in the virtual world can be a recurring and social exercise. Teachers should keep the collaboration purposeful by providing hints, clear role tasks, and structured response cycles to ensure that the collaboration remains targeted.

Another guideline is to balance synchronous and asynchronous activities. In real-time collaboration, writing during meetings stimulates rapid thinking and fosters a flow state. However, asynchronous reflection features, such as maintaining a digital diary or revising drafts outside of live sessions, allow for more deliberate language use. The combination of both modes ensures that students still benefit from time for significant analysis and processing from time to time. There is a need to cultivate digital reading skills with equally important linguistic literacy. Teachers should offer an orientation session on navigating metaverse platforms, managing avatars, and using interactive tools effectively. Without such preparation, technical challenges can hinder the achievement of learning goals. Starting small training programs or low-level tasks at the beginning of a course can help students become comfortable with the environment before working on more complex reading and writing projects. Finally, a formal evaluation should be built into immersive literature activities. Teachers can use multimodal evaluation methods, such as both text products (e.g., digital stories) and evaluating the processes behind them (e.g., colleague response, contribution, reflection log). This overall evaluation approach captures the memory and cooperative character of literacy in the metal areas, which may not be sufficiently reflected in traditional tests alone.

9 Adjust the Metaverse Activities with Course Goals

The integration of metacognitive activities should be based on the course overview to ensure that the development of literacy is average and relevant (Gee, 2003). Teachers should start by mapping specific course standards, such as reading strategies, writing flow, or significant interpretation of texts, in consecutive works. For example, if a course emphasizes identifying topics and symbols in target literature, students can discover a virtual world designed around symbolic imagination, as well as discuss interpretations by emptying the texts in the metaves.

It is also necessary for adjustment that immersive work is gradually done on the existing skills of students. Instead of changing traditional reading and writing exercises, metacognition should be supplemented by providing alternative methods of engagement. For example, a unit of motivation writing may include traditional essay writing and a collaborative debate in a virtual auditorium, where students co-produce arguments through shared documents and speeches led by an Avatar. This mixed approach ensures that students develop the main skills while benefiting from engaging improvements. When it comes to assessing assessments, teachers should ensure that the results of meta-based activities can be evaluated according to the existing grading rubric. If writing consistency and grammatical accuracy are central to course evaluation, digital history projects should include clear posts that address these criteria. Similarly, if the understanding of reading is evaluated through estimates and summaries, metacognitive activities should be structured to develop these skills, such as having students generate collaborative compositions of virtual history experiences (Lee et al., 2022).

It is also important that the syllabus adjustment should include and promote access. Not all students can have the same access to high-quality equipment or a stable internet connection. Teachers should design tasks that can be adapted to settings for lower peasant width in a flexible manner or complement offline material. In this way, metaverse-based literacy instructions support equity rather than increasing digital stratification. By engaging in readings and writing activities outlined in the syllabus, teachers can ensure that meta-stage integration is not a separate experiment, but a permanent educational strategy. This adjustment confirms the validity of the Metavors tool in formal education and provides students with reading skills that can be applied to references.

10 Conclusion

This chapter has explored the value of the metaverse in enhancing literacy instruction, particularly in reading and writing. As immersive learning studies have been used to support listening and speaking skills in the past, the results presented herein demonstrate that integrating literacy exercises into 3D worlds can yield desirable outcomes. When reading was placed in interactive, multimodal environments, students worked more richly with texts, and writing was an iterative, collaborative process through digital storytelling, crowdsourced writing, and peer feedback. The case study demonstrated quantifiable gains in reading comprehension and writing proficiency, accompanied by robust learner engagement and a sense of ownership over the learning process. Aside from performance measures, the metaverse has promoted creativity, critical thinking, and collaboration, reconceptualizing literacy as a participatory practice rather than an individual activity. For teachers and curriculum developers, the research offers actionable recommendations for folding immersive literacy activities into existing frameworks. For researchers, it offers new directions in scalability, availability, and long-term effects. Finally, the metaverse is designed as a visionary tool that not only inspires literacy skills but also improves digital literacy and group learning. By bridging pedagogy and immersive technologies, it creates new avenues of language learning in the digital world.

Acknowledgements I am grateful to the Management of KCG College of Technology, with whom I have been associated since 2017, for their continued support and commitment to students' growth. I also appreciate the encouragement and inspiration from my colleagues in the Department of Artificial Intelligence and Data Science. The insights gained through my ongoing research in Deepfake detection have further enriched my academic journey in teaching and research.

References

Alfadil, M. (2024). Immersive virtual reality: A novel approach to second language vocabulary acquisition in K-12 education. *Sensors, 24*(22), 7185. https://doi.org/10.3390/s24227185

Bailenson, J. (2018). *Experience on demand: What virtual reality is, how it works, and what it can do*. W. W. Norton & Company.

Çelik, F., & Baturay, M. H. (2024). The effect of metaverse-based language teaching on L2 vocabulary learning, engagement, and presence. *BMC Psychology, 12*, 58. https://doi.org/10.1186/s40359-024-01549-4

Chang, C. Y., Kuo, H. C., & Du, Z. (2023). The role of digital literacy in augmented, virtual, and mixed reality in popular science education: A review study and an educational framework development. *Virtual Reality, 27*(3), 2461–2479. https://doi.org/10.1007/s10055-023-00817-9

Cuocci, S., Fattahi Marnani, P., Khan, I., & Roberts, S. (2023). A meta-synthesis of technology-supported peer feedback in ESL/EFL writing classes research: A replication of Chen's study. *Language, 8*(2), 114. https://doi.org/10.3390/languages8020114

Damaševičius, R., & Sidekerskienė, T. (2024). Virtual worlds for learning in metaverse: A narrative review. *Sustainability, 16*(5), 2032. https://doi.org/10.3390/su16052032

Fan, L., & Chiang, J. (2023). A systematic review of the application of metaverse in language education: Prominent themes, research methods, impacts, and future challenges. *Journal of Language Teaching, 3*(10), 1–14. https://doi.org/10.54475/jlt.2023.026

Gee, J. P. (2003). What video games have to teach us about learning and literacy. *Computers in Entertainment, 1*(1), 1–4. https://doi.org/10.1145/950566.950595

Hwang, Y., Shin, D., & Lee, H. (2023). Students' perception on immersive learning through 2D and 3D metaverse platforms. *Educational Technology Research and Development, 71*(4), 1687–1708. https://doi.org/10.1007/s11423-023-10238-9

Ibrahim, A., Huynh, B., Downey, J., Höllerer, T., Chun, D., & O'Donovan, J. (2017). ARbis Pictus: A study of language learning with augmented reality [preprint]. *arXiv*. https://arxiv.org/abs/1711.11243

Kaplan-Rakowski, R., & Gruber, A. (2023). Motivation and reading in high-immersion virtual reality. In B. Arnbjörnsdóttir, B. Bédi, L. Bradley, K. Friðriksdóttir, H. Garðarsdóttir, S. Thouësny, & M. J. Whelpton (Eds.), *Intelligent CALL, granular systems, and learner data: Short papers from EUROCALL 2022* (pp. 208–213). Research-publishing.net. https://doi.org/10.14705/rpnet.2022.61.1460

Kaplan-Rakowski, R., & Gruber, A. (2024). An experimental study on reading in high-immersion virtual reality. *British Journal of Educational Technology, 55*(2), 541–559. https://doi.org/10.1111/bjet.13392

Kojić, T., Ali, D., Greinacher, R., Möller, S., & Voigt-Antons, J.-N. (2020). User experience of reading in virtual reality—Finding values for text distance, size and contrast [preprint]. *arXiv*. https://doi.org/10.48550/ARXIV.2004.01545

Kourtesis, P., et al. (2024). Multimodal XR applications, risks, and ethical challenges in the metaverse [preprint]. *arXiv*. https://arxiv.org/abs/2411.04508

Lan, Y.-J. (2020). Immersion into virtual reality for language learning. In K. D. Federmeier & H.-W. Huang (Eds.), *Psychology of learning and motivation* (Vol. 72, pp. 1–26). Academic. https://doi.org/10.1016/bs.plm.2020.03.001

Lee, S. M. (2023). Second language learning through an emergent narrative in a narrative-rich customizable metaverse platform. *IEEE Transactions on Learning Technologies, 16*(6), 1071–1081. https://doi.org/10.1109/TLT.2023.3267563
Lee, G., Healey, J., & Manocha, D. (2022). VRDoc: Gaze-based interactions for VR reading experience [preprint]. *arXiv*. https://arxiv.org/abs/2211.03001
Li, Y., Cui, Y., Li, W., Lv, T., Yuan, X., Simsek, M., & Dressler, F. (2022). When internet of things meets metaverse: Convergence of physical and cyber worlds [preprint]. *arXiv*. https://arxiv.org/abs/2208.13501
Li, K., Lau, B. P. L., Yuan, X., Ni, W., Guizani, M., & Yuen, C. (2023). Towards ubiquitous semantic metaverse: Challenges and opportunities [preprint]. *arXiv*. https://arxiv.org/abs/2307.06687
Muthmainnah, M., Cardoso, L., Marzuki, A. G., & Al Yakin, A. (2025). A new innovative metaverse ecosystem: VR-based human interaction enhances EFL learners' transferable skills. *Discover Sustainability, 6*(1), 156. https://doi.org/10.1007/s43621-025-00913-7
Nguyen, A., Huynh, L., Dang, B., Pohjolainen, S., Mattila, J., Paajala, I. J., Tikkanen, R., Lehto, E., Poikonen, F., & Karppinen, P. (2025). Conceptualizing and enhancing metaverse literacy for education. *Education and Information Technologies, 30*(12), 17133–17153. https://doi.org/10.1007/s10639-025-13486-9
Park, S., & Kim, S. (2022). Identifying world types to deliver gameful experiences for sustainable learning in the metaverse. *Sustainability, 14*(3), 1361. https://doi.org/10.3390/su14031361
Parmaxi, A. (2023). Virtual reality in language learning: A systematic review and implications for research and practice. *Interactive Learning Environments, 31*(1), 172–184. https://doi.org/10.1080/10494820.2020.1765392
Peterson, M. (2013). Computer games and learning. In M. Peterson, Computer games and language learning (pp. 33–50). Palgrave Macmillan US. https://doi.org/10.1057/9781137005175_3.
Prabakaran, N., Patrick, H. A., & Kareem, J. (2025). Enhancing English language proficiency and digital literacy through Metaverse-based learning: A mixed-methods study in higher education. *Journal of Information Technology Education: Research, 24*. https://doi.org/10.28945/5484
Qiu, Y., Isusi-Fagoaga, R., & García-Aracil, A. (2023). Perceptions and use of metaverse in higher education: A descriptive study in China and Spain. *Computers and Education: Artificial Intelligence, 5*, 100185. https://doi.org/10.1016/j.caeai.2023.100185
Tan, K. H., Naim, M. K., Wahi, W., Arham, A. F., & Yunos, N. (2024). Metaverse-based activities for enhancing communicative competencies among young learners. *International Journal of Interactive Mobile Technologies, 18*(21), 4–25. https://doi.org/10.3991/ijim.v18i21.47867
Wang, Z., Zou, D., Peng, P., Wang, F. L., Lee, L.-K., & Xie, H. (2025). Effects of mobile metaverse-based vocabulary learning on learners' perception and performance: A case study of Chinese EFL learners. *Journal of Computers in Education, 12*(4), 1333–1366. https://doi.org/10.1007/s40692-024-00348-5
Yudintseva, A. (2023). Virtual reality affordances for oral communication in English as a second language classroom: A literature review. *Computers & Education: X Reality, 2*, 100018. https://doi.org/10.1016/j.cexr.2023.100018
Zhang, H., Yang, Q., & Ju, Z. (2024). An experimental study on the reading experience and the comprehension effect in virtual reality reading device. *Proceedings of the 24th ACM/IEEE joint conference on digital libraries*, 1–5. https://doi.org/10.1145/3677389.3702498.

V. S. Krithikaa Venket is an assistant professor in Information Technology at KCG College of Technology, Chennai, India. She holds master's degrees in Information Technology and is pursuing a PhD in deepfake technology. Her research interests include artificial intelligence, machine learning, and deep learning applications in education. Venket contributes to studies on metaverse-enhanced literacy development through interactive and collaborative activities. She bridges technical innovation with pedagogical practice in immersive language learning.She earned her bachelor's and master's degrees in Information Technology from Dr. Sivanthi Aditanar College of Engineering. She is currently an Assistant Professor in the Information Technology department at KCG College of Technology, Chennai. In addition to her teaching role, she is pursuing a Ph.D. at Anna University, focusing on deepfake technology. Her research interests include, artificial intelligence, machine learning, Deep fake and deep learning.

R. Adline Freeda is an assistant professor with 18 years of teaching experience at KCG College of Technology, Chennai, India. She holds a PhD in Computer Science and Engineering, with research interests in machine learning, software engineering, and cloud computing. Freeda is a life member of the Computer Society of India and has published in international journals. Her work explores metaverse-based approaches to reading and writing skills. She emphasizes multimodal and collaborative literacy in virtual environments.She has 18 years of teaching experience and she has received the B.E Degree and M.E in Computer Science and engineering and completed her Ph.D. in Computer science and engineering from Hindustan Institute of Technology & Science, Tamil Nadu, India. Her current research interests include Machine learning, Software Engineering and Cloud Computing. She is a Life Member of Computer Society of India. And published research papers in International Journals.

Assessment Strategies for Metaverse-Enhanced Language Classrooms

Volkan Duran and Yaşar Barut

Abstract This chapter critically examines assessment strategies in metaverse-enhanced language education, combining theoretical perspectives and empirical developments to propose integrated frameworks for evaluating linguistic, intercultural, and digital competencies. In reimagining assessment for an immersive learning environment, this chapter introduces a range of innovative evaluation methods that go beyond conventional tests. It presents gamified assessments, performance-based tasks, and data analytics approaches designed to measure both language proficiency and the soft skills critical to modern communication. The chapter emphasizes how real-time feedback and adaptive evaluation methods can offer a more nuanced understanding of student progress, allowing educators to fine-tune instruction in ways that are in step with the dynamic nature of the metaverse. This chapter critically examines assessment strategies in metaverse-enhanced language education. Given that metaverse-based pedagogy is still emerging, assessment frameworks for these environments are likewise in their formative stages. This chapter therefore discusses both established assessment theories and their application to immersive contexts, while acknowledging that comprehensive frameworks specific to metaverse assessment require continued empirical development.

Keywords Assessment strategies · Metaverse · ELT · Metaverse based language classrooms

V. Duran (✉)
Psychology Department, Turkey: Iğdır University, Iğdır, Turkey
e-mail: volkan.duran8@gmail.com

Y. Barut
Ondokuz Mayıs University, Samsun, Türkiye
e-mail: ybarut@omu.edu.tr

F. Çelik and C. Yangın Ersanlı (eds.), *Metaverse-Based Language Learning and Teaching*, English Language Education 49,
https://doi.org/10.1007/978-3-032-31366-9_7

1 Introduction

By integrating metaverse technologies in language learning, we are facing a profound shift that leads us to reevaluate our assessment practices. Traditional assessment in language learning, which relies on written assessments as well as activities that are assessed separately and disconnected from the multi-contextual nature of communication in a digital environment, will not be sufficient, especially as digital environments become more complex. The metaverse allows for an unprecedented opportunity to develop genuine, real-world immersive assessment tasks that will closely resemble real-world language use. This type of assessment will produce a longitudinal snapshot of student engagement, performance, and development.

The move to the metaverse is not simply a response to a new technology. The shift in assessment towards development in the metaverse raises fundamental questions about how we assess competency in language education in the twenty-first century. Students today are not simply concerned with language itself, but also with digital literacy, spatial development, multitasking communication modalities, and cross-cultural/linguistic encounters within these spaces. This means assessment systems need to consider (and assess) grammaticality and appropriacy in addition to technical skills in collaboration tasks through immersive and dynamic avatar-based design, while simultaneously overlapping learning and assessment.

Evaluation in metaverse environments pursues two general aims: to support learning by providing ongoing formative feedback, and to provide more reliable and accurate summative assessment and accountability data (Bennett, 2011; Black & Wiliam, 1998). The utility of real-time feedback mechanisms, adaptive assessment approaches, and hidden assessments expands the potential for meaningful and supportive assessments of teaching and learning in measurements (Shute, 2008). In addition, the diverse nature of virtual learning spaces requires assessment methods that can encompass intercultural competence and global awareness in addition to fundamental language skills (Byram, 1997; Deardorff, 2006).

With the potential and excitement of virtual worlds, pressing issues related to reliability, fidelity, accessibility, and ethical use of evaluation in the metaverse emerge as academics and teachers begin to navigate a changing landscape. How to maintain fidelity in immersion evaluation? What frameworks should guide the development of a technologically sophisticated assessment that is pedagogically useful? How to address digital equity and avoid creating more barriers to equitable education in the metaverse? This chapter highlights these concerns with evidence-based approaches, theoretical frameworks, and practical considerations for application in language teaching classrooms enhanced through the metaverse. It suggests that the future of language evaluation lies not in choosing between traditional and innovative approaches but in their intentional integration within immersive digital environments. To ensure the fair and ethical implementation of assessment in metaverse environments, educators must address issues of digital equity, data privacy, and algorithmic transparency. Ethical evaluation requires establishing clear policies for data storage, bias detection, and inclusive access so that metaverse-based assessments do not reproduce existing educational inequalities.

2 Immersive Assessment Paradigm: Transitioning from Traditional Testing Approaches to Virtual Reality

A novel method evaluates abilities utilizing virtual reality for assessing abilities in more realistic contexts and diverges from old testing paradigms (Bower et al., 2020). The rationale behind this method is based on people learning best when actively engaged in a recreated real-life context (cf., Piaget, 1977; Vygotsky, 1978). In terms of language learning, this idea translates into the use of virtual environments to reproduce tools for genuine communication that mimic real-life language usages (Godwin-Jones, 2022). A natural evolution of assessment, assessing reality is moving away from typical testing measures that do not address real relevance and authenticity, and examining behavior and thought in more relevant paradigms (Chapelle & Voss, 2016).

While this involves a prominent shift in assessing cognition, mental states, and behavior, this shift to VR testing offers various advantages (e.g., Kourtesis et al., 2020; Parsons et al., 2013), and traditional exams often do not account for the level of complexity associated with real-life events and interactions. Specifically, VR tests can offer dynamic, interactive, and realistic contexts that approximate the daily lives of individuals, which can lead to more accurate and comprehensive assessments of behavior and thought (Kourtesis et al., 2020; Parsons et al., 2013).

Virtual environments, like a virtual supermarket or a virtual assessment lab, have been demonstrated to be more authentic and immersive experiences than traditional assessment techniques, resulting in better assessment outcomes (Kourtesis et al., 2020; Parsons et al., 2013). Moreover, recent studies have indicated that VR assessments can be better predictors of cognitive declines in performance, memory, and attention in real-world scenarios (Davison et al., 2017). This advancement is due to VR's ability to create complex circumstances, in which cognitive evaluations can be assessed simultaneously (Everard, Burton, & Van de Sype, et al., 2024; Terbeck et al., 2022). Critically, VR assessments also maintain accuracy and accessibility while remaining fun and engaging for individuals with ADHD, challenges associated with strokes, or age-related cognitive declines (Everard et al., 2024). The added dimension of hidden assessments within VR (i.e., subtle behaviours are monitored in real-time, which are not possible with traditional questionnaires) can assess psychological traits that traditional questionnaires cannot (Giglioli et al., 2017). Psychological assessments prioritise authentic, participant-centric, scientifically sound, and personally relevant assessment experiences.

3 Gamified Language Assessment: Theoretical Foundations of Motivation and Measurement Balance

An innovative method of teaching, gamified language assessment integrates the characteristics of games into language assessment to promote student engagement while preserving accurate assessment. This method is heavily influenced by self-determination theory (SDT) and flow theory, as both describe how natural motivation can be cultivated through autonomy, development of skill, and social connectedness (Muttaqin, Zuhdi, & Ridwan, 2025; Zhang & Crawford, 2023). Using these frameworks, educators can consciously engage each of these aspects in gamified assessment in an online context, creating systems that would be scientifically valid while maximizing natural motivation. This theory clarifies the idea of employing game-like components (e.g., points, rewards, challenges, feedback, etc.) to foster natural motivation and support deeper mental engagement with assessment tasks (Laksanasut, 2025; Ma, 2025).

The general premise is that features of games, such as points, badges, leaderboards, and storylines, could promote engagement in a way that is both fair and valid in assessment. Research demonstrates that, when utilized effectively, gamified assessments may alleviate testing anxiety and can provide a more detailed overview of language proficiency (Gee, 2003; Prensky, 2001).

The difficulty is in finding an ideal balance between enjoyment and educational aims, while ensuring the game components are designed to enhance rather than disrupt the assessment of learning outcomes (Deterding et al., 2011). There is also evidence to support this belief, as users of gamified assessments not only became more engaged but also demonstrated gains in vocabulary, language skills, and speaking (Casanova-Mata, 2023; Imron et al., 2024). Studies using gamified formative assessments, such as Quizizz, showed significant increases in motivation and acceptance of the learning objectives, and they discuss the value of motivational frameworks in assessment design (Zhang & Crawford, 2023). Nevertheless, one major concern is how to balance reliability in North American tests with motivation. Mechanisms that may offer poorly designed gamified systems can place too much emphasis on external reward rather than language performance, which will create the possibilities for compromised reliability (Kocadere & Çağlar, 2015; Li et al., 2024). That said, leaderboard illustrations may create a healthy competition but also create feelings of sentimental dismay for students with less successful performances. Gamification can also theoretically promote mental features such as attention spans and memory, which can lead to increased reliability in analyzing language assessment instruments; however, these features are usually short-lived, leading to continuous design (Al-Khresheh, 2025). In conclusion, although gamified language assessments are grounded in sound motivational theory, providing solid educational benefit, they must be crafted to operate within the framework of scientific and ideological integrity.

4 Multidimensional Competence Model: Holistic Evaluation of Language Skills in Metaverse Environments

The multidimensional competence framework builds on the communicative language ability framework from Bachman and Palmer (1996) and expands beyond the more traditional communicative language ability framework by including unique characteristics of virtual environments. The base principle of this framework is that language users in metaverse environments need linguistic knowledge, working in English, digital literacy, spatial apparatus, and the ability to work across different resources (Thorne & Smith, 2011). This model fuses together the communicative competence model of Canale and Swain (1980) with important 21st-century skills. This model contributes to expanded notions of linguistic ability and assessment of linguistic ability by including grammatical competence, sociolinguistic competence, discourse competence, and strategic competence. This insight shows that language and digital literacy are linked in today's communication.

Integrating metaverse technologies into language learning requires a change in how we assess student performance. We need a wider assessment strategy that considers thinking skills, language abilities, social awareness, and tech skills. Traditional language assessments often focus on grammar and vocabulary, which don't capture the interactive communication needed in virtual settings. A more comprehensive view recognizes that language proficiency includes using language correctly, understanding social signals, being culturally aware, and using language strategically (Shaik, 2024). In metaverse learning, where students interact through avatars in changing environments, these competencies are closely linked and depend on context.

Research shows that students in augmented and virtual reality settings not only improve their traditional language skills (reading, writing, and speaking) but also enhance their tech abilities and social skills (Prabakaran, Patrick, & Kareem, 2025). However, we must address challenges like equal access to technology and adequate training.

Effective metaverse instruction focuses on personalized, authentic scenarios and immediate feedback, helping develop flexible communication skills and collaborative problem-solving (Hong, 2025). As language use in virtual spaces increasingly reflects real-world interactions, educators need assessment methods that recognize multilingualism, intercultural understanding, and digital literacy (Belova & Kharkhurin, 2024).

The metaverse is changing not only how we teach but also what effective communication means in our connected, tech-driven world. Therefore, a multi-faceted competence model provides a useful framework for assessing language skills in ways that are relevant, inclusive, and prepare students for future challenges.

5 Real-Time Feedback Theory: Impact of Instantaneous Assessment on Learning Processes

The theory of real-time feedback in metaverse-based assessment builds on Shute's (2008) ideas about formative feedback and Hattie and Timperley's (2007) feedback model, which says that feedback should be given immediately after performance, presented in a clear way, and allow for adjustments based on individual performance. The foundation shows that virtual environments offer new ways for timely feedback, which can shorten the gap between performance and evaluation, making learning in specific subjects more effective (Butler & Winne, 1995). In language learning in metaverses, real-time feedback can come through various methods, like visual, auditory, or tactile signals, creating a rich information environment for immediate error correction and skill development (Clark & Mayer, 2016). The characteristics of real-time feedback in a metaverse also follow cognitive load theory by providing support when needed without overloading working memory (Sweller, 1988).

Immediate feedback, meaning assessment and guidance given right away during learning, is critical for how well people learn and what they gain from education. Research consistently shows that receiving feedback instantly helps learners because they can correct mistakes, change their strategies, and strengthen their understanding while they work. For example, in learning music, immediate feedback can enhance technical skills and motivation by offering various types of cues, like visual or touch signals, that guide practice in the moment (Johnson, 2014; Johnson et al., 2011). This allows students to adjust continuously without waiting for later feedback, making learning feel more natural and responsive. In classrooms, using immediate feedback tools can speed up teaching, boost teacher confidence, and create a more student-focused learning atmosphere. This happens because teachers can adjust their instruction based on what students report right away (Al-Mansouri, 2024). These tools can also reduce anxiety by making feedback a normal and supportive part of learning.

Real-time feedback can also benefit online learning. Feedback is a crucial, dynamic part of learning; its value lies not just in being an external stimulus, but in how learners construct feedback using their cognitive systems and other contextual factors (Peters et al., 2017). Thus, feedback is more than real-time input; it is shaped by both external and internal elements that aid in supporting cognitive processes and timing feedback delivery. Feedback should be seen as event-based rather than merely time-based, following Keiding and Qvortrup's (2014) argument. When we realize real-time feedback thoughtfully, it may enhance adaptive learning qualities, deepen engagement, improve learning results, and increase instructional effectiveness.

6 Adaptive Assessment Systems: Dynamic Test Adjustment Based on Individual Learning Pathways

Adaptive Assessment Systems (AAS) represent a shift in modern education by enabling real-time personalization of learning experiences through adjustments to assessments based on each learner's cognitive and behavioral profile. Adaptive systems use technologies like artificial intelligence, cognitive diagnosis models, and item response theory (IRT) to track learner performance as it changes and modify the difficulty of assessment items. In the metaverse, adaptive assessment systems employ both Item Response Theory (IRT) and Computer Adaptive Testing (CAT) to offer personalized assessment experiences (van der Linden & Glas, 2010). The core belief is that effective personalized learning happens when assessment difficulty matches the learner's current ability level, rooted in Vygotsky's (1978) Zone of Proximal Development.

Currently, an adaptive system provides automatic adjustments for task difficulty, individualized support, and custom assessment metrics in virtual language learning settings. This type of assessment provides accurate measurements with minimal time investment, enhancing the overall learning experience. It offers a more effective assessment that is user-centered, time-efficient, and cost-effective (Wainer, 2000). Adaptive systems allow learners to follow personalized learning paths while reflecting on their performance, skills, and challenges, automatically adjusting their pace and knowledge to ensure deeper understanding and mastery (Chau & Choi, 2025; Kumaresan, Jeyakarthic, & Devi, et al., 2025). By leveraging the advantages of artificial intelligence models with natural language processing, platforms can assess testing difficulty, suggest remedial content, and provide semi-guided learning activities in real-time (Cao, 2024; Malicse, 2025).

Indeed, adaptive frameworks have shown benefits in various contexts, such as language learning, engineering education, and cybersecurity talent development (Caratozzolo et al., 2025; Zhang et al., 2025). Importantly, when LLMs are used in personalized assessment systems, they help clarify students' true intentions and any misconceptions they may have, enabling systems to refine their feedback and evaluation measures (Huang et al., 2025). These adaptive and personalized approaches are vastly different from traditional static assessments. They allow learners to evaluate their learning based on changing cognitive states, leading to improvements in motivation, positivity, and retention. However, we must also consider ethical aspects and fairness, particularly in under-resourced situations (Sankaranarayanan, 2025). As adaptive assessment becomes more common, it is seen as a driving force that may reshape assessment practices to be more than mere measurement tools. They could become powerful vehicles for individualized learning.

7 Performance-Based Authentic Assessment: Real-Life Simulations in Virtual Environments

The theory behind performance-based authentic assessments in metaverse contexts mainly relies on Wiggins' (1993) model of authentic assessment. It places assessment within realistic tasks that mirror real-world language use. This approach focuses on evaluating language skills through various meaningful activities instead of isolated tasks (Brown & Hudson, 1998). The virtual spaces created by the metaverse offer new chances for authentic assessment that wouldn't be practical in traditional classrooms. Examples include virtual job interviews, international business meetings, and cross-cultural social interactions (Sykes & Reinhardt, 2013). The theory suggests that authentic assessment in virtual settings helps learners transfer their skills by practicing real communicative scenarios.

The concept of performance-based authentic assessment is rapidly becoming a common practice in education and professional training contexts as it is widely considered to provide a valuable opportunity for learners to apply their knowledge and skills in authentic, real-world situations. Virtual environments (VEs), including those that include immersive technologies such as virtual reality (VR), are an effective site for performance-based authentic assessments. VEs provide learners the opportunity to undertake tasks that resemble those carried out in a real-world setting and therefore offer the best potential for learners to demonstrate their skills, decision-making, and problem-solving dispositions relative to what is required in practice. For example, within teacher education, there is evidence that virtual simulations can help prepare preservice teachers for professional practice classrooms by providing a mirror experience of their placements, thus enabling preservice teachers to enhance their self-efficacy and add a common assessment of teaching (Ersozlu et al., 2021). Likewise, in criminology education, students may use gamified VR platforms, such as CrimOPS, to undertake activities in realistic scenarios as an authentic means of showcasing their ability to apply their knowledge within a crime scene investigation, which engages students and provides opportunities for further engagement and skill development (Gerard et al., 2022). VR simulations in particular have been shown to be effective for assessment purposes for their perceived authentic experience of learners and the manner in which they matched learners' experiences and world logic (Gilbert, 2017).

Performance-based assessments in XR and VR also support integrated and adaptive assessments, where learners' interactions with virtual agents and dynamic systems provide a deeper understanding of their performance (Ziker et al., 2020). Moreover, existing studies reveal that simulations can accurately reflect real-world performance in virtual environments, even in high-stakes or clinical settings. They save time while maintaining their ability to predict outcomes (Greenwood et al., 2016). When designed thoughtfully, the immersive experience creates chances to link theoretical understanding with practice, positioning 21st-century education and training as valuable resources. Thus, real-world simulations in virtual environments represent a significant change in performance-based assessment, enhancing the reliability and relevance.

8 Data-Driven Learning Analytics: Extracting Learning Insights from Metaverse Interactions

Understanding learning in metaverse assessment areas using data relies on theories from educational data analysis and established methods for studying human learning (Ferguson, 2012; Long & Siemens, 2011). This view enables students to grasp their learning process thoroughly through the detailed data generated during their engagement in virtual worlds. It tracks their progress and activities (Baker, Martin, & Rossi, 2016). This process involves collecting various types of data—like where they look, how they move, what they say, and their behaviors—to create detailed profiles for each student (Bienkowski et al., 2012). Importantly, this approach aims to convert raw data into useful information that improves lesson planning and customizes learning opportunities for individuals (Greller & Drachsler, 2012).

The introduction of metaverse technologies into the education sector has allowed for new techniques to collect and examine student data that can provide valuable data for educators/researchers. Many traditional learning analytics approaches struggle to account for the complexity, dynamics, and variety of learning in immersive environments. However, research about data-driven learning contexts in the metaverse can provide insight into all areas of the students' experiences in context. For example, based on their previous work, Song et al. (2024) developed a multimodal learning analysis (MMLA) framework that utilized eye-tracking data and AI-driven conversational agents to study student engagement and self-regulated learning in a metaverse. In a similar manner, Song et al. (2023) designed a visual system on the Learningverse platform that incorporates heatmaps and avatar behavior tracking for the examination of social presence, cognitive presence, and teaching presence to help educators understand patterns associated with engagement.

Text analysis techniques have also been beneficial for surface-level insights into open-ended student focus group responses and other unstructured information. Artificial intelligence in the metaverse education context is also an important consideration. For example, by using ChatGPT within virtual environments, Alfaisal et al. (2024) illustrated how to facilitate personalized learning, multilingual communication, and individual support in real-time and relevant interactions. These intelligent systems map user interactions, adjust strategies, and facilitate not only content delivery but also ongoing learning analysis.

Beyond personal thought processes, data-based methods have expanded to include structural analyses of metaverse systems. Casale-Brunet et al. (2023a) and (2023b) explored using daily transaction data and platform information, applying machine learning in blockchain-based metaverses to study user behavior, virtual land transactions, and social dynamics. This research demonstrates how different data sources in metaverse environments can offer practical insights in both educational and business contexts. Overall, these studies emphasize the considerable potential of data-driven learning analysis in metaverse environments—not just for evaluation but also for enhancing learning through immersive, flexible, and intelligent systems.

9 Social Interaction Assessment Model: Measuring Communication Skills in Virtual Environments

Principles from sociolinguistics and current views on communication skills guide our assessment of social skills in virtual settings. This approach acknowledges that learning a language in virtual worlds involves complex social interactions. It requires us to evaluate aspects such as understanding unspoken signals, cultural background, effective teamwork, and differences in communication (Byram, 1997; Hymes, 1972; Kramsch, 1986). Techniques like dialogue analysis help us assess the quality of social interactions in these environments (Sacks et al., 1974). Ultimately, we want to evaluate not just correct language use but also whether online communication is appropriate, effective, and respectful of different cultures (Crystal, 2001).

The growing interest in virtual environments in health, education, and job training offers new ways to evaluate and develop communication skills. Conventional evaluation approaches, such as interviews, observations, and surveys, often have similar biases and limitations in terms of objectivity and consistency. Virtual reality (VR) systems, on the other hand, offer controlled, repeatable, immersive settings to the evaluator in order to assess both spoken and unspoken communication in real time (Kim & Kim, 2011). These digital tools afford evaluators the opportunity to objectively observe behavior in consistent settings through the simulation of real social situations, and therefore increase the fidelity of evaluation. In mental health, for example, individuals with mental illness, such as autism spectrum disorder (ASD), may benefit from using virtual environments to enhance social communication. Three examples in particular highlight the usefulness of evaluating social communication in VR contexts. Some samples of virtual teamwork environments, administered by evaluators, were reported to map strongly to actual assessments of teamwork (Zhang et al., 2019). Similarly, VR systems that mimicked real-life interactions for autistic children enabled patients, caregivers, and therapists to assess the development of communication skills (Faita et al., 2017).

Moreover, automated systems involving virtual characters have also been developed to facilitate the teaching and measurement of social skills through structured conversations and feedback. For example, an automated social skills trainer addresses communication challenges by generating simulated experiences of communicating with another individual, mirroring traditional models of social skills training (Tanaka et al., 2016). Studies compare where skills may be evaluated in either a virtual modality or a traditional modality. These studies suggest virtual evaluation can be just as reliable as in-person evaluation across a variety of independent studies, while acknowledging participants' preferences for engaging in a traditional modality (VanLangen et al., 2021). Automated systems utilizing machine learning algorithms and real-time behavioral analysis are further advancements that researchers are exploring. For example, eye contact, paralinguistics, and movement can all be captured and evaluated in an interview, to a high degree of fidelity, and predict communicative skill (Rasipuram & Jayagopi, 2018). These developments suggest that virtual worlds are capable of a diagnostic and training role.

Many traditional assessment instruments like the Assessment of Communication and Interaction Skills (ACIS) have been successfully adapted to virtual contexts, generating a standardized approach for assessing social interaction (Forsyth et al., 1999; Kjellberg et al., 2003). The incorporation of virtual patients has been very effective at preparing clinicians for mental health practice, especially in the geriatric context, and has drawn attention to the value of authentic interactions for skill acquisition (Chaby et al., 2022). In an education context, educational technologies are also utilizing virtual models to develop communication skills with teachers and students, a learning opportunity that promotes the use of interpersonal and cross-cultural communication (Volchenkova et al., 2019). These sources indicate a solid foundation of work and flexibility of virtual worlds for evaluating and developing communication skills. In summary, by bringing together immersive technology, artificial intelligence, and behavioural science, we are developing an innovative approach to measuring social interaction and learning about human communication in various contexts.

10 Soft Skills Integration Theory: Parallel Assessment of Language Proficiency and Life Skills

The incorporation of soft skills into the assessment models of the metaverse is grounded in established frameworks for 21st-century skills and competency-based education (Pellegrino & Hilton, 2012; Trilling & Fadel, 2009). This theoretical framework suggests that meaningful participation in virtual worlds requires proficiency in language, as well as skills in analytical thinking, creativity, problem-solving, and working collaboratively. Building on the theories of multiple intelligences (Gardner, 1983) and emotional intelligence (Goleman, 1995), this framework advocates for a rich evaluation that integrates cognitive, emotional, and interpersonal skills, along with language abilities. The intent behind this theory is the intertwining of soft skills development and language acquisition, both of which are essential for successful communication, engagement, and participation in today's digital contexts.

The Soft Skills Integration Theory posits that a fuller and more impactful educative environment can be created by integrating and assessing language skills with critical life skills, commonly termed as soft skills. This integrated model meets the communication demands of the 21st century, in which language serves as a medium for communicating ideas, rather than simply a utilitarian instrument, and becomes a fundamental interconnected facet of cognitive, social, and emotional competencies (Gibb, 2014). Integrating soft skills into language teaching results in marked improvement in both areas, in a range of educational contexts. Take, for example, the effectiveness of implementing Active Learning and Problem-Based Learning (ALASPEM) pedagogical approaches that aim to improve students' oral communication skills, in conjunction with critical thinking, teamwork, information literacy, and creativity. This indicates a robust positive relationship between the two areas of soft skills development and improvements in language ability (Jariyathitinant, 2021). Reports of English language teaching experts in Thailand also indicate the prevalence of simultaneous development of curricula, including soft skills such as interpersonal communication, and adding digital literacy in anticipation of real-world context preparation for students (Boonmoh & Chanchay, 2024).

The research indicates that reading and comprehending experiences can be appropriate for taking on other important non-technical skills through reading and comprehension prospects. Curriculum specialists will be creating courses in oral communication that are clearly identified with life skills, with a focus on analytical reasoning and communication. This practice is based on the frameworks of NACE and P21 (Zuwanda et al., 2021), representing evidence that educational systems can address both objectives of development at once.

Theoretical constructs (attribution and control theories) have some correspondence to support this idea of language for language and personal development. Again, the framework of Kolb (1984)'s experiential learning offers some ability to situate social interactions consistent with the students' definitions of their ability, opportunity for both personal growth and language development (Gibb, 2014). Real outcomes noted by Moroccan engineering schools, beyond developing English language skills, showed the benefits of experiential learning based on Kolb's framework of developing skills critical to the workplace, such as negotiation and leadership (Baahmad, 2025).

The research also indicates that language fluency alone will not support social and professional integration, specifically regarding immigrants' education in Canada. Important dimensions of non-technical knowledge, such as the pragmatic character of communication and understanding culture, are necessary for participation in society (Derwing & Waugh, 2012). Overall, these studies support the fundamental principle of the Soft Skills Integration Theory: non-technical abilities and language competence are interconnected rather than separate areas of development that should be assessed and nurtured together. This approach ensures that students are adaptable, collaborative, and equipped to handle complex real-world communication scenarios alongside achieving fluency in language.

11 Multiple Intelligence-Based Metaverse Assessment: Measurement Approaches for Different Learning Styles

The foundation of Gardner's (1983) model of multiple cognitive capabilities and knowledge of learning styles (Dunn & Dunn, 1993; Fleming & Mills, 1992) suggests that the issue of assessment within the context of a metaverse invites multiple forms of assessment in order to honour the various cognitive capabilities and/or preferences learners bring to the process. Given that virtual environments can engage learners in different ways, this model suggests that virtual environments are form of assessment where learners can invest verbal skills, visual-spatial skills, physical skills, auditory skills, and skills in sociability at the same time, creating a more inclusive and accessible assessment experience (Gardner, 2006). If we consider aspects of universal design for learning (Rose & Meyer, 2002), the objective is access to assessment methods for students with different talents and preferences for learning. The idea is to provide various reasons for participants to demonstrate language acquisition while preserving the fidelity of the assessment.

The integration of Multiple Intelligence (MI) theory with metaverse-based learning contexts presents an excellent opportunity to create more fluid assessment tools that support a range of learning styles. Following the MI framework articulated by Howard Gardner, MI capabilities encompass a range of intelligences comprised of verbal, logical, visual-spatial, physical, auditory, social interactive, introspective, naturalistic, and existential domains of learning. This dimension of MI opens up learning in a variety of ways that advance instructional assessment beyond IQ measures (Tirri et al., 2013). Using immersive virtual reality (VR), AI, and fluid social engagement characters used in metaverse contexts, teachers could then begin to potentially conduct assessment exercises that align with their students' primary intelligences. For example, students with dominant auditory or social capabilities could participate in discussions related to the assessment, while students who are strongest in kinesthetic or hands-on experiences could exhibit learning using the metaverse in simulations that rely on their strengths using sound with avatars or interactive group assessment teams in the virtual environment with avatars (Putri et al., 2022; Solidum, 2022). Current studies provide more evidence supporting the idea that students display diverse cognitive abilities linked to specific learning styles. For example, intrapersonal skill often aligns with individual learning preferences, while interpersonal ability is commonly associated with group approaches. These findings underscore the importance of employing a variety of assessment methods (Qutab et al., & Zareen, 2024; Ridwan, 2018). Understanding student preferences enhances their engagement and success. Educational specialists have started integrating MI-informed techniques to tailor learning opportunities, and the metaverse offers a new and flexible platform for such initiatives (Silva, 2002).

Advancements in technology, such as artificial intelligence, further enhance assessment in metaverse settings. Using interaction data, intelligence-powered avatars and machine learning tools can measure and predict student performance. Research indicates that avatar-mediated simulations effectively assess interpersonal skills by capturing behavioral and emotional signals that traditional assessments might overlook. Additionally, models utilizing electroencephalography (EEG) and neural networks have demonstrated impressive accuracy in identifying learning preferences, showcasing the ability of objective physiological data to inform metaverse assessment tools (Ali & Amin, 2018).

Despite these advancements, there is ongoing debate regarding the evidentiary credibility of MI and learning preference models. It might be argued that teaching based on learning preferences conflated with Gardner's MI theory, often misinterpreted as lacking strong empirical backing and being merely a collection of learning styles rather than a distinct concept. It might be argued that teaching based on learning preferences is often conflated with Gardner's MI theory, which is frequently misinterpreted as lacking strong empirical backing and being merely a collection of learning styles rather than a distinct concept. Nevertheless, the key implication of MI theory, as Gardner emphasizes, is pedagogical diversification—teaching and assessment through various methods—which aligns with the multimodal capabilities of metaverse education. Customized engagement is the end goal (Tirri et al., 2013). Ultimately, the integration of MI theory and metaverse technology presents a compelling model for transforming educational assessment. By including behavioral, cognitive, and physiological measures within immersive environments, educators can better understand and support students' individual learning profiles across multiple styles.

12 Intercultural Competence Assessment: Measuring Cross-Cultural Communication in Global Virtual Environments

The evaluation of intercultural competence (ICC) in metaverse contexts is grounded in established frameworks in communication theory and global citizenship education. This approach incorporates assessment techniques that are suitable for evaluating cultural awareness as well as flexibility and a global frame of reference, given that virtual worlds present new opportunities for intercultural engagement. Drawing on critical cultural awareness theory and intercultural speaker models, this framework assesses learners' capabilities in engaging with cultural differences and mediating among various perspectives. It emphasizes the importance of evaluating not only surface cultural awareness but also deeper intercultural skills so that students are prepared to be global digital citizens in the world.

In the world we live in today, assessing ICC in virtual contexts for educators and institutions has become important. Traditional systems and generic self-assessment tools, which are often anchored in Eurocentric perspectives, have been critiqued for not being able to capture the important nuances of ICC, particularly in North-South education partnerships. New virtual global environments, such as Collaborative Online International Learning (COIL) and Global Virtual Teams (GVTs), intentionally develop intercultural communication skills through cognitive, emotional, and behavioral practices.

In summary, while many virtual exchanges support the development of ICC, successful elements of ICC generally require well-designed program contexts, pedagogically sound practices, and supportive learning eco-systems. Educators, whether trainers or facilitators, often come from different cultures and may not have the necessary knowledge of cultural differences, leading to miscommunication and/or biases in expectations that inhibit student learning. In addition to partly reflecting on their own reflective practices, there remain challenges, such as some students reporting greater anxiety or skepticism about intercultural communication and interactions, as well as some participants reporting that virtual exchanges did not affect their intercultural identities as researchers continue to refine theoretical models of ICC, some lines of inquiry place increasing emphasis on relational dynamics as well as with empathy and contextualized actions. Some aspects of more sophisticated, culturally responsive evaluation practices to support ICC development may be warranted, beyond simple evaluative assessments. For example, evaluations in global virtual exchange spaces should not only assess students' attitudes or knowledge development, but also whether students are able to evaluate and effectively engage in fast-paced, intercultural contexts with respect to their culturally learned social norms or circumstances. Integrating intercultural and soft-skill assessment frameworks within metaverse contexts strengthens the authenticity of language evaluation. Combining Deardorff's process model of intercultural competence with Gardner's multiple-intelligence theory allows educators to capture both cognitive and affective dimensions of communication, thus promoting a holistic understanding of global competence.

13 Discussion

The evaluative methods presented here do a good job of incorporating traditional and innovative, technology-enhanced methods by creating a new paradigm for evaluating language learning in metaverse-enhanced language learning contexts. Immersive assessment is at the heart of the new paradigm of assessment opportunities—from fixed, more traditional assessments that are not connected to communicative contexts to lively assessments that rely on assessment in virtual environments. This includes flexible assessments that are gamified and emphasize theoretical motivational principles like Self-Determination Theory and Flow Theory, in an effort to balance the action of assessment with the action of assessment. Gamified, more immersive assessments lead to less assessment-related stress but also improve overall proficiency outcomes. Although different contexts may provide different findings, these findings show that planning to avoid an overreliance on external rewards is necessary, and gamification holds potential to enhance intrinsic motivation and cognition.

In addition to gamified assessment, the complexity of the competence model allows the assessment opportunities to assess more than linguistic accuracy and include areas like digital literacies, cross-cultural and intercultural awareness, and adaptive capacities, to name just a few.

This corresponds to what contemporary educational frameworks indicate about communication capability, which must be aligned with essential skills for the 21st century. Directly integrating a real-time feedback theory into metaverse environments advances this integrated notion. Based on models of formative feedback, real-time feedback-based design encompasses immediate learning support aimed at closing the gap between performance and corrective behavior, without overloading cognitive resources. Research across domains, including music and debate training, indicates the benefits of immediate, multimodal feedback for enhancing self-efficacy and performing in adaptive ways. Likewise, adaptive evaluation systems and performance-based authentic assessments develop these constructs through personalizing assessments with item response theory and recreating authentic practice. This alignment supports individual learning trajectories and ultimately leads to assessing students' ability and understanding to apply that knowledge in a known, authentic situation. For instance, VR platforms such as VEGS and CrimOPS have shown improved predictive validity and engagement. Similarly, data-driven learning analytics lend support for these assessments by using multimodal integration and artificial intelligence to generate student engagement profiles and instructor intervention across interaction data.

The theory of soft-skills integration and the social interaction assessment model address the interpersonal aspects of metaverse learning through technologies that test the emotional skills, the practical, and collaborative dimensions. That is how global digital communication works. CRETA-like platforms verify and confirm the effectiveness of virtual assessment for controlled environment behavior evaluation. Assessments from multiple intelligences-based perspectives attempt to satisfy multiple preference directions through universal design that accommodates inclusiveness. Process-based frameworks capture strategic competence by giving importance to metacognitive strategies and learning trajectories through interaction logs.

While the chapter provides an extensive synthesis of existing assessment models, a more critical comparison is necessary. For instance, gamified and AI-driven models can be evaluated according to their validity, reliability, and scalability, using criteria derived from language-testing theory. Such analytical positioning transforms the discussion from descriptive to interpretive, clarifying how each paradigm advances or limits assessment practice. Because intercultural competence measurement and AI-based systems address cultural and technological complexities, the modularity framework focuses on adaptability. Learning and evaluation techniques within machine learning combine hybrid formative-summative ways, pouring in constant supervision alongside some accountability through stealth assessment for self-improvement. Metaverse-based portfolio assessments are finally gathered by documenting multimodal artefacts that nurture student agency and reflective practice.

The linked approach offers numerous advantages, including greater authenticity, personalization, and motivation. Nevertheless, there are some challenges. To affirm validity and reliability in an immersive environment, issues such as digital equity, ethical data management, and AI system bias must be addressed. Without first guaranteeing technological access, these methods could be a catalyst to further deepen existing educational inequities. Also, while local policies are evolving, balancing cutting-edge research with established educational principles is something that requires constant analysis to support the practice of these methods within diverse communities and settings.

The comparative Table 1 synthesizes the central features of the three leading assessment models that currently structure metaverse-enhanced language education. Each model rests on a distinct theoretical foundation and measures different dimensions of learner competence. Gamified assessment, grounded in self-determination and flow theories, prioritizes motivation and engagement by integrating elements of play into evaluative processes. Adaptive assessment, derived from item response theory and Vygotsky's zone of proximal development, focuses on cognitive and linguistic development through dynamic task adjustment that personalizes learning paths. Portfolio assessment, informed by reflective learning and digital literacy frameworks, captures process-based creativity and learner autonomy over time. While these models offer complementary advantages—motivation, personalization, and reflection—they also introduce challenges related to reliability, ethical fairness, and workload, highlighting the importance of combining them within a balanced, context-sensitive assessment ecosystem.

Table 1 Comparative overview of assessment models in metaverse-enhanced classrooms

Model	Theoretical basis	Type of competence measured	Advantages	Limitations
Gamified assessment	SDT, flow theory	Motivation, engagement	Reduces anxiety, increases participation	May affect reliability
Adaptive assessment	IRT, ZPD	Cognitive and linguistic ability	Personalised learning paths	Ethical and equity concerns
Portfolio assessment	Reflective learning, digital literacy	Process, creativity	Promotes learner autonomy	Time-consuming

14 Conclusion

On the whole, language assessment within metaverses needs to depart from standard testing. The subtle traits of modern communication skills allow assessment only if creative, flexible, and comprehensive measures are used. Game-based activities and real-time feedback systems are combined with data analytics and cross-cultural assessment to provide a more thorough, reliable insight into language and interpersonal skills. Essentially, this stance argues that preparing students for worldwide, tech-advanced interactions makes it imperative for language assessment to embrace the conscious adoption of these new modalities in virtual learning landscapes. More research and ethical considerations will be necessary to allow metaverse technologies to attain their full potential and thus be able to provide equitable, meaningful, and creative learning opportunities as they unfold.

References

Al-Khresheh, M. H. (2025). The cognitive and motivational benefits of gamification in English language learning: A systematic review. *The Open Psychology Journal, 18*. https://doi.org/10.2174/0118743501359379250305083002

Al-Mansouri, Jamal O. (2024). The impact of real-time feedback on optimizing teachers' classroom teaching pace. *Research and Advances in Education, 3*(11), 45–48. Retrieved from https://www.paradigmpress.org/rae/article/view/1392

Baahmad, Y. (2025). Enhancing soft skills in schools of engineering: The application of the experiential learning theory (ELCT). *Journal of English Language Teaching and Applied Linguistics, 7*(1), 216–229. https://doi.org/10.32996/jeltal.2025.7.1.20

Bachman, L. F., & Palmer, A. S. (1996). *Language testing in practice: Designing and developing useful language tests*. Oxford University Press.

Baker, R. S., Martin, T., & Rossi, L. M. (2016). Educational data mining and learning analytics. In A. A. Rupp & J. P. Leighton (Eds.), *The Wiley handbook of cognition and assessment*. https://doi.org/10.1002/9781118956588.ch16

Belova, A., & Kharkhurin, A. (2024). Analysing the factor structure of the plurilingual and pluricultural competence scale: Dimensionality, reliability, and validity of the adapted Russian version. *International Journal of Multilingualism, 22*, 669–692. https://doi.org/10.1080/14790718.2024.2326001

Bennett, R. E. (2011). Formative assessment: A critical review. *Assessment in Education: Principles, Policy & Practice, 18*(1), 5–25. https://doi.org/10.1080/0969594X.2010.513678

Bienkowski, M., Feng, M., & Means, B. (2012). Enhancing teaching and learning through educational data mining and learning analytics: An issue brief. U.S. Department of Education, Office of Educational Technology.

Black, P., & Wiliam, D. (1998). Assessment and classroom learning. *Assessment in Education: Principles, Policy & Practice, 5*(1), 7–74.

Boonmoh, A., & Chanchay, K. (2024). The integration of soft skills in language learning classroom: The perspective of Thai ELT teachers at a university of technology. *REFlections, 31*(1), 255–274. https://doi.org/10.61508/refl.v31i1.272794

Bower, M., DeWitt, D., & Lai, J. W. (2020). Reasons associated with preservice teachers' intention to use immersive virtual reality in education. *British Journal of Educational Technology, 51*(6), 2215–2233. https://doi.org/10.1111/bjet.13009

Brown, J. D., & Hudson, T. (1998). The alternatives in language assessment. *TESOL Quarterly, 32*(4), 653–675. https://doi.org/10.2307/3587999

Butler, D. L., & Winne, P. H. (1995). Feedback and self-regulated learning: A theoretical synthesis. *Review of Educational Research, 65*(3), 245–281. https://doi.org/10.2307/1170684

Byram, M. (1997). *Teaching and assessing intercultural communicative competence.* Multilingual Matters.

Caratozzolo, P., Chans, G. M., & Dominguez, A. (2025). Editorial: Continuing engineering education for a sustainable future. *Frontiers in Education, 10,* 1629507. https://doi.org/10.3389/feduc.2025.1629507

Cao, H. (2024). Development and application of an online autonomous learning platform based on artificial intelligence. In *Proceedings of 2024 4th International Conference on Mobile Networks and Wireless Communications (ICMNWC)*

Canale, M., & Swain, M. (1980). Theoretical bases of communicative approaches to second language teaching and testing. *Applied Linguistics, 1*(1), 1–47.

Casale-Brunet, S., Chiariglione, L., & Mattavelli, M. (2023a). Exploring the data of blockchain-based metaverses. In *2023 IEEE International Conference on Metaverse Computing, Networking and Applications (MetaCom)* (pp. 109–113).

Casale-Brunet, S., Mattavelli, M., & Chiariglione, L. (2023b). Exploring blockchain-based metaverses: Data collection and valuation of virtual lands using machine learning techniques. *Digital Business, 3*(2), Article 100068. https://doi.org/10.1016/j.digbus.2023.100068

Casanova-Mata, I. (2023). Enhancing English acquisition: Effects of among us game-based gamification on language competence, motivation, attention, and attitude towards the English subject. *Education Sciences, 13*(11), 1094. https://doi.org/10.3390/educsci13111094

Chaby, L., Benamara, A., Pino, M., Prigent, E., Ravenet, B., Martin, J.-C., Vanderstichel, H., Becerril-Ortega, R., Rigaud, A., & Chetouani, M. (2022). Embodied virtual patients as a simulation-based framework for training clinician-patient communication skills: An overview of their use in psychiatric and geriatric care. *Frontiers in Virtual Reality, 3.*

Chapelle, C. A., & Voss, E. (2016). 20 years of technology and language assessment in *Language Learning & Technology. Language Learning & Technology, 20*(2), 116–128. https://doi.org/10.64152/10125/44464

Chau, L. T., & Choi, K. C. (2025). AI personalized language learning application. In *Proceedings of the 2025 6th International Conference on Computer Engineering and Application (ICCEA 2025)* (pp. 1393–1398). Institute of Electrical and Electronics Engineers.

Clark, R. C., & Mayer, R. E. (2016). *E-learning and the science of instruction: Proven guidelines for consumers and designers of multimedia learning* (4th ed.). Wiley.

Crystal, D. (2001). *Language and the internet.* Cambridge University Press.

Davison, S. M. C., Deeprose, C., & Terbeck, S. (2017). A comparison of immersive virtual reality with traditional neuropsychological measures in the assessment of executive functions. *Acta Neuropsychiatrica, 30*(2), 79–89.

Deardorff, D. K. (2006). Identification and assessment of intercultural competence as a student outcome of internationalization. *Journal of Studies in International Education, 10*(3), 241–266. https://doi.org/10.1177/1028315306287002

Derwing, T., & Waugh, E. (2012). Language skills and the social integration of Canada's adult immigrants.

Deterding, S., Dixon, D., Khaled, R., & Nacke, L. (2011). From game design elements to gamefulness: Defining "gamification." In *Proceedings of the 15th international academic MindTrek conference* (pp. 9–15). ACM.

Dunn, R., & Dunn, K. (1993). *Teaching secondary students through their individual learning styles: Practical approaches for grades 7–12.* Allyn & Bacon.

Ersozlu, Z., Ledger, S., & Hobbs, L. (2021). Virtual simulation in ITE: Technology driven authentic assessment and moderation of practice. In T. Chaudhary (Ed.), *Authentic assessment and evaluation approaches and practices in a digital era: A kaleidoscope of perspectives* (pp. 39–58). Brill. https://doi.org/10.1163/9789004501577_003

Everard, G., Burton, Q., Van de Sype, V., et al. (2024). Extended reality to assess post-stroke manual dexterity: Contrasts between the classic box and block test, immersive virtual reality with controllers, with hand-tracking, and mixed-reality tests. *Journal of NeuroEngineering and Rehabilitation, 21*(1), 36. https://doi.org/10.1186/s12984-024-01332-x

Faita, C., Brondi, R., Tanca, C., Carrozzino, M., & Bergamasco, M. (2017). Natural user interface to assess social skills in autistic population. In *Virtual, Augmented and Mixed Reality* (pp. 144–154). Springer.

Ferguson, R. (2012). Learning analytics: Drivers, developments and challenges. *International Journal of Technology Enhanced Learning, 4*(5–6), 304–317.

Fleming, N. D., & Mills, C. (1992). Not another inventory, rather a catalyst for reflection. *To Improve the Academy, 11*(1), 137–155.

Forsyth, K., Lai, J., & Kielhofner, G. (1999). The Assessment of Communication and Interaction Skills (ACIS): Measurement properties. *The British Journal of Occupational Therapy, 62*(2), 69–74.

Gardner, H. (1983). *Frames of mind: The theory of multiple intelligences*. Basic Books.

Gardner, H. (2006). *Multiple intelligences: New horizons in theory and practice*. Basic Books.

Gee, J. P. (2003). *What video games have to teach us about learning and literacy*. Palgrave Macmillan.

Gerard, F. J., Mentzelopoulos, M., Economou, D., Khalish, Z., Ingram, J., & Ashley, E. (2022). Work-in-progress—CrimOPS—Gamified virtual simulations for authentic assessment in criminology. In *2022 8th International Conference of the Immersive Learning Research Network (iLRN)* (pp. 1–3).

Gibb, S. (2014). Soft skills assessment: Theory development and the research agenda. *International Journal of Lifelong Education, 33*(4), 455–471. https://doi.org/10.1080/02601370.2013.867546

Gilbert, S. B. (2017). Perceived realism of virtual environments depends on authenticity. *PRESENCE: Teleoperators and Virtual Environments, 24*, 322–324.

Giglioli, I., Parra, E., Cárdenas-López, G., Riva, G., & Raya, M. A. (2017). Virtual stealth assessment: A new methodological approach for assessing psychological needs. In *International Conference on Universal Access in Human-Computer Interaction* (pp. 1–11). Springer.

Godwin-Jones, R. (2022). Partnering with AI: Intelligent writing assistance and instructed second language acquisition. *Language Learning & Technology, 25*(1), 42–54. https://doi.org/10.64152/10125/73474

Goleman, D. (1995). *Emotional intelligence: Why it matters more than IQ*. Bantam Books.

Greenwood, K., Morris, R., Smith, V., Jones, A.-M., Pearman, D., & Wykes, T. (2016). Virtual shopping: A viable alternative to direct assessment of real-life function? *Schizophrenia Research, 172*, 206–210.

Greller, W., & Drachsler, H. (2012). Translating learning into numbers: A generic framework for learning analytics. *Educational Technology & Society, 15*(42), 42–57.

Hattie, J., & Timperley, H. (2007). The power of feedback. *Review of Educational Research, 77*(1), 81–112.

Hong, K. (2025). The development of a metaverse-based instructional model for enhancing university students' field practice competencies. *Korean Association For Learner-Centered Curriculum And Instruction, 25*(3), 291–308. https://doi.org/10.22251/jlcci.2025.25.3.291

Huang, M., Ma, J., & Bo, S. (2025). Design and implementation of a multi-level personalized teaching framework based on LLM. In *Proceedings of the IEEE International Conference on Educational Technology*.

Hymes, D. (1972). On communicative competence. In J. Pride & J. Holmes (Eds.), *Sociolinguistics* (pp. 269–293). Penguin Books.

Imron, A., Budi, B. S., & Mujayanah, S. (2024). Measuring the impact of gamification on motivation and English language learning outcomes: A case study. *INATESOL Journal, 1*(1). https://doi.org/10.30587/inatesol.v1i1.8936

Jariyathitinant, P. (2021). The integration of soft skills in English language teaching and learning through AL-ASPEM. *Psychology and Education Journal, 58*(2), 1234–1241.

Kumaresan, V., Jeyakarthic, M., & Devi, M. et al. (2025). Personalized AI-driven online education technologies for adaptive learning and cognitive skill enhancement. In *Proceedings of the 7th International Conference on Intelligent Human-Computer Interaction.*

Johnson, R. M. G. (2014). *In touch with the wild: Exploring real-time feedback for learning to play the violin* (Doctoral dissertation). University College London.

Johnson, R. M. G., Linden, J. V. D., & Rogers, Y. (2011). Real-time feedback for learning the violin. In *Proceedings of the 25th BCS Conference on Human-Computer Interaction* (pp. 535–538).

Jones, D. (2014). Reading students' minds: Design assessment in distance education. *Journal of Learning Design, 7*(1), 27–39.

Keiding, T. B., & Qvortrup, A. (2014). Feedback as real-time constructions. *E-Learning and Digital Media, 11*(2), 191–203.

Kim, J.-J., & Kim, J. (2011). Virtual reality-based assessment of social skills and its application to mental illnesses. In *Virtual reality* (pp. 105–116). IntechOpen.

Kjellberg, A., Haglund, L., Forsyth, K., & Kielhofner, G. (2003). The measurement properties of the Swedish version of the assessment of communication and interaction skills. *Scandinavian Journal of Caring Sciences, 17*(3), 271–277.

Kocadere, S. A., & Çağlar, Ö. Ş. (2015). The design and implementation of a gamified assessment. *Journal of e-Learning and Knowledge Society, 11*(3), 85–99. https://doi.org/10.20368/1971-8829/1070

Kolb, D. A. (1984). *Experiential learning: Experience as the source of learning and development.* Prentice Hall.

Kourtesis, P., Collina, S., Doumas, L. A. A., & MacPherson, S. E. (2020). Validation of the Virtual Reality Everyday Assessment Lab (VR-EAL): An immersive virtual reality neuropsychological battery. *Journal of the International Neuropsychological Society, 27*(2), 181–196.

Kramsch, C. (1986). From language proficiency to interactional competence. *The Modern Language Journal, 70*(4), 366–372.https://doi.org/10.2307/326815

Laksanasut, S. (2025). Gamification in ESL/EFL education: Transforming language learning and teaching through play. *TESOL and Technology Studies, 6*(1), 16–29. https://doi.org/10.48185/tts.v6i1.1562

Li, C., Fryer, L. K., & Chu, S. K. W. (2024). Utilising gamified formative assessment to support English language learning in schools: A scoping review. *Innovation in Language Learning and Teaching, 19*(3), 1–17. https://doi.org/10.1080/17501229.2024.2352789

Long, P., & Siemens, G. (2011). Penetrating the fog: Analytics in learning and education. *EDUCAUSE Review, 46*(5), 30–32.

Ma, X. (2025). Gamified EFL ınstruction: Empirical evidence for enhanced language proficiency, learner motivation, and ıdealized bilingual ıdentity. *Journal of Research in Vocational Education, 7*(3), 55–63. https://doi.org/10.53469/jrve.2025.7(03).13

Malicse, A. (2025). How AI can implement the universal formula in education and leadership training. *PhilPapers.*

Muttaqin, M., Zuhdi, H., & Ridwan, R. (2025). The use of gamification-based Duolingo application in increasing student motivation is reviewed from the theory of self-determination. *Al-Wijdan: Journal of Islamic Education Studies, 10*(1). https://doi.org/10.58788/alwijdn.v10i1.5844

Parsons, T. D., McPherson, S., & Interrante, V. (2013). Enhancing neurocognitive assessment using immersive virtual reality. In *2013 1st Workshop on Virtual and Augmented Assistive Technology (VAAT)* (pp. 27–34). IEEE.

Pellegrino, J. W., & Hilton, M. L. (2012). *Education for life and work: Developing transferable knowledge and skills in the 21st century.* National Academies Press.

Peters, S., van der Meulen, M., Zanolie, K., & Crone, E. (2017). Predicting reading and mathematics from neural activity for feedback learning. *Developmental Psychology, 53*(1), 149–159.

Piaget, J. (1977). *The development of thought: Equilibration of cognitive structures.* Viking Press.

Prabakaran, R., Patrick, H. A., & Kareem, J. (2025). Enhancing English language proficiency and digital literacy through metaverse-based learning. *Journal of Information Technology Education: Research, 24*, 1–20. https://doi.org/10.28945/5484

Prensky, M. (2001). *Digital game-based learning*. McGraw-Hill.
Putri, L. A., Deviyanti, R., & Suningsih, S. (2022). Teacher's perception of multiple intelligence. In *Proceedings of the Universitas Lampung International Conference on Social Sciences (ULICoSS 2021)*.
Qutab, L., Raza, A., Tabbassum, R., & Zareen, S. J. (2024). An investigation to study the relationship of multiple intelligence and students' learning styles. *Pakistan Journal of Humanities and Social Sciences, 12*(1), 123–135. https://doi.org/10.52131/pjhss.2024.v12i1.1924
Rasipuram, S., & Jayagopi, D. (2018). Automatic assessment of communication skill in interview-based interactions. *Multimedia Tools and Applications, 77*(14), 18709–18739.
Ridwan, A. (2018). The investigation of students' multiple intelligence to assess their learning style.
Rose, D. H., & Meyer, A. (2002). *Teaching every student in the digital age: Universal design for learning*. ASCD.
Sacks, H., Schegloff, E. A., & Jefferson, G. (1974). A simplest systematics for turn-taking. *Language, 50*(4), 696–735.
Sankaranarayanan, L. S. (2025). The global AI framework: Navigating challenges and societal impacts. *AI & Society*. https://doi.org/10.1007/s00146-024-02070-3
Shaik, S. S. (2024). Developing communication proficiency. *International Journal of Advanced Research*. https://doi.org/10.21474/ijar01/18829
Shute, V. J. (2008). Focus on formative feedback. *Review of Educational Research, 78*(1), 153–189.
Silva, D. E. (2002). *Teachers' handbook for implementing learning styles through multiple intelligences*.
Solidum, O. S. G. (2022). Multiple intelligence and learning styles. *Timor Leste Journal of Business and Management, 4*.
Song, Y., Cao, J., Tao, L., & Gašević, D. (2023). A holistic visualisation solution. In *International Conference on Computers in Education*.
Song, Y., Tao, L., Deng, H., & Fu, J. (2024). Developing a multimodal learning analytics approach. In *International Conference on Computers in Education*.
Sweller, J. (1988). Cognitive load during problem solving. *Cognitive Science, 12*(2), 257–285.
Sykes, J. M., & Reinhardt, J. (2013). *Language at play: Digital games in second and foreign language teaching and learning*. Pearson Education.
Tanaka, H., Sakriani, S., Neubig, G., Toda, T., Negoro, H., Iwasaka, H., & Nakamura, S. (2016). Teaching social communication skills through human-agent interaction. *ACM Transactions on Interactive Intelligent Systems, 6*(2), 1–26.
Terbeck, S., Case, C., Turner, J., Spencer, V., Bacon, A., Howard, C., & Howard, I. (2022). Assessing reactive violence using immersive virtual reality. *PLoS ONE, 17*(5).
Thorne, S. L., & Smith, B. (2011). Second language development theories and technology-mediated language learning. *CALICO Journal, 28*(2), 268–277.
Tirri, K., Nokelainen, P., & Komulainen, E. (2013). Multiple intelligences: Can they be measured? *Psychological Test and Assessment Modeling, 55*, 438–461.
Trilling, B., & Fadel, C. (2009). *21st century skills: Learning for life in our times*. Jossey-Bass.
VanLangen, K. M., Sahr, M., Salvati, L. A., Meny, L. M., Bright, D., & Sohn, M. (2021). Viability of virtual skills-based assessments focused on communication. *American Journal of Pharmaceutical Education, 85*(8), Article 8378.
van der Linden, W. J., & Glas, C. A. (Eds.). (2010). *Elements of adaptive testing*. Springer.
Volchenkova, K., Evsina, E., Elsakova, R., Serebrennikova, E. V., & Batina, E. (2019). Mastering interpersonal and virtual communication skills. In *2019 International Conference "Quality Management, Transport and Information Security, Information Technologies"* (pp. 648–652). IEEE.
Vygotsky, L. S. (1978). *Mind in society: The development of higher psychological processes*. Harvard University Press.
Wainer, H. (2000). *Computerized adaptive testing: A primer* (2nd ed.). Lawrence Erlbaum Associates.

Wiggins, G. P. (1993). *Assessing student performance: Exploring the purpose and limits of testing.* Jossey-Bass.

Zhang, L., Lu, W., Zhao, Y., Yuan, W., & Zhai, L. (2025). Integrating IRT and knowledge graphs for the selection of cybersecurity talent. In *2025 28th International Conference on Computer Supported Cooperative Work in Design (CSCWD)* (pp. 2430–2435). IEEE. https://doi.org/10.1109/CSCWD64889.2025.11033228

Zhang, L., Weitlauf, A., Amat, A. Z., Swanson, A., Warren, Z., & Sarkar, N. (2019). Assessing social communication and collaboration in autism spectrum disorder using intelligent collaborative virtual environments. *Journal of Autism and Developmental Disorders, 50*(1), 199–211.

Zhang, Z., & Crawford, J. (2023). EFL learners' motivation in a gamified formative assessment. *Education and Information Technologies, 29*, 6217–6239.

Ziker, C., Ydo, E., Zapata-Rivera, J. D., Hillier, M., & Casale, M. (2020). Special session – Challenges and opportunities for assessment in XR. In *Proceedings of the Immersive Learning Research Network Conference* (pp. 421–423).

Zuwanda, M. E., Sumarni, S., & Sulistyaningrum, S. (2021). Designing life and career skills-integrated speaking syllabuses. *SAGA: Journal of English Language Teaching and Applied Linguistics*

Volkan Duran is working at the Iğdır University. Dr. Volkan Duran is an Associate Professor at Iğdır University, Türkiye. His research focuses on applied linguistics, educational psychology, and foreign language education, with a particular interest in the integration of artificial intelligence, cognitive science, and optimisation algorithms into teaching and learning processes. He has contributed extensively to the fields of scale development, psychometrics, and mixed-methods research, especially in areas related to reasoning styles, transcendent thinking, and meta-university frameworks. Dr. Duran has served as an editor and reviewer for international journals and book projects, including volumes on AI-driven education, cultural immersion innovations, and digital twin applications in learning environments. His work often bridges theory and practice by developing interactive teaching modules, agent-based modelling platforms, and curriculum designs that align with national education standards. In addition to his scholarly publications, Dr. Duran is engaged in collaborative projects with global scholars across linguistics, psychology, physics education, and computer science. He actively mentors young researchers and contributes to international conferences, reflecting a commitment to advancing interdisciplinary approaches in education and science.

Yaşar Barut serves at Ondokuz Mayıs University, Faculty of Health Sciences, Department of Child Development. His academic expertise spans child development, educational psychology, and counselling, with a strong focus on psychological guidance and developmental education. He has authored more than 200 publications, including contributions indexed in Web of Science and Scopus, and his research has received considerable international recognition with citations across multiple databases. His academic impact is reflected in H-index scores in Web of Science, Scopus, Google Scholar, TrDizin, and Sobiad. In addition to his scholarly work, he has supervised graduate theses, coordinated national projects, and contributed to interdisciplinary collaborations. His work reflects a dedication to advancing psychological counselling, child development, and educational practices, and he continues to play an active role in both national and international academic communities.

Cultivating Critical Thinking and Creativity in Metaverse-Based Language Teaching: The CREATE–MBLT Framework

Hayriye Avara

Abstract The use of immersive environments for language education presents new ways of interacting with one another and working together; yet, it does not ensure the development of critical thinking and creativity, unless there are explicit instructions and intention behind the tasks within the platform designed to foster inquiry and interpretation by the learner. If the assignments direct participants toward visualization without providing sufficient structured inquiry, students may be limited in their ability to justify their interpretations. In the CREATE-MBLT paradigm, this difficulty is addressed by including students in the metaverse, moving from the original observation through a collaborative interpretation, then a creative production, and finally ending in reflective critique. The experience of moving through the five phases of Curiosity Activation, Immersion in Inquiry, Collaborative Ideation, Creative Production, and Critique and Reflective Revision builds on each previous phase, enabling progressively deeper interpretive engagement. Users communicate with one another in shared spaces through avatars. Learners are given opportunities to express themselves in multiple ways, which should make meaning-making easier. In this way, the students can demonstrate their capacity for critical thinking and creativity by observing, relating, supporting, and revising their interpretations of the environmental signs and the discussion. The theory and research that inform the framework within this chapter examine the immersive environment for its properties in stimulating creativity and critical thought in language learning. It places particular emphasis on task design, facilitation, as well as assessment/measurement in relation to these components. Additionally, the creative process is treated as a disciplined process of inquiry that deepens a learner's knowledge of a subject. The CREATE-MBLT theory identifies immersive language acquisition as a site of disciplined interpretive exploration rather than an area strictly concerned with the act of expression.

H. Avara (✉)
Amasya University, Amasya, Türkiye
e-mail: hayriyevara@gmail.com

F. Çelik and C. Yangın Ersanlı (eds.), *Metaverse-Based Language Learning and Teaching*, English Language Education 49,
https://doi.org/10.1007/978-3-032-31366-9_8

Keywords Critical thinking · Creativity · Metaverse-based language teaching · Immersive learning · Dialogic inquiry · Collaborative meaning-making · CREATE–MBLT framework

1 Introduction

The current approach to teaching foreign languages has created a complex environment combining language, culture, and technology, thereby requiring students to be adept at understanding meaning through many different mediums. Today's foreign language student has to interact with multiple text types, video, digital, and social networking sites to derive their understanding from many different sources, all with their own meanings and layers of symbolic and nuanced meaning, making it a difficult process to find a common ground across the multiple perspectives found on these different platforms. They will also need to navigate through a large amount of evidence and opinion, and develop their own conclusions from multiple perspectives. Consequently, critical thinking has migrated from an enrichment to a core component of competence. Viewing it through this lens, critical thinking involves more than simply analyzing data; it also includes examination of the implications of an individual's surroundings or environment by looking for clues that inform context. In addition, to make logical judgements based on the evidence collected, learners will also need to assess and evaluate the differing opinions and positions surrounding that information and how that information will ultimately impact their understanding of the subject matter (Zhang & Zou, 2022).

While the use of immersive environments in language learning has increased the avenues available for both interaction and multiple means of expression, there currently does not exist an established sequence of inquiry-based pedagogical practices within these immersive environments that supports the measured development of critical thinking via the systematic interpretation of evidence. Additionally, no principled methodology exists that will allow creative thinking to develop, build and improve upon creative thought and its representations, as opposed to continuing to be an unstructured, undefined form that has always been the case in traditional language class environments. To address this issue, CREATE-MBLT provides a pedagogical model based on research from immersive language education, inquiry-based pedagogies, teamwork, creativity and reflective practices as well as practitioners' observations of their classrooms. As a synthesis of ideas rather than an empirical study, the CREATE-MBLT Framework serves as a source for creating pedagogical frameworks for future research regarding language teaching in the metaverse.

Metaverse education provides an opportunity to learn languages in new ways due to its capability of enabling users to walk through shared virtual environments, use avatars as representational tools, and manipulate symbolic objects for the construction of meaning. The way learners process and reason through all of the different symbols and spaces around them is reflective of the processes they use to find their way within an environment, to place themselves in the space, and to create relationships with those objects. Thus, their decisions regarding where they place items, what routes they take, and how they depict those things with symbolic behavior are indications of not just their thought processes, but also of how they interpret their surroundings (Lan, 2020). A student's ability to demonstrate comprehension is not only through what they say, but through how they relate with things in their environment. For example, the way in which a student may adjust their avatar's lighting depending on the way they feel may differ from the way another student might adjust their props in order to indicate that they want to create some distance between themselves and a story when telling. This provides a greater opportunity to encourage engagement for students; however, if the students' tasks do not specifically encourage them to ask questions, justify their interpretations, and revise their claims with the evidence they collected, there is a chance that the systems of engagement will evolve into a performance-based assessment.

Therefore, in order to promote language learning in a manner that supports the culture of the metaverse, the tasks that students perform must be engineered with a focus on engaging students through observation, comparison, reasoning, reflection and adaptation. The role of the teacher will be a transition from one of solely presenting students with facts, to one in which the teacher is a facilitator, encouraging the student to generate their own questions and design experiences that guide the students in their thinking and, therefore, sus2021tain their engagement with the content. In this context, while developing critical thinking, the learning environment should use a structured process, rather than relying on one that is designed to transfer an individual skill (O'Dowd, 2021; Wells, 1999). While emerging research suggests promising connections between immersive environments and creative thinking development, the empirical evidence base for metaverse-based creative and critical thinking instruction remains limited. Most available evidence comes from small-scale studies or pilot programs. As this area develops, larger-scale comparative studies and longitudinal investigations will be essential to establish effective practices for cultivating higher-order thinking skills in metaverse contexts.

This chapter presents the CREATE-MBLT framework as a five-phase design for creating immersive learning in the metaverse, through which students can work through an iterative process, developing curiosity, inquiry, collaborative interpretation, multimodal representation, and critical thinking. The CREATE-MBLT framework does not consider the metaverse to be a fast track for language learning, but rather to be an open forum for students to collaboratively create, question and transform meaning, using conversation, cultural exchange and collaborative thinking. The overall goal of the CREATE-MBLT framework is to liberate the immersive learning process from the boundaries created by performance metrics, and replace them with a model of learning based on collective knowledge, rational evidence and explanation of context.

Thus, the purpose of this chapter is to discuss how the CREATE-MBLT framework may help students develop their thinking about language learning in the metaverse through a review of existing research on learning, interpretive reasoning, multimodal meaning making, and intercultural reflection and develop the CREATE-MBLT framework as an example of how critical thinking can be considered a socially situated, embodied, and reflective practice. Additionally, this chapter outlines the CREATE-MBLT framework and provides examples of pedagogical principles necessary to keep inquiry alive in the metaverse. The CREATE-MBLT framework should not simply be viewed as a new or exciting technology in the field of education, but as an environment where meaning is established, expressed and judged. The literature review presented below provides a critical examination of all dimensions of the CREATE-MBLT framework.

2 Literature Review

Creating an immersive, metaverse-like environment for use within the foreign language classroom opens up many different avenues of research. These include the sensation of presence experienced through virtual environments, the interactional dynamics associated with social engagement, as well as the encouragement of critical thought, multifaceted bodily-enacted comprehension, and the subtleties of intercultural/ethical interaction. Collectively, these areas of study suggest that the immersive nature of the environment can facilitate learner engagement with the content; however, unless the design of the educational experience compels learners to engage in inquiry, conversation, logical reasoning, and contemplation, such immersion risks being merely an exercise in description without authentic or critical connections to any substantive content. This section focuses specifically on key areas of research which are linked closely with the CREATE–MBLT framework.

2.1 Presence, Co-Presence, and Interaction in Immersive Environments

According to Shadiev and Yang (2020), a sense of presence is crucial for enhancing engagement, reducing communication anxiety, and promoting interaction through shared experiences within an immersive learning environment. With the use of avatars representing individuals, learners are able to adopt personas for purposes of showcasing their identity and exploring digital worlds. Through using an avatar to represent their identity or achieve a goal, learners may be more willing to express their ideas and use their foreign language in interactions. According to Lan (2020), students that feel uncomfortable interacting with others in real-life scenarios may feel more comfortable communicating through avatar-mediated interactions using virtual reality. The combination of the physical distance between themselves and the avatar, as well as the ability to visually represent themselves through the avatar's body language, can alleviate some of the stress associated with communication.

Research suggests that simply having access to immersive environments will not cause students to engage cognitively; without meaningful tasks, they will typically explore the environment passively. Therefore, teachers must provide both experiential and assignment-based learning in immersive learning environments to help students move beyond passive observation to active means of interpreting and justifying observations. To illustrate, through the collaborative development of authentic virtual worlds, students work together to refine their interpretations and engage with one another more critically (Makransky & Mayer, 2022). This provides greater opportunities for students to collaboratively engage with one another and use higher-order thinking skills than would be present if they were engaging only with themselves (Makransky & Mayer, 2022). Therefore, when students work together in virtual environments (using avatars) as collaborative teams, they can see, hear, feel, and experience the images and physical components of the virtual environments they will be creating, rather than only viewing them on-screen. Additionally, they can discuss, think critically, and work together on these virtual components, collaborating with teammates within those components (Radianti et al., 2020) to create and encourage deeper levels of learning rather than simply providing an immersive guided experience in the environment.

The Curiosity Activation and Immersion in Inquiry phases of CREATE-MBLT aim to make this transition from passive observation through some form of active interpretation or meaning-making possible by providing learners with experiences that support both forms of learning.

2.2 *Critical Thinking as Interpretive and Dialogic Practice in Language Education*

For a long time, critical thinking has been considered an aim; nonetheless, the role that it plays in language training has changed depending on the circumstances. Numerous educational systems, as reported by Zhang and Zou (2022), highlight the importance of communication competence. However, true critical thinking involves a greater level of complexity than just the ability to communicate; it requires learners to analyse and assess arguments, identify the underlying assumptions of those arguments, evaluate competing evidentiary sources and provide a rational basis for their conclusions (Zhang & Zou, 2022). There is a tendency for those capacities to develop most robustly when learners are seen as co-constructors of meaning rather than passive vessels for information (Wells, 1999). Through co-construction, learners have access to others' perspectives, enriching their understanding.

As "dialogism" in language education promotes collaborative communication over one-way transmission, dialogical communication involves active listening, feedback, and stakeholder awareness. Dialogic approaches to instruction maintain that learners' understanding deepens when they encounter a range of explanations and must justify why they accept or modify a claim (Byram, 1997). In a language learning environment, it is incumbent upon educators to devise assignments that provide opportunities for students to be exposed to multiple and valid interpretations of an object. This leads to the possibility of a discussion about a particular scene, event or venue, and can lead to several interpretations arising from the discussion. Learning occurs through the examination of these interpretations and how closely they match the facts that have been provided.

The term "critical thinking" does not denote an independent generic transferable skill, in other words, critical thinking does not automatically transfer from one environment/context to another. Stimulating or enhancing an individual's critical thinking is enabled through the process of structured dialogue within a framework where multiple interpretations or interpretations of the same event are evaluated and challenged. Universal instruction on 'how' to think critically will not have the same benefit. This is in line with the CREATE-MBLT model that advocates for providing a framework for students, rather than telling them what to think or how to think.

Importantly, critical thinking does not occur with every task in a language class, but rather becomes integral to specific tasks. Learners, when viewed as interpreters in their negotiations of meaning, are able to apply evidence in their engagement, rather than just memorising facts. Subsequently, this application of evidence is an integral part of the process of engaging critical thought into the development of communication. This transformation occurs more readily in an environment where everyone shares a common understanding and has access to directly observed experiences. By using the community experience to determine validity, learners gain firsthand experience in the ability to support their claims, and can consider multiple possibilities based upon what they have witnessed. Thus, thinking becomes a collaborative process of negotiating meaning amongst individuals rather than being an isolated process of an individual.

2.3 Multimodal Representation and Embodied Meaning-Making

The concept of meaning in the Metaverse is dynamic and continuously being created as the environment, and the way to create meaning within that environment shifts with the user's gestures or movement to a different viewpoint, the use of avatars, and the use of symbols when interacting with the environment through the use of multimedia sources (Kress & van Leeuwen, 2001). Through the changing and remaking of the environment, the user creates meaning from experiences the same way that people use to form spoken sentences. Research on multimodal sense-making has shown that visual and spatial cues can produce a range of interpretations (Kress & van Leeuwen, 2001).

According to Lin and Lan (2015), when learners do not have an opportunity to describe their choices in creating a representation of an idea, they will typically produce only an expressive and not an analytical piece of creative work. The authors contend that encouraging learners to engage in multimodal production through structured reflection can assist students in understanding the rationale for their innovative decision-making process. Thus, for educators, the goal is to encourage output while firmly linking the construction of the output to the deeper cognitive layers of understanding. This requires the learners to explain why they placed certain elements where they did; why they chose certain light, symbols, and organization; and how they conceptualized their relationship between symbols and image placement or between the physical attributes of their materials and spaces. In order to help learners create a framework for understanding, they should be guided in stages through a structured design framework. This involves brainstorming the idea and then developing a prototype (the building stage), then providing the learner with an opportunity to review the work through a feedback loop (the iterative phase).

Although VR language learning can be explored through research, the instructional supports that guide learners to reflect on their own reasoning when creating a visual representation of their language learning are overall absent from most studies related to virtual reality language learning (Lin & Lan, 2015). Without prompting to justify their reasoning, many learners create beautiful images but are lacking the logical reasoning for the creation and thus are weakly based. Therefore, the educational objective should be to create a fusion of representation and explanation for the student, helping them understand how spatial constructs, symbols, and physical gestures affect their interpretation of the material, thus allowing for reflection and discourse on the thought process instead of being mechanical in their process of creation. The primary aim of the Creative Production stage within CREATE-MBLT is to combine the use of representation and analysis.

2.4 *Embracing Intercultural and Ethical Interpretation in Immersive Contexts*

Immersive settings require us to deal with the issues of representation and identity, and there are ethical implications in their complexities. In class, students are regularly asked to play a role or create a representation that does not correspond directly to their real-world experience.

Role-play and cultural representation activities have great potential to foster empathy among learners, but they can also inadvertently reinforce stereotypes if they are not critically examined. In order to avoid this issue, learners should receive explicit guidance for analysing the underlying assumptions contained within their own cultural representations (Byram & Wagner, 2018).

Research in communication indicates that learners develop critical cultural awareness when they analyse the cultural artefacts and the meaning attached to them, and when they examine the ways their own pre-existing biases affect their interpretive decisions (Byram, 1997). Since the transfer of meaning often occurs through pathways, whether or not language is used, immersion in an environment enhances that transfer. For example, by placing a sign within a scene, the sign's relationship to its neighbouring objects may indicate a hierarchy, reverence, or marginalisation of that sign. Students are then able to use this information to create representations that are guided by the feedback they receive during a structured critique.

The ethical aspect of the CREATE-MBLT framework is created through the integration of understanding and reflective judgement. Therefore, critical thinking functions as both a method of analysis and a channel for developing moral and intercultural responsibility. In the context of cross-cultural understanding, the learner not only has to recognise different symbols or situations, but also needs to consider how the construction and exchange of meaning is affected by their depiction of the material they create. When students take time to reflect on how their cultural background influences how they see and interpret their surroundings, immersive spaces will no longer serve only as environments for occupying a point of view but rather as laboratories for investigating perspective. Consequently, critical thinking extends beyond the capacity to conduct analysis and includes the moral and intercultural element of judgement and emphasises that the responsibility for the interpretation and enactment of meaning is embedded in the creation of culture. In the Critique and Reflective Revision Phase of the CREATE-MBLT Model, the ethical aspect is explicitly addressed as students examine not only the cultural assumptions related to how they have represented information but also the cultural assumptions they have made in their own representational decisions.

2.5 *Embodiment, Identity Positioning, and Social Presence*

Research indicates that avatars can influence learners' feelings of identity and agency; how the learner sees themselves as an individual, their relationships with others, and their willingness to engage in risk-taking behaviours while communicating in the target language. The construction of meaning in a shared virtual environment can be viewed as a product of the integration of both bodily structures and verbal language. The avatar's posture and movement, closeness and spatial alignment carry communicative weight and significance that goes beyond that of spoken words (Lan, 2020). Learning occurs through activities whereby learners create and interpret meaning and communicate those interpretations to others. The distance between avatars indicates emotional tension or emotional implications associated with the interaction of the avatars. The embodiment of avatars increases the range of tools within the language-learning experience by increasing the range of the representation of the language-learning experience beyond spoken utterances.

The process of creating personalized avatars in a virtual reality language learning environment has recently become an area of study. Past research on virtual reality language learning indicates that learners' avatar identities influence how willing they are to engage with others in the target language and to perform new discourse functions using their avatars (Lin & Lan, 2015). Because avatars are stages for self-presentation, many students assume different physical postures than what they do in the physical classroom. These shifts in physical posture may result in the formulation of new viewpoints, alternative discourses, and new narratives and accounts of the experiences of the students. By selecting their avatars, students view themselves in ways that demonstrate their views of the world; therefore, it is important for educators to create an environment where students can think about what they have chosen to represent themselves, as this information can assist to define their identity and values more completely than words will ever be able to.

The CREATE-MBLT model views embodied expression as a means to engage in reasoning through embodied interaction with others. Through the act of placing their avatar, and co-existing within the same virtual space, learners communicate both emotionally and symbolically, rather than solely through language. The physical aspect of the creation of meaning forms a basis for the development of new ideas, based on a common, concrete experience, rather than through abstract verbal description only. This intertwining of embodied expressions of thought and reasoning nurtures the development of new ideas because it supports the building of new ideas using interpretations of experiences based in a shared physical context, rather than building on linguistic abstraction. The CREATE-MBLT framework incorporates the knowledge of avatar design and spatial positioning through the use of creative production, whereby evidence of interpretive reasoning is evidenced by embodied choices made while creating.

2.6 Shared Interpretation and Collective Reasoning Dynamics in Metaverse Spaces

Through immersion, students engage in collaborative meaning-making by using digital environments, or "metaverse environments". For instance, students can have debates in a metaverse environment such that those debates unfold spatially instead of merely verbally; thus providing students with a break from typical classroom conversation. Designed scaffolding protects against misunderstandings while providing opportunities for students to compare and juxtapose different perspectives as a framework for collaborative thinking (Lan, 2020). Collaborative thinking includes observing, proposing, defending, and refining ideas. As students pick up cues, all of their interpretations are contextually driven. Thus, multiple students can concurrently 'scan' the same environment but each produce different readings of the same perceptual cue. The process of exchanging readings produces cognition and provides insight into how an idea or proposal is becoming developed. In these types of environments, reasoning, interpretation, and meaning-making all play pivotal roles in the cognitive processes utilized to produce collaborative thinking.

The design of the virtual environment determines the way the user interprets the events happening and will influence the perceptions they have about the way the virtual world is laid out (Kress & van Leeuwen, 2001) by taking into consideration all the spatial configurations, the sequencing of the events, and the location of the avatars. An immersive environment can alter the configuration of the environment, provide symbolic cues, and change the presentation of an avatar, revealing nuances that cannot be expressed in static prose. This fluid dynamism enables learners to make their judgments on the fly and thus convert opaque reasoning into visible and adaptable reasoning; therefore, readings created as a result of the dialogues occurring in immersive environments are subject to critique and adjustment. From this perspective, critical thinking is a mechanism for refining and developing ideas rather than merely problem-solving in a linear manner.

Research has demonstrated that simply pairing students does not guarantee they will arrive at a shared interpretation of an event. If a guided-inquiry scaffold is not provided, it is often the case that students will coordinate with each other without pausing to consider how their actions relate to the significance of the task assigned to them. Makransky and Mayer (2022) assert that most students approach their assignments as if they were mainly concerned with simply completing their courses, rather than working on developing the cognitive skills needed to understand the material being taught. As a result, the educational challenge is to create an environment that supports collaboration between learners by providing opportunities for students to discuss, clarify, and reflect on their ideas. Therefore, it is important for students to explore how the cues they receive impact their statements, revisit multiple times the material being studied, and contemplate how their choices of representation influence the meaning of the material being studied.

Since any metaverse experience requires reasoning, educators rely on scaffolding to assist their students to develop their understanding of the ideas being studied. The rich capabilities of metaverse environments allow participants to collaboratively co-create meaning while also providing opportunities for digital exploration and inquiry. Therefore, the CREATE-MBLT paradigm is designed to encourage critical thinking by integrating curiosity, inquiry, comparison, and reflection, creating critical-thinking skills and resources. CREATE-MBLT offers an innovative approach in their Collaborative Ideation Phase. This phase organizes the way individuals interact and develop ideas together, allowing the growth of new understanding through discussion instead of simply completing a task as a group.

2.7 *Reflective and Metacognitive Insight in Immersive Learning Settings*

As research continues to grow, it has become apparent that immersive learning spaces can enhance the students' awareness of their own interpretation of the material as they are prompted to reflect in an immersive environment (Makransky & Mayer, 2022). A key component of reflection is embedding it within the process of creating meaning, rather than treating it separately after the fact. Through the process of reflecting, students can examine the underlying assumptions that shaped their reading and begin to explore other possible interpretations of the text. In order for students to develop critical cultural awareness, which means understanding how culture, power, and position affect meaning-making, they need to engage in the process of meta-cognitive reflection (Byram, 1997; Byram & Wagner, 2018). Thinking in a given context involves pulling apart the symbolisms or narrative strands of a piece of text and evaluating how the choices a student made in creating the representation of the text can influence how others perceive and understand that piece of text.

Lan (2020) argues that experiential anchors serve as a bridge between the task at hand and learners' engagement through a tangible, observable aspect of the environment. Deliberately created experiential anchors facilitate how learners seek and process feedback while completing the task. When the learner's experience is derived from observations of the physical world, it serves as an anchor that keeps learners engaged in the project or task by keeping them focused on what physically exists and is observable in the immediate environment, thereby reducing distractions from other stimuli. The task acts as the interpretive framework that directs learners to complete the task as it was designed.

Thus, CREATE-MBLT includes the integration of the Critique and Reflective Revision stage, which encourages students to process how their representational choices can shape other people's interpretations of the text. Ultimately, identifying the underlying beliefs that shape how people interpret texts is more important than attempting to find a "correct" interpretation. The focus is on developing an understanding of the processes by which meaning is created through textual analysis, rather than judging interpretations based on whether they are deemed appropriate.

2.8 How Scaffolding and Teacher Mediation Shape Immersive Critical-Thinking Contexts

Learners do not necessarily process information cognitively when they are fully engaged with their environment with their senses. Without any structured activities or teacher-directed mediation, learners will likely respond to what they experience rather than understand and interpret it; thus, while they move through an immersive environment, they may not comprehend what they are seeing or doing (Makransky & Mayer, 2022). In the absence of an instructional framework to guide learners in the processing of their immersive experiences, learners remain in a surface-level engagement, resulting in a fragmented and shallow level of engagement; hence, they are unable to develop an authentic interpretive understanding of their immersive experiences (Makransky & Mayer, 2022). The Instructional Strategy (Mediated Learning) provides students with a framework to articulate, rationally defend, and continually refine their claims based on the stimuli of their immersion experience through iterative refocus and adjustment. The incorporation of mediation strategies within Metaverse-based language courses provides scaffolding for learners through such strategies as suggestion, sequential cognitive phases, and reflective, conversational analysis. Instructor-influenced mediation strategies are shown to assist learners in distinguishing how immersive environments create meaning for them. According to Zou et al. (2023), structured social interaction prompts within a technology-enhanced language learning environment have been shown to have positive impacts on learners' ability to communicate effectively with others; in this case, learners must be able to explain their reasoning for why they believe what they do, justify their interpretations, and react to the interpretation(s) of other learners. The result of these activities is that the learners will be able to process the content they have read and heard in a more critical way (Zou et al., 2023). Evidence from studies conducted into the use of Virtual Reality for Language Learning supports this idea of encouraging learners through focusing their tasks towards an experience. By providing students with VR immersive environments which contain various ambiguous or multi-layered messages or cues, they allow for the development of multiple interpretations and deter them from jumping to conclusions (Lan, 2020).

Research on immersive VR confirms that learners lacking structured scaffolding often struggle to engage collaboratively with unfamiliar symbolic or spatial cues (Makransky & Lilleholt, 2018). A traditional first step in creating an instructional strategy for guided interpretation is to gradually release images for learners. Doing so allows students to begin to process the information over time, creating time and space for adjustment. At the same time, Lan (2020) describes a pedagogical practice of moving from simply observing information presented, to forming some sort of feasible hypothesis about that information, and then, finally, providing a meaningful justification for the hypothesis they have formed. In most cases, students learn something similar to what they think they have learned via mediated instruction by their teachers. Çakıroğlu and Kılıç (2023) state that the mental models constructed by learners are directly influenced by the quality of instruction received from their teachers. Specifically, when teachers possess strong pedagogical content knowledge and express themselves clearly, learners are better able to develop accurate mental representations of the tasks being taught to them.

By creating opportunities for students to compare and contrast various cultural perspectives, educators help their students raise their awareness of different cultures. The value systems and biases that students apply to intercultural interactions are primarily invisible, but they become apparent when students are asked to compare their experiences to those of others in comparative dialogue (Byram & Wagner, 2018). Language teaching should provide students with organised ways in which to critically self-reflect upon their interpretive lens and on how they view and engage in intercultural contexts.

Recent findings on how best practice should be followed for scaffolding within immersive environments indicate that scaffolds must not be constructed using a predetermined instructional sequence. Instead, scaffolds need to be designed and utilized in an intuitive manner, using data gathered from learner activity and feedback as a means of assessing what supports are required (Wang et al., 2024). Additionally, cognitive scaffolding is a critical element of iteratively developing thinking processes as students explore their hypotheses and refine ideas in metaverse-based learning environments. The design of scaffolding also provides opportunities for learners to ask questions in real time and models the reasoning behind decisions made.

Mediation should take precedence based upon the clarity of the concepts that are delivered to users to avoid the users of immersive environments interpreting the immense amount of imagery contained in immersive environments as fulfilling their need to make sense of an experience within an immersive environment (Makransky & Lilleholt, 2018). When scaffolding provides learners with structured opportunities to compare and reflect, they will notice patterns of significance across different types of sources and experience an increased level of conceptual understanding (Çakıroğlu & Kılıç, 2023). In order to effectively mediate student learning experiences when using immersive technology, educators must have knowledge of how to teach and an understanding of how to use the technology. This knowledge and understanding cannot be taken for granted and must be developed through a structured development programme (Çakıroğlu & Kılıç, 2023; Lee & Wu, 2024). Learners will generally be able to form meaning from overlapping experiences that take place in the same immersive environment by comparing between those experiences, rather than through instructional means. According to Lan (2020), observing the way peers navigate and represent meaning in a collaboratively built, virtual space enables learners to discern the meaning of choices they make as they navigate this space, including how the choices they make with respect to spatial design and symbols relate to interpretation.

During the Critique and Reflective Revision phase of the CREATE-MBLT model, students connect their observations of the immersive environment to the analytical interpretations they create based on those observations (Makransky & Mayer, 2022). Structured discourse role frameworks may promote learners' ability to use regulatory thinking in research (Zhou et al., 2024). Within a process of ideation, the roles of interpreter proposer and alternative perspective challenger can serve as tools that help learners engage in responsible conversation rather than just descriptive language and should thus provide both initial and ongoing opportunities to think critically. Lastly, learners can use immersion to expose the shared values that create common ground across cultural groups.

3 Theoretical Foundations

The CREATE-MBLT Framework is based on four different theories: sociocultural theory, dialogic reasoning, distributed and embodied cognition, and reflective and ethical reasoning. All of these philosophies converge on the notion that critical thinking does not develop through the repetitive practice of cognitive skills in isolation from the environment or others but rather develops through collaborative meaning-making in which people create, question, and revise their interpretations collectively.

Immersive learning environments provide a multimodal- involving multiple ways to communicate and process information- shared space for learners who then create, question, and revise their understanding of the world using language, non-verbal communication (e.g., body language), use of space (e.g., body placement), and symbols (e.g., written text, art, etc.) as they negotiate meaning with each other. Therefore, the CREATE-MBLT framework represents thinking as a collaborative interpretive process continually shaped by how people interact with their environment and one another, not as a sterile abstract skill that can be applied uniformly to every setting.

3.1 Sociocultural Theory and the Co-Construction of Meaning

Sociocultural theory indicates that learning consists of a process of developing knowledge resulting from collaborative participation of different cultures with various tools, not just through an exchange of information from one mind to another (Wells, 1999). As a tool for thought and a basis for interpreting information, language provides learners with a way to give meaning to their thoughts, compare and contrast ideas or points of view, and reach agreements on what is intended by the other person. In a virtual environment, as an example of the metaverse, the various forms of mediation used are not solely in the use of language, but also through physical actions such as positioning a learner's avatar, controlling physical characteristics of the objects in their virtual environment, and configuring their surroundings (Lan, 2020). With the assistance of all of these forms of mediation, learners have the opportunity to bring their ideas out in the open so they can participate and build upon those ideas together.

Consider how learners form groups around an object, build a large image of a symbol, or line up their avatars either side by side or at a distance from each other; each of these configurations reflects a particular way of creating meaning. Through the experience of placing their avatars in various positions while working together as a group, learners create a communal visual representation of their ideas and thoughts, enabling them to work collaboratively on the development of one another's thoughts and ideas. As noted previously, scaffolding for learners helps them understand these types of mediation through their experiences and provides them with a clear understanding of where and how they will create meaning when they work in a community.

3.2 Dialogic Reasoning and the Encounter of Interpretive Perspectives

As dialogic theory posits, dialogic understanding is achieved by having our own perspectives challenged through exposure to and negotiation of the multiple divergent viewpoints of others (Byram, 1997; O'Dowd, 2021). Critical thinking involves more than stating a position but requires weighing different pieces of evidence, considering alternative viewpoints, and modifying the learner's point of view based on the evidence available. While engaging in dialogue, dialogic reasoning occurs when learners have a visual-spatial reference system to base their thinking upon, thus eliminating ambiguity and linking their perspective to what is observable.

The educators' situational context anchors learners' viewpoints in terms of their immediate environment and provides them a tangible means to express the significant gaps between each other's interpretations. This will allow them to avoid abstract arguments, instead relying upon their immediate location along with the repeating symbols and narrative elements which are visible to them all, to refer to when communicating and negotiating their differing interpretations. Having this common reference point provides a foundation for a justification-based reasoning style, where learners support their claims rather than merely state them. The Collaborative Ideation stage in the CREATE-MBLT model puts into practice the idea of collaboration in terms of its ability to assist learners in developing new ideas about topics they are investigating through paired discussions about two different interpretations of their ideas.

3.3 Distributed and Embodied Cognition in Immersive Learning

Research in the area of Embodied Cognition indicates that thought is generated internally, and that it is influenced by external factors such as the learners' environment, tools, and bodily presence (Lan, 2020); therefore, these external factors have great ramifications for how students create meaning when engaged with three-dimensional (3D) virtual worlds. When they interact with others within a 3D virtual world, they use their avatars to communicate. The embodiment of their avatars allows thoughts to be represented visually. The physical presence of their avatars allows them to display their thoughts through their positioning, movement, and actions. The representation of their avatars can also allow for individual representation; for example, an avatar's distance from another can signify differing levels of emotional connection between them. Conversely, the movement and manipulation of avatars can indicate where the avatar's physical focus is shifting within the conversation.

These two types of avatar movement (moving apart from others or using parts of an object to manipulate and rotate them) can indicate how learners are thinking and what they are feeling about each other, their partner, and the object. Thus, the CREATE–MBLT process situates the avatars' physicality within the creative production phase, the point in time when they create a structure for creative expression. The Creative Production and Critique phases of the CREATE-MBLT framework are largely based on this ability to re-evaluate and develop the physical manifestation of mental processes. This phase of the framework is where students will take a pathway of reasoning through the final stage and make their reasoning visible. From there, students will have the opportunity to put their reasoning to the test in a structured manner.

3.4 *Reflective and Ethical Reasoning in Intercultural Interpretation*

Assumptions, values and previous experience constantly play a role in how every interpretation is made; therefore, each interpretation will be impacted by these varied influences. The idea of communicative competence means that all interpreters need to develop an insight into their culture by analysing the manner in which meaning is constructed and how selecting different representations can affect the understanding of that meaning. Some environments may intensify this dynamic because cultural signs are very often incorporated into the spatial/visual design (unknown to the reader) of that environment (Byram, 1997).

It is important to consider what placing the cultural symbol at the centre of the learners' design represents to the viewer. Viewing their cultural symbol located in the centre may demonstrate that they are placing great value on this symbol or it could also indicate to the viewer that this symbol holds a higher position than all other symbols surrounding it. If that cultural symbol is at the very edge of the design, this may signal to the viewer that the cultural symbol has been marginalised (Byram & Wagner, 2018). The CREATE-MBLT framework includes cultural awareness as a component in the Critique/Reflective Revision part of the process. In this context, the learner can reflect on how each of their own interpretative decisions affects the final product. Further, learners may also investigate other possible interpretations for the same "symbol" and reflect on how those different forms may evoke either an alternative or additional meaning or interpretation of the same symbol. Through this process, learners must not only reflect on what they did through the many different steps of the creation process, but must also practice how they would interpret a work from another culture (as part of an overarching ethical practice).

3.5 *Synthesis*

Through these lenses, the four perspectives on theory discussed in this chapter share a common notion of learning as being inherently social, embodied, dialogic and reflective. Through sociocultural understanding, meaning is created through collaborative participation. The means used to participate in learning are mediated through social relations, including the use of tools and environments (Wells, 1999). According to Byram (1997), dialogical reasoning allows students to create a deeper knowledge construct through the interaction of diverse perspectives. Instead of simply sharing knowledge, dialogical reasoning allows students to test their interpretations against the perspectives of others and reshape their beliefs by doing so. Distributed cognition and embodied cognition take these ideas one step further by asserting that cognition is not just the result of mental thought processes, but is also a result of the physical experiences associated with cognition and the interaction of a learner's body with the physicality of the world (Kress & van Leeuwen, 2001; Lan, 2020). Lastly, reflective and moral reasoning grounds all of these processes in the understanding that learning and interpretation are culturally biased and affect learners' ability to effectively evaluate their experiences and make decisions based on those experiences (Byram & Wagner, 2018).

All four perspectives exist within the context of the previous three, establishing an argument for collaboration, which creates an opportunity for dialogue; dialogue provides a context in which to see reasoning; embodied action provides an opportunity to make reasoning "real" by physically engaging with it; and reflection gives learners the potential to assign meaning and interpretative understanding to their experiences. The CREATE-MBLT Framework was designed as a pedagogical response to this convergence of theoretical perspectives. Each of the proposed elements, Curiosity Activation, Immersion in Inquiry, Collaborative Ideation, Creative Production and Critique and Reflective Revision, is derived from at least one of the theoretical principles and will be used to demonstrate the processes of collaborative construction through critical self-evaluation. CREATE-MBLT views the underlying principles of its theory not just as an influencing factor in the context of the overall design, but also as key to helping learners to engage meaningfully at all levels throughout their learning journey.

4 The CREATE–MBLT Framework

The CREATE–MBLT model is a framework for teaching and learning through a series of experiences that guide students through a progressive learning journey from initial observation, through exploration and collaboration, culminating in the creation of new products based on their knowledge and understanding. The model consists of five interconnected elements (see Table 1): (1) Activate Curiosity, (2) Immerse in Inquiry, (3) Collaborate on Ideation, (4) Create a Product, and (5) Critique and Reflective Revision. The sequential development of each phase provides a structured pathway for learners to transition from observation into evidence-based interpretation and ethical reflection. Creativity is also emphasized as a disciplined process involving the creation of new ideas and products through teamwork and collective brainstorming.

Within immersive language learning, the primary obstacle is that the environment will not determine how well, or how deeply, a learner will be able to engage in interpretive communication. The immersive environment serves to enhance the learner's focus on tasks within that environment and allows for expanded options for expressive communication; however, an immersive experience in an environment will not automatically help in cognitive processes that are required for either analytical reasoning or reflective judgement.

Instead, the CREATE-MBLT Framework provides learners with a structured path for progressing through a series of phases of engagement and interpretation of concepts and ideas, ultimately to enable them to re-evaluate their interpretations using concepts and ideas encountered previously within the metaverse. Each phase of engagement will build the learner's interpretive skills in increasing intensity, and

Table 1 CREATE–MBLT phases and pedagogical focus

Phase	Primary thinking focus	Creativity focus	Typical evidence/output
Curiosity activation	Notice patterns; suspend premature closure	Generate questions; imagine multiple possibilities	Observation notes; exploratory prompts
Immersion in inquiry	Link claims to observable cues; build hypotheses	Explore alternatives; test 'what if' readings	Evidence-based explanations; annotated cues
Collaborative Ideation	Justify, compare, refine interpretations dialogically	Co-create options; re-combine ideas	Reasoned dialogue; alternative readings
Creative production	Make reasoning visible through multimodal representation	Design symbolic/ spatial representations	Scenes, artifacts, layouts, avatar choices
Critique and reflective revision	Evaluate coherence, ethics, and evidence; revise	Iterate and improve representations	Peer critique; reflective commentary; revised product

the initial engagement phases of the CREATE-MBLT Framework provide the basis for developing the perceptual and conceptual skills required for interpreting future documents and materials and developing the reasoning ability necessary to create an informed opinion on anything related to language.

4.1 Activating Curiosity

In the first stage of inquiry, learners are encouraged to observe and derive multiple meanings or interpretations, rather than being expected to provide a specific analysis immediately. They are invited to simply watch, observe, and experience the environment in which they find themselves, to look at its layout, its symbols, and to notice anything unusual or out of place without trying to give a specific interpretation to what they see. During this experience, students develop an exploratory and not a judgmental mindset; therefore, curiosity grows when there is an inkling of an explanation but it is not yet defined. In being asked to hold off on defining meaning and interpretation during this initial phase, learners can maintain a larger view of the discovery process and not limit their understanding or insights too early in the process. This initial phase of inquiry serves as a foundation for learners to build their understanding based on reflective thought; therefore, students will be able to develop their inquiry based on an analytical and careful consideration rather than by guessing. The ability to observe openly and to be naturally curious serves as the foundation of an evidence-based inquiry process that will occur in the next phase.

4.2 *Diving Deep into Inquiry*

Students start to adopt an interpretive perspective, and develop an initial hypothesis of how: what is physically in the environment; the relationship between things, and what the environment physically communicates to people, each of which contributes to meaning. They have to move from just naming what is in the environment, to connecting that to its interpretive significance. The development of what is seen, is the first part of the process for students to create meaning, and then to create meaning through consideration of what all of these elements suggest. The main part of developing interpretive meaning requires that students' interpretations be based on physical evidence in their environment. The environment will influence their understanding of meaning. The role of the instructor is to provide support for inquiry while refraining from offering any conclusions so that students can choose their own paths for further investigation. By asking learners open-ended questions the instructor encourages them to provide justification for the reasoning used but does not provide answers. Evidence collected at this point is commonly in annotated observations or verbal explanations of the learner's view of what the environment is providing. Once students can use observable evidence to validate the interpretation of an event, they can then begin testing those interpretations against the interpretations and opinions of others in collaborative discussions.

4.3 *Co-creative Conceptualization*

The third phase of making sense of things allows for social interaction and discussion. Here, learners can express their thoughts and then compare them to each other to see how they hold up in conversation. All people in the metaverse space have an identical starting point when putting forward ideas, which makes it easy for everyone to see how the ideas relate to each other. Because they use the same information and common vantage point, there is greater accountability for people when making interpretations, since every interpretation must go back to evidence from the environment.

During brainstorming, emphasis is placed on logical reasoning versus simply agreeing to agree. The goal during this stage is not necessarily to agree with one another but to develop a learner's ability to make an informed decision by comparing different ways of interpreting the same thing according to the way that each person's interpretation holds up when contrasting it with all others' interpretations or to see if they can support or eliminate each other.

As participants craft their arguments, they will begin to understand their own beliefs and preconceived notions regarding the way of interpreting something. The participants are also engaging in conversation in a more productive way, which allows them to notice where their interpretations overlap with other participants' and to also better identify the arguments and justifications currently being used in the discussions. This approach fosters what is often referred to as "creative accountability," or the idea that the representation of ideas is not limited to a learner's own personal opinion; it is also subject to evaluation and reassessment based on how people view that representation collectively. After engaging in collaborative discussions with peers to create and justify their understanding of a topic, students no longer think an idea is simply an idea; instead, they will have created a product based on their personal expression of that topic using physical mediums.

4.4 Creative Production

In this step, learners transition from thinking of something conceptually to creating it physically or digitally. The artefact created does not only demonstrate creativity but also indicates a learner's thought processes (through their choice of space, symbols selected, and the way they represented the concept). By taking the time to create something based on their thoughts, the learner shows how they have understood the material studied. As such, meaning is conveyed not only through language but also through intentionality when designing an artefact using various forms and spaces along with their associated symbols. In the last phase, the visible representation of reasoning will now be the focus of critical review.

4.5 Critique and Reflective Revision

At the closing phase, an audit of the assembly of the representation, including the interpretive point of view, is made. Reflection should be made at this stage to determine whether the representation effectively communicates the desired meaning as well as to consider whether the representation clarifies, obscures, or conceals any point of view. The reflection stage directs attention to the concept of responsibility. In other words, all produced representations have cultural, relational, and ethical implications. The revision stage does not involve correcting mistakes but instead, an opportunity to gain deeper insight into the representation and the interpretive point of view which produced it. In this respect, the scope of reflection is broadened; at this point, the learners are able to see that interpretation is a continuous process that goes through several stages before reaching the final product. The five interconnected phases create a cohesive and unified process where every step is required and cannot be separated from the entire process.

4.6 Conceptual Coherence of the Framework

The CREATE-MBLT Framework relies on the interconnectedness of each stage to maintain consistency throughout its various stages. Curiosity inspires an initial perception; that perception leads to inquiry, followed by interpretive reasoning, which then informs collaborative ideation (i.e., developing ideas with others) through interaction that helps to further develop an idea. Creative production allows for the 'making of' the concept and critique and revision allow the participants to emphasize responsibility for their interpretation. Therefore, each stage sets up the next one. For example, when curiosity is skipped, it affects the efficacy of the inquiry; if no inquiry is made, collaboration will suffer, and so on. Finally, learners' interpretive awareness develops progressively through their experiences with CREATE-MBLT, not in a linear sequence from beginning to end, but rather as a continuum, as there will be reflections upon each of the progressive experiences along the continuum. Interpretive awareness will only develop through reflective experiences.

4.7 The Framework as Pedagogical Orientation

The structure of the CREATE-MBLT framework is important not only in terms of its ability to create conditions for collaborative meaning-making, but in terms of how the framework supports the learning process. The framework provides the instructor with multiple methods to support learner engagement through methods that create opportunities for developing interpretive awareness. In this manner, interpretation becomes an active process for learners to construct, articulate and critique their own interpretations, rather than just following the instructor's direction. The Metaverse will not simply be a stage on which to present interpretations but will also serve as a collective forum where learners can present their interpretations and participate in collaborative meaning-making. Under this model, immersive learning becomes a space for developing nuanced and deliberate interpretations and critical analysis of language in order to support the purpose of continued cultural enrichment and reflective engagement through language learning.

5 Pedagogical Implications

Developing the CREATE–MBLT framework into an institutionalized method of learning requires a structured approach to teaching that incorporates immersive interaction with reasoning development. The metaverse, with its potential for new interactions and multiple modes of representation, is an attractive platform for teaching through; however, technology and the functions that it provides will not guarantee that students will think critically. The primary factor enabling the students to become deeply engaged in their learning is related to how inquiry is organized and mediated by opportunities to engage in discourse and scaffolded reflection. In the succeeding sections, how instructional planning and practices that facilitate students' opportunities to continually participate in and develop interpretive engagement in immersive language learning environments will be discussed.

5.1 Designing and Facilitating Interpretive Engagement in Metaverse-Driven Language Learning

In the CREATE-MBLT framework, instruction is the priority, and the instructional design comes before technology. Although the metaverse offers the setting, utilizing learning scaffolds such as the order in which tasks are completed, reflective questions posed, and the sequencing of learning tasks is what allows learners to really get involved critically with their learning. While the metaverse can function as a space to argue about what meaning is, it is ultimately the instructional design that determines if learners will skim the surface of the meaning or really delve into it. Therefore, teachers must guide students on where their attention should be focused, the order of inquiry steps to follow and how to support students as they cultivate and develop their ideas.

In addition, the order of tasks is critical. The five-stage framework moves students from observation through joint investigation, then representation to reflection. In the initial assignments, observation is where the main focus of students should be so they can develop a list of the most significant points, opposing viewpoints and metaphorical meanings they find in the immersive environment. Curiosity is an essential motivation for the process of inquiry; thus, the learner's need for time and distance from their observations is required for complete reflection on their experiences before being influenced to form specific inferences. Collaborative exposition and comparative analysis should occur after the inquiry: skipping the order of steps provides students with insight but does not help develop substantial theoretical constructs.

Another goal of the CREATE-MBLT is to help students build their ability to have structured reasoning conversations by communicating through speech and listening to each other with an emphasis on logical reasoning rather than emotional reasoning. When people reason together and have discussions, they are likely to achieve a higher level of critical thinking. Classrooms that promote this approach frequently require students to alternate between listening and speaking to legitimatize their claims, support them with evidence and assign comparison tasks to show how differences exist among readings or interpretations of the same visual evidence. The metaverse provides an environment for argumentative structures based on observable behaviours so that participants can see their differences and build reasoning based on their interpretations rather than only opinions.

Furthermore, assessment methods should reflect the purposes of the CREATE-MBLT framework. Evaluations should include the scaffolding of choice used by learners to represent their understanding and the artefacts they created and manipulated within a virtual setting. While revising work, rubric-based evaluations may help measure how clearly learners articulate their position, the relationship between the form of their representation and its intended meaning, how receptive learners are to contradictory information, and how deeply defined their viewpoint is. Participation in reflective commentary, dialogic exposition and comparative critique gives students an opportunity to express their interpretations and provide evidence for their choices.

The instructor has a critical role within the CREATE-MBLT framework. Instead of being the sole bearer of interpretations, instructors have the opportunity to stimulate curiosity and reflection by asking students to slow down in their thinking, to explore what they read and to challenge the long-held beliefs they have developed. While helping to develop this curiosity and reflection, the instructors assist in converting the metaverse from being primarily an individual performance environment into one where collaboration can take place to create and recreate culturally aware meanings.

5.2 *Illustrative Classroom Snapshots and Facilitation Strategies*

The CREATE-MBLT framework is based on a systematic ordering of the inquiry and layering of supports so that learners can express their rationale for their interpretations. Real-life scenarios provide examples of how sequencing inquiry, thought, and multimodal representations can maintain cognitive depth, while allowing the learner to create their own meaning from them through a gradual empowerment.

An immersive environment for critical thinking can provide students with the impetus to increase their awareness of fine detail in a given environment. Students may be asked to map connections, decode symbolic themes, or assess the emotional character of an animated cultural market area, a historically important street scene, or a co-produced narrative world. At this point, the learner moves from a focus on perceiving objects to an interpretive analysis of all the objects' components and how they collectively provide meaning. Research on VR language learners has demonstrated that this shift is essential to achieving greater levels of engagement and is considered a critical factor contributing to success when using immersive environments for foreign language studies (Lin & Lan, 2015). By asking, "What do you notice that may influence how people feel in this environment?" the instructor has made the intentional decision to delay the learner's conclusion until the learner has had sufficient time to examine the details.

The second scenario describes how the instructor can lead the learners in coming to conclusions after they have made their observations. In this phase, students will typically be working in small groups to explore how various cultures and societies view the world around them. The instructor's role is to guide the conversation of the group so that their interpretations are supported by evidence and not merely by opinion. Lan (2020) demonstrates that when a learner is responsible for producing an output based on collaborative thought and collaboration, a teacher-student construct of learning evolves into a genuine dialogue, resulting in deeper learning outcomes.

The instructor may prompt the students to create multimodal depictions of their learning after several readings (or experiences). A variety of modifications are available for teams to use in order to visually represent their ideas and produce new forms of communication. In addition to this ability, modifying or changing an avatar provides the opportunity for teams to use the information created through these visual representation approaches to create a more comprehensive understanding of the meanings or interpretations that their team members have regarding the text or artifacts associated with the team members.

Zhou et al. (2024) support this method of using peer feedback (in real time or through an avatar) to motivate students to reflect on their interpretation and improve their understanding. In this process, the instructor plays an essential role by providing prompts for students to take a new perspective and become aware of other ways to represent ideas. For example, when prompted with "What did you change in your scene?" students are asked to consider how the decisions they made in creating it, influenced the way people viewed it, and when prompted with "How do you think someone from a different cultural background would interpret this?" students are challenged to develop interpretive empathy, the ability to step out of a learner's viewpoint and see how meaning can be viewed differently from another person's point of view (or another culture). The combination of student interaction with peers through feedback and structured questioning allows students to move from descriptive interpretations of their work toward critical, culturally-informed interpretation as described in the Critique and Reflective Revision phase of CREATE-MBLT.

Reflective practice is based on the idea of the learner developing a representational sensibility. This is the learner's awareness of how they create meaning- through selecting different forms, symbols, spaces- for others to interpret what they create (Kress & van Leeuwen, 2001). Creating does not mean we automatically become aware of how our representation will be received and understood. Learners need the opportunity to step back from their creation, to reflect on it as communication and not simply as self-expression. Learners are guided to think beyond, "What does my representation show?" and consider what it communicates, to whom, and from what cultural position. Asking these questions promotes the development of critical self-awareness and, ultimately, distinguishes genuine interpretive practice from unreflective production (Byram & Wagner, 2018).

Therefore, the CREATE-MBLT framework provides students with opportunities to investigate the use of the method in creating multimedia representations within immersive environments. It is a process whereby students start with observation of details and then continue to create tentative hypotheses and develop the co-creation of meaning and ultimately complete a reflective appraisal of their ability to create a range of interpretations and have an awareness of the ethical ramifications of the representation of their thinking in multimodal environments.

5.3 *Challenges and Limitations of Implementation*

Although the CREATE-MBLT model is designed to be flexible with the context of the teaching and learning situation, the effectiveness of the CREATE-Method depends, somewhat, on conditions (i.e., teachers may require the time and training to develop the skill sets necessary for the dialogue and engagement that is expected to take place in immersive environments). According to research, educators need to have access to structured professional development and supportive mentoring to support them in developing confidence in successfully facilitating both critical conversation and the interpretive interactions required by immersive learning contexts (Lee & Wu, 2024). Factors such as metaverse access and technical stability will both play a role in determining students' effective use of the CREATE-MBLT method, and students have varying levels of comfort with using avatars, multimodal representations, and participating in critique of each other's work. Although these limitations do not detract from the effectiveness of the CREATE-MBLT framework, they indicate the areas that require careful planning (i.e., how to provide scaffolded support and pacing) in order to ensure that creativity is purposeful and critical thinking is based on evidence.

6 Conclusion

The CREATE–MBLT approach focuses on how learners can continuously evolve, assess, and refine their interpretive abilities through shared multimodal interaction, creating a through-line in how they learn about the world through multiple channels of communication. Immersion alone is not an indicator of cognitive development; rather, the learning activities that occur during immersion represent ways to shape interpretive awareness in learners. As with the CREATE-MBLT framework, curiosity, inquiry, comparison, representation and reflection all serve to reinforce a learner's interpretive stance. By placing immersive technologies at the centre of language teaching, the CREATE-MBLT Framework avoids the traps of limiting learning to either exploration or production, where learners view interpretation as negotiable and adapt it continually throughout the learning process.

In language acquisition, the CREATE-MBLT framework promotes intelligent, introspective, and ethical dialogue about language learning. Instead of just being a tool to learn languages the metaverse is most helpful when seen as a place that helps people understand various interpretations of how one can get meaning about something; the learning occurs in an atmosphere of collaboration, in which the learners collaborate to create, compare and amend their respective understandings, interpretations and meaning of their experiences. Learners are actively involved in creating their own meanings through the CREATE-MBLT framework by crossing the bounds between their first and target languages. CREATE-MBLT views the metaverse as a semiotic environment; in this environment, learners do not merely 'experience' the virtual world, but rather engage in active processes to create, challenge and change the meaning of what they have experienced.

The success of CREATE-MBLT relies on the degree to which an instructor organizes the order of instructional methods, moderates two-way discussions rather than directing outcomes and offers repeated opportunities for students to think about their own interpretations. Therefore, in practice, it is recommended that teachers not rely on mere didactic instruction or corrective feedback and that they teach students to ask questions and to reflect on themselves and their interpretations rather than simply telling them to examine their conclusions.

The most valuable types of assessments for practitioners will provide evidence both of the final multimodal product created by learners and of the reasoning process that created it. In addition to the final multimodal product, practitioners should use assessments that include the quality of evidence-based claims, the openness to alternative interpretations of the work, the ethical sensitivity of the work's representations, and the quality of revisions made by the learner throughout the cycle of development. There is evidence available for practitioners implementing CREATE-MBLT through various types of documentation: rubrics, reflective commentaries, and dialogic transcripts. Each of these types of documentation reflect not only the quality of the outcome produced but also the complexity of the reasoning processes used to prepare for that final outcome. As such, the curriculum should allow learners to take their time in learning and progressing through interpretive cycles rather than rushing to conclusions based on impression or expectation. The reflective component of the CREATE-MBLT framework is often the most important aspect when crossing boundaries of international communication and representation. The act of creating a representation and how it is interpreted carries significant ethical ramifications, ultimately altering relationships. As such, students creating representations of their interpretations should consider how those representations may be interpreted across cultures or languages and serve to support or oppose existing stereotypes.

As a conceptual contribution, this chapter presents a theoretical model rather than detailing outcomes from a study of an intervention. Future empirical research could investigate CREATE-MBLT in terms of the levels of proficiency and types of tasks and cultural environment in which the model is used; teacher mediation and peer critique influence on critical thinking and creativity outcomes; and the ability of particular kinds of multimodal evidence to capture the evolving understanding of learners. Future research may substantially reshape the CREATE-MBLT framework for language learners, further developing their interpretive reasoning through digitally based and/or multimodal evidence sources, thus, promoting better instructional practice for teachers of language education. Further research comparing different instructional environments (immersive vs. non-immersive) may provide insight into how an immersive learning environment will influence students' interpretive reasoning and ability to work collaboratively with others.

References

Byram, M. (1997). *Teaching and assessing intercultural communicative competence.* Multilingual Matters.

Byram, M., & Wagner, M. (2018). Making a difference: Language teaching for intercultural and international dialogue. *Foreign Language Annals, 51*(1), 140–151. https://doi.org/10.1111/flan.12319

Çakıroğlu, Ü., & Kılıç, S. (2023). Assessing teachers' PCK to teach computational thinking via robotic programming. *Interactive Learning Environments, 31*(2), 818–835. https://doi.org/10.1080/10494820.2020.1811734

Kress, G., & van Leeuwen, T. (2001). *Multimodal discourse: The modes and media of contemporary communication.* Arnold.

Lan, Y.-J. (2020). Immersion, interaction and experience-oriented learning: Bringing virtual reality into FL learning. *Language Learning & Technology, 24*(1), 1–15. https://doi.org/10.64152/10125/44704

Lee, S.-M., & Wu, J. G. (2024). Preparing teachers for the future: Microteaching in the immersive VR environment. *ReCALL.* Advance online publication. https://doi.org/10.1017/S0958344024000089

Lin, T.-J., & Lan, Y.-J. (2015). Language learning in virtual reality environments: Past, present, and future. *Journal of Educational Technology & Society, 18*(4), 486–497. https://www.jstor.org/stable/jeductechsoci.18.4.486

Makransky, G., & Lilleholt, L. (2018). A structural equation modeling investigation of the emotional value of immersive virtual reality in education. *Educational Technology Research and Development, 66*(5), 1141–1164. https://doi.org/10.1007/s11423-018-9581-2

Makransky, G., & Mayer, R. E. (2022). Benefits of taking a virtual field trip in immersive virtual reality: Evidence for the immersion principle in multimedia learning. *Educational Psychology Review, 34*, 1771–1797. https://doi.org/10.1007/s10648-022-09675-4

O'Dowd, R. (2021). Virtual exchange: Moving forward into the next decade. *Computer Assisted Language Learning, 34*(3), 209–224. https://doi.org/10.1080/09588221.2021.1902201

Radianti, J., Majchrzak, T. A., Fromm, J., & Wohlgenannt, I. (2020). A systematic review of immersive virtual reality applications for higher education: Design elements, lessons learned, and research agenda. *Computers & Education, 147*, Article 103778. https://doi.org/10.1016/j.compedu.2019.103778

Shadiev, R., & Yang, M. (2020). Review of studies on technology-enhanced language learning and teaching. *Sustainability, 12*(2), Article 524. https://doi.org/10.3390/su12020524

Wang, W.-S., Lin, C.-J., Lee, H.-Y., Huang, Y.-M., & Wu, T.-T. (2024). Integrating feedback mechanisms and ChatGPT for VR-based experiential learning: Impacts on reflective thinking and AIoT physical hands-on tasks. *Interactive Learning Environments, 33*(2), 1770–1787. https://doi.org/10.1080/10494820.2024.2375644

Wells, G. (1999). Dialogic inquiry: Toward a sociocultural practice and theory of education. *Cambridge University Press.* https://doi.org/10.1017/CBO9780511605895

Zhang, R., & Zou, D. (2022). Types, purposes, and effectiveness of state-of-the-art technologies for second and foreign language learning. *Computer Assisted Language Learning, 35*(4), 696–742. https://doi.org/10.1080/09588221.2020.1744666

Zhou, X., Teng, D., & Al-Samarraie, H. (2024). The mediating role of generative AI self-regulation on students' critical thinking and problem-solving. *Education Sciences, 14*, Article 1302. https://doi.org/10.3390/educsci14121302

Zou, B., Guan, X., Shao, Y., & Chen, P. (2023). Supporting speaking practice by social network-based interaction in artificial intelligence (AI)-assisted language learning. *Sustainability, 15*(4), Article 2872. https://doi.org/10.3390/su15042872

Hayriye Avara is a researcher at Amasya University, Türkiye. Her work focuses on fostering critical thinking and creativity in immersive language learning environments. Avara developed the CREATE-MBLT framework for structured inquiry and collaborative meaning-making in metaverses. She emphasizes task design, facilitation, and assessment for higher-order skills. Her contributions provide pedagogical models for dialogic and multimodal language education.

Enhancing Communication and Collaboration in Metaverse-Based Language Teaching and Learning

Roberto Figueroa Jr., Mehrasa Alizadeh, and Aya Fukuda

Abstract Metaverse platforms are revolutionizing language learning by expanding traditional virtual exchanges into immersive, three-dimensional environments. Unlike conventional online tools, these spaces allow learners to co-create, collaborate, and engage with digital twins of real-world objects while also experiencing cultural simulations tied to the target language. Such environments make abstract concepts more concrete, promote authentic communication, and strengthen intercultural competence. By allowing students to learn in realistic cultural settings, metaverse-based teaching methods create new and exciting ways to learn languages that are both interesting and relevant. This chapter presents two conceptual models of metaverse-based immersive open pedagogies designed to support language learning and intercultural communication courses based on institutional practice. By examining their processes, challenges, and outcomes, it is hoped that the discussion will serve as a valuable guide for future instructional designers, highlighting common pitfalls, offering practical solutions, and demonstrating the improvements that can be achieved through thoughtful integration of metaverse-based pedagogies.

Keywords Metaverse · Intercultural communication · Collaborative Learning · COIL · Immersive open pedagogies · Immersive learning

R. Figueroa Jr. (✉)
University of the Philippines—Open University, Laguna, Philippines
e-mail: robertojr.figueroa@up.edu.ph

M. Alizadeh
Otemon Gakuin University, Ibaraki, Osaka, Japan
e-mail: m-alizadeh@otemon.ac.jp

A. Fukuda
Tokyo University of Foreign Studies, Tokyo, Japan
e-mail: fukuda_aya@tufs.ac.jp

F. Çelik and C. Yangın Ersanlı (eds.), *Metaverse-Based Language Learning and Teaching*, English Language Education 49,
https://doi.org/10.1007/978-3-032-31366-9_9

1 Introduction

Communication and collaboration are two very essential 21st-century skills that learners, regardless of their field of study, need to master to be successful in their future careers. More specifically, experts claim that the source of second language learning is collaborative dialogue, which is a form of languaging (Swain & Watanabe, 2012). Their argument highlights the importance of interactive environments that promote intercultural communicative exchanges with speakers of the target language. However, conventional classrooms often lack opportunities for spontaneous, unscripted discourse using the target language, which restricts the development of communicative competence (Çelik & Baturay, 2024; Kits & Meristo, 2025; Loewen & Sato, 2018). It is generally difficult to provide a diversity of perspectives and authentic communication with speakers of the target language due to logistical constraints and resource limitations (Salmanova, 2025). These constraints have prompted educators to explore alternative learning designs that extend language use beyond the physical classroom and mitigate limitations of time, space, and access. In response, digitally mediated pedagogies have increasingly been leveraged to create opportunities for authentic interaction and intercultural exchange.

Fortunately, these digitally mediated pedagogies powered by information and communication technology (ICT) have also become more accessible in the past five years because of increasing Internet speeds across the globe and decreasing device costs. Virtual exchanges have become abundant in the form of tandem learning (Silva & Figueiredo, 2015) and collaborative online international learning (COIL). These learning activities have been reported to have a positive impact on increasing engagement, especially in classes where a second language is being taught or used as a medium of instruction (Vahed & Rodriguez, 2020). While these intercultural activities mediated by ICT have usually been dominated by text-based or video conferencing platforms, the advent of metaverse technologies offers new avenues for more immersive and interactive communicative experiences (Lee & Ahn, 2024), potentially bridging geographical and cultural divides in novel ways. These immersive virtual environments facilitate active engagement and collaborative learning by allowing instructors to mediate knowledge transfer through physical models and visual materials, akin to real-world interactions (Lataifeh & Ahmed, 2024). However, obstacles in implementing this very technology often include the technical complexities of platform development, ensuring equitable access for all learners, and integrating these virtual spaces effectively into existing curricula to maximize their pedagogical impact (Cowie & Alizadeh, 2022).

It is also important to determine ways to effectively combine metaverse platforms and metaverse-based teaching methods to improve language immersion and encourage cross-cultural communication in second language learning situations (Montes & Lázaro, 2023). In this chapter, we attempt to explore how metaverse-based language teaching can enhance communication and collaboration by explaining how the technological features of these platforms, combined with pedagogical strategies and approaches, facilitate authentic communicative and collaborative interactions.

These are embodied by two models resulting from synthesizing recurring design patterns, instructional strategies, and implementation challenges observed in real courses, programs, and cross-institutional collaborations that we led over multiple iterations, reflecting our institutional practice of metaverse-enhanced pedagogies to enhance linguistic immersion and promote intercultural communication in learning environments.

One unique contribution of this chapter lies in presenting immersive open pedagogies as an emerging framework within which the two pedagogical models are situated, drawing from sustained institutional implementations rather than isolated technological demonstrations. These models emphasize the importance of careful teaching planning, understanding different cultures, and designing for accessibility as key elements for effective learning in immersive settings.

The following learning questions guide the chapter's orientation:

1. How can learners use the affordances of metaverse platforms to engage in authentic, collaborative, and interculturally situated language use beyond conventional ICT-mediated exchanges?
2. How can metaverse-based immersive open pedagogical designs support learners' progression from guided interaction to learner-driven intercultural collaboration?
3. What challenges related to access, design, and implementation do learners and educators encounter in MBLL environments, and how can these challenges be addressed to promote equitable participation?

Together, these learning questions frame the chapter's discussion of metaverse-based language learning guided by immersive open pedagogical principles, leading to the deliberate design and development of immersive environments to foster communication, collaboration, and intercultural competence.

While the chapter is primarily conceptual and intended as a guide for teachers, it is grounded in both our institutional experience and prior studies, exemplified through case illustrations, some of which are preliminary and employ both quantitative and qualitative methods. It is also important to note that design principles for collaboration in metaverse environments are still emerging. Thus, although the discussion builds on research from virtual environments and computer-supported collaborative learning, the specific application of these principles to metaverse-based language teaching remains an active area of investigation. Educators who are keen to employ these recommendations are encouraged to view them as emerging best practices rather than prescriptive or universally applicable solutions. This means that adaptation may be required based on their specific contexts and learner populations.

2 The Metaverse in Communication and Collaboration

The metaverse is an immersive and interactive virtual environment that acts as a dynamic platform for authentic language practice and collaborative learning (Lee & Ahn, 2024; Zhang et al., 2022). It allows for the creation of simulated, vivid learning contexts where learners can engage in role-plays and dialogue practice with avatar partners or intelligent non-player characters, mirroring real-world scenarios not feasible in physical classrooms (Zhang et al., 2022). Furthermore, the metaverse facilitates constructivist learning by enabling students to explore virtual environments, manipulate digital objects, and interact with peers and artificial intelligence in ways that promote contextualized language learning (Çelik & Baturay, 2024; Lee & Ahn, 2024).

Unlike conventional online platforms that rely to a significant extent on video conferencing or text-based interaction, metaverse platforms enable embodied communication through avatars, spatial audio, and interactive virtual objects. These features allow learners to engage in more natural communication enriched with gesture use and proxemics, which are often lost in two-dimensional online spaces (Dalgarno & Lee, 2009).

One of the most significant advantages of the metaverse for language learning lies in its ability to situate communication within meaningful and context-rich scenarios, which enhance learners' engagement and spatial presence (Çelik & Baturay, 2024). Spatial presence in a virtual environment, in turn, has a positive influence on learner motivation (Figueroa & Jung, 2025). Furthermore, this heightened sense of presence and immersion can foster a more authentic communicative experience, allowing for real-time practice and interaction that more closely mimics real-world language use (Zhang et al., 2022). For instance, a group of culturally diverse learners can collaboratively solve a problem in a virtual environment or navigate a culturally themed environment that requires negotiating meaning in the target language. Such tasks in immersive environments foster intercultural communicative competence by embedding learners in contexts that mirror authentic intercultural interactions (Gruber et al., 2023).

The theoretical foundation of metaverse-enhanced learning corresponds with Vygotsky's notion of mediation (Ghassemzadeh, 2005), which posits that cognitive development arises from the tools, symbols, and social interactions that organize human activity. Ghassemzadeh (2005) continued to discuss that Vygotsky (1967) defined signs as "artificially created stimuli" (p. 29) that serve as stimulants for the brain to form new reflex connections. Immersive environments like the metaverse, therefore, serve as advanced mediational instruments that would facilitate these signs for supporting higher forms of learning and collaboration. Such an environment facilitates the practical application of the principles of the Constructivist Learning Theory, where learners actively construct knowledge through interactive engagement within virtual worlds and with other participants through their avatars or digital representations. Furthermore, Metaverse-based learning environments and activities support the implementation of Context Learning Theory, which posits that situational experiences facilitate authentic learning more effectively than abstract teaching methods. (Jiao et al., 2024). This contextualization is crucial for language acquisition, as it enables learners to grasp linguistic and cultural semiotics through direct interaction with the environment and other participants (Nuesser et al., 2024).

In the metaverse, collaboration extends beyond engaging in conversations. Learners can co-construct artifacts such as posters, 3D models, or even performances within the virtual space. These joint projects necessitate negotiation, decision-making, and role assignment, thereby promoting communicative functions beyond information exchange that tap into higher-order thinking skills (Chen et al., 2023). Moreover, because learners interact through avatars, they often report lower levels of communication anxiety, which may lead to increased willingness to communicate compared to traditional classroom or videoconference settings (Hwang & Lee, 2024).

Another dimension worth highlighting is cross-cultural collaboration. By linking classrooms from different geographical locations, metaverse-based exchanges provide an arena for intercultural dialogue that goes beyond text chats or video calls (Valizadeh & Morady Moghaddam, 2025). Learners can engage with peers in environments that simulate culturally significant practices such as festivals and ceremonies or urban spaces, enabling more profound discussions about cultural values and perspectives. These immersive contexts can create shared reference points that make intercultural communication more vivid and memorable.

In this section, we present two models that locate themselves in the continuum of immersive open pedagogies, which can collectively be described as an educational approach based on the philosophies of immersive learning and open pedagogy. The term "immersive open pedagogies" was first used to describe the use of immersive technologies in open and distance e-learning settings. However, Figueroa and Flor (2024) went deeper into incorporating the philosophy of open pedagogy, which emphasizes the co-creation of immersive open educational resources (IOER) with learners. Thus, immersive open pedagogies feature a spectrum of various levels of learner participation in the creation of IOER. Metaverse platforms offer various tools for creating environments and crafting 3D objects, which is why immersive open pedagogies are often embedded in MBLL activities.

Together, they illustrate the metaverse-based facilitation and promotion of collaboration and communication activities in the Philippines and Japan.

3 Model 1: Virtual Exhibits in the Metaverse

The first model involves curating digital media from global experts from various fields, with an individual or a small team of instructors and designers setting up a virtual exhibit in the metaverse that features these works. In this model, the instructor team curates media created by learners through their assignments or past activities, allowing them to receive feedback from these experts. This approach leverages customizable metaverse platforms, enabling instructors to design unique virtual spaces tailored to specific educational objectives. What follows are small events that would encourage learners to interact with these experts and creators in a target language.

These interactions can take the form of virtual workshops, Q&A sessions, or guided tours, providing authentic communicative practice within a specialized

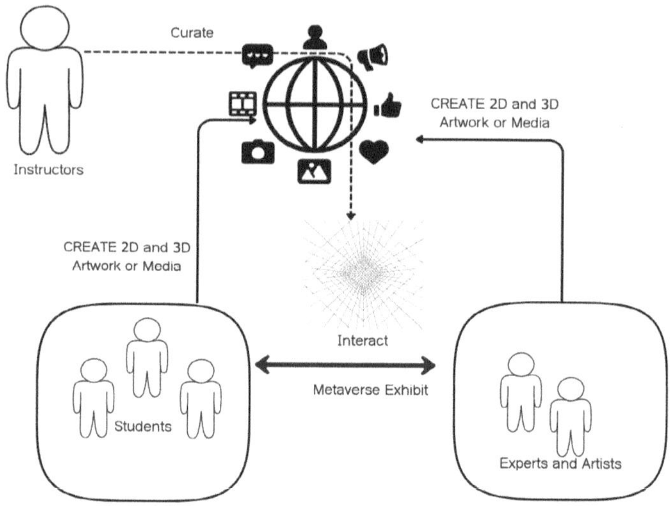

Fig. 1 Flow of activities in model 1

domain. Figure 1 illustrates the flow of activities and the relationship between components and actors in the model.

This model capitalizes on the metaverse's capacity to host diverse digital content, integrating technologies for enhanced user interaction and guidance (Çelik & Baturay, 2024). By allowing learners to interact with experts and creators using a global language like English, it fosters an environment where linguistic proficiency is directly applied and refined through meaningful, domain-specific communication (Wu et al., 2022). The pedagogical implications extend to fostering cross-cultural understanding, as learners from varied backgrounds can jointly engage with exhibitions and participate in discussions led by global experts (Shonfeld et al., 2021). They can reap similar benefits from using simple videoconferencing platforms, which is something to keep in mind. However, discussing actual 3D models in a shared virtual space through their avatars offers a more immersive and interactive experience that enhances contextual comprehension and promotes inclusive learning among learners (Esguerra et al., 2024a; Figueroa et al., 2025).

3.1 Case Report 1: The National Conference on Open and Distance eLearning Virtual Exhibit

A co-curricular initiative at the University of the Philippines Open University (UPOU) exemplifies this model. In this initiative, a team of instructors curated and presented student-created videos in a metaverse-based exhibit. Experts from different countries were invited to share their 2D and 3D art and engage with students.

This virtual exhibition fostered cross-cultural interaction and facilitated communication regarding artistic interpretations and linguistic nuances embedded within the displayed works. The format provided a unique opportunity for learners to practice language skills in an authentic, low-stakes environment while gaining exposure to diverse cultural perspectives.

More specifically, the course at the University of the Philippines Open University (UPOU) focused on fundamental topics related to information technology concepts. During this term, there was a national conference that had a virtual exhibit. This event was the university's first attempt to hold an exhibit in the metaverse, as it coincided with a period when everyone was just emerging from the lockdowns in 2022 and in-person gatherings were still unpopular (Esguerra et al., 2024b). For this exhibit, FrameVR (https://framevr.io/) was used to create a 3D environment that mimicked an expo featuring various panels for displaying posters and products. The metaverse-based exhibit was conceptualized to feature university publications, digital learning materials, and exemplary student projects. Exemplary student projects were curated from submitted assignments where students created short videos published with a Creative Commons License about what they had learned from YouTube during the pandemic. In the same exhibit, two contributors from Europe were invited to showcase their work. One contributor featured digital art of her Persian heritage, while a Dutch artist created a three-dimensional animated contraption. Figure 2 displays these works.

Both international experts were invited to visit the exhibit and share their comments through a feedback form embedded in some of the panels. The experts also scheduled presentations, inviting available students to participate and ask questions. This arrangement facilitated not only passive reception of information but also

Fig. 2 Three-dimensional digital art installations by international artists

active engagement, allowing students to articulate queries and engage in dialogue with international experts using English, thereby enhancing their communicative competence in a specialized academic context. While the students were learning the basics of information technology, they were in fact studying to become multimedia specialists, which is why interacting with the international artists was important.

Figure 3 shows screenshots of interactions between the students and the artist. From this interaction, many of them were not only able to articulate their questions and ideas in English, but they were also able to learn technical vocabulary as well as platforms that are needed to create 3D art, like Blender. This real-world application of linguistic skills within a technical domain illustrates the ability of metaverse platforms to provide contextualized learning experiences that extend beyond traditional classroom settings. Furthermore, even without meeting with the two resource persons, they were able to explore the various audio-visual objects offered by exhibitors in the environment.

While English is a second language in the Philippines and is widely used in academic settings, using it in a more global context with international speakers was expanded by this activity for the students at UPOU, especially when students were located in various geographical parts of the country, and gathering them physically in one place with global experts would have been difficult and expensive.

The comments from a survey form embedded in the exhibit were thematically analyzed, resulting in six themes, one of which is relevant to MBLL: *Multimodal communication enhances enjoyment and meaning-making,* as exemplified by representative comments such as

> The different paths to take as well as the narration for each area were very entertaining and informative.

Fig. 3 Dutch artist giving a presentation to students about blender

It was particularly enjoyable to be able to open links to the work and experience some VRs with playable audio.

I appreciate the effort of including some URL directory or YouTube links on some entries to fully understand the message they would like to convey.

I appreciate how the artist explained the process and the connection of their digital painting to RM's song 'Moonchild.'

4 Model 2: Collaborative Online International Learning in the Metaverse

The second model involves a type of virtual exchange that is often integrated into the lesson plan of a course, often referred to as Collaborative Online International Learning (COIL). COIL is a teaching model introduced by Jon Rubin that connects two or more classrooms from different countries to work on shared learning activities and assignments. It emphasizes the co-creation of syllabi by instructors, cross-cultural interaction among students, and the development of global perspectives within credit-bearing courses. Through COIL, learners engage with disciplinary content and enhance their intercultural competence by collaborating with peers who bring diverse life experiences and viewpoints (Rubin, 2017).

This pedagogical approach extends beyond typical digital pen-pal initiatives by fostering deeper collaborative projects that build competencies in interpersonal, international, intercultural, and language-learning proficiencies through technology (Minei et al., 2021). In the context of MBLT, COIL can be leveraged to create immersive, collaborative learning environments where students from different countries can interact in virtual spaces to complete joint projects, thereby enhancing their communicative skills and intercultural competence (Ying-jie & Shirley, 2021).

The model can have three primary configurations. One configuration can involve a pre-made environment created by the instructors. Students from participating universities can use the environment to collaborate on tasks using the target language or accomplish them with their groupmates. The roster of the groups would ideally be culturally heterogeneous to promote intercultural communication.

Another configuration involves students from one university creating the virtual environment or its interactive elements, which encourages greater ownership and creative expression while practicing language skills in a constructive context and presenting their exhibits in the metaverse with their foreign partners online using their avatars.

Finally, the third configuration can involve having a group of students from one university co-create a virtual environment with their foreign partners, who may not be familiar with the technology but may be able to provide input during the creation process. Various levels of collaboration can happen in this model, depending on the comfort levels of the students from the partner university.

Table 1 shows a summary of the three configurations of this model. The first configuration has the lowest level of co-creation because the instructors are the ones

Table 1 Summarized comparison of the three configurations of model 2

Dimension	Configuration 1:	Configuration 2:	Configuration 3:
Description	Instructor-designed environment	Single Student-group authorship with audience-oriented interaction	Distributed Student-group authorship through sustained inter-institutional collaboration
Level of co-creation	Low	Medium	High
Overall complexity	Simple	Intermediate	Advanced

who created or assigned the metaverse environment, which served as a venue for the students from collaborating universities to meet and interact. It is also the simplest to implement among the three configurations.

The second configuration has medium co-creation because students from one group or university are the ones developing their metaverse environment. However, the other group would only serve as audience and feedback-givers during the presentation of the student-created metaverse exhibits. The complexity of this model is also deemed intermediate because it would require training the student-creator group.

The last configuration has the highest level of co-creation because participants from both universities are involved in the development of the student-created metaverse exhibit at varying levels depending on their level of comfort. This configuration also has the most advanced level of complexity and effort because both universities will work to facilitate interaction and collaboration between their students during the conceptualization and development of the metaverse exhibit. It may also require training both groups of students in basic metaverse-environment design and development (Table 1).

4.1 Case Report 2.1: COIL Between UPOU and Toyo University

The first configuration was used in a previous COIL implementation between UPOU and Toyo University. However, what transpired in this COIL collaboration was inviting participants from both universities to an exhibit curated by the instructor, where they were asked to interact with the curated videos on second language learning apps, which were previously submitted by Toyo University students as an assignment. The videos became focal points for discussion among the students. Afterwards, as they interacted, students had the opportunity to contribute assets and create drawings on virtual whiteboards. They were also asked to move from one group to another to talk to other peers in English. A qualitative study that synthesized instructor reflections was conducted during this collaboration, with detailed findings to be presented in a forthcoming article.

4.2 Case Report 2.2: COIL Between UPOU and TUFS

The second configuration was exemplified when UPOU students were asked to create their own exhibits in the metaverse about ICT innovations in the Philippines and Filipino innovators. They were also asked to design the space using Filipino themes, icons, motifs, and textures. They were then asked to provide an online tour of their exhibits to students from the partner university. This scenario happened in another subject where UPOU students showcased similar exhibits to graduate students taking language and literacy education, as well as some members of the Filipino program of TUFs in the metaverse.

4.3 Case Report 2.3: Twinning COIL Between UPOU and TUFS

The final project for UPOU students in a twinning COIL course exemplified the third configuration. TUFS and UPOU collaboratively offered the course Digital Platforms for Intercultural Communication, adapting its content and delivery to suit each institution's unique context. At TUFS, where students already knew Japanese, the Japanese modules were replaced with more advanced topics on digital technologies and intercultural communication. At UPOU, on the other hand, the course kept both Japanese lessons and introductory intercultural communication modules. Unlike at TUFS, synchronous classes at UPOU were not mandatory; instead, students could voluntarily join the twinning sessions with TUFS peers.

The project involved forming groups and working with TUFS students as cultural resource persons for an exhibit that they would design in the metaverse about similarities and differences in terms of a certain cultural theme between two to three countries of their choice. Since some of the TUFS students were also from countries like Russia, Egypt, and Rwanda, this gave the UPOU students more access to other cultures. Some groups chose food, while others chose mythology or objects of fear. The interaction between UPOU and TUFS students varied. Some groups engaged extensively with their partners asynchronously. Others met online or even interacted in person during physical meetups.

Figure 4 shows some of the metaverse exhibits co-created by the students. The culminating activity was a hybrid exhibit presentation.

Some participants from the collaborating universities either joined the metaverse exhibit or presented from within the metaverse, while others gathered in one of the seminar rooms at UPOU on-site. In the in-person setup, exchange students from Osaka University and TUFS were invited as guests to interact with the Filipino presenters and to provide immediate feedback on their presentations, further enriching the cross-cultural dialogue. Some Filipino presenters also practiced their Japanese greetings with the Japanese guests, while the guests who were majoring

Fig. 4 Metaverse exhibits on intercultural themes co-created by students

in Filipino tried to practice Filipino while interacting with the Filipino presenters in person and in the metaverse.

During the last weeks of the term, students were asked to fill out a post-course evaluation survey that included items related to intercultural communication skills and concepts that they may have developed through the COIL activities. The relevant study where the survey was conducted received institutional ethics approval (No. 2024–006). Participation was voluntary, and informed consent was obtained prior to data collection. All identifiers were removed, pseudonyms were used in reporting, and data were securely stored and retained only in accordance with institutional policy.

Table 2 presents the mean and standard deviation of participant ratings for each item in the survey.

Items were rated on a 5-point Likert scale (1 = strongly disagree, 5 = strongly agree). Analytic interpretations summarize overall response tendencies and are intended to contextualize the mean scores as a descriptive snapshot.

In this particular case, learners were surveyed on several aspects of intercultural communication. The results showed that the participants reported strong development of intercultural communication skills among 11 participants, as reflected in high mean scores across several items. Students reported being "better able to communicate with different cultures" (M = 4.55, SD = 0.69) and "more aware of those from different nationalities" (M = 4.55, SD = 0.69), demonstrating increased sensitivity and adaptability in cross-cultural interactions. The highest rating, "course helped me understand global issues" (M = 4.91, SD = 0.30), further emphasizes how the course broadened students' perspectives and deepened their awareness of global

Table 2 Descriptive statistics of survey items

Survey item	M	SD	Analytic interpretation
Better able to communicate with different cultures	4.55	0.69	Indicating increased sensitivity and adaptability in cross-cultural interaction
More aware of those from different nationalities	4.55	0.69	
Course helped me understand global issues	4.91	0.30	Indicating how the course broadened students' perspectives and deepened their awareness of global interconnectedness
Global/intercultural fluency	4.64	0.50	Indicating enhanced students' ability to navigate cultural differences and essential competencies for effective communication and collaboration in diverse professional settings
Teamwork	4.64	0.50	
Professionalism	4.82	0.40	

interconnectedness. The consistently high scores for "global/intercultural fluency" ($M = 4.64$, $SD = 0.50$), "teamwork" ($M = 4.64$, $SD = 0.50$), and "professionalism" ($M = 4.82$, $SD = 0.40$) show that the COIL experience not only helped students understand and deal with cultural differences but also gave them the skills they need to communicate and work well with people from different backgrounds in a professional setting.

In the same survey, we asked students to state the challenges that they have encountered while partaking in the COIL activities. We then analyzed the responses and grouped them into themes related to the challenges faced. There were four themes that emerged. First was *Perspective Expansion*, which meant that collaboration broadened their worldview and deepened their appreciation for cultural diversity. Second was *Relationship Building*, which meant that forming friendships with peers from another country was one of the program's most rewarding outcomes. The third was *Skill Development,* representing improvements in communication, leadership, and digital collaboration skills, reinforcing what we found in the quantitative results. Finally, *Collaboration Challenges* were also identified, which pertained to schedule and time-zone difficulties, language differences, and technological issues.

Next, we will discuss the issues with using the metaverse in COIL activities and the solutions we found.

5 Challenges and Solutions

The challenges and solutions presented in this section do not only stem from the themes in the recent example but also from our past studies and iterations. We present four categories of such challenges.

5.1 Technological Challenges

One major problem is that not everyone has access to technology or knows how to use it. Immersive platforms often require advanced hardware such as VR headsets or PCs with high processing power and stable network connections. Learners from low-resource contexts may encounter difficulty in participating fully, which can exacerbate digital divides and limit the inclusivity of collaborative projects (Gonzalez & Ng, 2023). Numerous metaverse-based activities provided to the students have demonstrated this phenomenon. In the recent preliminary study that we described earlier, some students reported that their devices could not handle rendering the virtual exhibit platform well during our national conference, as illustrated by the earlier case regarding a virtual exhibit that exemplified the first model. Here are sample remarks from them:

> My laptop didn't handle it well because there is quite a delay in moving and in loading the visuals but I was still able to go around and have some fun.
>
> Luckily I was able to explore enough of the exhibit despite the lack of framerates. Even my phone was screaming in pain
>
> Its nice to experience the metaverse... although it was very laggy from my side, its probably my laptop

Schools and universities with well-equipped labs will not have a problem, but those with infrastructure and tech issues, as well as those that teach remotely, may be at a disadvantage. In such cases, it is important to provide alternative activities or frame the metaverse-based activity as a supplement, especially in cases where students will be using their devices. Equipping e-centers with more advanced equipment can help alleviate this barrier. However, as metaverse platform developers are aware of the problem and are pushing the boundaries to provide inclusive access to their products (Dudley et al., 2023), we are hopeful that this issue will be addressed in the near future.

5.2 Platform Challenges

The second issue can stem from platform-specific obstacles that can limit how instructors and learners communicate and collaborate in the metaverse. Users may face a challenging learning curve when navigating avatar-based immersive environments, which initially hinders rather than facilitates communication, even with available technological access.

Furthermore, the lack of standardization across various metaverse platforms can create interoperability issues, making it difficult for educators to seamlessly integrate diverse tools and content, thereby complicating collaborative efforts (Onu et al., 2023). Concerns also exist regarding the data storage practices of these platforms. Students sharing their data through their portfolios can give rise to ethical issues.

Moreover, sustainability is a significant concern because the longevity of these platforms and their ability to preserve all student creations is uncertain. Mozilla Hubs' announcement of its shutdown in 2024 is a well-known example of how sustainability has become an issue for maintaining virtual environments hosted by cloud-based metaverse platforms. (Binotti & Chambless, 2024).

Another challenge concerns nonverbal communication. While avatars facilitate the use of gestures and proxemics, their representations often fall short when compared to real-life nonverbal communication. Learners may struggle to interpret subtle facial expressions, gaze direction, or body language. In intercultural collaboration, such gaps can lead to miscommunication or reduced pragmatic awareness (Alizadeh & Cowie, 2024). Furthermore, the anonymity and reduced social cues in avatar-mediated interactions may encourage some learners to disengage, raising questions about the capability of the metaverse in enhancing communication. Anonymity may also foster an environment where misbehavior, cheating, bullying, harassment, or disruption can thrive (Cheong, 2022). In real life, social cues, peer pressure, and institutional authority discourage such actions. In the metaverse, however, the veil of anonymity removes these deterrents, making proactive safeguards necessary in educational design.

In the COIL cases we mentioned, the lack of nonverbal communication was reported as a challenge in expressing how students felt while communicating with their partners. The first few runs of COIL with FrameVR limited the use of gestures and emojis. However, more recently, the incorporation of emojis and gestures has lessened the stoic feel of the avatars. Another challenge was encountered when we considered using a bespoke metaverse platform that was co-developed by international partners. The Metaverse Academic Nexus for Global Opportunities (MANGOs) platform, which was initiated by Chulalongkorn University and shared with UPOU and other collaborating universities, was considered for future COIL sessions. We held workshops to develop UPOU's digital twin, capable of hosting COIL sessions using the first configuration (Figueroa et al., 2025). However, despite being free and self-hosted, the lack of co-creating access given to students discouraged them from using it. The environment can be edited in Unity and needs to be relaunched on the server before any changes are reflected, limiting real-time collaborative development and immediate feedback essential for dynamic learning environments, contrary to what FrameVR can provide. However, the MANGOs researchers and developers are continuously working to make the platform more flexible for in-world creation while providing a sustainable way for universities to host their virtual campuses in the metaverse.

5.3 Pedagogical Challenges

Our third concern lies in collaborative task design and management. Learners sometimes treat metaverse spaces as entertainment rather than learning environments, which can distract them from pedagogical goals. Teachers, therefore, face the dual challenge of designing tasks that take advantage of immersion and embodiment while also ensuring that learners remain focused on meaningful communicative objectives. Instructors may also struggle to monitor multiple simultaneous conversations in spatialized environments, making it harder to provide timely feedback or corrective input.

In COIL contexts, matching students from different universities can be a challenge because of temporal and administrative differences. Academic calendars can be different for each university, so determining overlapping schedules for collaborative activities requires careful coordination and flexibility. Furthermore, the number of students participating in the COIL activities from each university can vary greatly, leading to uneven group compositions and other grouping-related challenges.

For one COIL project, UPOU students faced challenges in inviting international collaborators for their metaverse projects because of their vastly uneven numbers. The issue was resolved by inviting participants from a short exchange initiative with another university, where a group of students from Japan stayed in the Philippines for one week for academic and cultural exchange. There were also exchange students from Japan who were invited to participate in a hybrid forum where groups that did not have international partners presented their work to the foreign students.

5.4 Physiological, Psychological, and Affective Challenges

Finally, there are physiological, psychological, and affective challenges. While some studies highlight reduced language anxiety in avatar-mediated communication (Chen, 2022), others report disorientation, cybersickness, or feelings of alienation when learners interact in unfamiliar virtual settings (Wu & Hung, 2022). Without sustained training and support, learners may disengage or fail to transfer skills developed in the metaverse to real-world communication. These factors collectively emphasize that it takes careful pedagogical design and robust technical infrastructure to maximize the benefits of metaverse-based language learning (MBLL) while mitigating potential drawbacks.

In some of our case examples, we noticed that cybersickness was common when using head-mounted displays (HMDs). That is why, when inviting students to the virtual exhibit and conducting COIL activities in the metaverse, we ensured that they could also access the metaverse platform using their laptops or phones through a web browser. This gave them an alternative way to engage with the metaverse.

In other instances, students often felt lost when they first entered the metaverse exhibits. That is why, before actually using the metaverse for collaborative or communication activities, a separate session should be conducted where students can simply play, explore, and experiment with the environment. Once we did this, the students became less anxious during the main task, as they were already familiar with the platform and navigating the environment.

In line with what we observed in our implementations, recent empirical work suggests that immersive, avatar-mediated environments do not automatically reduce affective barriers in language learning. Li and Yu (2023), in a systematic review of literature, reported that learners with low levels of digital literacy may experience technology anxiety. Their findings underscore the idea that the metaverse can function as a double-edged space: while the environment may be engaging and motivating, the immediacy of real-time, public speaking through avatars can also heighten evaluative pressure and cognitive strain especially if they are not technologically prepared. These findings resonate with our experiences, where students sometimes felt disoriented or anxious when first entering virtual exhibits or when using HMDs for the first time. As a result, our decision to offer browser-based access and to conduct separate sessions for play and exploration before the main tasks can be treated not only as technical onboarding but also as intentional affective and cognitive scaffolding. By allowing students to become familiar with the environment before engaging in high-stakes interaction, we observed reduced anxiety and smoother participation, supporting the view that careful pedagogical design is essential for mitigating the psychological demands of MBLL.

6 Immersive Open Pedagogies: From Curation to Co-Creation

The two models may seem entirely different, but they can actually be situated in a continuum of immersive open pedagogies. Immersive open pedagogies are educational approaches that leverage immersive technologies for learning online and emphasize co-creation. Thus, researchers can draw a framework from the two variables unique to immersive open pedagogies, immersion and co-creation, that situate the two models and the three configurations of the second model. Immersion or immersive capability, influences spatial presence, which can lead to motivation and learning gains in a virtual environment (Figueroa, 2023), while co-creation is a feature of open pedagogies (Sahyoni et al., 2025).

Figure 5 illustrates a two-dimensional conceptual model for positioning immersive open pedagogies along the intersecting continuum of immersion and co-creation. Curated virtual exhibits are situated toward the lower end of co-creation, typically implemented through screen-based or mobile devices, while collaborative online international learning (COIL) in student-crafted metaverse environments occupies the upper end of the spectrum, characterized by high levels of learner co-creation and immersive engagement through virtual reality environments.

Model 1 is positioned on the left side because of its lack of co-creation activities with the students. However, depending on the platform or devices used to experience the metaverse environment, its implementations can range from high to low immersion. In the recent case example mentioned, most students used their computers and mobile devices to navigate the metaverse exhibit and interact with the guest artists.

Model 2 might be situated on the higher end of co-creation. However, the first configuration may be similar or close to the position of Model 1 because initially,

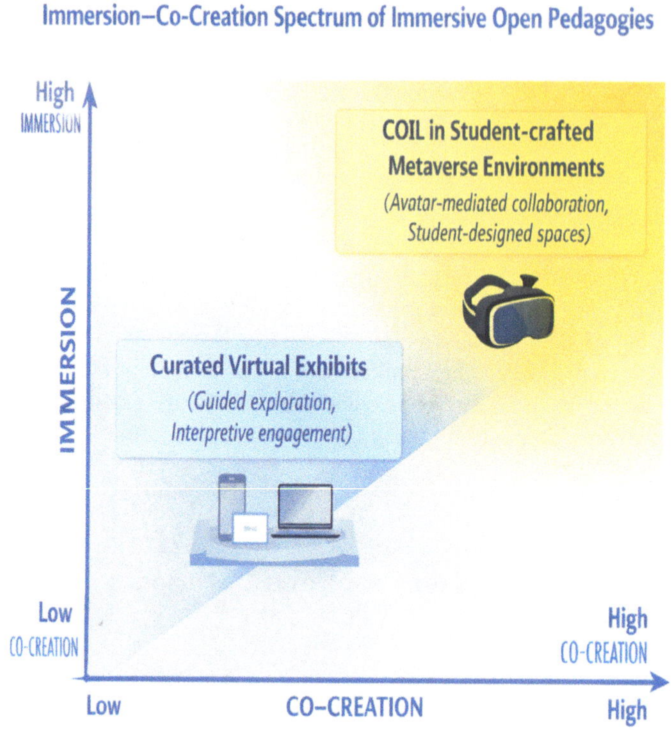

Fig. 5 Immersion–co-creation spectrum of immersive open pedagogies

the environment would be instructor-created. However, once they add objects in the environment or draw on the interactive whiteboards during the COIL activities, the level of co-creation increases dramatically. The second configuration would be on the higher end of co-creation because one group of students would be tasked to create their metaverse environment, while the third configuration would have the highest co-creation level because all participating students will have a hand in co-creating the metaverse exhibits. Like Model 1, all three configurations of Model 2 can have implementations that can vary along the immersion axis depending on the platform and device they are using during co-creation and actual interaction. If they co-create and interact using HMDs, then immersion would be high. However, in our case examples, only a few students used HMDs to navigate the metaverse exhibits. These circumstances would probably change in the future as HMDs become more and more affordable and accessible.

FrameVR, which was employed across all case examples, affords flexible levels of immersion as a web-based metaverse platform that supports both access and content creation using a wide range of devices, from standard smartphones and laptops to head-mounted displays (HMDs). This design works with any device, so teachers can adjust the level of immersion based on their teaching goals, the readiness of the students, and the limitations of the infrastructure. This makes it especially useful for open and distance learning. Table 3 shows how FrameVR compares to other popular virtual communication platforms like Zoom and more fully immersive virtual reality environments. It focuses on differences in embodiment, interaction, and co-presence.

Within this continuum, FrameVR occupies a pedagogically productive middle ground. It offers greater social presence, opportunities for spontaneous interaction, and support for situated and embodied language use than conventional videoconferencing platforms like Zoom, while remaining significantly more accessible, scalable, and institutionally feasible than fully immersive VR systems that rely on specialized hardware. As such, FrameVR enables meaningful communicative engagement and collaborative practices without imposing prohibitive technical or logistical barriers, aligning well with the principles of immersive open pedagogies.

Table 3 Comparison of platform affordances for communication and language practice

Pedagogical goal	FrameVR	Zoom	Fully immersive VR
Social presence	Shared 3D environment with avatars supports spatial co-presence	Presence limited to video tiles; non-spatial	High embodied presence through immersive, avatar-based interaction
Spontaneous oral interaction	Real-time voice chat enables informal, unscripted conversation	Interaction is largely turn-based and moderated	Highly conducive to spontaneous, overlapping dialogue
Multimodal communication	Embedded images, audio, video, and links support shared meaning-making	Screen sharing is presenter-centered	Rich multimodal and 3D object interaction
Situated language use	Spatial navigation supports contextualized and experiential language use	Minimal spatial context for communication	Strong support for embodied, context-sensitive language use
Learner contribution	Student-created exhibits serve as discussion anchors	Contributions are temporary and screen-bound	Extensive co-creation, but requires advanced skills and equipment
Intercultural exchange (COIL)	Browser-based access supports cross-border participation with social presence	Highly accessible but socially formal	Highly immersive but limited by hardware access
Accessibility versus immersion	Medium immersion with high accessibility	High accessibility, low immersion	High immersion, low accessibility

7 Conclusion

The metaverse presents a promising frontier for language education by enabling immersive, socially situated, and interculturally rich learning experiences that extend beyond conventional digital platforms. This chapter demonstrates how distinct pedagogical configurations, specifically curated virtual exhibits and collaborative online international learning (COIL) environments, can serve complementary functions in supporting language use and intercultural competence, rather than positioning metaverse-based language learning (MBLL) as a single or uniform approach.

Synthesizing insights from both models reveals a continuum of learner engagement and co-creation that moves from curated and guided, artifact-centered interaction toward sustained, avatar-mediated collaboration and co-creation with international peers. Across this continuum, learning outcomes are shaped less by technological novelty than by intentional pedagogical design, scaffolding, facilitation, and opportunities for reflection. The comparison further indicates that both models are underpinned by shared design principles, including structured interaction, meaningful social presence, and reflective engagement, while also facing common challenges related to access, interoperability, learner safety, and data governance. These problems have a direct effect on fairness, participation, and the long-term viability of learning environments that use the metaverse.

From a research perspective, the models situated along an immersive open pedagogical framework point to the need for longitudinal and comparative studies that examine how varying degrees of immersion and co-creation can influence linguistic development, intercultural competence, and learner identity formation in MBLL. As more advanced implementations evolve into cyber-physical systems (Figueroa et al., 2025), future research should also explore how integrated metaverse ecosystems shape affective, cognitive, and social dimensions of second language learning across diverse contexts and learner populations.

For teacher education and professional development, the findings highlight the importance of preparing educators not only to use metaverse platforms but also to design, facilitate, and ethically manage immersive learning experiences. This includes developing competencies in instructional design for immersive environments, intercultural facilitation, learner support in avatar-mediated spaces, and critical awareness of platform affordances and limitations.

At the policy level, the chapter stresses the importance of institutional and national frameworks that address infrastructure investment, accessibility standards, data privacy, learner protection, and quality assurance in metaverse-based education. Clear policies and guidelines will be essential to support responsible adoption and to ensure that MBLL initiatives align with broader educational goals and equity commitments.

Finally, this chapter positions the metaverse not as a replacement for existing pedagogies but as an evolving learning environment that, when thoughtfully designed, adequately supported, and ethically governed, can meaningfully expand opportunities for intercultural communication, collaboration, and language learning in global academic contexts.

7.1 Statement on the Use of AI Tools.

Jenni.ai assisted in portions of the literature review workflow, including preliminary summarization of located articles and reference formatting checks. The tool was used only to (a) draft preliminary prose for paragraph scaffolds that the authors then verified, rewrote, and fully attributed, and (b) examine APA 7 reference formatting against items the authors had already located. ChatGPT 5.2 and Quillbot were used to support illustration and diagram generation and to improve some sentences' structure, readability, and grammar, but the authors read and validated every suggestion. All claims, interpretations, and final wording are the authors' own. Every cited source in the manuscript was manually retrieved and read; quotations and paraphrases were verified against the original works. AI outputs were screened for accuracy, fabrication (hallucinated citations), and plagiarism using manual checks and standard academic integrity tools. The authors take full responsibility for the final published chapter, including the accuracy of the content, the interpretation of sources, and all claims and conclusions presented, regardless of the use of AI tools during earlier drafting or editing stages.

References

Alizadeh, M., & Cowie, N. (2024). Investigating the impact of online learning platforms on student engagement and learning outcomes: Comparing Zoom with VR. In T. Cochrane, V. Narayan, E. Bone, C. Deneen, M. Saligari, K. Tregloan & R. Vanderburg (Eds.), *Navigating the Terrain: Emerging frontiers in learning spaces, pedagogies, and technologies. Proceedings ASCILITE 2024* (pp. 437–441). https://doi.org/10.14742/apubs.2024.1180

Binotti, L., & Chambless, A. (2024). Work in progress—The Piazza Italiana as a site of VR-based linguistic and cultural learning. In *Academic Proceedings of the 10th International Conference of the Immersive Learning Research Network (iLRN2024)* (pp. 258–268). https://doi.org/10.56198/u6c0wvike

Çelik, F., & Baturay, M. H. (2024). The effect of metaverse on L2 vocabulary learning, retention, student engagement, presence, and community feeling. *BMC Psychology, 12*(1). https://doi.org/10.1186/s40359-024-01549-4

Chen, X., Zou, D., Xie, H., & Wang, F. L. (2023). Metaverse in education: Contributors, cooperations, and research themes. *IEEE Transactions on Learning Technologies, 16*(6), 1111–1129. https://doi.org/10.1109/tlt.2023.3277952

Chen, Y. (2022). Effects of technology-enhanced language learning on reducing EFL learners' public speaking anxiety. *Computer Assisted Language Learning, 37*(4), 789–813. https://doi.org/10.1080/09588221.2022.2055083

Cheong, B. C. (2022). Avatars in the metaverse: Potential legal issues and remedies. *International Cybersecurity Law Review, 3*(2), 467–494. https://doi.org/10.1365/s43439-022-00056-9

Cowie, N., & Alizadeh, M. (2022). The affordances and challenges of virtual reality for language teaching. *International Journal of TESOL Studies, 4*(3), 50–65. https://doi.org/10.46451/ijts.2022.03.05

da Silva, S. V., & de Figueiredo, F. J. Q. (2015). Teletandem language learning in a technological context of education: Interactions between Brazilian and German students. *DELTA, 31*(3), 729–762. https://doi.org/10.1590/0102-445068781234723614

Dalgarno, B., & Lee, M. J. W. (2009). What are the learning affordances of 3-D virtual environments? *British Journal of Educational Technology, 41*(1), 10–32. https://doi.org/10.1111/j.1467-8535.2009.01038.x

Dudley, J., Yin, L., Garaj, V., & Kristensson, P. O. (2023). Inclusive immersion: A review of efforts to improve accessibility in virtual reality, augmented reality and the metaverse. *Virtual Reality, 27*, 2989–3020. https://doi.org/10.1007/s10055-023-00850-8

Esguerra, J. R., Figueroa, R. B., Rodríguez, F., Fukuda, A., & Anzai, Y. (2024a). Collaborative online international learning: A reflexive thematic analysis of narratives from the metaverse. *International Journal in Information Technology in Governance Education and Business, 6*(1), 100–108. https://doi.org/10.32664/ijitgeb.v6i1.140

Esguerra, J. R., Mangubat, L., Macaldo, H. G., Figueroa, R. B., & Núñez, A. (2024b). The design and evaluation of a conference exhibit in the metaverse. *International Journal on Open and Distance E-Learning, 10*(1), 97–111. https://doi.org/10.58887/ijodel.v10i1.280

Figueroa, R. B., Jr. (2023). Immersive capability and spatial presence in virtual reality photo-based tours: Implications for distance education. *Asian Association of Open Universities Journal, 18*(3), 201–217. https://doi.org/10.1108/AAOUJ-12-2022-0171

Figueroa Jr., R. B., Budi Santoso, H., Makino, M., Sasithong, P., Noisri, S., Wuttisittikulkij, L., Deepaisarn, S., Vanichchanunt, P., Saadi, M., Leevangtou, K., Kovintavewat, P., Nendya, M. B., Tandianus, B., Dendy Senapartha, I. K., Saengthongkam, S., & Ali, M. (2025). Building capacity for the collaborative development of an educational ecosystem in the metaverse in the ASEAN Region. In *2025 22nd International Conference on Electrical Engineering/Electronics, Computer, Telecommunications and Information Technology (ECTI-CON)* (p. 1). https://doi.org/10.1109/ecti-con64996.2025.11101025

Figueroa Jr., R. B., & Flor, A. G. (2024). Immersive open pedagogies in the university of the future. In M. F. Lumanta, P. B. Garcia & R. T. Bagarinao (Eds.), *University of the future: Perspectives, transformations, and sustainability* (pp. 115–128). University of the Philippines Open University. https://www.researchgate.net/publication/383543102_Immersive_Open_Pedagogies_in_the_University_of_the_Future

Figueroa Jr., R. B., & Jung, I. (2025). Integrating VR tours in online language learning: A design-based research study. *Australasian Journal of Educational Technology, 41*(1), 70–87. https://doi.org/10.14742/ajet.9498

Ghassemzadeh, H. (2005). Vygotsky's mediational psychology: A new conceptualization of culture, signification and metaphor. *Language Sciences, 27*(3), 281. https://doi.org/10.1016/j.langsci.2004.04.003

Gonzalez, A. F., & Ng, P. (2023). Round the table, education without the 2d frame constraints: A WebVR experience from a glocal perspective. In *Blucher Design Proceedings* (pp. 1017–1028). https://doi.org/10.5151/sigradi2022-sigradi2022_272

Gruber, A., Canto, S., & Jauregi-Ondarra, K. (2023). Exploring the use of social virtual reality for virtual exchange. *ReCALL, 35*(3), 258–273. https://doi.org/10.1017/S0958344023000125

Hwang, Y., & Lee, J. H. (2024). "Yes, I am more confident with my avatars": Integrating EFL students' speaking practice into metaverse. *RELC Journal*. https://doi.org/10.1177/00336882241251952

Jiao, Y., DeWitt, D., & Razak, R. B. A. (2024). Exploring the potential of metaverse-based platforms for enhancing English as a Foreign Language (EFL) learning: A comprehensive systematic review. *International Journal of Information and Education Technology, 14*(2), 231–239. https://doi.org/10.18178/ijiet.2024.14.2.2044

Kits, K., & Meristo, M. (2025). Fostering oral creativity in the foreign language classroom. *Discover Education, 4*(1), 417. https://doi.org/10.1007/s44217-025-00882-z
Lataifeh, M., & Ahmed, N. (2024). Metamorphosis of EduX: A comparative study for education in the metaverse. *Frontiers in Computer Science, 6*. https://doi.org/10.3389/fcomp.2024.1423768
Lee, S.-M., & Ahn, T. Y. (2024). L2 learner experiences in a playful constructivist metaverse space. *ReCALL, 37*(1), 129–145. https://doi.org/10.1017/s0958344024000235
Li, M., & Yu, Z. (2023). A systematic review on the metaverse-based blended English learning. *Frontiers in Psychology, 13*, 1087508. https://doi.org/10.3389/fpsyg.2022.1087508
Loewen, S., & Sato, M. (2018). Interaction and instructed second language acquisition. *Language Teaching, 51*(3), 285–329. https://doi.org/10.1017/S0261444818000125
M. Minei, E., Razuvaeva, T., & Dyshko, D. (2021). Modern day digital pen pals: A semester-long Collaborative Online International Learning (COIL) project. *Communication Teacher, 35*(4), 336–344. https://doi.org/10.1080/17404622.2021.1887906
Montes, C. S., & Lázaro, O. J. (2023). Digital Language Immersion (DLI) and virtual exchanges. In *Routledge eBooks* (p. 267). Informa. https://doi.org/10.4324/9781003146391-14
Nuesser, M., Zheng, D., & Dong, J. (2024). Optimizing affordances of high immersive virtual reality for language learning. *Journal of China Computer-Assisted Language Learning*. https://doi.org/10.1515/jccall-2023-0006
Onu, P., Pradhan, A., & Mbohwa, C. (2023). Potential to use metaverse for future teaching and learning. *Education and Information Technologies, 29*(7), 8893–8924. https://doi.org/10.1007/s10639-023-12167-9
Rubin, J. (2017). Embedding Collaborative Online International Learning (COIL) at higher education institutions. *Internationalization of Higher Education, 2*, 27–44.
Sahyoni, S., Damanik, L. A., & Oktarina, H. (2025). Co-creation in English teaching: Enhancing student engagement and learning in an English language education program. *Journal of Language and Pragmatics Studies, 4*(1), 52–65. https://doi.org/10.58881/jlps.v4i1.51
Salmanova, S. (2025). Communicative approach in foreign language teaching: Advantages and limitations. *EuroGlobal Journal of Linguistics and Language Education, 2*(1), 79–88. https://doi.org/10.69760/egjlle.250009
Shonfeld, M., Cotnam-Kappel, M., Judge, M., Ng, C., Ntebutse, J. G., Williamson-Leadley, S., & Yildiz, M. N. (2021). Learning in digital environments: A model for cross-cultural alignment. *Educational Technology Research and Development, 69*(4), 2151–2170. https://doi.org/10.1007/s11423-021-09967-6
Swain, M., & Watanabe, Y. (2012). Languaging: Collaborative dialogue as a source of second language learning. *The Encyclopedia of Applied Linguistics*. https://doi.org/10.1002/9781405198431.wbeal0664
Vahed, A., & Rodriguez, K. (2020). Enriching students' engaged learning experiences through the collaborative online international learning project. *Innovations in Education and Teaching International, 58*(5), 596–605. https://doi.org/10.1080/14703297.2020.1792331
Valizadeh, M., & Morady Moghaddam, M. (2025). Metaverse magic: Improving language learners' intercultural understanding through virtual reality. *Journal of Multilingual and Multicultural Development, 46*(7), 2062–2081. https://doi.org/10.1080/01434632.2025.2538691
Vygotsky, L. S. (1967). Play and its role in the mental development of the child. *Soviet Psychology, 5*(3), 6. https://doi.org/10.2753/rpo1061-040505036
Wu, J. G., Feng Teng, M., & Lindsay, M. (2022). Challenges in a mobile English telecollaborative project: Towards a conceptual model. *Australasian Journal of Educational Technology, 38*(1), 1–19. https://doi.org/10.14742/ajet.6371
Wu, Y.-H.S., & Hung, S. A. (2022). The effects of virtual reality infused instruction on elementary school students' English-speaking performance, willingness to communicate, and learning autonomy. *Journal of Educational Computing Research, 60*(6), 1558–1587. https://doi.org/10.1177/07356331211068207

Ying-jie, L., & Shirley, T. (2021). Without crossing a border: Exploring the impact of shifting study abroad online on students' learning and intercultural competence development during the COVID-19 pandemic. *Online Learning*, *25*(1). https://doi.org/10.24059/olj.v25i1.2471

Zhang, X., Chen, Y., Hu, L., & Wang, Y. (2022). The metaverse in education: Definition, framework, features, potential applications, challenges, and future research topics. *Frontiers in Psychology*, *13*. https://doi.org/10.3389/fpsyg.2022.1016300

Dr. Roberto Figueroa Jr. is the Dean of the Faculty of Information and Communication Studies (FICS) at the University of the Philippines Open University (UPOU), where he also serves as the Program Leader of Immersive Open Pedagogies (IOP) at the Immersive Spatial Technologies and Realities Laboratories (ISTaR Labs). His research focuses on expanding access to education and fostering global collaboration through immersive technologies, open pedagogy, and intercultural communication. He is one of the pioneering Filipino members of the metaverse Academic Nexus for Global Opportunities (MANGOs) initiative and one of the managing editors of the International Journal for Educational Media and Technology. He is also a visiting research fellow at Meiji University and a Transpacific Bridge Fellow at the Tokyo University of Foreign Studies (TUFS), where he actively coordinates and implements various Collaborative Online International Learning (COIL) activities as well as faculty, staff, and student exchanges between UPOU and partner universities in Japan and USA.

Dr. Mehrasa Alizadeh is Associate Professor at Otemon Gakuin University in Ibaraki, Osaka, Japan, where she teaches English as a foreign language to Japanese students. Mehrasa's research interests include mobile learning, immersive learning, and the use of virtual reality in language education. She has published and presented extensively on immersive learning in international conferences and journals.

Dr. Aya Fukuda is a lecturer at Tokyo University of Foreign Studies, Japan. She obtained her Master of Arts from the Institute of Education, University of London (The UCL Institute of Education, the faculty of education and society, University College London). Then, she obtained her Doctor of Philosophy from International Christian University, Tokyo, Japan. She was engaged in international education and development projects and international exchange programs. She is now actively engaged in projects for collaborative online international learning (COIL) with universities in the US, the Philippines, Cambodia, India, Indonesia, Norway, Pakistan and Sri Lanka. Her areas of interests include learning outcomes of COIL, education for peace, experiential learning and promoting mutual understanding online.

Socio-Emotional, Ethical, and Sustainable Dimensions

Critical Perspectives on the Potential and Challenges of Metaverse-Based Language Teaching and Learning

Neda Fatehi Rad, Zuraina Ali, Hamed Barjesteh, and Shaghayegh Shirzad

Abstract This study investigates the challenges of integrating Artificial Intelligence (AI), particularly ChatGPT, into English language education in Iran, and positions these challenges within the broader framework of Metaverse-Based Language Learning (MBLL).Semi-structured interviews were conducted with 20 Iranian EFL university teachers, purposively selected from diverse institutions. Data were analyzed through systematic thematic analysis using MAXQDA software. Eight major challenges emerged: filtering-related restrictions, lack of privacy, plagiarism concerns, overdependence on AI, inadequate safeguards, reduced self-efficacy, lack of institutional policy, and unequal access to technology. These challenges highlight the socio-technical barriers that shape AI adoption in restricted contexts. The findings reveal the urgent need for clear policies, safeguards, and equitable access to harness AI responsibly in language education. They also suggest that AI-related challenges are not confined to local restrictions but have global parallels, offering insights into how MBLL could be adapted for low-resource and politically constrained contexts.

Keyword Artificial Intelligence · Challenge · Chat GPT · English language education

N. F. Rad
Department of English Language, Ke.C., Islamic Azad University, Kerman, Iran

Z. Ali
Department of English, Universiti Malaysia Pahang Al-Sultan Abdullah (UMPSA), Pekan, Malaysia
e-mail: zuraina@umpsa.edu.my

H. Barjesteh (✉)
Department of English Language, Am.C., Islamic Azad University, Amol, Iran
e-mail: Hamed.Barjesteh@iau.ac.ir

S. Shirzad
Eiman Narimani Marketing Management Co. L. L.C., Dubai, UAE

F. Çelik and C. Yangın Ersanlı (eds.), *Metaverse-Based Language Learning and Teaching*, English Language Education 49,
https://doi.org/10.1007/978-3-032-31366-9_10

1 Introduction

The earth is currently experiencing a quick and remarkable shift towards the 'Fourth Industrial Revolution' (4th IR). According to Ross and Maynard (2021), this word was introduced in Germany's 2030 strategy plan. As put by Schwab (2018), the 4th IR is considerably different from other human experiences with regard to scale, breadth, and complexity, and this is what helps it transform human life, work, and social interactions. The 4th IR integrates physical, digital, and biological technologies, including biotechnology, artificial intelligence (AI), nanotechnology, robotics, and the Internet of Things (IoT) (Catal & Tekinerdogan, 2019).

The enumerated technologies of the 4th IR are influencing different aspects of society, including its industrial, agricultural, economic, and educational aspects. The traces of the 4th IR have been revealed and are predicted to reach their climax in 2030. There is evidence that with such quick transformations, Fifth, Sixth, and subsequent Industrial Revolutions are also not far from mind. While the future is always volatile, uncertain, complex, and ambiguous, what is clearly expected is that various dimensions of human life will be influenced by significant changes, transformations, opportunities, and challenges (Chivu et al., 2022).

Various domains of education, including English language education, have been influenced in various degrees by the rapid advancement of artificial intelligence (AI) technologies (Rasul et al., 2023; Yan, 2023). The emergence of AI-driven language models such as ChatGPT is considered clear evidence for this claim. AI-driven language models have the potential to generate coherent text, engage in interactive dialogue, and assist in a multitude of educational tasks, including language learning (Cao et al., 2023; Labruna et al., 2023; Mahmut & Şen, 2023; Moustaghfir & Brigui, 2024; Mohamed, 2023; Otani et al., 2023; Wang et al., 2023a, 2023b, 2023c; Xiao & Zhi, 2023). This is why we see the integration of AI into different areas of English education, including teaching and research domains (Vaccino-Salvadore, 2023). English education systems are influenced by AI, which is predicted to bring important positive transformations to educational plans, instructional processes, and learning opportunities (Aiken & Epstein, 2000; Kim et al., 2023; Kostka & Toncelli, 2023; Rukiati et al., 2023; Wei, 2023).

The popularity of AI technologies is due to customized feedback, individualized learning styles, enhanced motivation and autonomy of users, and the diversity of tasks they use (Liu & Ma, 2024). This makes AI a promising tool for empowering learners, especially those with limited access to native English speakers. Moreover, in today's global era, communication and interaction across horizons and time zones have become increasingly pervasive thanks to the emergence of AI. Besides, the introduction of e-learning platforms and remote work arrangements has highlighted the importance of English language learning for effective AI-based interactions and communications. The trend toward remote and digital communication is also seen in more general studies in education and the workplace. The widespread use of digital platforms in contemporary communication and education is highlighted by studies on social media influencer marketing (Fauzi et al., 2024a, 2024b) and the investigation of learning management systems such as Blackboard for language training (Nasim et al., 2024). Research on workplace stress in higher education (Fauzi et al., 2024a, 2024b) also emphasizes the changing difficulties that educational institutions face as they undergo this digital transformation. The whole picture of these studies depicts an increasingly digitizing educational world, which is crucial background information for comprehending the high risks involved in integrating AI. English proficiency, in such an era, is characterized by more conducive AI-based communications with individuals with different backgrounds and helps the removal of problems that are rooted in language deficiencies (Dugošija, 2024).

Despite these advantages, the implementation and use of AI in language education in Iran are prohibited. In fact, still, threadbare educational methods and tools are prevalent in Iran. At first glance, it may seem that since overreliance on AI may hinder the development of critical thinking and autonomous learning skills (Vasconcelos et al., 2023), Iranian researchers, teachers, and learners are deprived of AI. However, the problem is more complex than this. Filtering and prohibition are here to stay and, in turn, influence various educational circles, including language education. Delving into this issue requires a local study with Iranian participants, allowing for the unraveling of the hidden layers of the unequal war between AI and traditional methods. To this end, this study aimed to explore the challenges of implementing AI in the English language education system in Iran. This chapter presents critical perspectives that are important for balanced understanding of metaverse-based language learning. However, given that the field is still emerging, many of these challenges may be addressed or mitigated through future technological advances, improved pedagogical practices, or better institutional support. The intention is not to discourage innovation but rather to encourage thoughtful, evidence-based implementation that is attentive to both opportunities and risks.

While the study primarily examined the challenges of using AI in English language education in Iran, these findings can also be positioned within the broader framework of Metaverse-Based Language Learning (MBLL). The immersive and interactive affordances of metaverse environments, such as virtual classrooms and 3D learning spaces, are powered by AI-driven tools that facilitate real-time interaction and adaptive feedback. Thus, understanding Iranian teachers' concerns about AI—ranging from filtering and access restrictions to ethical safeguards—also sheds light on the readiness and constraints that may influence the implementation of MBLL. Integrating AI challenges into metaverse contexts highlights that AI is not only a precursor but also a critical enabler of sustainable MBLL initiatives.

2 Literature Review

This study is conceptually built upon educational technology (ET). ET is the effective planning of any methods, procedures, and outcomes to achieve specific educational objectives (Smyrnova-Trybulska et al., 2019). This involves systematic recognition of the objectives of education, acceptance of the variety of learners' needs, learning context, and different measures needed for each need. Designing efficient systems that make use of suitable teaching–learning techniques in order to accomplish predetermined goals is a major challenge in educational technology. Studies examining the effective use of diverse digital technologies to achieve particular learning objectives make this notion clear. For example, studies have demonstrated that preschool teachers can effectively manage their knowledge using YouTube (Ali et al, 2022a, 2022b), that children can benefit from using devices for learning (Ali et al, 2020), and that Google Docs and other platforms can motivate collective online writing (Shahidan et al., 2022). Additionally, the examination of video resumes shows how students' professional self-presentation abilities can be enhanced through the use of technology (Ali et al., 2022a, 2022b). These examples demonstrate a global trend of using accessible technologies to address a range of educational needs; this tendency contrasts strongly with Iran's restrictive environment, where the process of systematic integration is a major barrier. Therefore, the solution to this problem is an appreciation of the role of ET as an agent of change in the classroom, which includes not only the teacher and the teaching–learning process but also systemic issues like reach, equity, and quality (McPherson & Bacow, 2015).

AI and AI-driven systems are primarily designed to generate original outputs based on identification and replication patterns from extensive datasets. They are characterized by an architecture that is built upon deep learning techniques, including attention mechanisms for processing and generating contextually adaptive responses (Schukow et al., 2024). AI synthesizes novel outputs, enabling it to perform diverse tasks such as natural language generation, machine translation, and question answering (Olivas-Padilla et al., 2024).

In language learning, AI is especially influential thanks to its capability to simulate human-like interactions and provide users with customized assistance. It is helpful for students in different areas, including grammar correction, composition writing, and vocabulary building, through customized feedback based on user input (Hayawi et al., 2024). Moreover, it has the potential to analyze and summarize vast amounts of data, help content comprehension, and support data-driven learning (Ray, 2023). However, it should not be missed that it works based on pre-training patterns rather than fundamental understanding, meaning it is devoid of human understanding and reasoning (Wu et al., 2023).

In sum, the application of AI in language education has surged due to its potential to enhance individualized learning experiences, its adaptability to individual learners, the provision of customized feedback, and resources adapted to students' needs (Zawacki-Richter et al., 2019). Additionally, it provides opportunities to practice language skills in interactive and low-pressure environments. It can simulate authentic conversational scenarios, offer immediate feedback, and foster learner autonomy (Amin, 2023; Sumakul et al., 2022; Tahir & Tahir, 2023).

Beyond language learning, AI's applications extend to areas such as homework assistance, research, and writing assignments. For teachers, AI can mechanize grading and scoring, leaving more time for customized instruction (Alqahtani et al.,

2023). This integration of AI promises to make education more efficient and accessible. This implies that AI's applications are not confined to one group and encompass different groups of stakeholders, including learners, teachers, and researchers. Despite these benefits, the use of AI is prohibited in Iran. As such, using AI in Iran for educational purposes is a challenging task. With a view to the transformative potentials of AI for language learning, this scenario may have negative implications for Iranian learners, teachers, and researchers. Accordingly, some people have taken different tricks to use AI for educational purposes. Although a key step in removing this prohibition is fostering collaboration and thoughtful policies of top-level authorities, exploring challenges of using AI may uncover hidden layers of this phenomenon. Filling this research gap is the primary mission of the present study.

Earlier studies also provide valuable context for the current challenges. Warschauer (1996) underscored issues of digital equity in CALL, foreshadowing the digital divide that persists in AI and metaverse contexts. Similarly, Selwyn (2011) emphasized the socio-political dimensions of educational technology, reminding us that adoption is often constrained by policy and cultural factors. These classic perspectives enrich contemporary debates by showing that today's AI and metaverse challenges echo earlier concerns about equity, access, and institutional readiness.

3 Methodology

3.1 Participants

The study recruited 20 Iranian EFL university teachers, purposively selected from teachers working with AI for teaching and research purposes. They were selected from different Iranian universities, permitting the extraction of diverse views. Their mean age was 50. They had from 5 to 20 years of teaching experience.

Of the 20 participants, 12 were male and 8 females, representing a range of disciplines within English language education, including applied linguistics, translation studies, and TEFL. They were affiliated with both public and private universities across Iran, reflecting institutional diversity. Such demographic variation enriches the interpretation of findings by ensuring that perspectives are drawn from different institutional types and teaching experiences.

3.2 Instruments

The data collection instrument employed in this study was semi-structured interviews, due to their potential to facilitate in-depth investigation of participants' perceptions and views while keeping a structured approach (Creswell & Clark, 2007). The planning of the interview guide was based on a rigorous process, including literature review and expert consultations to ensure its comprehensiveness. The interview questions addressed the challenges of using AI for teaching, learning, and research purposes in English language education in Iran. The sequence of questions was carefully structured from simple to challenging to build rapport and encourage nuanced reflections, avoiding unanticipated ethical problems. Rigor and trustworthiness in interview data entail credibility, transferability, dependability, and confirmability of the research findings (Creswell & Clark, 2007). To confirm the credibility of the findings, low-inference descriptors were employed. To this end, for each theme, two quotations were provided to observe credibility issues. To observe transferability, a rich and detailed description of the research participants, data collection, data analysis, and findings was provided, so that the readers could judge the similarity and relevance of the study to their own situations or interests. Concerning dependability, when the themes were extracted, some themes were randomly checked with the participants to verify the interpretation of their sayings. Finally, to confirm the confirmability of the findings, the ethical issues and dilemmas that arose during the research, such as informed consent, anonymity, and data confidentiality, were considered.

3.3 Data Collection

To collect the data, semi-structured interviews were conducted with the Iranian EFL teachers. To facilitate the interviews, social networks were used so that they could be conducted either as audio discussions or visual meetings over the internet. Participants were provided with enough time to share their views freely, and their permission was taken to record the interview sessions for further transcription and analysis. During the interviews, the researcher took some notes on non-verbal cues, which might be helpful in subsequent thematic analysis. The semi-structured approach permitted a merge of systematic questioning and open conversation, enabling the participants to discuss peripheral issues and express new ideas without repetition.

3.4 Data Analysis

The data collected from the interviews were analyzed using MAXQDA software via a systematic thematic analysis approach, consisting of four steps, including transcript creation and data familiarization, code selection, theme development, and development of a conceptual model (Creswell & Clark, 2007; Kallio et al., 2016). To this end, the files of the transcribed interviews were entered into the 'document system' of the MAXQDA by importing the existing data from the menu. Then, each file was meticulously read line by line for familiarization purposes. Afterwards, to do coding, keywords were identified as open codes. When each code was identified, it was entered into the 'code system'. Next, the evidence related to each code was selected from the 'retrieved segments' option in the MAXQDA and copied to be provided as evidence of each theme. Finally, through the 'creative coding' option in the 'visual tools' option in the menu, the map of the extracted themes was drawn.

4 Results

Thematic analysis was conducted to examine the data and uncover underlying patterns systematically. This process enabled the identification of recurring ideas and concepts that were clustered into overarching categories. As a result, the following key themes emerged, which are presented below as the central findings of the study:

- *Filtering-Related Problems*
- *Lack of Privacy*
- *Plagiarism Concerns*
- *Users' Overdependence on AI*
- *Lack of Strong Safeguards*
- *Undermining Users' Self-Efficacy*
- *Lack of Institutional Policy and Responsibility*
- *Inaccessibility of Technology*

Theme 1: Filtering-Related Problems

The quotations highlight the filtering-related problems expressed by participants regarding the challenges of using AI in Iran. The main codes of this theme were "filtering of AI" and "the need to filter breaker". Participants referred to filtering as a main challenge of using AI. In Iran, AI is filtered, and using it requires a filter breaker. This makes using AI a challenging task. The following quotations show some reflections on filtering-related problems:

> T12: *"As you know, AI is filtered in our country. This makes AI a prohibited tool."*
>
> T8: *"Using AI requires filter breaking, and this imposes extra costs on AI users."*
>
> T17: *"AI is banned in Iran. This is why it cannot be used freely. Inevitably, VPN must be used."*

Theme 2: Lack of Privacy

The following statements highlight the privacy concerns expressed by participants regarding the use of AI. The principal codes of this theme were "lack of privacy of personal information" and "lack of confidentiality of information". Participants believed that personal information of users is not kept private and confidential when using AI.

> T11: *"When using AI, there is danger of leaking personal information of users. There seems to be no definite privacy policy for keeping their personal information."*

T19: *"Private data is not confidential with AI. It is endangered and this irritates users."*

T5: *"I feel that my private information may be revealed by AI. This gives me a bad feeling."*

Theme 3: Plagiarism Concerns

Participants were worried that users could plagiarize the AI's responses without any proficiency. The main codes of this theme were "danger of copying" and "lack of users' engagement". Participants highlighted the danger of users' coping AI-generated materials without their own real engagement.

T13: *"A significant issue is that users can easily plagiarize the AI's materials and repurpose them as human-generated content."*

T10: *"The danger of users' coping AI-generated materials without their own real engagement is a challenge of using AI."*

T9: *"It cannot be made sure that the work is truly human-made and not generated by the AI."*

Theme 4: Users' Overdependence on AI

Participants expressed their concerns about users' overdependence on AI, becoming passive and inactive. Two main codes of this theme were "users' overuse of AI" and "users' passivity and inactivity", as highlighted in the following direct quotations. Users may overuse AI and this makes them passive and inactive.

T7: *"Users may become over dependent on AI. This can surpass analysis and thinking in them. Overuse of AI should not be kept far from mind."*

T2: *"I think that AI can make users passive. If not correctly used, AI leads to users' passivity, which is a major problem."*

T11: *"AI is a valuable tool as long as it does not make users inactive. Users' inactivity is a negative extreme that should be cautiously dealt with."*

Theme 5: Lack of Strong Safeguards

Participants voiced major concerns about the lack of strong safeguards to prevent the risks of AI. The primary themes of this topic were "misusing AI" and "cheating." As shown in the following quotes, the lack of strong safeguards to prevent these risks is an important challenge that cannot be missed.

T1: *"My main concern is that users might use AI to cheat because of a lack of strong safeguards. This technology must be appropriately used, otherwise, its risks overweigh its merits."*

T14: *"Misusing AI is a problem which is big enough to reduce effectiveness of this tool. If not used in its right place, AI can be a means of generating fake information. This needs preventive programs which are currently missing in the system."*

T19: *"If users do not resort to cheating in the absence of controlling policies, AI turns into a tool for cheating."*

Theme 6: Undermining Users' Self-Efficacy

Participants expressed concerns about remarkable reductions in users' self-efficacy as a consequence of using AI. The principal codes of this theme were "reduced self-efficacy" and "increased anxiety". It was perceived that overreliance upon AI can reduce users' self-efficacy and increase their anxiety.

T20: "*Relying too much on AI undermines users' self-efficacy because it weakens human function and performance.*"

T18: "*Using AI increases anxiety in some users. This reduces their self-efficacy.*"

T12: "Reduced *self-efficacy is a negative side effect of using AI. This contributes to other problems that are debilitating.*"

Theme 7: Lack of Institutional Policy and Responsibility

Participants voiced their concerns about the lack of institutional policy and responsibility to support the use of AI in Iran. No organization is accountable to users in this regard. The following extracts show that the main codes of this theme are "lack of institutional policy" and "lack of institutional responsibility".

T9: "*In Iran, you cannot find any registered organization that takes the responsibility to support users in using AI. There is no institutional policy to guide users.*"

T6: "*A well-designed support system is crucial for operationalization of any new application. This is while you cannot find any policy for governance of AI use. Accountability and responsibility are missing links.*"

T15: "*Because of sanction as well as its related problems, no organization has been assigned the task of policy development for applying AI. Therefore, users are confused when faced with a problem.*"

Theme 8: Inaccessibility of Technology

Participants expressed concerns that, due to unequal distribution of facilities among users, some users do not have access to the technological requirements for the use of AI. This implies that users' unequal access to technology makes using AI challenging. The principal codes of this theme were "inaccessibility of smartphones" and "inaccessibility of VPN".

T1: "*My biggest concern is that those who cannot afford the premium version of these tools cannot utilize them to their full potential.*"

T14: "*Students with the means to use it have an advantage over their peers who can't afford it or don't have the necessary.*"

T3: "*In some countries like ours, many of these chatbots, like ChatGPT, are not available, and we cannot buy unlimited versions of them.*"

Figure 1 illustrates the Max map of the extracted themes, along with their corresponding codes.

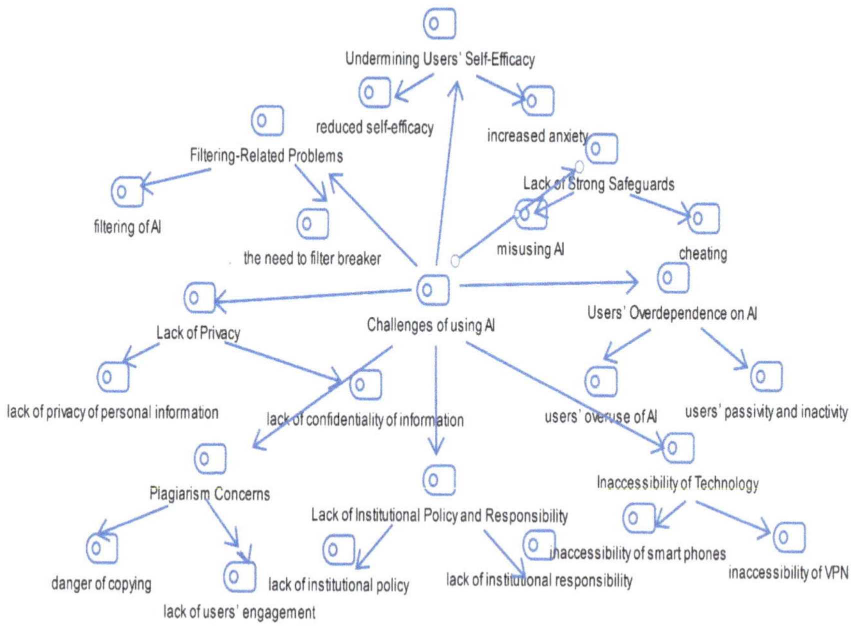

Fig. 1 The Max map of the extracted themes and their odes

5 Discussion

This study explored the challenges of using AI in the English language education system in Iran from EFL teachers' viewpoints. The findings highlight the following themes and codes as challenges of using AI in the English language education system in Iran: Filtering-related problems (codes: filtering of AI, the need to filter breaker), lack of privacy (codes: lack of privacy of personal information, lack of confidentiality of information), plagiarism concerns (codes: danger of copying, lack of users' engagement), users' overdependence on AI (codes: users' overuse of AI, users' passivity and inactivity), lack of strong safeguards (codes: misusing AI, cheating), undermining users' self-efficacy (codes: reduced self-efficacy, increased anxiety), lack of institutional policy and responsibility (codes: lack of institutional policy, lack of institutional responsibility), and inaccessibility of technology (codes: inaccessibility of smart phones, inaccessibility of VPN).

Beyond Iran, similar challenges have been reported in other restricted or low-resource contexts. For example, teachers in China have reported difficulties with platform filtering and ethical concerns in AI-assisted learning, while educators in parts of Africa face barriers linked to cost and unequal access to high-speed internet. In contrast, teachers in well-resourced countries highlight issues of overdependence and plagiarism but benefit from clearer institutional policies. Positioning Iran's case within this global picture underscores both the uniqueness of its political constraints and the universality of AI-related educational dilemmas.

Lack of privacy emerged as a challenge of using AI in English language education in Iran, aligning with prior studies. This concern for safe and moral technology use is consistent with broader issues in the sector, such as evaluations of technology management and the educational value of digital learning platforms (Ali et al., 2022a, 2022b; Nasim et al., 2024). Prinsloo and Slade (2016) and Stahl and Eke (2020) emphasized the empty place of privacy in some educational technologies, which resonates in the Iranian EFL context. Godwin-Jones (2019) delved into privacy in CALL and found low degrees of privacy within this area. The findings also refine Guo et al.'s (2024) insistence on mitigating privacy risks in AI-powered education.

Plagiarism concerns associated with AI tools were also prominently discussed in previous studies. Crews (1993) and Rane et al. (2023) showed that AI-generated content questions academic honesty. Plagiarism concerns highlight the need for effective measures to promote responsible use of AI, reflecting intellectual reasoning in the digital age (Crews, 1993). Users' overdependence on AI is consistent with Bok and Cho (2023) and Heejoo (2023). It also resonates with Hasanein and Sobaih's (2023) concept of "cognitive offloading," implying students' lack of deep engagement. This study reflects the paramountcy of balanced AI use to avoid debilitating development of human performance. The urgent need for safeguards to avoid risks of misusing AI echoes Hua et al.'s (2023) research on AI governance, reflecting how strategic control may avoid risks associated with AI. Apparently, regardless of context, safeguards are necessary for preventive purposes. Otherwise, the risk of AI misuse is high.

Undermining users' self-efficacy as a negative psychological impact of AI was also noted by Ajlouni et al. (2023) and Ngo (2023). It highlights the need for planning ethical guidelines that target preventing the negative side effects of AI on users. Ethical guidelines help mitigate such reverse effects. Lack of institutional policy and responsibility aligns with Jeyaraman et al. (2023) and Stahl and Eke (2020), who emphasized the specific need for institutions to develop AI-sensitive policies to promote and support AI use. Similarly, Ulla et al. (2023) called for institutional leadership in confronting AI's problems and complexities. The inaccessibility of technology echoes Warschauer and Matuchniak's (2010) emphasis on the digital divide, and Gottschalk and Weise's (2023) highlighting of unequal opportunities in technology use. This study corroborates these findings by reporting unequal access to technology in Iran. Closely related to this, Massala (2023) referred to justice in the distribution of technology. Additionally, Mehrabi et al. (2021) warned against disparities in technological systems and bias in access to educational AI. Lastly, Wang and Siau (2019) emphasized the importance of fairness and inclusivity in AI-driven education. This difficulty is not unique to AI; rather, it is a basic problem of resource distribution equity, which is also evident in studies on educational resources and across multidisciplinary domains, including material science, where access to cutting-edge data and materials is essential (Ruslan et al., 2024).

6 Conclusion

The integration of AI in English language education has proven to be a multifaceted landscape rife with challenges demanding careful attention. This study has identified several key issues that encapsulate the following challenges: filtering-related problems, lack of privacy, plagiarism concerns, users' overdependence on AI, inadequate safeguards, undermining users' self-efficacy, lack of institutional policy and responsibility, and inaccessibility of technology. Unfortunately, as long as filtering-related problems are not solved, there is little hope of coping with other challenges. Iranian educational and political policymakers are required to take appropriate measures to remove the filtering of AI as an invaluable tool for educational purposes. Stakeholders of educational circles, including teachers, students, and researchers, are the main losers in this game because they lag behind recent educational improvements with the current threadbare methods that are here to stay in Iran. These findings have far-reaching implications for various stakeholders. Top-level policymakers in Iran should take regulatory measures to remove the filtering of AI and facilitate its use in English education. For teachers, it necessitates a shift in their approaches from traditional methods to AI-driven ones. This may turn into a demanding act that obliges authorities to remove the filtering. Policy-making organizations must develop regulatory policies to govern AI use to avoid AI misuse. Finally, AI designers should incorporate governance considerations in designing AI to control plagiarism and address such ethical concerns. The study opens up new avenues for further research, such as futurology of English education under the shadow of AI, developing anti-filtering AI-driven pedagogical methods, exploring the psychological and motivational aspects of AI integration, and assessing AI literacy of Iranian teachers, students, and researchers.

Future research should move beyond AI in isolation and explicitly investigate how AI-mediated challenges intersect with metaverse-based language learning. Studies might, for example, examine how Iranian EFL teachers and learners adapt to immersive 3D classrooms, or how policy restrictions influence the integration of AI-powered avatars and virtual simulations. Exploring these directions will align the research more closely with the overarching theme of metaverse-based education and provide concrete pathways for future practice and policy.

References

Aiken, R. M., & Epstein, R. G. (2000). Ethical guidelines for AI in education: Starting a conversation. *International Journal of Artificial Intelligence in Education, 11*(2), 163–176.

Ajlouni, A. O., Wahba, F. A. A., & Almahaireh, A. S. (2023). Students' attitudes towards using ChatGPT as a learning tool: The case of the University of Jordan. *International Journal of Interactive Mobile Technologies, 17*(18). https://doi.org/10.3991/ijim.v17i18.41753

Ali, Z., Abu Bakar, N., Ahmad Tilwani, S., & Ajanil, B. (2022). Knowledge management and technology management: The use of YouTube among preschool teachers. *Education Research International*. https://doi.org/10.1155/2022/3166476

Ali, Z., Ali, A. Z. M., Harbi, S., Hassan, S. A. J., Nor, A. N. M., & Sahar, N. S. (2022b). Help me to find a job: An analysis of students' delivery strategies in video resume. *Asian Journal of University Education, 18*(2), 489–498. https://doi.org/10.24191/ajue.v18i2.18002

Ali, Z., Anuar, A. M. B. M., Mustafa, N. A. B., Halim, K. N. B. A., & Sivabalan, K. (2020). A preliminary study on the uses of gadgets among children for learning purposes. *Journal of Physics: Conference Series, 1529*(5). https://doi.org/10.1088/1742-6596/1529/5/052055

Alqahtani, T., Badreldin, H. A., Alrashed, M., Alshaya, A. I., Alghamdi, S. S., bin Saleh, K., Albekairy, A. M., et al. (2023). The emergent role of artificial intelligence, natural learning processing, and large language models in higher education and research. *Research in Social and Administrative Pharmacy, 19*(8), 1236–1242. https://doi.org/10.1016/j.sapharm.2023.05.016

Amin, M. Y. M. (2023). AI and Chat GPT in language teaching: Enhancing EFL classroom support and transforming assessment techniques. *International Journal of Higher Education Pedagogies, 4*(4), 1–15. https://doi.org/10.33422/ijhep.v4i4.554

Bok, E., & Cho, Y. (2023). Examining Korean EFL college students' experiences and perceptions of using ChatGPT as a writing revision tool. *Journal of English Teaching through Movies and Media, 24*(4), 15–27. https://doi.org/10.16875/stem.2023.24.4.15

Catal, C., & Tekinerdogan, B. (2019). Aligning education for the life sciences domain to support digitalization and industry 4.0. *Procedia Computer Science, 158*, 99–106. https://doi.org/10.1016/j.procs.2019.09.032

Cao, Y., et al. (2023). A comprehensive survey of AI-Generated Content (AIGC): A history of generative AI from GAN to ChatGPT. *ArXiv*, abs/2303.04226. http://arxiv.org/abs/2303.04226

Chivu, R. G., Popa, I. C., Orzan, M. C., Marinescu, C., Florescu, M. S., & Orzan, A. O. (2022). The role of blockchain technologies in the sustainable development of the students' learning process. *Sustainability, 14*(3), Article 1406. https://doi.org/10.3390/su14031406

Creswell, J. W., & Plano Clark, V. (2007). *Designing and conducting mixed methods research.* Sage.

Crews, K. D. (1993). *Copyright, fair use, and the challenge for universities: Promoting the progress of higher education.* University of Chicago Press.

Dugošija, T. (2024). Benefits and challenges of artificial intelligence in English language teaching. KNOWLEDGE – *International Journal, 62*(2), 275–280.

Fauzi, M. A., Ali, Z., Satari, Z., Ramli, P. A. M., & Omer, M. (2024a). Social media influencer marketing: Science mapping of the present and future trends. *International Journal of Quality and Service Sciences, 16*(2), 199–217. https://doi.org/10.1108/IJQSS-10-2023-0174

Fauzi, M. A., Rahamaddulla, S. R., Lee, C. K., Ali, Z., & Alias, U. N. (2024b). Work pressure in higher education: A state of the art bibliometric analysis on academic work–life balance. *International Journal of Workplace Health Management, 17*(2), 175–195. https://doi.org/10.1108/IJWHM-01-2023-0002

Godwin-Jones, R. (2019). Responsible data Collection and management in language learning research. *Language Learning & Technology, 23*(3), 1–7.

Gottschalk, F., & Weise, C. (2023). *Digital equity and inclusion in education: An overview of practice and policy in OECD countries.* OECD Education Working Papers No. 299. https://doi.org/10.1787/7cb15030-en

Guo, J., Ma, Y., Li, T., Noetel, M., Liao, K., & Greiff, S. (2024). Harnessing artificial intelligence in generative content for enhancing motivation in learning. *Learning and Individual Differences*, 102547. https://doi.org/10.1016/j.lindif.2024.102547

Hasanein, A. M., & Sobaih, A. E. E. (2023). Drivers and consequences of ChatGPT use in higher education: Key stakeholder perspectives. *European Journal of Investigation in Health, Psychology and Education, 13*(11), 2599–2614. https://doi.org/10.3390/ejihpe13112599

Hayawi, K., Shahriar, S., & Mathew, S. S. (2024). The imitation game: Detecting human and AI-generated texts in the era of ChatGPT and BARD. *Journal of Information Science*, 01655515241227531. https://doi.org/10.1177/01655515241227531

Heejoo, I. (2023). A study on learners' perceptions and attitudes toward the use of ChatGPT in general English classes. *Culture and Convergence, 45*(9), 1335–1342. https://doi.org/10.33645/cnc.2023.09.45.09.1335

Hua, S., Jin, S., & Jiang, S. (2023). The limitations and ethical considerations of ChatGPT. *Data Intelligence*, 1–38. https://doi.org/10.1162/dint_a_00186

Jeyaraman, M., Ramasubramanian, S., Balaji, S., Jeyaraman, N., Nallakumarasamy, A., & Sharma, S. (2023). ChatGPT in action: Harnessing the potential of artificial intelligence and addressing ethical challenges in medicine, education, and scientific research. *World Journal of Methodology, 13*(4), 170. https://doi.org/10.5662/wjm.v13.i4.170

Kallio, H., Pietilä, A. M., Johnson, M., & Kangasniemi, M. (2016). Systematic methodological review: Developing a framework for a qualitative semi-structured interview guide. *Journal of Advanced Nursing, 72*(12), 2954–2965. https://doi.org/10.1111/jan.13031

Kim, S., Shim, J., & Shim, J. (2023). A study on the utilization of ChatGPT as a second language learning tool. *Journal of Multimedia Information System, 10*(1), 79–88. https://doi.org/10.33851/JMIS.2023.10.1.79

Kostka, I., & Toncelli, R. (2023). Exploring the applications of ChatGPT in English language teaching: Opportunities, challenges, and recommendations. *Tesl-Ej, 27*(3), Article n3. https://doi.org/10.55593/ej.27107int

Labruna, T., Brenna, S., Zaninello, A., & Magnini, B. (2023). *Unraveling ChatGPT: A critical analysis of AI-generated goal-oriented dialogues and annotations.* https://arxiv.org/abs/2305.14556

Liu, G., & Ma, C. (2024). Measuring EFL learners' use of ChatGPT in informal digital learning of English based on the technology acceptance model. *Innovation in Language Learning and Teaching, 18*(2), 125–138. https://doi.org/10.1080/17501229.2023.2240316

Liu, M., Ren, Y., Nyagoga, L. M., Stonier, F., Wu, Z., & Yu, L. (2023). The future of education in the era of generative artificial intelligence: Consensus among Chinese scholars on the applications of ChatGPT in schools. *Future in Educational Research, 1*(1), 72–101. https://doi.org/10.1002/fer3.10

Mahmut, D., & Şen, D. Ş. (2023). Reflection of artificial intelligence applications on students' critical and analytical abilities. *Proceedings of the3rdInternational Scientific and Practical Conference, Science and Education in Progress, Ireland, 184*, 459–467. https://archive.interconf.center/index.php/conference-proceeding/article/view/5124

Massala, K. (2023). Navigating bias and ensuring fairness: Equity unveiled in the AI-powered educational landscape. *Apprendre Et Enseigner Aujourd'hui, 13*(1), 37–41. https://doi.org/10.7202/1107542

McPherson, M. S., & Bacow, L. S. (2015). Online higher education: Beyond the hype cycle. *The Journal of Economic Perspectives, 29*(4), 135–153. https://doi.org/10.1257/jep.29.4.135

Mehrabi, N., Morstatter, F., Saxena, N., Lerman, K., & Galstyan, A. (2021). A survey on bias and fairness in machine learning. *ACM Computing Surveys (CSUR), 54*(6), 1–35. https://doi.org/10.1145/3457607

Mohamed, A. M. (2023). Exploring the potential of an AI-based Chatbot (ChatGPT) in enhancing English as a Foreign Language (EFL) teaching: Perceptions of EFL Faculty Members. *Education and Information Technologies*, 1–23. https://doi.org/10.1007/s10639-023-116881

Moustaghfir, S., & Brigui, H. (2024). Navigating critical thinking in the digital era: An Informative exploration. *International Journal of Linguistics, Literature and Translation, 7*(1), 137–143. https://doi.org/10.32996/ijllt.2024.7.1.15

Nasim, S. M., Mujeeba, S., AlShraah, S. M., Khan, I. A., & Ali, Z. (2024). Exploring pedagogical perspectives of EFL instructors: advantages, disadvantages, and implications of Blackboard as an LMS for language instruction. *Cogent Social Sciences, 10*(1). https://doi.org/10.1080/23311886.2024.2312659

Ngo, T. T. A. (2023). The perception by university students of the use of ChatGPT in education. *International Journal of Emerging Technologies in Learning (Online), 18*(17), 4–19. https://doi.org/10.3991/ijet.v18i17.39019

Olivas-Padilla, B. E., Manitsaris, S., & Glushkova, A. (2024). Explainable AI in human motion: A comprehensive approach to analysis, modeling, and generation. *Pattern Recognition*, 110418. https://doi.org/10.1016/j.patcog.2023.110418

Otani, N., Araki, J., Kim, H., & Hovy, E. (2023). On the under-specification of situations in open-domain conversational datasets. In *Proceedings of the 5th Workshop on NLP for Conversational AI (NLP4ConvAI 2023)* (pp. 12–28).

Prinsloo, P., & Slade, S. (2016). Student vulnerability, agency, and learning analytics: An exploration. *Journal of Learning Analytics, 3*(1), 159–182. https://doi.org/10.18608/jla.2016.31.10

Rane, N. L., Choudhary, S. P., Tawde, A., & Rane, J. (2023). ChatGPT is not capable of serving as an author: Ethical concerns and challenges of large language models in education. *International Research Journal of Modernization in Engineering Technology and Science, 5*(10), 851–874. https://doi.org/10.54926/IRJMETS23.10.851

Rasul, T., Nair, S., Kalendra, D., Robin, M., de Oliveira Santini, F., Ladeira, W. J., Heathcote, L., et al. (2023). The Role of ChatGPT in higher education: Benefits, challenges, and future *research directions. Journal of Applied Learning and Teaching, 6*(1), 3888–3894. https://doi.org/10.37074/jalt.2023.6.1.18

Ray, P. P. (2023). ChatGPT: A comprehensive review on background, applications, key challenges, bias, ethics, limitations, and future scope. *Internet of Things and Cyber-Physical Systems*. https://doi.org/10.1016/j.iotcps.2023.100022

Ross, P., & Maynard, K. (2021). Towards a fourth industrial revolution. *Intelligent Buildings International, 13*(3), 159–161. https://doi.org/10.1080/17508975.2021.1873625

Rukiati, E., Wicaksono, J. A., Taufan, G. T., & Suharsono, D. D. (2023). AI on learning English: Application, benefit, and threat. *Journal of Language, Communication, and Tourism, 1*(2), 32–40. https://doi.org/10.25047/jlct.v1i2.3967

Ruslan, H. N., Muthusamy, K., Mat Yahaya, F., Fauzi, M. A., Ismail, M. A., & Ali, Z. (2024). Review on performance of self-compacting concrete containing solid waste and bibliometric properties: A review. *Journal of Building Engineering, 86*. https://doi.org/10.1016/j.jobe.2024.108752

Schukow, C., Smith, S. C., Landgrebe, E., Parasuraman, S., Folaranmi, O. O., Paner, G. P., & Amin, M. B. (2024). Application of ChatGPT in routine diagnostic pathology: Promises, pitfalls, and potential future directions. *Advances in Anatomic Pathology, 31*(1), 15–21. https://doi.org/10.1097/PAP.0000000000000417

Schwab, K. (2018). *Shaping the future of the fourth industrial revolution*. Crown Currency.

Shahidan, S. N., Ali, Z., & Tilwani, S. A. (2022). Fostering motivation in ESL collaborative online writing through Google Docs. *World Journal of English Language, 12*(7), 166–178. https://doi.org/10.5430/wjel.v12n7p166

Smyrnova-Trybulska, E., Morze, N., & Boiko, M. (2019). The impact of educational trends on the digital competence of students in Ukraine and Poland. In E. Smyrnova-Trybulska (Ed.), *E-learning and STEM education, e-learning* (pp. 365–379). Studio Noa for the University of Silesia.

Stahl, B. C., & Eke, D. O. (2020). Artificial intelligence for learning? A systematic literature review of artificial intelligence applications in learning. *Systems Research and Behavioral Science, 37*(5), 807–821. https://doi.org/10.1002/sres.2719

Sumakul, D. T. Y., Hamied, F. A., & Sukyadi, D. (2022). Artificial intelligence in EFL classrooms: Friend or foe?. LEARN Journal: *Language Education and Acquisition Research Network, 15*(1), 232–256. https://so04.tci-thaijo.org/index.php/LEARN/index

Ulla, M. B., Perales, W. F., & Busbus, S. O. (2023). To generate or stop generating response: Exploring EFL teachers' perspectives on ChatGPT in English language teaching in Thailand. *Learning: Research and Practice, 9*(2), 168–182. https://doi.org/10.1080/23735082.2023.2186465

Vaccino-Salvadore, S. (2023). Exploring the ethical dimensions of using ChatGPT in language learning and beyond. *Languages, 8*(3), 191–201. https://doi.org/10.3390/languages8030191

Vasconcelos, H., Jörke, M., Grunde-McLaughlin, M., Gerstenberg, T., Bernstein, M. S., & Krishna, R. (2023). Explanations can reduce overreliance on AI systems during decision-making.

Proceedings of the ACM on Human-Computer Interaction, 7(CSCW1), 1–38. https://doi.org/10.1145/3545969
Wang, T., Lund, B. D., Marengo, A., Pagano, A., Mannuru, N. R., Teel, Z. A., & Pange, J. (2023a). Exploring the potential impact of artificial intelligence (AI) on international students in higher education: Generative AI, chatbots, analytics, and international student success. *Applied Sciences, 13*(11), 6716. https://doi.org/10.3390/app13116716
Wang, W., & Siau, K. L. (2019). Artificial intelligence, machine learning, automation, robotics, future of work and future of humanity: A review and research agenda. *Journal of Database Management, 30*, 61–79.
Wang, X., Liu, Q., Pang, H., Tan, S. C., Lei, J., Wallace, M. P., & Li, L. (2023b). What matters in AI-supported learning: A study of human-AI interactions in language learning using cluster analysis and epistemic network analysis? *Computers & Education, 194*, Article 104703. https://doi.org/10.1016/j.compedu.2022.104703
Wang, Y., Pan, Y., Yan, M., Su, Z., & Luan, T. H. (2023c). A survey on ChatGPT: AI-generated content, challenges, and solutions. *IEEE Open Journal of the Computer Society*. https://doi.org/10.1109/OJCS.2023.3300321
Warschauer, M., & Matuchniak, T. (2010). New technology and digital worlds: Analyzing evidence of equity in access, use, and outcomes. *Review of Research in Education, 34*(1), 179–225. https://doi.org/10.3102/0091732X09349791
Wei, L. (2023). Artificial intelligence in language instruction: Impact on English learning achievement, L2 motivation, and self-regulated learning. *Frontiers in Psychology, 14*, 1–14. https://doi.org/10.3389/fpsyg.2023.1261955
Wu, T., He, S., Liu, J., Sun, S., Liu, K., Han, Q. L., & Tang, Y. (2023). A brief overview of ChatGPT: The history, status quo and potential future development. *IEEE/CAA Journal of Automatica Sinica, 10*(5), 1122–1136. https://doi.org/10.1109/JAS.2023.0120252
Xiao, Y., & Zhi, Y. (2023). An exploratory study of EFL learners' Use of ChatGPT for language learning tasks: Experiences and perceptions. *Languages, 8*(3), 212–220. https://doi.org/10.3390/languages8030212
Yan, D. (2023). Impact of ChatGPT on learners in a L2 writing practicum: An exploratory investigation. *Education and Information Technologies, 28*(11), 13943–13967. https://doi.org/10.1007/s10639-023-11603-x
Zawacki-Richter, O., Marín, V. I., Bond, M., & Gouverneur, F. (2019). Systematic review of research on artificial intelligence applications in higher education: Where are the educators? *International Journal of Educational Technology in Higher Education, 16*(1), 1–27. https://doi.org/10.1186/s41239-019-0171-0

Neda Fatehi Rad is an assistant professor of English Language Teaching at Islamic Azad University, Kerman Branch, Iran. She is also the director of the Journal on New Trends in English Language Teaching (JNTELL). She mainly teaches language testing, research methodology and research at the graduate level and her main areas of interest include teachers' education, cooperative learning, language testing and research. She has published 62 papers in international and national academic journals. She has published five books in the field of translation, language learning, and teaching.

Zuraina Ali is an Associate Professor of English at the Centre for Modern Languages in Universiti Malaysia Pahang (UMP). She is the Dean of the Centre for Modern Languages, UMP. She has co-authored several English textbooks that are used in the university. She has also contributed to writing academic papers on vocabulary learning and the use of technology at the tertiary level in second language learning. Her research interests include Technology-related issues in language teaching, ESL/EFL education, especially with beginners in an e-Learning environment, and the use of new web-based learning environments to support learning and vocabulary learning among language learners. A trainer of English courses for adult and research methodology in and outside the university, she conducted language and research courses training. Currently, she is active in providing seminars/webinars on the learning of language and research methodology courses. She was invited by associations and universities for talks in her country, besides Oman, India, Pakistan, and the King of Saudi Arabia, Bangladesh.

Hamed Barjesteh is an Associate Professor of Applied Linguistics with over 20 years of experience in teacher education, academic leadership, and research. He has served as head of the English department and a rector. He has published extensively in Scopus-, ESCI-, and SSCI-indexed journals, focusing on critical pedagogy, educational, and positive psychology. He has delivered keynotes and chaired sessions at international conferences, supervised numerous M.A. and Ph.D. theses, served on the editorial boards of leading journals, and acted as an external Ph.D. examiner and a member of the national entrance exam committee. His academic influence extends through global collaborations, editorial service, and knowledge-based projects in TESOL and Applied Linguistics.

Shaghayegh Shirzad holds a Ph.D. in Teaching English as a Foreign Language (TEFL). She currently works as a teacher-training consultant at various English language institutes, where she supports professional development initiatives and advances effective pedagogical practices. Dr. Shirzad has actively participated in numerous national and international seminars, conferences, trainings, and workshops, focusing on research in applied linguistics and language communication. Her scholarly interests include language learning strategies, the cultivation of critical thinking skills, and the integration of critical pedagogy in language education. Through her work, she seeks to bridge the gap between theory and practice in English language teaching, promoting reflective teaching practices that empower both learners and educators.

Sustainable Education with Metaverse Based Language Teaching

Kumutha Raman, Wei Lun Wong, and Nur Izzati Khairuddin

Abstract This systematic literature review, guided by PRISMA protocols, synthesizes findings from 25 high-impact studies published between 2020 and 2025 to explore the convergence of Metaverse-Based Language Teaching (MBLT) and the principles of sustainable education. In response to global calls for inclusive, equitable, and engaging learning pathways aligned with SDG 4, this review investigates how the metaverse is conceptualized and implemented to create lifelong language learning opportunities. The analysis reveals that the educational metaverse is characterized by immersion, advanced computing, and socialization, enabling experiential learning in safe, simulated environments. Findings indicate that MBLT significantly enhances student engagement, motivation, and collaborative skills, with applications ranging from virtual language exchanges to STEM and teacher training. However, the review also identifies critical challenges, including variable impacts on specific learning outcomes like oral proficiency, significant concerns regarding privacy and cybersecurity, and the risk of exacerbating digital inequalities. This chapter concludes that while the metaverse holds substantial promise for enriching education through immersive and equitable learning experiences, its sustainable integration requires a measured, pedagogically-driven approach. Future efforts must prioritize addressing ethical concerns, ensuring equitable access, and explicitly linking metaverse implementations to the goals of education for sustainable development.

Keywords Metaverse · Language teaching · Sustainable education · Systematic literature review · Educational technology · SDG 4

K. Raman · N. I. Khairuddin
INTI International University, Nilai, Malaysia

W. L. Wong (✉)
Faculty of Education, Universiti Kebangsaan Malaysia, Bangi, Malaysia
e-mail: colinw@ukm.edu.my

F. Çelik and C. Yangın Ersanlı (eds.), *Metaverse-Based Language Learning and Teaching*, English Language Education 49,
https://doi.org/10.1007/978-3-032-31366-9_11

1 Introduction

This fast-paced world has witnessed tremendous digital transformation in education. Emerging technologies and frameworks have shaped the current pedagogy to foster more effective teaching and learning practices. Equally important is the global call for sustainability in education that is in line with Sustainable Development Goal (SDG) 4, where educators and learners adopt new methods to reimagine their teaching and learning pathway to ensure inclusive and equitable quality education. Particularly, language learning and teaching have gained popularity through immersive experiences across the world, especially language learning and teaching through metaverse. This chapter explores the connection between sustainable education and Metaverse-based language teaching (MBLT), which, together, creates equitable, engaging and lifelong learning opportunities.

As the world faces challenges of access, quality, and inclusivity in education, integrating the metaverse; a network of interconnected virtual worlds that enable real-time interaction offers an innovative pathway to achieve the goals of sustainable education (Díaz et al., 2020). Metaverse-based language teaching (MBLT) can support the development of global competence and linguistic proficiency, while at the same time promoting the broader sustainability agenda by immersing learners in rich, interactive environments where communication and collaboration occur naturally.

This study aims to systematically review and synthesize the scholarly literature from 2020 to 2025 on the use of metaverse technologies in education. In particular, the review focuses on exploring how metaverse platforms are being utilized in teaching and learning with an emphasis on English language education and examining how these emerging practices align with the goals of sustainable educational development. Through this objective, the study seeks to identify key themes, applications, benefits, challenges, and gaps at the intersection of metaverse technology, language learning, and sustainable education.

1.1 Research Questions

1. How is the "metaverse" defined and conceptualized in the context of education between 2020 and 2025?
2. In what ways are metaverse technologies being applied in teaching and learning environments, particularly in language education contexts?
3. What impacts on student learning outcomes, engagement, or other educational indicators have been reported when using metaverse-based learning approaches?
4. What key factors influence the adoption and acceptance of metaverse platforms in educational settings (e.g. student attitudes, teacher readiness, technical or security considerations)?

5. To what extent does current research connect metaverse-based education to the goals of sustainable education or Education for Sustainable Development (ESD), and what gaps remain in this area?

1.2 Definition of Key Terms

The term 'sustainable education' refers to an approach to teaching and learning that prioritizes quality, equity, accessibility, and lifelong learning, altogether encompassing environmental responsibility and social inclusion as well as economic viability in education systems (Agbedahin, 2019). In the context of language learning, sustainable education means creating systems that enable learners from all backgrounds to develop communicative skills that empower them to participate meaningfully in global society, regardless of socioeconomic status or location (Zygmunt, 2016).

The metaverse is broadly defined as an interconnected digital ecosystem of immersive virtual worlds that combine elements of extended reality (XR), including virtual reality (VR), augmented reality (AR), and mixed reality (MR) (Mystakidis, 2022). Within these environments, users interact through avatars, the digital representations of themselves, in persistent, shared spaces that simulate authentic social and cultural experiences. The metaverse is not confined to entertainment; it is increasingly recognized as a transformative educational platform that enables experiential and collaborative learning.

The terms—metaverse, virtual worlds, and extended reality (XR) are used to describe immersive digital environments designed for learning. To ensure conceptual clarity, this review adopts the term metaverse-based learning environments (MBLEs) as an umbrella construct encompassing a range of technologies and platforms that share core characteristics: immersion, interactivity, persistence, and real-time social engagement. Metaverse typically refers to a persistent, shared digital space that integrates various immersive technologies, including virtual reality (VR), augmented reality (AR), and artificial intelligence (AI), with social presence features such as avatars and real-time interaction (Godwin-Jones, 2023; Ng, 2022; Ortega-Rodríguez, 2022).

Virtual worlds, such as Second Life or Gather, represent earlier or narrower forms of the metaverse that enable users to interact via avatars in 3D or 2D environments. While not always labeled as "metaverse," these platforms often fulfill similar pedagogical roles (Novak, 2022). XR (Extended Reality) is a technical umbrella that includes VR, AR, and mixed reality (MR). Some scholars treat the metaverse as an evolution or convergence of XR technologies (Hsiao et al., 2025).

For the purpose of this review, the term metaverse is used in an inclusive sense, provided the study involves immersive, interactive digital environments used for educational purposes. This pragmatic categorization enables a coherent synthesis of findings across studies that may use slightly different terminologies but share overlapping technological and pedagogical assumptions.

Metaverse-based language teaching (MBLT) refers to the application of metaverse technologies for second or foreign language instruction. In this mode, learners enter immersive environments where they can communicate, collaborate, and complete tasks in the target language through avatars and virtual interactions (Wu et al., 2023). For example, students might visit a simulated marketplace to practice transactional dialogues, participate in virtual international exchanges, or collaborate on problem-solving tasks with peers from different countries. These environments promote authentic communicative use, intercultural competence, and learner autonomy (Hatmanto et al., 2023), aligning directly with the principles of sustainability in education.

This chapter focuses primarily on language education within the metaverse while centering on pedagogical, theoretical, and sustainability perspectives which eventually offers a holistic understanding of how metaverse-based approaches can transform language learning into a sustainable and future-ready educational practice.

2 Rationale for Integrating Sustainable Education, Language Learning, and Metaverse Technologies

The shared vision of creating accessible, inclusive, and transformative educational experiences for all learners is achieved through the integration of sustainable education, language learning, and metaverse technologies. In today's interconnected and multilingual world, language competence has become more than a skill. It is a pathway to global citizenship, intercultural understanding, and lifelong learning (Fujioka et al., 2024; Zhou et al., 2024). As societies strive toward the SDGs, educators are reimagining teaching practices to ensure that learning is effective, equitable, and future-ready. The metaverse is an emerging digital ecosystem that connects learners through immersive, interactive, and persistent virtual spaces offers an innovative avenue to realize these goals by transcending geographical, economic, and social barriers (Damaševičius & Sidekerskienė, 2024; Godwin-Jones, 2023).

From a sustainability perspective, education is no longer confined to the physical classroom or limited by institutional resources. Sustainable education emphasizes that learning opportunities should be continuous, inclusive, and environmentally responsible. It calls for leveraging technology to reduce inequalities, enable flexible access, and optimize resources (Suiçmez & Ozansoy, 2024). Within this framework, MBLT aligns perfectly where it creates virtual learning environments that are scalable, resource-efficient, and adaptable to different contexts. For instance, virtual classrooms can host learners from various regions, eliminating the need for travel and extensive physical infrastructure, while promoting meaningful cultural exchange through shared immersive experiences (Li & Yu, 2023).

Language learning benefits significantly from the integration of sustainable education, language learning, and metaverse technologies. As pointed out by Richards (2015) and Skiada (2021), traditional classroom environments often struggle to provide authentic linguistic and cultural immersion, especially for second- or foreign-language learners. The metaverse addresses this gap by enabling experiential, context-rich communication in simulated real-world settings (Bhuiyan & Islam, 2025). Learners can role-play in virtual communities, engage in intercultural dialogues, or collaborate on problem-solving tasks, all within the target language. These immersive experiences foster motivation, engagement, and retention, the key components of effective language acquisition (Saritaş & Topraklıkoğlu, 2022). Moreover, the metaverse cultivates intercultural competence by connecting learners globally. It creates a strong cornerstone of sustainable education that values empathy, diversity, and shared understanding.

The connection between sustainability, language education, and metaverse technologies also lies in their potential to democratize learning. The access to qualified language teachers or communicative environments remains limited in many parts of the world. Metaverse-based systems can bridge these gaps by offering equitable participation through affordable or open-access platforms (Pradana & Elisa, 2023). As educational institutions and governments explore digital-inclusion strategies, MBLT stands out as a model for inclusive and resilient learning ecosystems, the ones that uphold social sustainability by empowering learners from diverse socioeconomic and linguistic backgrounds.

Adopting a metaverse-supported approach to language education encourages a broader paradigm shift toward lifelong and future-oriented learning. Educators and learners can both prepare themselves for an evolving world that demands adaptability, digital literacy, and social responsibility by combining the goals of sustainable education with the affordances of immersive technologies. The convergence of these three domains—sustainability, language learning, and metaverse—marks a pivotal evolution in educational practice. This initiative transforms how languages are taught and learned as well as reinforces education's role as a driver of sustainable development and human connection in a rapid digital world.

3 Methodology

This study adopts a systematic literature review (SLR) approach following PRISMA (Preferred Reporting Items for Systematic Reviews and Meta-Analyses) guidelines to ensure transparency and reproducibility (Page et al., 2021). Importantly, this review was guided by the Community of Inquiry (CoI) framework (Garrison et al., 2001), which conceptualizes online learning as an interplay of cognitive, social, and teaching presence. Given the immersive and interactive nature of metaverse environments, this framework provided a lens to examine how presence and engagement are facilitated in language teaching contexts. The CoI framework helped shape the thematic coding and interpretation of findings related to interaction, learning design, and student outcomes.

The literature review followed a systematic approach using the Web of Science (WoS) database. The search was conducted in November 2025 and focused on publications from 2020 through 2025 to capture the surge of interest in educational applications of the metaverse in recent years. A combination of keywords was used to identify relevant studies: "metaverse" (and related terms like "metaverse technology," "metaverse education," "virtual world," "immersive learning") AND terms related to language education (such as "language teaching," "ESL," "EFL") AND terms related to sustainable education (including "sustainable development education," "sustainability," "education for sustainable development"). This strategy was intended to retrieve studies at the intersection of metaverse technology, language learning, and sustainable education.

The initial search generated a total of 65 records in WoS. Since only one database was used, no duplicates were found in this set (Fig. 1). Then, the titles and abstracts of these records were screened to determine their relevance. At this stage, studies that did not clearly relate to metaverse applications in educational contexts like papers focusing purely on technical aspects of virtual reality without an education focus were excluded. Also, sources that were not scholarly peer-reviewed articles such as opinion pieces or news articles and those not written in English were excluded. After title and abstract screening, 30 records were excluded as irrelevant or out of scope, leaving 35 articles for more detailed evaluation.

For the remaining 35 articles, the full texts were obtained and assessed to determine eligibility. The inclusion criteria prioritized studies that were published in high-quality journals such as those indexed in SSCI/SCIE or known high-impact educational technology journals, as well as those that had made a significant impact in the field. To gauge impact, the number of citations as an indicator was considered; specifically, papers were most frequently cited by other scholars were noted. Also, it is ensured that the studies explicitly addressed the use of metaverse or immersive virtual worlds in an educational setting with an emphasis on language learning or broader educational outcomes. During full-text review, an additional 10 articles were excluded. The reasons for exclusion at this stage included: the studies were not actually utilizing metaverse or immersive environments, they were focusing on unrelated outcomes which were pure technical development with no learner-centric evaluation, or the articles were appearing in venues of questionable quality. It is also found that very few articles directly connected metaverse technology with education for sustainable development or sustainability themes and those that did not make any such connection and were not top cited were set aside in favor of more influential works.From this screening process, 25 articles were identified to have met all criteria and were included in the review (Fig. 1). All 25 selected studies are peer-reviewed journal articles published between 2020 and 2025, aligning with the period of rising academic interest in the metaverse in education. Notably, these articles represent a range of educational domains with a significant subset focusing on language education, as per our search intention and cover diverse research methodologies such as quantitative studies on technology acceptance, experimental and quasi-experimental studies on learning outcomes, qualitative explorations in teacher education, as well as conceptual papers).

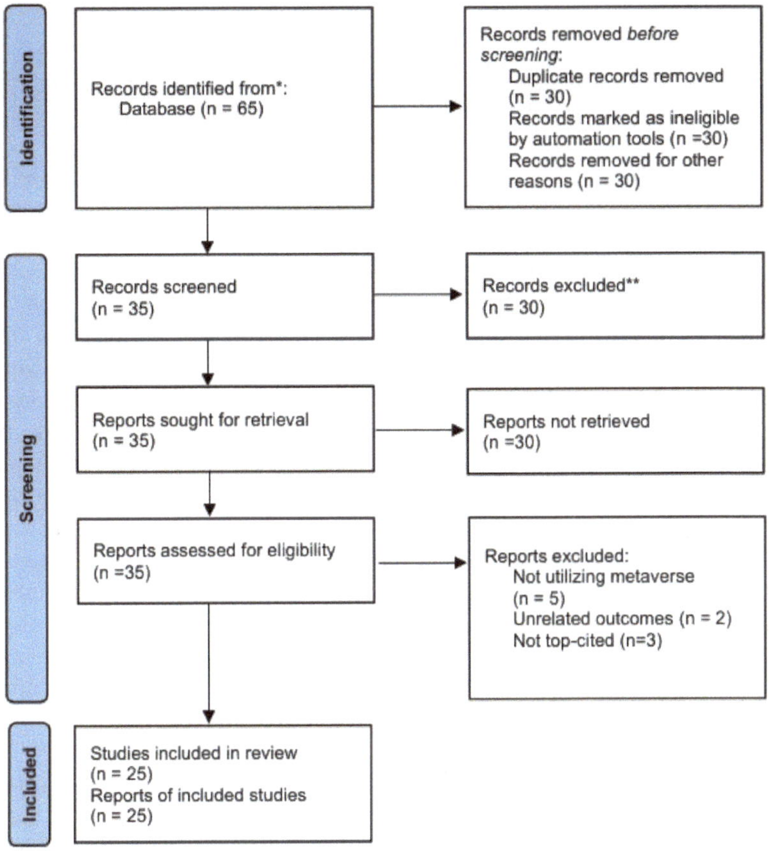

Fig. 1 PRISMA flow diagram of the literature screening process

The intention of this review was not to capture every publication on the topic, but to analyze the most influential and methodologically rigorous studies at the intersection of metaverse, language education, and sustainability. Therefore, the inclusion of only WoS-indexed studies allowed a focused synthesis of literature that has demonstrable academic impact and visibility, ensuring depth over breadth. To mitigate potential omission bias, this review applied strict inclusion criteria focused on peer-reviewed, top-cited studies indexed in SSCI/SCIE journals. A structured screening process following PRISMA guidelines was used to ensure relevance and transparency. Although a single database was used, the methodological rigor of screening and quality-focused inclusion criteria reduce the risk of selection bias. The following sections on Findings and Discussion are organized around the key themes and insights derived from these 25 studies.

4 Findings

4.1 Conceptualizing the Metaverse in Education

One recurring theme in existing literature is the definition and conceptualization of what the metaverse means in an educational context. The term "metaverse" itself originated in science fiction (Stephenson's 1992 novel Snow Crash) and has been reintroduced into popular discourse following Facebook's rebranding as Meta in 2021. However, researchers note that the concept is not entirely new. Instead, it builds on decades of work with virtual worlds and simulations in learning. For instance, Novak (2022) provides a historical overview, tracing the use of virtual worlds for learning back to the 1990s and noting that the idea of immersive online environments for education has long-standing foundations. Ng (2022) similarly remarks that the metaverse gained sudden prominence around 2020 but lacks a unified definition in the scholarly community. In an exploratory review of 19 studies, Ng (2022) identified key elements that various authors associate with the metaverse: immersion (the sense of presence in a virtual space), advanced computing (the infrastructure enabling rich virtual environments, such as AR/VR and AI), socialization (multi-user interaction and community building), and decentralization (often referring to user ownership and possibly blockchain use). These four elements were mapped to existing educational theory using the Community of Inquiry framework, suggesting that metaverse learning environments can support cognitive, social, and teaching presence in new ways (Ng, 2022).

Across the surveyed literature, there is consensus that the metaverse involves more than just VR goggles or 3D graphics; it is envisioned as an ecosystem of technologies and experiences. Several authors highlight that metaverse applications can include virtual reality (VR) and augmented reality (AR), but also other emerging technologies. For example, blockchain or decentralized platforms for value exchange are sometimes mentioned as part of the metaverse. This is illustrated by Hsiao et al. (2025), who developed a competency scale including the mastery of "decentralized value exchange" as one dimension. Artificial intelligence (AI) is another component, enabling intelligent virtual agents or chatbots within metaverse spaces. This is exemplified by Hwang et al. (2025) and Godwin-Jones (2023), who integrated AI chatbots into a metaverse environment for language learning. Thus, the metaverse in education can be thought of as a convergence of extended reality (XR) technologies, AI, and internet communication tools to create persistent, immersive learning worlds. Some authors use the term extended reality (XR) as an umbrella for VR/AR/MR and view the metaverse as an evolution of XR with greater connectivity and persistence (Ortega-Rodríguez, 2022). Ortega-Rodríguez (2022) emphasizes that while XR has already demonstrated benefits for teaching and learning, especially via increased immersion and presence, the metaverse could amplify these but also brings new challenges such as ethical concerns and identity protection in virtual spaces.

4.2 Applications in Teaching and Learning Contexts

The selected studies show that metaverse technologies have been applied in diverse educational contexts, ranging from K-12 to higher education, and spanning various disciplines. A significant subset of the literature focuses on language education, which is likely due to our search targeting ESL/EFL contexts. For example, English as a Foreign Language (EFL) teaching has been a testbed for metaverse-based learning innovations. Hwang et al. (2025) conducted an experiment with pre-service English teachers, where one group taught using AI chatbots within a 3D virtual world that functioned as a metaverse classroom, and another group taught using the same chatbots in a traditional classroom. They found that the metaverse setting encouraged more authentic and interactive language tasks like the virtual context (e.g. role-playing scenarios in a virtual environment) allowed these trainee teachers to create richer communicative situations for language learners. In a similar vein, Lee et al. (2025) explored having Korean pre-service teachers interact with AI chatbots in a metaverse as the means to raise their awareness of Global Englishes. This study found that using a 3D metaverse platform for role-playing conversations increased the teachers' confidence and willingness to incorporate global English perspectives, more so than a conventional classroom presentation task. These examples suggest that metaverse environments can provide language learners and teachers with a safe, immersive space to practice communication, potentially reducing anxiety via the use of avatars and virtual identities, and enabling scenarios that would be hard to simulate in a real classroom.

Beyond language learning, researchers have piloted metaverse-based approaches in other subject areas as well. For instance, science and engineering education have seen innovative uses of virtual worlds. Rahman et al. (2024) developed a Virtual Chemistry Classroom in VR for teaching chemical bonding. Their system, which is called VC3B, uses game-based learning elements, allowing students to manipulate atoms and molecules in an immersive game to learn how chemical bonds form and compose chemical formulas within the virtual environment. When compared to traditional learning methods such as textbook study or video lectures, the VR game approach significantly increased student engagement and helped make an abstract topic more concrete and enjoyable. In computing education, Chen and Huang (2024) introduced a metaverse-based collaborative platform for teaching elementary students programming. They combined the Jigsaw cooperative learning method with a metaverse virtual space where students were represented by avatars that could work together on programming puzzles in Scratch. The study found that students in the metaverse-supported collaborative learning group had higher programming achievement and more positive attitudes than those in a traditional classroom, illustrating the potential for immersive platforms to enhance teamwork and motivation in STEM learning. Similarly, Yang et al. (2023), in an art education context, created an "art metaverse" for art appreciation, in which college students could step into a VR reconstruction of an art gallery and interact with virtual characters inside paintings. The immersive art experience led to improved attitudes towards art and even higher attention levels among the students, as measured by electroencephalogram (EEG), during subsequent art-making activities, compared to a control group viewing art on a 2D screen. These disciplinary applications underscore that the metaverse can be a versatile medium for education, enabling experiential learning in chemistry, fostering collaborative problem-solving in programming, providing immersive cultural experiences in art, and more.

Another prominent application area is teacher training and professional development. A few studies in the sample specifically examine how metaverse environments can help pre-service or in-service teachers build skills. Lee and Kim (2024) implemented a "learning by design" project where pre-service teachers in Korea had to design virtual classrooms in a metaverse platform and conduct micro-teaching within those 3D spaces. Through this process, the aspiring teachers reportedly improved their understanding of student needs and learned to better integrate pedagogical theory with practice. The virtual classroom design exercise pushed them to consider how layout, interactive objects, and virtual context can affect learning, therefore bridging the gap between knowing teaching principles and actually applying them in a classroom setting. Chen (2023) also studied pre-service English teachers, using a platform called Gather, a 2D retro-style virtual world for lesson planning activities. That study found that working together in a virtual environment on lesson design improved the participants' sense of social presence and collaboration compared to traditional in-class planning. Interestingly, even though both high-achieving and low-achieving trainees benefited, the more proficient group reported a stronger sense of immersion and presence in the metaverse than the less proficient group (Chen, 2023). This might imply that some initial digital literacy or confidence could magnify the benefits of metaverse training; nonetheless, both groups preferred the metaverse platform over standard video conferencing for online collaboration. Overall, these findings from teacher education suggest that metaverse platforms can serve as safe training grounds where teachers practice and experiment with teaching strategies in realistic simulations, which is especially valuable when real classroom access is limited, as was the case during the COVID-19 pandemic.

4.3 Impacts on Learning Outcomes and Engagement

A key question driving much of the research is whether MBLT actually makes a measurable difference in student outcomes and engagement. According to the surveyed studies, the general trend is that introducing immersive and interactive elements through the metaverse tends to enhance student engagement, motivation, and, in some cases, learning outcomes, although results can vary depending on the context and the implementation of the technology.

Several experimental studies reported improvements in learning performance when using metaverse or virtual world interventions. Chen and Huang (2024) observed significantly better programming project scores for the 5th-graders who learned in the metaverse-supported collaborative setting versus those who learned via traditional lecture. Similarly, the VR art appreciation study by Yang et al. (2023) noted improved post-activity performance in terms of art attitude assessments and attention levels for the VR group. In the domain of formal curriculum learning, Chen et al. (2024) integrated an online metaverse platform into middle and high school classrooms in China, covering standard subjects like math, literature, history, and chemistry. In their controlled study with 278 students, they found notable gains in academic achievement for the classes that used the metaverse platform compared to those that did not. For example, seventh graders in the metaverse-backed classes scored higher on tests in mathematics and history than their peers in traditional settings, and their engagement and motivation levels were also significantly higher. This suggests that even for core academic content, a well-designed metaverse environment can boost outcomes, potentially by increasing student interest and time-on-task through gamified or immersive features.

Another significant trend detected from the literature was that motivation and enjoyment are commonly reported benefits of metaverse learning. Many studies cite qualitative feedback from learners that the virtual environments make learning "more fun" or engaging. Rahman et al. (2024) found that middle school students described VR-integrated chemistry games as more interactive and motivating than simply reading or watching online content. In Chen and Huang's (2024) study, students in the metaverse group expressed greater enjoyment in working with peers in the virtual space and appreciated the timely help from teammates, something that can be orchestrated through the collaborative affordances of the platform. Metaverse learning often incorporates elements of gamification, such as points, quests, and avatars, and immersive storytelling, which can drive higher intrinsic motivation. From the teacher's perspective, these features translate to students who are more willing to participate and less afraid of failure. This is supported by Lee and Ko (2025), who reported reduced peer pressure in metaverse-mediated activities, where self-conscious students felt more comfortable represented by avatars and thus engaged in increased oral practice.

However, the impact on cognitive learning outcomes is not always straightforward. For instance, Lee and Ko (2025) compared three modes of EFL instruction—metaverse-based, face-to-face, and textbook-based—and found that while the metaverse class excelled in keeping students engaged, it did not outperform face-to-face instruction in speaking skill gains. The face-to-face group still achieved the best speaking proficiency improvements, likely because the teacher could provide more personalized feedback and scaffolding in person. This highlights that metaverse approaches may need to be blended thoughtfully with traditional methods to harness the best of both worlds. Additionally, not all studies found significant differences in hard outcomes such as test scores. Chen and Huang (2024) reported no significant difference in the development of computational thinking skills between the metaverse group and the control group; both improved similarly, perhaps because the curriculum content was effectively learned in both conditions. In such cases, the value of the metaverse might lie more in affective or social benefits rather than purely academic scores.

Another facet of impact is a sense of presence in three key forms: social, physical, and self-presence, all of which can influence learning. Chen (2023) measured multiple types of presence in the Gather-based virtual classroom and found that students generally felt physically present (i.e., having a sense of "being there" in the virtual space) and socially present with peers, which can be conducive to collaborative learning. High-engagement levels are often linked to this feeling of presence. This has been intensely supported by Godwin-Jones (2023) that language learners could enhance their communication and interaction skills in real and virtual spaces. From a neuroscience perspective, Yang et al. (2023) demonstrated that students in an immersive art environment exhibited higher attention levels as recorded by EEG, which may imply deeper engagement. These insights suggest that one mechanism by which metaverse experiences improve learning is by capturing students' attention and imagination more fully than traditional media, thereby potentially enabling deeper processing of the material when designed well.

4.4 Factors Influencing Metaverse Adoption in Education

Even with promising outcomes, the widespread adoption of metaverse technology in education is not guaranteed. Multiple studies in our review tackle the question of what drives or hinders the acceptance of metaverse platforms among students and educators. A number of these works applied or extended technology acceptance models, primarily the Technology Acceptance Model (TAM) and the Unified Theory of Acceptance and Use of Technology (UTAUT), to the context of metaverse-based learning, often surveying university students.

Perceived usefulness emerges as a critical factor in almost all models. Chanda et al. (2024) examined higher education learners' attitudes and found that students' behavioral intention to use metaverse for learning was strongly predicted by how useful they thought it would be for their studies. According to them, if students believe that engaging in a metaverse platform will help them learn more effectively or achieve better outcomes, they are more likely to embrace it. This aligns with the classic TAM constructs which are perceived usefulness and perceived ease of use—originally proposed by Davis (1989). In Chanda et al.'s (2024) study, both usefulness and ease of use had significant effects on attitude, but usefulness had a stronger impact on intention. In a similar vein, Al-Adwan et al. (2023) extended TAM by adding personal and environmental factors and found that students' perceived enjoyment and personal innovativeness in IT also positively influenced the intention to use metaverse learning platforms. Notably, their findings revealed that the classic ease-of-use factor was not a significant direct predictor of intention once other factors were considered. This is possibly because today's students, as digital natives, are less deterred by new technology interfaces when they perceive high value and enjoyment in them.

Beyond individual attitudes, social influence and cultural context also play significant roles. Al-Adwan and Al-Debei (2024) focused on Gen Z students in Jordan and applied the UTAUT2 model, examining factors like social influence, performance expectancy, effort expectancy, facilitating conditions, and personal innovativeness. They found that, except for social influence, all other UTAUT2 factors, which include performance expectancy, effort expectancy, facilitating conditions, and hedonic motivation, were significant in explaining students' intention to use the metaverse in a higher education context. This implies that students are inclined to adopt the system if they perceive performance benefits in their learning, find it easy to use, receive institutional support, and enjoy the experience. The lack of significance for social influence might suggest that in this context, the decision to use an educational metaverse was more individually driven than by peer or teacher opinions. However, other studies (e.g., Wiangkham & Vongvit, 2023) did find social influence to be a significant factor for engineering students, indicating that peer attitudes or the sense that "…others expect me to use this…" can matter in some cases.

A standout theme, which is less typical in general technology adoption studies but very salient for the metaverse, is privacy and cybersecurity concerns. Because metaverse platforms often involve avatars, interactions in real-time, and potentially the exchange of personal data or even digital assets, students may worry about security risks. In the study by Al-Adwan et al. (2023), perceived cyber risk was identified as the main inhibitor of students' intention to adopt metaverse learning. Likewise, Wiangkham and Vongvit (2023) included trust and cybersecurity in an extended UTAUT model and found cybersecurity to have the strongest effect among all factors on behavioral intention—even outweighing performance expectancy. These findings highlight that while students may be excited about the possibilities of immersive learning, their willingness to participate can be undermined by fears of data breaches, privacy invasion, or general uncertainty about the safety of these new platforms. This underscores the need for institutions to address security and privacy issues proactively. This includes choosing platforms with robust safety protocols and clearly communicating how student data and interactions are protected.

Technical accessibility and ease of access are also influential practical factors. Some qualitative insights reveal that infrastructure issues (e.g., needing special hardware like VR headsets, or high-bandwidth internet) and the digital divide could limit adoption. Mahmoud (2024), in an analysis of public comments on social media, found a mix of excitement and concern among the public regarding metaverse in education. People often raised issues of accessibility and inclusion, fearing that not all students or schools have the resources to participate, which could exacerbate inequalities. Likewise, in Akyürek et al. (2024)'s interviews with tourism educators, participants acknowledged the engaging potential of the metaverse but pointed out challenges like insufficient technology infrastructure and the learning curve associated with using complex virtual platforms. In Hwang et al. (2023) user experience study, even when undergraduates tried multiple platforms (such as Ifland, Gather Town, and Frame VR), their sentiments varied—some platforms were perceived as easier or more enjoyable than others. This suggests that platform design and usability can significantly affect user sentiment; a clunky or overly technical interface might turn students off before they can appreciate the educational benefit.

Finally, educators' acceptance is just as crucial as students'. While not the primary focus of most studies in our sample, a few insights emerged regarding teacher perspectives. Priest (2023) offers a forward-looking reflection, arguing that despite all the hype, educators in fields like outdoor and experiential learning remain skeptical that a metaverse can replace the value of real-world experiences—at least in the near term. This highlights a pedagogical belief factor: teachers need to be convinced not only of the utility, but that these technologies align with their educational values and goals. If a teacher views learning in nature or face-to-face interaction as fundamentally superior, they may resist investing in virtual alternatives. On the other hand, some educators are optimistic. Novak (2022) points out emerging trends and encourages exploration, implying that with proper training and evidence, teachers could be engaged to leverage the metaverse effectively. The challenge is to avoid technophilia that Ortega-Rodríguez (2022) warns about and instead cultivate a balanced understanding among educators of when and how the metaverse adds value to learning.

5 Discussion

Overall, literature paints a picture of the educational metaverse as a promising but nascent frontier. In our review of 25 high-impact studies from 2020 to 2025, we found a broad consensus that metaverse technologies can enrich education through enhanced immersion, interaction, and motivation. However, the findings also underscore that realizing this potential on a broad scale will require addressing practical challenges and pedagogical considerations.

One major point of discussion is the unique value proposition of metaverse learning environments. What can be done in a metaverse that was previously difficult or impossible in conventional or even earlier online learning? The studies suggest a few clear advantages. First, the metaverse enables immersive simulations and experiential learning at low cost and risk. Students can perform virtual experiments, visit historical or fantasy environments, and practice skills in realistic scenarios without the logistical constraints of the real world. For example, language learners can engage in conversation with AI avatars from different cultural backgrounds, or chemistry students can experiment with virtual chemicals safely. These experiences align with experiential learning theory—learning by doing—in context which can deepen understanding and retention. Second, the metaverse supports a sense of presence and community even among geographically distributed learners. This is particularly relevant during the post-COVID era, as educators seek online platforms that go beyond the flat experience of video conferencing. Studies such as Chen (2023) and Díaz et al. (2020) provide empirical evidence that key social dynamics of a physical school or campus, such as students clustering for discussion and collaboratively exploring shared spaces, can be replicated in a metaverse environment. In particular, Díaz et al. (2020) demonstrate that metaverse-based learning can also mimic teacher–student rapport, thereby supporting sustained engagement in online courses. Third, metaverse platforms often integrate gameful and social media-like features, such as avatars, customization, virtual rewards, and real-time chat, meeting the younger generation's expectations for digital interaction. This can make learning feel more like an adventure or a game, potentially tapping into both students' intrinsic and hedonic motivation (Al-Adwan & Al-Debei, 2024; Chen et al., 2024; Wiangkham & Vongvit, 2023). The study by Mahmoud (2024) suggests hints that the public views innovative learning methods and the future of skills on such platforms, but also rightly tempers that enthusiasm with concerns.

Indeed, striking a balance between enthusiasm and caution is a recurring theme. While many students and teachers find metaverse learning enjoyable and novel, researchers also urge critical reflection. Ortega-Rodríguez (2022) cautions against a technophile approach assuming that more immersion is always better without solid evidence of learning gains or consideration of developmental effects. It is important to remember that not all outcomes in our review were positive or significantly better than traditional methods. For instance, face-to-face instruction outperforms metaverse for speaking skills (Lee & Ko, 2025): a clear reminder that technology should supplement, not necessarily replace, effective pedagogy. While the metaverse excels at creating stress-free conversation practice for shy students and enabling gamified content drilling, it may be less effective for objectives such as developing complex oral communication, which depends on immediate human feedback. Therefore, educators and researchers need to delineate where metaverse tools add the most value in the learning process. This includes identifying the profiles of learners who benefit most; for example, some evidence suggests that students who are already confident with technology or with the subject matter might leverage virtual environments more fully. This was seen in Chen's (2023) study, where higher-achieving pre-service teachers reported a greater sense of presence than their lower-achieving peers. This could imply a need to scaffold less-prepared learners when introducing them to such platforms, so that the benefits are more equitably experienced.

Another discussion point is the implications for educational equity and sustainability. Our initial intent was to explore literature connecting metaverse education with sustainable development goals (e.g., quality education for all, reduced inequalities, etc.). It was found that few of the top-cited studies explicitly address sustainability or education for sustainable development (ESD). This appears to be a gap in the current research: the metaverse is often touted as the "future of the internet" or a key part of Education 4.0, but its specific role in advancing sustainability goals, such as promoting inclusive access to education or furthering environmental education, remains under-examined. That said, some implicit connections can be drawn from the findings. For example, the themes from Mahmoud's (2024) social media analysis, which are accessibility and inclusion, speak to the idea that if metaverse education is to be sustainable and equitable, it must be accessible to diverse populations, including those with limited resources or differing abilities. The public's concerns about the digital divide signal that without careful policy and support, the metaverse could inadvertently widen educational inequalities: for example, it may become a tool accessible only to well-funded schools or students who can afford expensive hardware. On the flip side, when implemented thoughtfully, metaverse learning could increase inclusion by connecting learners across distances and providing alternative ways to participate; for example, a student who is homebound or in a remote area could attend a virtual class trip to a museum within the metaverse. As for environmental sustainability, the literature is largely silent, though one might consider that virtual activities could reduce the need for physical materials or travel, it also raises concerns about energy use of servers and devices. These are areas ripe for future research: examining the carbon footprint of large-scale metaverse adoption and how it compares to physical educational activities, as well as how metaverse could be leveraged to teach sustainability concepts (e.g., virtual simulations of climate change scenarios).

A related aspect is the development of digital competencies and literacy. If the metaverse is to become part of mainstream education, students and teachers alike will need certain competencies to navigate and learn effectively in these spaces. Hsiao et al. (2025)'s creation of a Metaverse Competency Scale is a step toward identifying what those skills are and notably, the ability to manage digital avatars, engage in immersive experiences, and understand virtual economies or decentralized systems. Their finding that these competencies correlate with higher motivation to participate suggests that training in metaverse-related skills could encourage more fruitful use of technology. In practical terms, educational institutions may need to invest in professional development for teachers, covering topics such as how to facilitate a class in VR and how to design virtual activities aligned with learning objectives, as well as orientation programs for students, addressing areas like digital citizenship in virtual worlds and the basic troubleshooting of AR/VR hardware. Without such support, even if the infrastructure is available, users may not fully capitalize on it. Several studies in the set indirectly support this. For example, Lee and Kim (2024) found that pre-service teachers gained significant confidence from designing and using a virtual classroom, underscoring that hands-on experience is key. If teachers have never seen a metaverse environment, they may naturally be hesitant or simply use it suboptimally, like treating it as a glorified video chat.

Ethical and safety considerations constitute another critical discussion point. As highlighted by a few sources (e.g. Al-Adwan et al., 2023; Mahmoud, 2024; Ortega-Rodríguez, 2022), the metaverse brings forth issues of privacy, data security, and even identity. Educational use means potentially having minors or young adults interacting in online virtual spaces, sometimes with user-generated content or external participants, which raises questions of moderation and appropriate behavior. Developing an ethical code of conduct for metaverse interactions in educational settings is advisable and this might cover guidelines on respectful communication, academic integrity in virtual simulations, protection of one's and others' personal data, and avoidance of harmful content. Furthermore, platform providers should ensure compliance with privacy laws (like GDPR or FERPA) when deploying metaverse solutions in schools. Some researchers call for interdisciplinary collaboration between technologists and educators to address these challenges (Ortega-Rodríguez, 2022), suggesting that a purely technical solution is not enough and that it must be coupled with pedagogical strategies and policies that safeguard learners. Cybersecurity, as the adoption studies showed, can make or break user trust as it plays a vital role in shaping users' behavior intention to use the technology themselves (Wiangkham & Vongvit, 2023). Therefore, discussion among stakeholders, which involve educators, IT professionals, policymakers, parents, and students, is needed to navigate these challenges so that the metaverse can be a safe and supportive environment for learning.

Finally, it is worth discussing the future research directions indicated by this review. Given that scholarly interest in metaverse and education only sharply increased around 2021–2022, many questions remain open. The systematic review by George-Reyes et al. (2023) points out that research has only just begun to explore complex thinking skills in relation to metaverse use and there is room to study how immersive environments might cultivate critical thinking, creativity, and problem-solving more effectively than traditional settings. He et al. (2025) took a step in this direction by examining creative thinking and collaboration within a metaverse teaching scene, finding positive effects via increased immersion and situational context. This line of inquiry could be expanded to different age groups and subject matters, helping researchers understand if metaverse-based learning does not just improve test scores or engagement, but also higher-order thinking and twenty-fist-century skills. Another direction is the longitudinal impact: most studies to date have focused on short-term interventions or one-time surveys. Thus, the long-term effects of metaverse-based learning have yet to be established. For example, do students who regularly use educational virtual worlds develop better self-regulated learning habits? Does their novelty wear off, or do they continue to find value over semesters and years? Longitudinal studies and observations would be valuable. Moreover, as technology evolves like more advanced AI, better VR hardware, more open metaverse platforms, continuous research is needed to reassess what is pedagogically possible. The notion of a truly open, interoperable educational metaverse, one where students from different institutions can seamlessly roam various learning environments, is still largely conceptual; studying small-scale implementations that move in this direction could inform future infrastructure. Research should also not shy away from critically examining downsides such as potential physical discomfort such as VR sickness, distraction issues, or social isolation if overused, so that we have a balanced understanding of how to best integrate the metaverse in a sustainable educational ecosystem.

It is important to note that interpreting the studies through the CoI lens reveals how metaverse platforms foster cognitive presence through immersive simulations, social presence through avatar-based interaction, and teaching presence through instructor-designed tasks. However, gaps remain in how consistently these presences are supported across platforms, and how they contribute to sustainable learning outcomes. In summary, the discussion around metaverse in education is one of optimism edged with caution. This optimism is fueled by early evidence of enhanced engagement, novel learning opportunities, and positive student attitudes. The caution stems from practical and ethical challenges and the realization that any new technology must serve pedagogy, not overshadow it. Through these collective insights of these pioneering studies, educators and decision-makers can better navigate the path forward by adopting metaverse innovations in ways that truly enrich learning experiences, while also ensuring equity, security, and pedagogical soundness.

6 Conclusion

This literature review examined 25 influential studies (2020–2025) on the use of metaverse and immersive virtual environments in education, with particular attention to language learning contexts and considerations of sustainable educational development. Our review highlights that the metaverse, often characterized by technologies like VR/AR, 3D virtual worlds, and AI-driven avatars, has demonstrated considerable potential to enhance educational experiences. Key benefits reported in increased and greater learner engagement, enhanced motivation, opportunities for authentic practice, secure and safe virtual settings, and innovative methods for collaboration and interaction that transcend physical classroom limitations. In fields ranging from language teaching to STEM, art, and teacher training, metaverse implementations have led to positive outcomes such as higher achievement scores, increased confidence, and more enthusiastic participation.

At the same time, the findings urge a measured and strategic approach to integrating metaverse technology into education. Not all traditional methods are inferior to metaverse-based ones, for certain skills and in certain conditions like developing spoken fluency or personalized coaching, face-to-face interaction remains crucial. The metaverse should be seen as an augmentation of the educational toolkit, not a wholesale replacement. Educators are encouraged to leverage its strengths for immersion, simulation, and social presence for appropriate objectives, while still guiding and scaffolding students in ways that align with sound pedagogy.

While this review was conducted with methodological care and guided by the PRISMA protocol, several limitations must be acknowledged. First, the review relied solely on the Web of Science (WoS) database. While WoS is a high-quality, curated index of peer-reviewed scholarship, the use of a single database may have limited the breadth of the literature included and introduced potential publication bias. Future reviews should consider incorporating additional databases such as Scopus, ERIC, or Google Scholar to enhance comprehensiveness.

Second, while the review focused on highly cited and peer-reviewed journal articles to ensure quality, a formal quality appraisal like using tools like CASP or MMAT was not conducted. This limits our ability to systematically assess the methodological rigor of the included studies. Third, because metaverse research in education is still emerging, many included studies were exploratory, conceptual, or lacked longitudinal data. This restricts the generalizability of findings and suggests the need for caution in drawing firm conclusions about long-term impacts. Lastly, although the synthesis was organized thematically and supported by a guiding theoretical framework (CoI), the interpretive nature of thematic analysis introduces subjectivity. Efforts were made to ensure transparency and rigor, but bias in interpretation cannot be fully eliminated. Nonetheless, the review offers a grounded and theoretically informed synthesis of the most influential work to date and highlights important directions for future research.

Crucially, for metaverse-based education to be sustainable and widely adopted, issues of access, equity, and safety need to be addressed. The current research not only identifies factors like perceived usefulness and enjoyment as drivers of student adoption but also points to barriers such as cybersecurity fears and potential unequal access. Stakeholders must ensure that infrastructure is in place, ensuring access is not limited to a privileged few, and that robust policies are established to protect privacy and promote positive behaviors. Future research should address a notable gap in literature by explicitly linking the metaverse to Education for Sustainable Development (ESD), particularly exploring its potential to advance inclusive, quality education and tackle global issues through experiential learning.

Finally, it is worth reiterating that research on sustainable practices, specifically within metaverse-based education, remains in its infancy. The recommendations offered in this chapter are therefore grounded in broader sustainability principles from educational technology research, supplemented by emerging insights from early metaverse implementations. As institutions gain longer-term experience with sustained metaverse programmes, evidence-based sustainability practices tailored to metaverse-based language learning will become clearer.

Acknowledgements We truly appreciate the comments given by the reviewers and the guidance given by the editors.

Appendix

Paper ID	Refs.	Source	Title	Citations
P1	Novak, K. (2022)	TechTrends	Introducing the metaverse, again!	15
P2	Ng, D. T. K. (2022)	Australasian Journal of Educational Technology	What is the metaverse? Definitions, technologies and the community of inquiry	86
P3	George-Reyes, C. E., Peláez Sánchez, I. C., Glasserman-Morales, L. D., & López-Caudana, E. O. (2023)	Frontiers in Education	The Metaverse and complex thinking: Opportunities, experiences, and future lines of research	10
P4	Al-Adwan, A. S., Li, N., Al-Adwan, A., Abbasi, G. A., Albelbisi, N. A., & Habibi, A. (2023)	Education and Information Technologies	Extending the technology acceptance model (TAM) to predict university students' intentions to use metaverse-based learning platforms	279

(continued)

(continued)

Paper ID	Refs.	Source	Title	Citations
P5	Hwang, Y., Lee, S., & Jeon, J. (2025)	Education and Information Technologies	Integrating AI chatbots into the metaverse: Pre-service English teachers' design works and perceptions	33
P6	Wiangkham, A., & Vongvit, R. (2023)	Education and Information Technologies	Exploring the drivers for the adoption of metaverse technology in engineering education using PLS-SEM and ANFIS	28
P7	Al-Adwan, A. S., & Al-Debei, M. M. (2024)	Education and Information Technologies	The determinants of Gen Z's metaverse adoption decisions in higher education: Integrating UTAUT2 with personal innovativeness in IT	76
P8	Díaz, J., Saldaña, C., & Avila, C. (2020)	International Journal of Emerging Technologies in Learning	Virtual world as a resource for hybrid education	153
P9	Chen, G., Jin, Y., & Chen, P. (2024)	Education and Information Technologies	Development of a platform for state online education services: Design concept based on meta-universe	23
P10	Ortega-Rodríguez, P. J. (2022)	Teoria de la Educacion	From extended reality to the metaverse: A critical reflection on contributions to education	18
P11	Yang, X., Cheng, P. Y., Liu, X., & Shih, S. P. (2023)	Education and Information Technologies	The impact of immersive virtual reality on art education: A study of flow state, cognitive load, brain state, and motivation	26
P12	Chen, C. M., & Huang, M. Y. (2024)	International Journal of STEM Education	Enhancing programming learning performance through a Jigsaw collaborative learning method in a metaverse virtual space	15
P13	Lee, S. M., & Kim, S. Y. (2024)	British Journal of Educational Technology	Preservice teachers' learning by design through space construction in the metaverse	26

(continued)

(continued)

Paper ID	Refs.	Source	Title	Citations
P14	Lee, S., Jeon, J., & Choe, H. (2025)	TESOL Quarterly	Enhancing pre-service teachers' global Englishes awareness with technology: A focus on AI chatbots in 3D metaverse environments	26
P15	Rahman, H., Wahid, S. A., Ahmad, F., & Ali, N. (2024)	Education and Information Technologies	Game-based learning in metaverse: Virtual chemistry classroom for chemical bonding for remote education	18
P16	Godwin-Jones, R. (2023)	Language Learning & Technology	Emerging spaces for language learning: AI bots, ambient intelligence, and the metaverse	48
P17	Chen, H. J. (2023)	Education and Information Technologies	Gather in the metaverse: Learning outcomes, virtual presence, and perceptions of high- and low-achieving pre-service teachers of English as a Foreign Language	64
P18	Hsiao, K. L., Chen, M. Y., & Liao, Y. R. (2025)	Education and Information Technologies	Development and evaluation of a metaverse competency scale for university students	10
P19	Lee, J., & Ko, Y. (2025)	Education and Information Technologies	Comparing metaverse and face-to-face instruction for enhancing English skills and attitudes among EFL adolescents	10
P20	Akyürek, S., Genç, G., Çalık, İ., & Şengel, Ü. (2024)	Journal of Hospitality Leisure Sport & Tourism Education	Metaverse in tourism education: A mixed method on vision, challenges and extended technology acceptance model	9
P21	Hwang, Y., Shin, D., & Lee, H. (2023)	ETR&D—Educational Technology Research and Development	Students' perception on immersive learning through 2D and 3D metaverse platforms	8
P22	Chanda, R. S., Pabalkar, V., & Sharma, S. (2024)	Journal of Applied Research in Higher Education	Attitude and behavioral intention for using metaverse in education: Learner's perspective	8

(continued)

(continued)

Paper ID	Refs.	Source	Title	Citations
P23	Mahmoud, A. B. (2024)	British Educational Research Journal	Exploring the public's beliefs, emotions and sentiments towards the adoption of the metaverse in education: A qualitative inquiry using big data	6
P24	Priest, S. (2023)	Journal of Adventure Education and Outdoor Learning	Predicting the future of experiential and adventurous learning in the metaverse	6
P25	He, T. L., Zhang, C. C., Huang, Z. Q., & Qin, F. (2025)	Thinking Skills and Creativity	Investigating the impact of situational cognition, emotions, and self-efficacy on creative thinking and collaborative intention in metaverse teaching scene	2

References

Agbedahin, A. V. (2019). Sustainable development, education for sustainable development, and the 2030 agenda for sustainable development: Emergence, efficacy, eminence, and future. *Sustainable Development, 27*(4), 669–680. https://doi.org/10.1002/sd.1931

Akyürek, S., Genç, G., Çalık, İ, & Şengel, Ü. (2024). Metaverse in tourism education: A mixed method on vision, challenges and extended technology acceptance model. *Journal of Hospitality, Leisure, Sport & Tourism Education, 35*, Article 100503. https://doi.org/10.1016/j.jhlste.2024.100503

Al-Adwan, A. S., & Al-Debei, M. M. (2024). The determinants of Gen Z's metaverse adoption decisions in higher education: Integrating UTAUT2 with personal innovativeness in IT. *Education and Information Technologies, 29*(6), 7413–7445. https://doi.org/10.1007/s10639-023-12080-1

Al-Adwan, A. S., Li, N., Al-Adwan, A., Abbasi, G. A., Albelbisi, N. A., & Habibi, A. (2023). Extending the technology acceptance model (TAM) to Predict University Students' intentions to use metaverse-based learning platforms. *Education and Information Technologies, 28*(11), 15381–15413. https://doi.org/10.1007/s10639-023-11816-3

Bhuiyan, S. I., & Islam, N. (2025). Virtual immersion and global learning: The future of education through the metaverse. In N. Islam & I. Salami (Eds.), *Metaverse innovation. Applied innovation and technology management*. Springer. https://doi.org/10.1007/978-3-031-97080-1_5

Chanda, R. S., Pabalkar, V., & Sharma, S. (2024). Attitude and behavioral intention for using metaverse in education: Learner's perspective. *Journal of Applied Research in Higher Education, 16*(5), 2168–2184. https://doi.org/10.1108/JARHE-07-2023-0307

Chen, C. M., & Huang, M. Y. (2024). Enhancing programming learning performance through a Jigsaw collaborative learning method in a metaverse virtual space. *International Journal of STEM Education, 11*(1), 36. https://doi.org/10.1186/s40594-024-00495-2

Chen, G., Jin, Y., & Chen, P. (2024). Development of a platform for state online education services: Design concept based on meta-universe. *Education and Information Technologies, 29*(17), 23605–23629. https://doi.org/10.1007/s10639-024-12792-y

Chen, H. J. (2023). Gather in the metaverse: Learning outcomes, virtual presence, and perceptions of high-and low-achieving pre-service teachers of English as a Foreign Language. *Education and Information Technologies, 29*(7), 8549–8577. https://doi.org/10.1007/s10639-023-12135-3

Damaševičius, R., & Sidekerskienė, T. (2024). Virtual worlds for learning in metaverse: A narrative review. *Sustainability, 16*(5), 2032. https://doi.org/10.3390/su16052032

Davis, F. D. (1989). Perceived usefulness, perceived ease of use, and user acceptance of information technology. *MIS Quarterly, 13*(3), 319–340. https://doi.org/10.2307/249008

Díaz, J., Saldaña, C., & Avila, C. (2020). Virtual world as a resource for hybrid education. *International Journal of Emerging Technologies in Learning (iJET), 15*(15), 94–109. https://doi.org/10.3991/ijet.v15i15.13025

Fujioka, M., Reimer, K., & Saito, E. (2024). 'It wasn't just Japanese': A tertiary language programme to help students prepare for the next stage of life. *International Journal of Lifelong Education, 43*(5), 540–552. https://doi.org/10.1080/02601370.2024.2368155

Garrison, D. R., Anderson, T., & Archer, W. (2001). Critical thinking, cognitive presence, and computer conferencing in distance education. *American Journal of Distance Education, 15*(1), 7–23.https://doi.org/10.1080/08923640109527071

George-Reyes, C. E., Peláez Sánchez, I. C., Glasserman-Morales, L. D., & López-Caudana, E. O. (2023, May). The Metaverse and complex thinking: Opportunities, experiences, and future lines of research. *Frontiers in Education, 8*, 1166999. https://doi.org/10.3389/feduc.2023.1166999

Godwin-Jones, R. (2023). Emerging spaces for language learning: AI bots, ambient intelligence, and the metaverse. *Language Learning & Technology, 27*(2), 6–27. https://doi.org/10.64152/10125/73501

Hatmanto, E. D., Pratolo, B. W., & Intansari, M. (2023). Metaverse magic: Unveiling the pedagogical potential and transformative effects on intercultural communication in English language Teaching. *English Language Teaching Educational Journal, 6*(1), 14–31. https://doi.org/10.12928/eltej.v6i1.8627

He, T. L., Zhang, C. C., Huang, Z. Q., & Qin, F. (2025). Investigating the impact of situational cognition, emotions, and self-efficacy on creative thinking and collaborative intention in metaverse teaching scene. *Thinking Skills and Creativity, 56*, Article 101723. https://doi.org/10.1016/j.tsc.2024.101723

Hsiao, K. L., Chen, M. Y., & Liao, Y. R. (2025). Development and evaluation of a metaverse competency scale for university students. *Education and Information Technologies*, 1–26. https://doi.org/10.1007/s10639-025-13520-w

Hwang, Y., Lee, S., & Jeon, J. (2025). Integrating AI Chatbots into the metaverse: Pre-service English teachers' design works and perceptions. *Education and Information Technologies, 30*(4), 4099–4130. https://doi.org/10.1007/s10639-024-12924-4

Hwang, Y., Shin, D., & Lee, H. (2023). Students' perception on immersive learning through 2D and 3D metaverse platforms. *Educational Technology Research and Development, 71*(4), 1687–1708. https://doi.org/10.1007/s11423-023-10238-9

Lee, J., & Ko, Y. (2025). Comparing metaverse and face-to-face instruction for enhancing English skills and attitudes among EFL adolescents. *Education and Information Technologies, 30*(6), 8215–8244. https://doi.org/10.1007/s10639-024-13162-4

Lee, S., Jeon, J., & Choe, H. (2025). Enhancing pre-service teachers' global Englishes awareness with technology: A focus on AI Chatbots in 3D metaverse environments. *Tesol Quarterly, 59*(1), 49–74. https://doi.org/10.1002/tesq.3300

Lee, S. M., & Kim, S. Y. (2024). Preservice teachers' learning by design through space construction in the metaverse. *British Journal of Educational Technology, 56*(1), 208–230. https://doi.org/10.1111/bjet.13493

Li, M., & Yu, Z. (2023). A systematic review on the metaverse-based blended English learning. *Frontiers in Psychology, 13*, 1087508. https://doi.org/10.3389/fpsyg.2022.1087508

Mahmoud, A. B. (2024). Exploring the public's beliefs, emotions and sentiments towards the adoption of the metaverse in education: A qualitative inquiry using big data. *British Educational Research Journal, 50*(5), 2320–2341. https://doi.org/10.1002/berj.4026

Mystakidis, S. (2022). Metaverse. *Encyclopedia, 2*(1), 486–497. https://doi.org/10.3390/encyclopedia2010031

Ng, D. T. K. (2022). What is the metaverse? Definitions, technologies and the community of inquiry. *Australasian Journal of Educational Technology, 38*(4), 190–205. https://doi.org/10.14742/ajet.7945

Novak, K. (2022). Introducing the metaverse, again! *TechTrends, 66*(5), 737–739. https://doi.org/10.1007/s11528-022-00767-0

Ortega-Rodríguez, P. J. (2022). From extended reality to the metaverse: A critical reflection on contributions to education. *Teoría de la Educación: Revista Interuniversitaria, 34*(2), 189–208. https://doi.org/10.14201/teri.27864

Page, M. J., McKenzie, J. E., Bossuyt, P. M., Boutron, I., Hoffmann, T. C., Mulrow, C. D., Shamseer, L., Tetzlaff, J. M., Akl, E. A., Brennan, S. E., Chou, R., Glanville, J., Grimshaw, J. M., Hróbjartsson, A., Lalu, M. M., Li, T., Loder, E. W., Mayo-Wilson, E., McDonald, S., ... Moher, D. (2021). The PRISMA 2020 statement: An updated guideline for reporting systematic reviews. *BMJ, 372*. https://doi.org/10.1136/bmj.n71

Pradana, M., & Elisa, H. P. (2023). Metaverse in education: A systematic literature review. *Cogent Social Sciences, 9*(2), 2252656. https://doi.org/10.1080/23311886.2023.2252656

Priest, S. (2023). Predicting the future of experiential and adventurous learning in the metaverse. *Journal of Adventure Education and Outdoor Learning, 24*(1), 21–34. https://doi.org/10.1080/14729679.2023.2220835

Rahman, H., Wahid, S. A., Ahmad, F., & Ali, N. (2024). Game-based learning in metaverse: Virtual chemistry classroom for chemical bonding for remote education. *Education and Information Technologies, 29*(15), 19595–19619. https://doi.org/10.1007/s10639-024-12575-5

Richards, J. C. (2015). The changing face of language learning: Learning beyond the classroom. *RELC Journal, 46*(1). https://doi.org/10.1177/0033688214561621

Saritaş, M. T., & Topraklıkoğlu, K. (2022). Systematic Literature Review on the Use of Metaverse in Education. *International Journal of Technology in Education, 5*(4), 586–607. https://doi.org/10.46328/ijte.319

Skiada, M. (2021). The implementation of authentic language input in second language (L2) teaching: Pedagogical arguments. *Training, Language and Culture, 5*(1), 86–96. https://doi.org/10.22363/2521-442X-2021-5-1-86-96

Suiçmez, İ, & Ozansoy, K. (2024). Development of sustainable education environments in higher education with metaverse applications. *Sustainability, 16*(23), 10331. https://doi.org/10.3390/su162310331

Wiangkham, A., & Vongvit, R. (2023). Exploring the drivers for the adoption of metaverse technology in engineering education using PLS-SEM and ANFIS. *Education and Information Technologies, 29*(6), 7385–7412. https://doi.org/10.1007/s10639-023-12127-3

Wu, J. G., Zhang, D., & Lee, S. M. (2023). Into the brave new metaverse: Envisaging future language teaching and learning. *IEEE Transactions on Learning Technologies, 17*, 44–53. https://doi.org/10.1109/TLT.2023.3259470

Yang, X., Cheng, P. Y., Liu, X., & Shih, S. P. (2023). The impact of immersive virtual reality on art education: A study of flow state, cognitive load, brain state, and motivation. *Education and Information Technologies, 29*(5), 6087–6106. https://doi.org/10.1007/s10639-023-12041-8

Zhou, R., Samad, A., & Perinpasingam, T. (2024). A systematic review of cross-cultural communicative competence in EFL teaching: Insights from China. *Humanities and Social Sciences Communications, 11*, 1750. https://doi.org/10.1057/s41599-024-04071-5

Zygmunt, T. (2016). Language education for sustainable development. *Discourse and Communication for Sustainable Education, 7*(1), 112–124. https://doi.org/10.1515/dcse-2016-0008

Kumutha Raman is a senior lecturer at INTI International University and holds a PhD in TESL from Universiti Kebangsaan Malaysia (UKM). With over 12 years of experience in high school education and 3 years in higher education, her expertise lies in technology-enhanced language learning, particularly integrating Virtual Reality (VR) to elevate ESL classroom engagement and outcomes.

Wei Lun Wong is a senior lecturer of TESL at Faculty of Education, Universiti Kebangsaan Malaysia. His research interests are TESL, applied and corpus linguistics. He has published in prestigious Scopus and WoS journals such as Scientific Reports, SAGE Open, and CALL-EJ.

Nur Izzati Khairuddin is a lecturer of English Language and Business Communication at INTI International University, Malaysia. Her research focuses on AI-enhanced language learning, project-based pedagogy, and assessment in higher education. She is actively involved in cross-institutional research collaborations and has also received multiple international innovation awards for developing impactful, learner-centred, and technology-driven instructional solutions.

Future Directions

Emerging Trends and Innovations in Metaverse-Based Language Learning and Teaching

Ayfer Su-Bergil

Abstract The purpose of this chapter is to investigate the numerous ways in which metaverse technology has altered the process of language teaching and learning. The rationale for metaverse as pedagogical acceptance in EFL/ESL education is presented first, followed by an examination of the learning environment and language learning through metaverse and how to place it in EFL/ESL education. Following this, the accompanying section concentrates on the dimensions of the metaverse and reflections of the "7-Layer Metaverse Value Chain" on the processes of learning and teaching foreign and second languages. Then, how the metaverse has changed the roles and competencies of EFL/ESL teachers and learners has been displayed from both stakeholders' conditions. With the current trends in metaverse use in EFL/ESL teaching, the use of metaverse-based applications in EFL/ESL instruction has been shown to improve students' communication abilities, cultural awareness, and motivation, according to recent research and proven methodology. At the end of the chapter, trends in future EFL/ESL teaching and possible metaverse areas for development present a discussion regarding the ethical, pedagogical, and technical problems that are related to the utilization of metaverse applications for the purpose of language instruction. In addition to being a unique technology, the metaverse is a significant arena for academic studies that is transforming the nature of EFL/ESL education in the digital era by revolutionizing how people think about the language education.

Keywords Metaverse · Language learning · EFL/ESL education · Value chain · EFL/ESL teachers · EFL learners · Roles and competencies · Virtual learning environments · Metaverse trends

A. Su-Bergil (✉)
Amasya University, Amasya, Türkiye
e-mail: ayfersubergil@amasya.edu.tr

F. Çelik and C. Yangın Ersanlı (eds.), *Metaverse-Based Language Learning and Teaching*, English Language Education 49,
https://doi.org/10.1007/978-3-032-31366-9_12

1 Introduction

Technology is rapidly becoming an integral part of education as a means to help students learn in ways that are more engaging, beneficial, and personalized to their needs. Nowadays, students may learn a lot more than they could in a regular classroom thanks to internet resources, interactive learning tools, VR, and AR (Urbaite, 2024). This will allow students to access the course materials more efficiently and thoroughly. A notable advantage of technology-enhanced education is that it enables students to learn at their own pace. The convenience of having course materials available at your fingertips at all times makes online learning a more adaptable option. As a result, students could feel less anxious and have a stronger desire to learn (Chisunum & Nwadiokwu, 2024). In addition, technology has the ability to enhance equal access to education. Thanks to technology, students have the opportunity to connect with a wider range of people. Within this framework, the metaverse and related technologies hold great promise for enhancing education and influencing students' knowledge acquisition practices.

As is known, it was already important for educators to employ modern and technological tools in the classroom before emergent situations, such as pandemics and earthquakes, etc. But it is accepted that those emergent situations hastened the shift to online education and made it quite clear that technology must be a part of classroom instruction (Rof et al., 2022). Even while the COVID-19 epidemic was difficult to live through, it was also an opportunity to turn adversity into strength. During this time, IT companies prioritized offering several training options to help employees learn new skills and tackle old problems in novel ways. Because innovative methodologies in educational institutions were inevitable, certain children may acquire English more effectively through the utilization of these innovative techniques.

All in all, these issues have forced educators to conduct new research and use technology to help learners improve their reading, writing, listening, and speaking language skills. To overcome these challenges and make foreign language learning successful, several alternative ways have been tried in Türkiye at the national level, as in other countries. All of those efforts show how important it is to incorporate technology into "English as a foreign/second language" (EFL/ESL) classroom (Zengin & Aksu, 2017). After the consideration of the pros and cons at that time, it is agreed upon that that the technology plays a crucial role in solving problems associated with English language instruction, especially in those urgent conditions. Because, in spite of the problems with the learning environment and insufficient practice opportunities, meticulously crafted learning environments provide learners with the opportunity to acclimatize to their new surroundings and prepare them for life beyond the schools. These experiences remarked the idea that the educators must make the required adjustments to the learning settings while keeping current technology in mind in order to achieve the programs' or schedules' goals (Zhang, 2022). Only in that way, the system guarantees that the learners get an excellent and potential education at the point of teaching foreign/second languages, which is the scope of this chapter.

Furthermore, the lightning-fast development of digital technology has outpaced the ways to describe pedagogical approaches that include tech, such as "technology-assisted language learning" (TALL), "computer-assisted language learning" (CALL), and "mobile-assisted language learning" (MALL). As a result, we are failing to meet the needs of students enrolled in other courses, as well as those who are making steady progress in learning a foreign/second language. Since this is the case, people are continually coming up with different technology use approaches pedagogically. As an example, the so-called "online 4.0" technologies are a huge step forward for the web since they personalize and engage users beyond their usual online habits. This innovative approach to leveraging the internet has significantly facilitated the process of learning and teaching English for both learners and educators (Procel et al., 2024). Applications that make use of "augmented, virtual, and mixed reality" (AR, VR, and MR) have seen a consistent uptick in user engagement over the last several years within this context. The use of metaverse learning environments is also on the rise, and these applications are becoming more commonplace. As a result of the metaverse-based modifications and enhancements to these technologies, there has been a substantial impact on group and individual language learning situations.

Especially when we think of the conditions of individuals, "digital natives" who have grown up with technology, the metaverse and increasing number of new technologies are promising for the improvement of EFL/ESL education. At this point, Hyun (2021) reminds us the immersive aspects of the metaverse need to be realized because it has the potential to create virtual English-speaking environments and real-life experiences for language teaching and learning conditions in an authentic way. So, this transmits the language education further from the traditional classrooms, where the learners are provided with real-life language conditions that will help them develop more confidence and better communication skills in the target language.

When all of these impacts are taken into consideration, the intensified technology integration with the metaverse seems unavoidable because it offers novel viewpoints and applications not only for the realm of education but also specifically for EFL/ESL education, which is what is focused on, here. For this purpose, this chapter aims to depict the rationale behind the integration of the metaverse in the context of EFL/ESL education by highlighting the basic principles of it that can be associated with teaching and learning a language. While I attempt to highlight the significance of the metaverse in language learning in different aspects of the following part, here we'll take a look at and remind the origins of the metaverse idea very briefly, its educational value, and its uses in EFL/ESL education. Moreover, the transformation of the roles and competencies of language teachers and learners will be addressed by clarifying how the metaverse could help English language teachers and teacher educators as well as the language learners through their journey in learning and teaching a foreign or/and second language.

2 The Rationale for Metaverse as Pedagogical Acceptance in EFL/ESL Education

As known, the phrase "metaverse" that denotes a digital domain that surpasses the confines of the physical world (Cheng et al., 2022), derived from the Greek "meta" and the English "universe". This notion defines an immersive three-dimensional virtual environment accessible via technologies like virtual and augmented reality and was initially presented in Neal Stephenson's, 1992 novel Snow Crash. In this interconnected environment that Stephenson (1992) depicted, the users, or the participants, as being digital avatars, have the abilities to communicate, cooperate, learn, play, and participate in different and creative endeavors. In addition to these facilities, as reflected in the literature, metaverse has extended beyond entertainment, healthcare, military training, and business so that its increasing significance in modern digital culture is very obvious (Ali et al., 2023; Rostami & Maier, 2022). At this point, its amalgamation of interactivity, immersion, and connectedness develops its transformative potentials for education sector as well. In detail, as for EFL/ESL context, it can be declared that the immersive and communicative capabilities of the metaverse suggest various kinds of fascinating pedagogical environments and promote authentic language usage, intercultural interaction, and learner engagement in different ways for both learners and teachers in language education as opposed to conventional classroom facilities.

Initially, the production of fertile instructional resources for language education takes attraction with the incorporation of metaverse into EFL/ESL education. Because of this, as Ghoulam and Bouikhalene (2024) displayed, the metaverse, a continuous digital environment, overlaps effectively with fundamental language education principles such as interactivity and engagement. Furthermore, with its opportunity of "sense of presence," it fosters student engagement that much research conducted in various countries reflected as having potential for increased vocabulary acquisition, retention, and motivation (Çelik & Baturay, 2024; Seock & Shin, 2025).

Another major benefit of metaverse-based learning environments is that they encourage contextual and experiential learning conditions, providing language learners with opportunities for authentic and collaborative interaction facilities and context. This benefit corresponds with Vygotsky's social constructivist theory, increasing the social presence and communicative abilities (Al-kfairy et al., 2025; Çelik & Ersanlı, 2025) of language learners today's conditions and realities align with the 21st-century skills. So, by promoting collaborative learning and intercultural communication, metaverse enables the language learners to engage with various classmates worldwide, which result in the enhancement of communication and global cultural awareness (Hatmanto et al., 2023).

According to Pérez-Jorge et al. (2025), flexibility and personalization serve as other notable advantages that metaverse environments adapt the learning pathways to accommodate personal learner profiles to reduce anxiety and increase the accessibility conditions in the teaching and learning process. As a result of these advantages, we can conclude that the teacher's position evolves from being a "conventional knowledge disseminator" to a "learning architect" assigned to design interactive and engaging pedagogical encounters for learners (Negre et al., 2025).

All of these insights highlight that the metaverse has the potential to transform EFL/ESL education by enhancing engagement, providing context-rich learning experiences, fostering collaboration, enabling customization, and altering instructional methods effectively responding to personal needs and profiles of the learners. Besides, the metaverse has the potential to establish innovative educational frameworks that aim to improve EFL/ESL education from different perspectives by recognizing the accurate evaluation of technical infrastructure, educator training, ethical implementation, and content development.

3 Learning Environment and Language Learning Through Metaverse

The potential educational benefits of the metaverse are being recognized by many individuals and researchers as its popularity grows. Numerous educational institutions have tested it to see if it improves students' ability to absorb and retain material through the use of situational realism. The lecture series "Virtual Human," developed and led by Bailenson (2024), took place solely within a VR environment. This allowed them to go to many different places that they never would have had the chance to visit in the flesh. Embry-Riddle Aeronautical University is building a virtual crash lab to help with safety research (Burgess & Moran, 2015). Improving educational fairness is facilitated by the capacity to engage in virtual interactions, which is useful for learning languages and medicine. In order to enhance the metaverse experience, anatomy lectures are incorporating extended reality technology as an additional application. VR has been integrated into the curriculum, allowing students to receive instruction in a digital setting (Ibili et al., 2024). Not only does this make learning more fun for learners, but it also helps them become better tech users. Beyond the constraints of physical space, the metaverse encourages participatory learning and employs immersive technology like AR to make learning more fun and practical. Promoting interaction amongst individuals in the same setting allows this to happen as well (Damaševičius & Sidekerskienė, 2024).

The following are some example scenes for metaverse-based language learning environments of how students can benefit greatly from using metaverse virtual worlds to improve their English language skills through increased engagement with course content and peer support. It provides synchronous, competency-based teaching that aids students in expanding their vocabulary and improving their grammar skills in engaging, lifelike settings that mimic traditional classrooms. Students not only improve their academic performance but also broaden their understanding of the world when they interact with one another through avatars. Wonderful, individually-tailored experiences can also be given to students by their instructors. Even if the learners feel lonely outside of the metaverse, they are still encouraged to exercise

Fig. 1 Illustrations for metaverse-based language learning environment

because of the three-dimensional communication it provides. On a more specific note, this tool is useful for figuring out how to motivate individuals to study English. Changes in approach usually result in a more pleasant learning experience. As illustrated below, the learners can learn new languages in a variety of places in the metaverse (Fig. 1).

4 Metaverse and EFL/ESL Education

To better comprehend how to use EFL/ESL in the metaverse, it is vital to have a fundamental understanding of the metaverse and its value chain. The metaverse is an online community where users can share knowledge and interact with one another. The four parts that comprise the metaverse are a contrast between within and outside, technologies that center on personal identity, and augmentation and simulation, as shown in Fig. 2. When new features, functions, graphics, or designs are added to existing systems through the use of technology, this process is called augmentation, and it is a continuous process. In contrast, simulation technology models the actual world to generate its own universe.

Second Life, Roblox, Minecraft, and Zepeto are just a few instances of technologies that prioritize user identity. With these tools, a person's identification and the task they do are all that are really important. The majority of the time, when it comes to external technologies, the focus is on the environment and the environment around the user. These technologies give the user information about and control over their immediate surroundings. There are two main categories of programs and tools in these two frameworks, the internal and the external. The former helps the user concentrate on their inner world, while the latter helps them focus on the world around them.

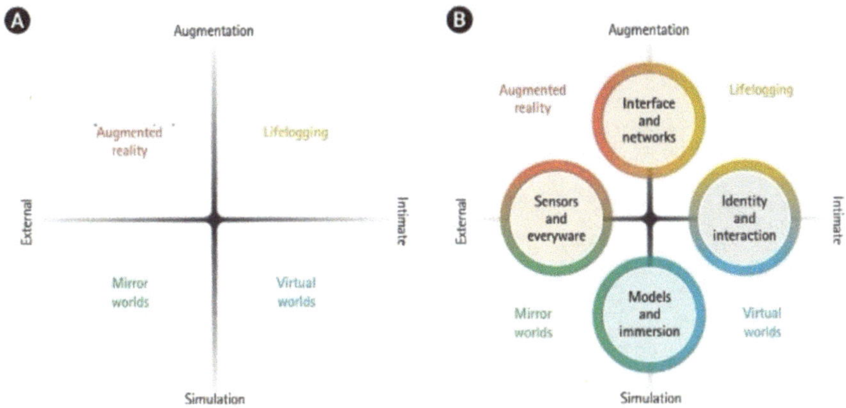

Fig. 2 The dimensions of the metaverse (Kye et al., 2021; Smart et al., 2007)

Programs and tools of both kinds are at your disposal. The use of 3D virtual environments is common in educational settings because they provide a unique constructivist experience, are easy to access, and create a feeling of presence. Whether working alone or with others, there are a variety of modeling methodologies that may be used to mimic the way real-life communities' function. It is now possible to take on a whole new persona in a virtual environment like Google Earth thanks to simulations. The External and Simulation Axis Mirror Worlds are digital recreations of actual locations that have been enhanced with recent data. Simulated environments and mirror worlds mean the same thing. In addition to sensors, location-aware technologies, and life-logging capabilities, they have enhanced tools for virtual mapping, modeling, and annotating. There are currently functional mirror worlds such as Google Earth and geographic information systems (GIS). Metaverse technology can incorporate networked data into our usual view of the world by means of location-aware systems and interfaces. This phenomenon is known as AR when seen through the lens of the external and augmented axis. This results in the creation of improved educational settings whose enhanced environments allow users to interact with digital elements seamlessly integrated into their physical surroundings. Consequently, it opens up new possibilities for education, entertainment, and productivity, transforming the way we perceive and engage with reality.

As a result, technology creates new opportunities for education, enjoyment, and productivity, altering our perception and interaction with reality. Radoff (2021) delineated a seven-tiered value chain for the metaverse in the following figure, which reflects the transition that also facilitates creative methodologies across multiple settings of language learning and teaching (Fig. 3).

As depicted in the figure of a value chain for the metaverse, there are seven levels to Radoff's "Metaverse Layers" model: "infrastructure, human interface, decentralization, spatial computation, producer economy, exploration, and experience." The first layer is "infrastructure" (5G, WiFi 6, 6G, Cloud Computing,

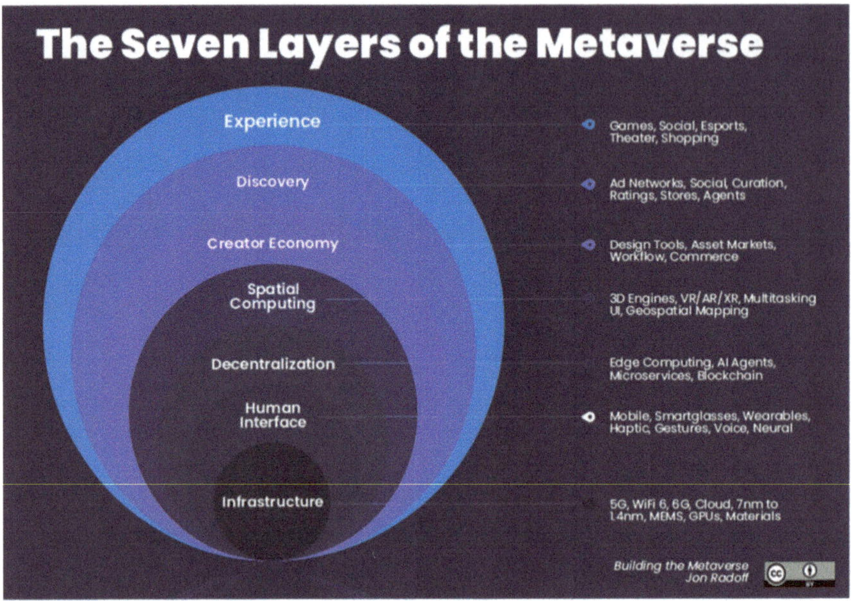

Fig. 3 A 7-layer value chain for the metaverse (Radoff, 2021)

Micro-Electromechanical Systems, GPU-Graphics Processing Unit), the second layer addresses "Human Interface" (Wearable Tech, Smart Glasses, Mobile Tech, Touch, Gestures, Voice, Neural Networks), the third layer reflects "Decentralization" (Edge Computing, AI, Intelligent Agents, Microservices, Blockchain), the fourth layer displays "Spatial Computing" (3D, AR, VR, MUIs, and GM), the fifth layer entails "Creator Economy (Design Tools, Asset Markets, Workflow, Commerce), the sixth layer reflects "Discovery (Ad Networks, Social, Curation, Ratings, Stores, Agents), and finally, on the very last layer "Experience" (Games, Social, Esport, Theater, Shopping) is placed. According to Thakur et al. (2023) since infrastructure is the most crucial layer, it must provide a strong base before any of the other improvements occur in the system or applications of metaverse. Combined and interacted with other layers, in the experience layer the individuals/learners will be free to have their own experience that is totally unique to them without any kind of material or physical constraints.

Thus, the transfer of the value chain perspectives on language education is essential for adjusting to the changes the learners experience and have in their surroundings. Through engagement with immersive technologies, learners acquire opportunities to refine language skills in genuine circumstances that will augment their communicative competencies in their practices. Moreover, the amalgamation of virtual reality with gamified educational platforms can facilitate collaborative learning experiences. Then, it will be observed that his method fosters learner engagement with varied linguistic and cultural viewpoints, enhancing comprehension of language application in different circumstances. After that, educators can utilize these technology innovations to develop customized learning experiences that cater to individual needs. By doing so, they may guarantee that language instruction remains pertinent and efficacious in an increasingly digital landscape.

5 Dimensions of the Metaverse and Reflections of the "7-Layer Metaverse Value Chain" on the Processes of Learning and Teaching Foreign and Second Languages

Smart et al. (2007) and Kye et al. (2021) proposed that the metaverse is such a complex and dynamic space that fosters discovery, enriches language learning, and helps individuals explore their own identities throughout the learning process. On account of this, it cannot be accepted just as an advanced technological system. Instead of this, this complex system illustrates the pedagogical value with the concept of the value chain, and it offers new opportunities for EFL/ESL contexts. Ultimately, whatever the metaverse suggests for EFL/ESL education will support both teachers and learners with virtual worlds, mirror worlds, augmented reality, and life-tracking applications. In this way, it can be argued that teachers and learners will be able to reshape how they connect in and interact on social, emotional, and cognitive levels of the target language by incorporating the opportunities the metaverse offers for EFL/ESL contexts. Because metaverse is not only an up-to-date perspective on language education but also expands the potential for exploring its role in EFL/ESL contexts.

Furthermore, it can be inferred that the dimensions of the metaverse deeply shape the way individuals learn a new language. Because its virtual language learning environments provide learners steps into immersive 3D spaces where the learners can instantly interact with native speakers and other speakers of the target language from different settings and backgrounds. In traditional classrooms, these kinds of settings are frequent, and they serve multiple functions, including assisting students in gaining a respect for diversity, enhancing their communication skills, and gaining knowledge about other cultures. For instance, with the "mirror world" referring to a virtual environment that looks exactly like the actual world, students will be able to practice the language in authentic settings. A person who is learning English can get additional knowledge about the language and culture "in situ" by interacting with a digital London. Via the AR the learning process by incorporating digital components into the physical environment can be enhanced. Students demonstrate a great willingness to acquire new words, enhance their pronunciation, and improve their language skills through the completion of these steps. On the other hand, life logs enable students to learn on their own by enabling them to monitor their progress in personalized digital profiles while they are in school. This approach allows students to learn independently. As a consequence of this, educators are able to immediately investigate the progress of their students and devise innovative approaches to instructing them.

The "7-Layer Metaverse Value Chain" is a detailed guide that shows us how to build and maintain a language learning space (Thakur et al., 2023). This system is constantly evolving, and it fits in perfectly with that. Virtual language courses can only work on devices that have 5G, cloud computing, and the ability to use AI. People can now connect in more than one language thanks to this technology, which allows for high-quality audio and video conversations and tools for real-time translation interpretation. In the human interfaces layer, students can engage with language by means of virtual reality goggles, motion sensors for their hands, and voice recognition software. By doing so, you may make the learning process more interactive and immersive. The idea behind decentralization is to make education more accessible and democratic by ensuring that no one entity controls the whole body of knowledge. In addition, they can create their own learning spaces. The teacher is doing more than just relaying facts in this case; they are actively improving the students' capacity to absorb the material.

With the advent of spatial computing and the growth of the creator economy, there have been profound changes in the functions of digital learning settings. For students to fully immerse themselves in the languages they are learning and to actively participate as creators, it is feasible to provide them with realistic, three-dimensional surroundings. Because it can help teachers and students in the real and virtual worlds at the same time and offers a great deal of promise as an educational tool. This results in a classroom environment that is conducive to learning for everyone involved teachers and students alike (Guo & Gao, 2022). Furthermore, it may open doors that can be used to improve EFL and ESL curricula. From this vantage point, it's critical to remember that utilizing avatars in the metaverse for educational purposes has the ability to mask traits like gender, ethnicity, and physical disabilities (Duan et al., 2021). This perspective holds that the metaverse can greatly benefit inclusive education in contexts where English is a foreign or second language.

While advanced algorithms are used in the discovery layer to make information more personalized for each user, language and cultural engagement are combined in the experience layer. Because it may aid learners in understanding language as a medium of communication and their digital identities, which makes learning a second or foreign language very beneficial. Thus, the huge change has occurred in the way we educate with the arrival of the digital era. This is mostly attributable to the fact that educators are crucial in providing learners with engaging and relevant lessons and contents. Herein, the metaverse offers a new area where people can learn a language without worrying about physical distance or time constraints (Park & Kim, 2022). Through the integration of cutting-edge technology propelled by AI, the metaverse holds the promise of fulfilling all desires in language education.

6 The Changing Roles and Competencies of EFL/ESL Teachers with Metaverse

According to Kennedy and Sundberg (2020), after the emergence of the internet in 1980s, the Information Age revolutionized the communication process for everyone, and the 21st-century skills such as critical thinking, creativity, and collaboration come to the forefront in diverse areas of education. Also, globalization itself has accelerated the development of similar skills, such as communication and digital literacy skills in the education arena among teachers and learners (Sahlberg, 2004). Especially with the trends of Industry 4.0, Society 5.0, and Education 4.0, in addition to the rapid technological advances such as cloud computing, artificial intelligence, and the Internet of Things, the traditional conditions gave way to the innovation and student-centered pedagogies in education addressing the transformation of the roles and competencies of EFL/ESL teachers (Ibrahim, 2021; Lampropoulos et al., 2019; McKinsey, 2020; Soboleva et al., 2018).

So, it can be asserted that the metaverse and the accompanying digital transformation are still expanding the boundaries of the traditional classroom and conditions in language teaching by encouraging language learning environments to become dynamic and interconnected (Bibri & Jagatheesaperumal, 2023; Fang & Shen, 2021; Nair et al., 2024). In this way, this transformation and change put forward the vital importance of the role and competencies of language teachers. Thus, language teachers, one of the most important practitioners, are motivated to create flexible, technology-enhanced environments that will encourage participation and adaptability. Meanwhile, even as digital learning environments continue to evolve, it is expected that continuous professional development and innovative teaching practices will become more aligned with the needs of EFL/ESL teachers and will be more closely integrated into sustainable processes so that this transformation can adequately equip language teachers in the long term.

In the metaverse, immersive technologies such as virtual augmented reality and mixed reality are continuing the transformation of educational environments by enabling language learners to experience globally connected experiences alongside more engaging and local connections (Heider, 2021). For this transformation and change to take place, practitioners of EFL/ESL will need to modify their roles and skills, shifting from being knowledge transmitters to facilitators and guides in digital contexts. AR, VR, and AI are examples of technologies that can be used in education to create dynamic learning environments that have the potential to prioritize a student-centered, discovery-oriented approach to language teaching and learning.

The proliferation of digital resources has compelled teachers of English as a foreign language and English as a second language to rethink their roles within the classroom (Rahimi & Oh, 2024). It is necessary for educators to integrate their pedagogical, technological, and design skills in order to facilitate successful student interactions in virtual learning environments, as stated by Adera (2025).

Onu et al. (2024) identify essential competencies for teachers in metaverse environments as robust digital and metaverse literacy, adaptability in instructional strategies, and facilitation of intercultural communication among students. Considering the technological aspects of these competencies, the EFL/ESL teachers need to have learning analytics abilities to carry out and adapt such kinds of learning experiences and interactions of the students while making them familiar with the importance of ethics, security, and digital citizenship to navigate them responsibly for their virtual interactions (Tabassum & Qadir, 2024; von Gillern et al., 2024).

To sum up, the challenges that hinder teachers from adapting to new environments, such as technological limitations and unequal student access (Chasubuta & Ndibalema, 2024; Memon & Memon, 2025), need to be addressed pedagogically for practitioners by integrating the metaverse itself and the technological content into teachers' training programs. In that way metaverse literacy, infrastructure improvement, the development of the specialized assessment tools will be possible to be implemented by the teachers as they build their teacher competencies (Ajani, 2024). Hence, the metaverse reshapes teaching, demanding enhanced digital, pedagogical, and ethical skills for effective teaching and learning facilitations (Iqbal & Ali, 2024). In addition to the other roles and competencies mentioned in this part, following a comprehensive approach regarding all of these aspects is essential for EFL/ESL teacher training programs.

7 The Changing Roles and Competencies of EFL/ESL Learners with Metaverse

Remembering that the rapid advancement of digital technologies has significantly transformed language teaching methods, with the metaverse emerging as a prominent example, this immersive environment, which combines virtual and augmented reality, allows learners to engage in three-dimensional, interactive experiences (Al-Ansi et al., 2023). At this point, the roles and competencies of EFL/ESL learners are also evolving as the teachers in the same context.

The technological advances come up with major transformational shifts in EFL/ESL learners (Yıldız, 2024). Although the language learners are often passive recipients of the information in the traditional classroom, which is at its least amount compared to the other subject fields, especially with the development of smart technologies as metaverse, here, the active learner roles such as being active content producers, participants of task and social interactions via avatars, are the prominent condition of the EFL/ESL learners transformation. This transformation in roles and competencies of EFL/ESL learners is provided with some research samples from the literature, indicating not only how metaverse-based vocabulary learning enhances student engagement, enjoyment, and community feeling, but also highlighting the cognitive and emotional benefits of the new roles and competencies (Çelik & Baturay, 2024; Wang et al., 2025).

Additionally, learners transition from being dependent on teachers to becoming self-directed. The metaverse provides a flexible learning ecosystem where students can manage their learning processes, set personal goals, and achieve higher retention rates compared to traditional methods (Muthmainnah et al., 2025; Omar & Gómez, 2025). In this way, both independence and responsibility in learning a target language have potential to be fostered under the influence of the self-directed approach.

The sense of community is another competency that the EFL/ESL learners can develop through the use of metaverse (Chen, 2024). The metaverse environment provide language learners various conditions where they can interact with peers from different backgrounds. By being the participants of these interactions, the levels of language learning motivation and senso belonging will also enhance at national and international stances. As a result, EFL/ESL learners will be the active members of versatile multicultural communities rather than isolated and limited language learning conditions (Çelik, 2025; Singh et al., 2024).

When the roles and conditions of language learning are evolving so do the competencies of the learners that are the requirements of what metaverse has brought to the language education field. Apart from the above-mentioned ones, linguistic competencies are another type of requirements that can be reinforced via task-based interactions being simulated through real-life scenarios by improving not only verbal communication but also realistic interactional skills as well (Yao et al., 2024; Yusupalieva, 2024). However, the digital literacy skills and competencies need to be seen as essential for the language learners to navigate virtual environments by utilizing different types of technological tools in a practical and effective ways (Thelma et al., 2024; Wei, 2024).

Moreover, metacognitive skills are seen as having its vital place in metaverse-based environments because it directs the learners in a way that they should be responsible for their own learning, defining personal-specific goals, following their own progress, and accommodate the strategies they are utilizing while learning the target language (Mazari, 2025; Suvorova & Demirbilek, 2025). Additionally, with the influence of metacognitive skills, again the competencies of collaboration and intercultural competence will find conditions to develop, underlying the importance of cultural awareness and teamwork (Mutchima et al., 2025; Muthmainnah et al., 2025).

Despite the new roles and competencies that metaverse language learning environments provide in terms of language learning, it is beneficial to remind learners of certain important pedagogical and ethical considerations (Onu et al., 2024; Wardat & Akour, 2024). As language learners continue to develop their evolving roles and competencies in this context, it is more crucial than ever that they be guided by teachers and provided with structured tasks and equal learning opportunities to enhance effective learning environments, addressing issues such as healthy access to technology, anxiety in digital environments, privacy of personal data, and ethical use of their own and others' data (Damaševičius & Sidekerskienė, 2024; Onu et al., 2024).

In summary, it is clear that metaverse learning environments are reshaping the landscape of EFL/ESL education by redefining learner roles and competencies

(Butvilas & Kołodziejski, 2024; Mansueto & Temprosa, 2025). As language learners become more active, self-directed, and community-oriented, educational institutions and their stakeholders may move away from viewing metaverse learning environments solely as technological tools and instead view them as an effective pedagogical ecosystem (Bobko et al., 2024; Meepung, 2025). Therefore, future research is expected to increase in quality, including findings that can reveal long-term examples and impacts of metaverse-based language learning from different perspectives, and to make lasting contributions to EFL/ESL education.

8 Current Trends in Metaverse Use in EFL/ESL Teaching

Parallel to the changing roles and competencies with metaverse, there is still room for improvement in the field of metaverse-supported EFL/ESL instruction. Nevertheless, it would be beneficial to have a look at the trends that have already emerged in the field of foreign language teaching, are acknowledged in the existing body of literature, and have the potential to be useful in the future. Many of these tendencies can be summarized as follows:

1. Applications that are designed to improve vocabulary and memory: A study conducted in Turkey by Çelik and Baturay (2024) demonstrated the positive impact of metaverse-based instruction on the acquisition and retention of vocabulary in a second language (L2). The study highlighted the benefits of increasing student engagement and fostering a sense of social presence and community.
2. Exercises in simulation and role-playing utilizing virtual reality and augmented reality: Sadigzade (2025) explored the experiences of language learners with actual situations that took place within virtual and augmented reality contexts. In the study it was demonstrated that the use of applications for activities such as ordering food at a cafe, requesting directions, and shopping has the potential to assist individuals in learning a foreign language by making them more fluent, conversational, and involved.
3. Gamification and apps that enhance motivation: In their research, Anggraeni et al. (2025) employed game elements such as incentives, leaderboards, leveling up, and avatar customization to assist individuals in getting better at learning a new language. It was emphasized that the incorporation of these elements into the instruction of foreign languages resulted in students having a greater interest in utilizing the language.
4. Applications for learner-community and social interaction: Chen (2024) found in their research that the metaverse creates a "sense of presence" in the setting of learning a foreign language. This "sense of presence" strengthens social characteristics such as a sense of community. Specifically, it was emphasized that students inhabit similar virtual worlds not just as individuals who consume information but also as individuals who interact with one another and learn together.

5. Teacher roles and development of teaching models: According to Kern (2024), the utilization of the metaverse in the teaching of foreign languages transforms teachers into guides, facilitators, and managers of technology. This is among the roles and activities that teachers engage in while constructing instructional models. Additionally, during this process of evolution, individuals have the ability to take on several roles, such as those of content creators, organizers of virtual environments, and specialists who influence the learning experience. He stated that the EFL/ESL teachers need to have a greater understanding of how to use technology in the classroom.
6. The establishment of technical infrastructure, including VR gear, AR tools, fifth generation (5G) networks, and even the incorporation of AI: Muthmainnah et al. (2025) highlighted the proliferation of tools, such as affordable virtual reality headsets, enhanced lightweight augmented reality tools, artificial intelligence-driven chatbots, voice recognition technology, and real-time feedback systems. They also highlighted the necessity for EFL and ESL students to acquire the necessary skills for these infrastructures.

9 The Trends in Future EFL/ESL Teaching and Possible Metaverse Areas for Development

The teaching of foreign/second languages through the use of the metaverse is still in its infancy; nevertheless, technological advancements, pedagogical innovations, and the incorporation of artificial intelligence are beginning to have an impact on the future of this field. In the not-too-distant future, it is projected that language learning experiences will develop into formats that are more individualized, interactive, and culturally richer. The following is a list of the most significant developments that are perhaps going to take place in the near future in the field of foreign/second language training that is supported by the metaverse:

As the Fig. 4 depicts above, with the integration of smart technologies, one of which is the metaverse in this chapter, the integration of the content and local culture, learner-specific learning paths, natural language use, practices, and experiences integrated with the spoken conditions of the target language, and different kinds of metaverse-integrated hybrid options for both learners and teachers, digital certification systems that are accepted all around the world, ethics including both privacy and data security for all of the individuals utilizing the tech-based environments in terms of teaching and learning, various models of affording the tech-based tools and environments via subscription or any other ways will be more prominent for foreign/second language education.

Local Culture & Content Integration
In Metaverse environments, culture is as important as language; local expressions, idioms, and cultural contexts are expected to be taught more effectively in virtual worlds. Localization of this content facilitates student engagement (Tafazoli, 2024).

Personalized Learning Paths
AI-based learning analytics enable educators to create individualized roadmaps for each student, provide learning environments tailored to their preferred styles, and optimize tasks, content, and other instructional elements according to their unique strengths and weaknesses (Muthmainnah et al., 2024).

Natural Language & Speaking Practice
Learners can benefit from more frequent encounters with 'daily life' scenarios in Metaverse worlds, including participation in chat groups within virtual environments, conversations with interactive NPCs, and culturally grounded role-playing practices (Sumon et al., 2024).

Proliferation of Hybrid Models
Traditional classroom and Metaverse/VR/AR-supported instructional combinations enrich the learning process by blending physical classroom education with immersive virtual experiences. (Ha, 2024).

Blockchain & Certification Systems
Securely recording the skills and achievements learners acquire in the Metaverse, as well as verifying internationally recognized certificates or digital badges through blockchain-like systems, enhances trust and transparency in digital learning credentials (Lee & Hwang, 2023).

Compatible Content & Accessibility
Solutions that function across different devices—such as mobile phones, low-cost VR headsets, and browser-based VR/AR—and remain usable in regions with low internet speeds, while also providing content adapted for students with disabilities, help ensure inclusive and accessible learning experiences (Mourtzis & Mystakidis, 2022).

Ethics, Privacy & Data Security Issues
Issues such as how learner data is used, how student privacy is protected, how identity and avatars are managed in virtual environments, and how content is controlled will become increasingly prominent (Kaddoura & Al Husseiny, 2023).

Changing Economic/Education Models
The models—such as subscriptions, micropayments, and content marketplaces—will continue to expand, allowing users to pay for the content or virtual tools they want and creating a clearer distinction between free and premium offerings. (Godwin-Jones, 2024).

Fig. 4 The future metaverse trends for EFL/ESL education

10 Conclusion

The emerging trends and innovations discussed in this chapter represent current developments in the rapidly evolving metaverse landscape. However, it is important to recognize that technological change is accelerating. New platforms, tools, and affordances will likely emerge that were not anticipated at the time of writing.

Educators and researchers should view this chapter as providing a snapshot of current trends while remaining open to rapid changes and new developments in the field.

In addition to being a novel approach to learning and teaching foreign/second languages, the metaverse also brings about a shift in the way EFL/ESL teachers instruct. So, students are afforded opportunities to learn that extend beyond what they are able to accomplish in the actual world thanks to the digital realm, which enables them to have linguistic and cultural connections in a variety of different ways. The teaching profession is undergoing a transformation as a result of this new learning ecosystem, which is being constructed concurrently with digitalization and other technological improvements mentioned in this chapter. As a result, it is increasingly important for practitioners, especially EFL/ESL teachers and learners, to acquire the skills necessary and competencies to utilize metaverse in addition to the other digital tools in the classroom and transfer them beyond the classrooms. As declared, the "7-Layer Metaverse Value Chain" alters the manner in which EFL/ESL language education progresses from the creation of information to the experience of the learner. This contributes to the whole process of bringing foreign/second language instruction into the digital environment in a manner that is sustainable.

Particularly, it is possible that the use of the metaverse in EFL/ESL education will improve both the teachers' and students' conditions, as well as providing extra opportunities for them that could be better for their own situations. In the near future, having the ability to teach foreign/second languages in the metaverse may not only be a possibility, but it may also be an essential component of education in this digital age. Consequently, the stakeholders of EFL/ESL education, including both the educational institutions and the researchers, need to take an active role in utilizing the educational potential offered by the metaverse, taking into consideration the ethical, pedagogical, and technical aspects of this rising arena.

References

Adera, N. (2025). Innovative learning spaces and blended learning: Quest for 21st century competency teaching and learning approaches. In G. Areba, B. Gisore, & E. Njurai (Eds.), *Creating dynamic space in higher education: Modern shifts in policy, competencies, and governance* (pp. 139–174). IGI Global Scientific Publishing. https://doi.org/10.4018/979-8-3693-6930-2.ch006

Al-Ansi, A. M., Jaboob, M., Garad, A., & Al-Ansi, A. (2023). Analyzing augmented reality (AR) and virtual reality (VR) recent development in education. *Social Sciences & Humanities Open, 8*(1), Article 100532. https://doi.org/10.1016/j.ssaho.2023.100532

Ali, M., Naeem, F., Kaddoum, G., & Hossain, E. (2023). Metaverse communications, networking, security, and applications: Research issues, state-of-the-art, and future directions. *IEEE Communications Surveys & Tutorials, 26*(2), 1238–1278. https://doi.org/10.1109/COMST.2023.3347172

Ajani, O. A. (2024). Enhancing pre-service teacher education: Crafting a technology-responsive curriculum for modern classrooms and adaptive learners. *Research in Educational Policy and Management, 6*(2), 209–229.

Al-kfairy, M., Sendaba, O., & Alfandi, O. (2025). Understanding trust in educational metaverse: The role of social cognitive theory constructs and perceived risks. *Kybernetes*.
Anggraeni, S. W., Sunendar, D., & Cahyani, I. (2025). Gamification as an innovation in enhancing language skills in the digital era. *KnE Social Sciences, 10*(12), 18–28. https://doi.org/10.18502/kss.v10i12.18857
Bailenson, J. (2024). Virtual reality. In M. C. Frank & A. Majid (Eds.). *Open encyclopedia of cognitive science*. https://doi.org/10.21428/e2759450.83209e91
Bibri, S. E., & Jagatheesaperumal, S. K. (2023). Harnessing the potential of the metaverse and artificial intelligence for the internet of city things: Cost-effective XReality and synergistic AIoT technologies. *Smart Cities, 6*(5), 2397–2429. https://doi.org/10.3390/smartcities6050109
Bobko, T., Corsette, M., Wang, M., & Springer, E. (2024). Exploring the possibilities of edu-metaverse: A new 3-D ecosystem model for innovative learning. *IEEE Transactions on Learning Technologies, 17*, 1278–1289. https://doi.org/10.1109/TLT.2024.336490
Burgess, S., & Moran, K. (2015). Use of virtual environments for simulation of accident investigation.
Butvilas, T., & Kołodziejski, M. (2024). Education policy strategies and applications for metaverse environments in teaching. *Multidisciplinary Journal of School Education, 13*(2), 169–190.
Chasubuta, A., & Ndibalema, P. (2024). Barriers hindering effective engagement in online assessment for teacher education in Tanzania: Perspectives from two teachers' colleges. *Journal of Issues and Practice in Education, 16*(1), 31–48.
Chen, H. J. (2024). Gather in the metaverse: Learning outcomes, virtual presence, and perceptions of high-and low-achieving pre-service teachers of English as a foreign language. *Education and Information Technologies, 29*(7), 8549–8577. https://doi.org/10.1007/s10639-023-12135-3
Cheng, R., Wu, N., Chen, S., & Han, B. (2022). Will metaverse be nextg internet? Vision, hype, and reality. *IEEE Network, 36*(5), 197–204. https://doi.org/10.1109/MNET.117.2200055
Chisunum, J. I., & Nwadiokwu, C. (2024). Enhancing student engagement through practical production and utilization of instructional materials in an educational technology class: A multifaceted approach. *NIU Journal of Educational Research, 10*(2), 81–89.
Çelik, F., & Baturay, M. H. (2024). The effect of metaverse on L2 vocabulary learning, retention, student engagement, presence, and community feeling. *BMC Psychology, 12*(1), 58. https://doi.org/10.1186/s40359-024-01549-4
Çelik, F. (2025). The impact of game-based metaverse on language learning motivation, anxiety, and vocabulary. *International Journal of Applied Linguistics*.
Çelik, F., & Ersanlı, C. Y. (2025). Developing and integrating metaverse into EFL listening skills to increase learners' self-determination based on social constructivist theory. *Journal of Computer Assisted Learning, 41*(6), Article e70151.
Damaševičius, R., & Sidekerskienė, T. (2024). Virtual worlds for learning in metaverse: A narrative review. *Sustainability, 16*(5), 2032.
Duan, H., Li, J., Fan, S., Lin, Z., Wu, X., & Cai, W. (2021). Metaverse for social good: A university campus prototype. In *Proceedings of the 29th ACM International Conference on Multimedia (MM '21)*. Association for Computing Machinery. https://doi.org/10.1145/3474085.3479238
Fang, L., & Shen, H. (2021). Changes in technology and civilization—A conceptual study of the metaverse. *Metaverse*, 2(2), 18. e 2, 18 pages. https://doi.org/10.54517/met.v2i2.1785
Ghoulam, K., & Bouikhalene, B. (2024). From classrooms to cyberspace: Understanding pedagogical approaches and outcomes in Metaverse learning environments. *Advances in Mobile Learning Educational Research, 4*(1), 983–993.
Guo, H., & Gao, W. (2022). Metaverse-powered experiential situational English-teaching design: An emotion-based analysis method. *Frontiers in Psychology, 13*, Article 859159. https://doi.org/10.3389/fpsyg.2022.859159
Hatmanto, E. D., Pratolo, B. W., & Intansari, M. (2023). Metaverse magic: Unveiling the pedagogical potential and transformative effects on intercultural communication in English language teaching. *English Language Teaching Educational Journal, 6*(1), 14–31.

Heider, K. L. (2021). Isolation, burnout, and a lost sense of belonging: Combating the challenges of distance education during a pandemic. *Distance Learning, 18*(1), 25–35. https://www.proquest.com/scholarly-journals/isolation-burnout-lost-sense-belonging-combating/docview/2551716178/se-2?accountid=25074

Hyun, J. J. (2021). A study on education utilizing metaverse for effective communication in a convergence subject. *International Journal of Internet, Broadcasting and Communication, 13*(4), 129–134.

Ibili, E., Ölmez, M., Ibili, A. B., Bilal, F., Cihan, A., & Okumuş, N. (2024). Assessing the effectiveness and student perceptions of synchronous online flipped learning supported by a metaverse-based platform in medical English education: A mixed-methods study. *Education and Information Technologies, 29*(14), 18643–18673.

Ibrahim, A. K. (2021). Evolution of the Web: From Web 1.0 to 4.0. *Qubahan Academic Journal, 1*(3), 20–28. https://doi.org/10.48161/qaj.v1n3a75

Iqbal, S., & Ali, A. (2024). Education and professional development: Opportunities and challenges for in-service teachers: A review. *Gomal University Journal of Research, 40*(1), 117–133.

Kennedy, T. J., & Sundberg, C. W. (2020). 21st century skills. In *Science education in theory and practice: An introductory guide to learning theory* (pp. 479–496). Springer International Publishing. https://doi.org/10.1007/978-3-030-43620-9_32

Kern, N. (2024). A vision for a humanising and sustainable future of language learning with the metaverse. *Journal of Futures Studies, 28*(4), 67–82. https://doi.org/10.6531/JFS.202406_28(4).0005

Kye, B., Han, N., Kim, E., Park, Y., & Jo, S. (2021). Educational applications of Metaverse: Possibilities and limitations. *Journal of Educational Evaluation for Health Professions, 18*, 1–13. https://doi.org/10.3352/jeehp.2021.18.32

Lampropoulos, G., Siakas, K., & Anastasiadis, T. (2019). Internet of things in the context of industry 4.0: An overview. *International Journal of Entrepreneurial Knowledge, 7*(1). https://doi.org/10.37335/ijek.v7i1.84

Mansueto, R., & Temprosa, M. A. (2025). Evaluating language policy and planning for english as a second language in Siquijor's basic education: A translanguaging perspective on school leadership and instructional practices. *Available at SSRN 5386866.*

Mazari, N. (2025). Building metacognitive skills using AI tools to help higher education students reflect on their learning process. *RHS: Revista Humanismo y Sociedad, 13*(1), 2.

Mckinsey. (2020). COVID-19: Implications for business in 2020. https://www.mckinsey.com/capabilities/risk-and-resilience/our-insights/covid-19-implications-for-business-2020

Meepung, T. (2025). A digital learning ecosystem through metaverse experiences to develop modern digital entrepreneurs competencies. *Journal of Education and Learning, 14*(1), 94–114.

Memon, F. N., & Memon, S. N. (2025). Digital divide and equity in education: Bridging gaps to ensure inclusive learning. In *Impact of digitalization on education and social sustainability* (pp. 107–130). IGI Global.

Mutchima, P., Leelakitpaisarn, Y., Pijitkamnerd, B., Phiwma, N., & Pantrakool, S. (2025). The effect of metaverse technology on multicultural learning: Strengthening the social attitudes, cultural awareness and critical thinking skills of secondary school students. *Journal of Education and e-Learning Research, 12*(1), 21–30.

Muthmainnah, M., Cardoso, L., Marzuki, A. G., & Al Yakin, A. (2025). A new innovative metaverse ecosystem: VR-based human interaction enhances EFL learners' transferable skills. *Discover Sustainability, 6*(1), 156. https://doi.org/10.1007/s43621-025-00913-7

Nair, A. J., Manohar, S., Mittal, A., & Chaudhry, R. (2024). Unleashing digital frontiers: Bridging realities of augmented reality, virtual reality, and the metaverse. In *The metaverse dilemma: Challenges and opportunities for business and society* (pp. 85–112). Emerald Publishing Limited. https://doi.org/10.1108/978-1-83797-524-220241006

Negre, Y., Patrício, R., & Ricarte, É. (2025). 20 teachers' perspectives. In *Handbook of design and industry: Scenarios for sustainable futures* (p. 323).

Omar, K., & Gómez, J. M. (2025, April). Metaverse-enhanced learning ecosystem (MELE) Framework. In *2025 1st International Conference on Computational Intelligence Approaches and Applications (ICCIAA)* (pp. 1–7). IEEE.

Onu, P., Pradhan, A., & Mbohwa, C. (2024). Potential to use metaverse for future teaching and learning. *Education and Information Technologies, 29*(7), 8893–8924.

Park, S., & Kim, S. (2022). Identifying world types to deliver gameful experiences for sustainable learning in the Metaverse. *Sustainability, 14*(3). https://doi.org/10.3390/su14031361

Pérez-Jorge, D., Olmos-Raya, E., González-Contreras, A. I., & Pérez-Pérez, I. (2025, March). Technologies applied to education in the learning of English as a second language. In *Frontiers in Education* (Vol. 10, p. 1481708). Frontiers Media SA.

Procel, G. J. O., Medina, M. L. F., Sotomayor, D. J., & Sanchez, M. A. (2024). *Using technology in English teaching.* Ciencia Latina Internacional. https://doi.org/10.37811/cli_w1048

Radoff, J., (2021, 7 Nisan). *The Metaverse value-chain.* https://medium.com/building-the-metaverse/the-metaverse-value-chain-afcf9e09e3a7

Rahimi, R. A., & Oh, G. S. (2024). Rethinking the role of educators in the 21st century: Navigating globalization, technology, and pandemics. *Journal of Marketing Analytics, 12*(2), 182–197.

Rof, A., Bikfalvi, A., & Marques, P. (2022). Pandemic-accelerated digital transformation of a born digital higher education institution. *Educational Technology & Society, 25*(1), 124–141. https://www.jstor.org/stable/48647035

Rostami, S., & Maier, M. (2022). The metaverse and beyond: Implementing advanced multiverse realms with smart wearables. *IEEE Access, 10*, 110796–111080. https://doi.org/10.1109/ACCESS.2022.3215736

Sadigzade, Z. (2025). Immersive and gamified approaches: VR/AR in language learning. *Porta Universorum, 1*(6), 15–24. https://doi.org/10.69760/portuni.0106002

Sahlberg, P. (2004). Teaching and globalization. *Managing global transitions*, *2*(1), 65. https://www.proquest.com/scholarly-journals/teaching-globalization/docview/902707207/se-2

Seock, Y. K., & Shin, J. (2025). Beyond the classroom walls: Leveraging virtual platform to enhance student engagement and learning. *International Journal of Fashion Design, Technology and Education*, 1–14.

Singh, M., Sun, D., & Zheng, Z. (2024). Enhancing university students' learning performance in a metaverse-enabled immersive learning environment for STEM education: A community of inquiry approach. *Future in Educational Research, 2*(3), 288–309.

Smart, J., Cascio, J., Paffendorf, J., Bridges, C., Hummel, J., Hursthouse, J., & Moss, R. (2007). A cross-industry public foresight project. *Proceeding of Metaverse Roadmap Pathways 3DWeb*, 1–28.

Soboleva, E. V., Karavaev, N. L., Shalaginova, N. V., & Perevozchikova, M. S. (2018). Improvement of the robotics cross-cutting course for training of specialists in professions of the future. *European Journal of Contemporary Education*, *7*(4), 845–857. https://doi.org/10.13187/ejced.2018.4.845

Stephenson, N. (1992). *Snow crash* (2011th ed.). Penguin.

Suvorova, T., & Demirbilek, M. (2025). Beyond adaptive learning: Harnessing AI for metacognitive skill development. In J. Zhao, V. Kumar, P. Katina, & J. Richards (Eds.), *Humans and generative AI tools for collaborative intelligence* (pp. 1–24). IGI Global Scientific Publishing. https://doi.org/10.4018/979-8-3693-8332-2.ch001

Tabassum, A., & Qadir, J. (2024). A critical AI approach for managing the risks in educational metaverses. In *EDULEARN24 Proceedings* (pp. 9578–9586). IATED.

Thakur, S. S., Bandyopadhyay, S., & Datta, D. (2023). Artificial intelligence and the metaverse: Present and future aspects. In A. E. Hassanien, A. Darwish, & M. Torky (Eds.), *The future of metaverse in the virtual era and physical world* (Studies in Big Data, Vol. 123, pp. 169–184). Springer. https://doi.org/10.1007/978-3-031-29132-6_10

Thelma, C. C., Sain, Z. H., Shogbesan, Y. O., Phiri, E. V., & Akpan, W. M. (2024). Digital literacy in education: Preparing students for the future workforce. *International Journal of Research, 11*(8), 327–343.

Urbaite, G. (2024). The role of technology in modern language education. *EuroGlobal Journal of Linguistics and Language Education, 1*(1), 3–10.

von Gillern, S., Rose, C., & Hutchison, A. (2024). How students can be effective citizens in the digital age: Establishing the teachers' perceptions on digital citizenship scale. *British Journal of Educational Technology, 55*(5), 2093–2109.

Wang, Z., Zou, D., Peng, P., Wang, F. L., Lee, L. K., & Xie, H. (2025). Effects of mobile metaverse-based vocabulary learning on learners' perception and performance: a case study of Chinese EFL learners. *Journal of Computers in Education*, 1–34.

Wardat, S., & Akour, M. (2024). Investigating the adoption of metaverse-based immersive learning in TESOL. *Emerging Science Journal, 8*, 396–409. https://doi.org/10.28991/ESJ-2024-SIED1-023

Wei, Z. (2024). Navigating digital learning landscapes: Unveiling the interplay between learning behaviors, digital literacy, and educational outcomes. *Journal of the Knowledge Economy, 15*(3), 10516–10546.

Yao, C., Kanjanakate, S., & Jantharajit, N. (2024). Enhancing ESL learners' executive function and cognitive ability: A hybrid approach of situated learning and task-based language teaching. *Australian Journal of Applied Linguistics*, *7*(2), 1522. https://doi.org/10.29140/ajal.v7n2.1522

Yıldız, T. (2024). The future of digital education: Artificial intelligence, the Metaverse, and the transformation of education. *İstanbul Üniversitesi Sosyoloji Dergisi, 44*(2), 969–988.

Yusupalieva, S. (2024). Developing students communicative competence using authentic materials with information technologies. *International Journal of Industrial Engineering, Technology & Operations Management, 2*(2), 59–62.

Zengin, Ö., & Aksu, M. (2017). A review study on the integration of technology into foreign language education in Turkey. *Ankara University Journal of Faculty of Educational Sciences (JFES), 50*(2), 79–104. https://doi.org/10.1501/Egifak_0000001398

Zhang, W. (2022). The role of technology-based education and teacher professional development in English as a foreign language classes. *Frontiers in Psychology, 13*, Article 910315. https://doi.org/10.3389/fpsyg.2022.910315

Ayfer Su-Bergil is a researcher at Amasya University, Türkiye. Her work investigates the transformative impact of metaverse technologies on EFL/ESL education. Su-Bergil examines the 7-Layer Metaverse Value Chain and its reflections on language teaching processes. She analyzes changing roles and competencies for teachers and learners. Her contributions highlight future trends, ethical concerns, and innovative applications in virtual learning environments.

Research Trends and Research Agenda for Metaverse-Based Language Teaching and Learning

Pan Qi and Hassan Abuhassna

Abstract With the rapid advancement of technology and innovation, metaverse technologies have revealed great potential to transform different sectors, such as education. Although several studies have investigated the integration of metaverse technologies into education, a comprehensive overview of its current status in language education remains absent. To address this gap, this study conducted a bibliometric analysis of 840 articles published between 2000 and 2024. This study aims to describe the application and the influence of integrated metavese technologies in language education. Using performance analysis, this study identified the publication trends, the most influential articles, and the productive countries in this field. Using science mapping, this study revealed four major theme clusters: (1) virtual reality-based language learning, (2) augmented reality and mobile-assisted language learning, (3) eye-tracking and vocabulary acquisition in VR, and (4) emerging immersive environments for vocabulary learning. These themes collectively shed light on the intellectual structure of this field. At the end, based on the results, this study proposed a research agenda for future work, emphasizing the need for integrating AI to further explore personalized learning, students' emotions, and ethical issues in immersive learning environments, which contributes to the theory and practice of this field.

Keywords Metaverse · Language education · Bibliometric analysis · Research trends · Research agenda

P. Qi (✉)
School of Foreign Languages, Zao Zhuang University, Zao Zhuang, China
e-mail: panqi@graduate.utm.my

H. Abuhassna
Faculty of Social Sciences and Liberal Arts, UCSI University, Kuala Lumpur, Malaysia

F. Çelik and C. Yangın Ersanlı (eds.), *Metaverse-Based Language Learning and Teaching*, English Language Education 49,
https://doi.org/10.1007/978-3-032-31366-9_13

1 Introduction

Metaverse, first introduced in 1992 through the science fiction novel Snow Crash written by Neal Stephenson (Aydın, 2022), is not a new concept. The metaverse is mainly linked to Virtual Reality (VR), which is a three-dimensional environment that allows students to enter, make friends, shop, communicate, and interact with others. Essentially, the Metaverse is a virtual environment where people can establish social connections similar to those in reality.

In recent years, metaverse technologies have also been widely used in the field of education (Almeman et al., 2025). This is because the metaverse combines communication, entertainment, and gamification, which allows students to engage in their learning process, interact with their classmates and instructors, and stimulate their learning motivation. Although the metaverse became prominent in education after 2020, this study expanded the definition of the metaverse, including the metaverse applications and immersive technologies.

Metaverse particularly aligns with language learning. Recent studies have demonstrated that metaverse technologies can decrease students' anxiety (Yu & Duan, 2024) and provide contextualized and immersive environments (Cantone et al., 2023) for language learning. Based on such an immersive environment, students can engage in situated practice, thereby enhancing their oral proficiency, communication skills, and vocabulary acquisition (Darmawansah et al., 2025; Xie et al., 2025).

Previous reviews have concentrated on narrow dimensions of metaverse applications in education rather than offering an entire view of this field (Table 1). For example, earlier reviews focused on adoption, acceptance, and the IS model for metaverse application in education (Al-kfairy et al., 2024; Alfaisal et al., 2024a, 2024b; Chua & Yu, 2024). Several reviews proposed the strategic frameworks for incorporating metaverse technologies into educational ecosystems (De Felice et al., 2023; Li & Yu, 2023; Panda et al., 2024; Roy et al., 2023). In addition, some reviews have addressed the applications and challenges of metaverse tools in language education (Fan & Chiang, 2023; Parmaxi, 2023). In particular, Han et al. (2023) examined a specific platform, such as the application of Roblox in learning.

Although existing reviews demonstrated diverse perspectives on metaverse tools in education, their scope is delimited, and most of the reviews are qualitative. As the body of knowledge of metaverse-based language education remains fragmented, it is necessary to provide a holistic overview of this field. In this regard, bibliometric analysis, which mainly relies on statistical methods, is capable of providing a comprehensive map of the present body of knowledge and research agenda for future work (Chandra et al., 2022). As noted by Donthu et al. (2021), the technique of bibliometric analysis was categorized into two main sections: performance analysis and science mapping. Based on this analytic approach, the present study aims to identify critical research gaps and outline key priorities for advancing the field of metaverse-based language teaching and learning. Besides mapping the existing body of knowledge, this study also seekss to outline the research the agenda that highlights current understanding of important questions requiring need investigation. As

Table 1 Past reviews on metaverse-based language education

No	Author(s) (year)	Review type	Review focus
1	Al-kfairy et al. (2024)	Systematic review	Factors influencing the adoption and acceptance of Metaverse technologies in education
2	Panda et al. (2024)	Systematic review	Present status and future directions for the Metaverse in higher education
3	De Felice et al. (2023)	Systematic review	The role of the metaverse as a tool in education from the academic perspective
4	Parmaxi (2023)	Critical review	Features of VR used for different types of activities for language learning
5	Roy et al. (2023)	Systematic review	Framework of Metaverse in Education
6	Han et al. (2023)	Systematic review	The benefits and challenges of using Roblox for learning
7	Fan and Chiang (2023)	Systematic review	Research topics, methodologies, common tools, impacts, and challenges of Metaverse tools in language education
8	Li and Yu (2023)	Systematic review	Integrate the evidence to generate a model that links the education-based metaverse
9	Alfaisal et al. (2024a, 2024b)	Systematic review	To evaluate research from information systems (IS) models to guide future research
10	Chua and Yu (2024)	Systematic review	The acceptability of the use of the Metaverse in education

the field develops and initial studies are completed, new research priorities will likely emerge. The goal of this agenda is to guide the research community in building a robust empirical foundation for MBLTL while remaining responsive to new challenges and opportunities that arise as both technology and pedagogy continue to evolve.

In the absence of a comprehensive review that examines metaverse-based language education, as listed in Table 1, and given the widely acknowledged role of metaverse technologies in shaping the future of education, this review seeks to address the following research questions:

RQ1: What is the publication trend of research on metaverse-based language education?
RQ2: What are the most influential articles on metaverse-based language education?
RQ3: What are the productive countries in metaverse-based language education?

RQ4: What are the keywords and themes of metaverse-based language education?
RQ5: What is the research agenda for metaverse-based language education?

2 Methodology

In contrast to the systematic literature review, which often relies on manual screening and qualitative synthesis, Bibliometric analysis relies on scientific and quantitative techniques to analyze patterns (publication, relevant source, authors, institutions), relationships (co-citation, co-word, co-authorship), and trends (keywords co-occurrence) of the body of knowledge (İri & Ünal, 2024). This study adopts bibliometric analysis to map the performance and science mapping of the literature on metaverse-based language education. According to Donthu et al. (2021), the procedure of conducting bibliometric analysis comprises four steps, including defining the aims and scope of the bibliometric study, choosing the techniques for bibliometric analysis, collecting the data for bibliometric analysis, running the bibliometric analysis, and reporting the findings.

Step 1: Defining the aims and scope of the bibliometric analysis

Defining the aims and scope is a crucial step in conducting bibliometric analysis. The objective of the bibliometric analysis should involve performance analysis, which examines productivity, while science mapping refers to the intellectual structure of a field, including major themes and topics. The scope of this study is to elucidate the landscape of metaverse-based language education.

Step 2: Choosing the techniques for bibliometric analysis

Following the first step, the second step involves the selection of the appropriate bibliometric analysis techniques. The objective of this study is to create a roadmap of metaverse-based language education. To achieve this, this study conducts the performance analysis employing a series of bibliometric results, such as publication trend, citation, h-index, cite score, etc. In the meantime, science mapping, including co-occurrence and co-citation analysis, is utilized to uncover the key themes and topics of the field.

Step 3: Collecting the data for bibliometric analysis

The third step seeks to collect data for bibliometric analysis. This study uses the Scopus database as the main database due to its comprehensive coverage of peer-reviewed journals relevant to educational technology and its ease of integration with bibliometric analysis tools such as VOSviewer and Biblioshiny (Abuhassna et al., 2022). In addition, to ensure a systematic methodological approach, this study employs the PRISMA (Preferred Reporting Items for Systematic Reviews and Meta-Analyses) framework proposed by Moher et al. (2009) to guide the retrieval of the data. Two independent reviewers screened all records using the criteria and checked the results to ensure accuracy. After the initial research based on a set of well-defined

Table 2 Keywords applied

Database	Search queries
Scopus	TITLE-ABS-KEY (metaverse OR "virtual reality" OR "augmented reality" OR "extended reality" OR XR OR VR OR AR OR "virtual world*" OR "immersive learning" OR "virtual environment*")AND ("language learning" OR "language education" OR "language acquisition" OR "second language" OR "foreign language" OR EFL OR ESL OR "multilingual education")

Table 3 Inclusion and exclusion criteria for study selection

Inclusion criteria	Exclusion criteria
11. Filtered by relevant keywords	
21. Publication from 2000 to 2024	11. Publications before 2000 were not accepted, and as 2025 is not yet over, publications in 2025 were also not accepted
31. Articles written in the English language	21. Articles written in any other languages
41. Subject areas related to (Computer science, arts and humanities, social science)	31. Any other subject areas
51. The article type was "articles" only	41. Conferences, blogs, thesis, and book chapters

keywords, 2077 articles were identified, and then some inclusion and exclusion criteria were applied. To ensure the data quality, only peer-reviewed journal articles indexed in Scopus were included. Conference papers, book chapters, and any other publications were excluded. As a result, 840 articles were retained for the final analysis of this study. The complete list of these 840 included studies is provided in Supplementary File A. The keywords applied, the inclusion and exclusion criteria, as well as the PRISMA framework, are presented in Tables 2, 3, and Fig. 1, respectively.

Step 4: Running the bibliometric analysis and reporting the findings

The final step involves running the analysis and reporting the findings. Biblioshiny and VOSviewer were used for performance and network visualization. The findings of the bibliometric analysis are presented and discussed in the following sections.

3 Performance Analysis of Metaverse-Based Language Education Research

The findings presented as follows correspond to research questions from one to three, focusing on publication trends, influential articles, and productive countries.

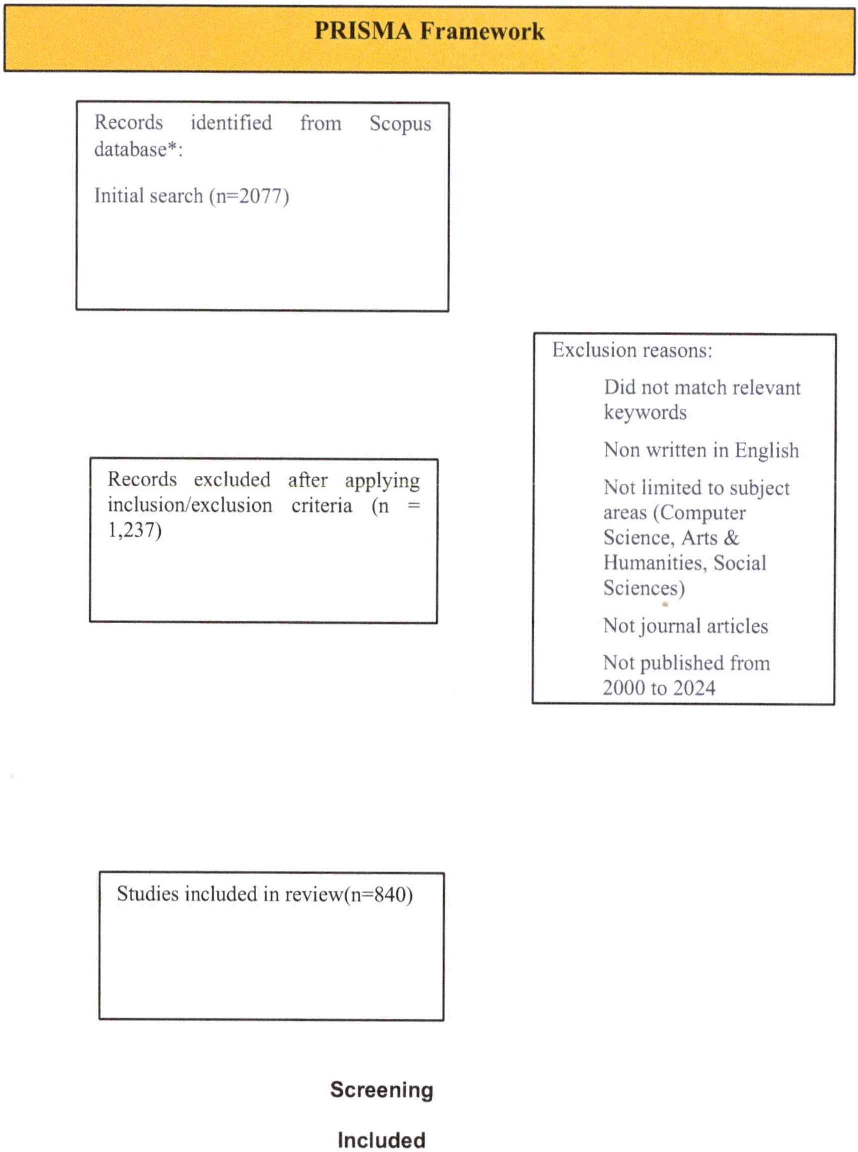

Fig. 1 Prisma framework for this review

3.1 Publication Trends for Metaverse-Based Language Education Research

To answer Research Question 1, the researchers analyzed the total publications in this field from 2000 to 2024. The researchers chose the timespan from 2000 to 2024

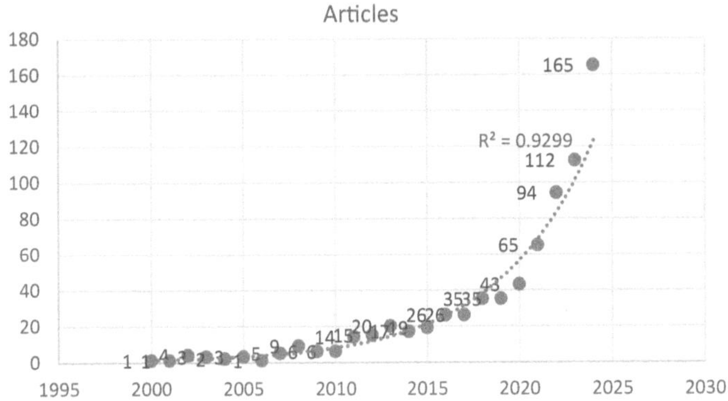

Fig. 2 Publication trends

to comprehensively capture technological and conceptual evolution from immersive technologies to recent metaverse-based learning environments. Although the term metaverse was widely used after 2020, earlier studies on immersive technologies, such as VR, provided a strong foundation in both pedagogy and technology, which helped to shape the later research in this field.

According to Fig. 2, the development of this field experienced three distinct phases. In phase 1 (2000 to 2010), the annual publication of metaverse-based language education remained below 10, indicating that its development was only in its initial phase. During the second phase (2011 to 2019), the publication demonstrates a steady growth every year, meaning that metaverse-based language education was gaining attention gradually among researchers.

Noteworthily, in the third phase (2020 to 2024), the publication witnessed a remarkable growth, beginning with 43 publications in 2020, and reaching a peak of 165 in 2024, highlighting the significant expansion ($R^2 = 0.9566$) and rapid development of this field in the past five years. This growth reflected not only the acceleration of technological integration into education but also the wide applications of metaverse technologies into language education (Gruber et al., 2023; Tan et al., 2024).

3.2 *Most Influential Articles for Metaverse-Based Language Education Research*

To address research question 2, the researchers employed R software to conduct a performance analysis of total citations across the 840 included articles. Table 4 presents the influential articles for metaverse-based language education research by total citation. Thorne et al. (2009)'s article on the second language use, socialization, and learning in gaming learning environment listed as the most influential article, with

364 citation, followed by Chien et al. (2020)'s article on effects of peer assessment within the context of s virtual reality on language education and Kessler (2018)'s article on Technology and the future of language teaching with 298 and 285 citation, respectively.

Thorne et al. (2009) explored how the learners used technology for second language practice in spaces between formal instruction and informal contexts.

Table 4 Top-cited original articles on metaverse-based language education

Rank	Title	Author(s)	Journal	TC	C/Y
1	Second Language Use, Socialization, and Learning in Internet Interest Communities and Online Gaming	Thorne et al. (2009)	The Modern Language Journal	364	22.75
2	Effects of peer assessment within the context of spherical video-based virtual reality on EFL students' English-speaking performance and learning perceptions	Chien et al. (2020)	Computers & Education	298	59.6
3	Technology and the future of language teaching	Kessler (2018)	Foreign language annals	285	40.7
4	Gaming as extramural English L2 learning and L2 proficiency among young learners	Sylvén and Sundqvist (2012)	ReCALL	266	20.5
5	The symbolic dimensions of the intercultural	Kramsch (2011)	Language Teaching	258	18.4
6	Learning English with Augmented Reality: Do learning styles matter?	Hsu (2017)	Computers & Education	237	29.6
7	Virtual reality in language learning: a systematic review and implications for research and practice	Parmaxi (2023)	Interactive Learning Environments	225	112.5
8	A context-aware ubiquitous learning environment for language listening and speaking	Liu (2009)	Journal of Computer-Assisted Learning	214	13.4
9	Language Learning in Virtual Reality Environments: Past, Present, and Future	Lin and Lan (2015)	Educational Technology & Society	190	19
10	Cross-cultural analysis of users' attitudes toward the use of mobile devices in second and foreign language learning in higher education: A case from Sweden and China	Viberg and Grönlund (2013)	Computers & Education	179	14.9

TC = Total Citation C/Y = Citation per Year

Through a comprehensive review, the researcher stated that the language socialization into sophisticated communicative practices required an extended period, during which creative expressions can serve as a tool to facilitate identity development and management. Their study offered valuable insights into language use and identity from a sociocultural perspective. Chien et al. (2020) developed a spherical video-based virtual reality (SVVR) environment to situate students in authentic English-speaking contexts. Furthermore, the researchers applied the peer assessment (PA) strategy for guiding students to provide comments on peers' speaking and to make reflections on their performance. The results revealed that the peer-assessment-based SVVR approach significantly improved learners' English speaking, learning motivation, and critical thinking, while also reducing their learning anxiety. Chien et al. (2020) provided strong evidence to examine the effect of immersive VR learning on language learning. Kessler (2018) emphasized that technological advancements, like big data, augmented reality (AR), virtual reality (VR), and computer-mediated communication (CMC), are transforming language education. They highlighted the need to create an interactive, immersive, and student-centered learning environment using these technologies. The authors also called for teacher preparation to address the challenges associated with integrating technology into language education. The contribution of these studies is not only that they are the earliest publications in this field, but also because they shaped theoretical and methodological foundations for later research.

3.3 Most Productive Countries for Metaverse-Based Language Education Research

Research question 3 pertains to identifying the most productive countries in metaverse-based language education. Figure 3 illustrates the most productive countries in this domain. Notably, China stands out from any other country in this field with 367 publications. The USA ranks second with 172 outputs. Then Iran and Spain follow, each with 61 publications, while Turkey and Australia contributed 60 and 59 publications, respectively. Other active countries like Saudi Arabia, 43 publications; the UK, 42 publications; and Canada, 36 publications. Several Asia countries also hold sustainable research in this area, such as Malaysia, with 58 publications, South Korea, 57 publications, Indonesia, 51 publications, Japan, and Thailand, 39 publications, respectively.

These findings demonstrate a growing global interest in metaverse-based language education. The dominant role of China and the USA might be due to continuous investment from the government and institutions in digital education, and high publication pressures within the academic system. In the meantime, European and Asia–Pacific countries such as Spain, Turkey, and South Korea also show emerging engagement. This can be attributed to international collaborations and policy-driven efforts in this field. However, the dominant output in a few countries also demonstrates

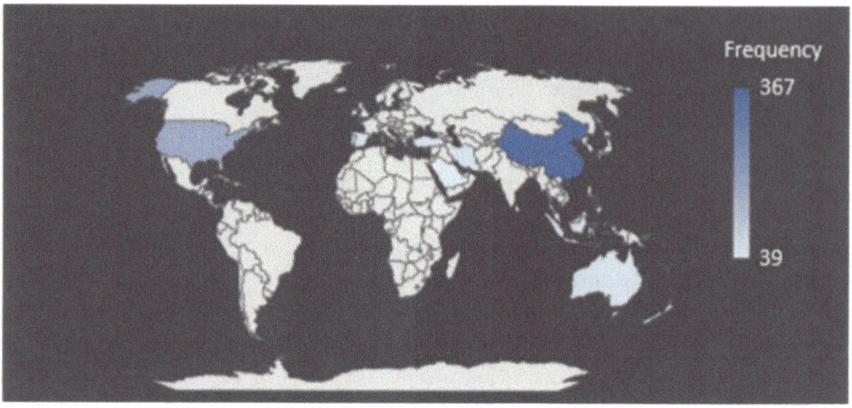

Fig. 3 Most productive countries in metaverse-based language education

geographic disparities and calls for international collaboration and participation in metaverse-based language research.

4 Science Mapping of Metaverse-Based Language Education Research

This section presents findings related to research questions four and five, with an emphasis on publication key themes and ways forward for metaverse-based language education.

4.1 Keywords and Themes of Metaverse-Based Language Education Research

(1) Keywords of Metaverse-Based Language Education Research

This section aims to answer the first part of RQ4: What are the keywords of metaverse-based language education research?—The researchers conducted a co-occurrence analysis of author keywords using VOSviewer software. The author's keyword analysis is essential for bibliometric analysis, as it helps shape the knowledge within the research field (Pearson, 2024). The keyword occurrences and their network visualisation are illustrated in Table 5 and Fig. 4.

The top 20 keywords according to their occurrences are illustrated in Table 5. Before conducting the analysis, synonymous and variant terms, such as "VR", "Virtual Reality", "Augmented Reality", "Virtual Environments", and "Vocabulary

Table 5 Top keywords by occurrence

Keyword(s)	Occurrence(s)
Virtual reality	158
Augmented reality	150
Language learning	93
Virtual worlds	59
Second life	33
Metaverse	25
Vocabulary learning	31
EFL	24
Second language acquisition	20
Computer-assisted language learning	20
Immersive learning	20
Motivation	19
Educational technology	17
Mobile learning	15
Higher education	14
gamification	13
Collaborative learning	12

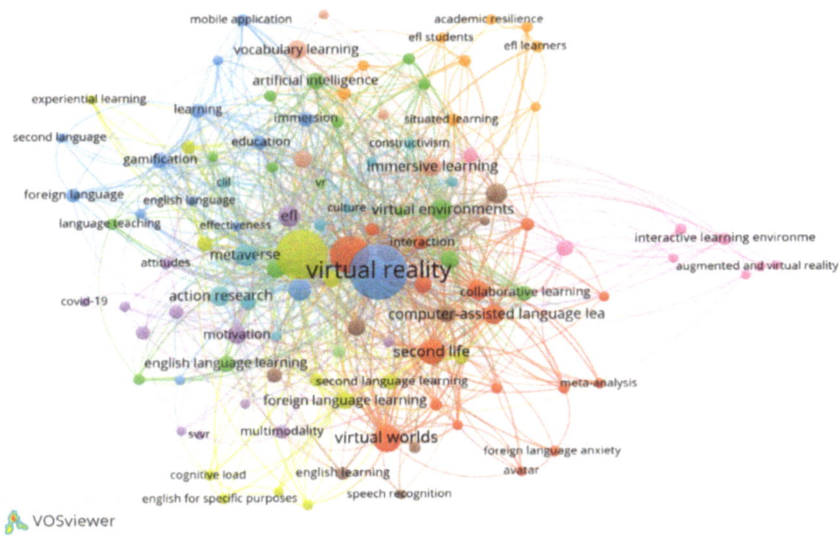

Fig. 4 Keyword co-occurrence network

Acquisition" and were merged. In doing so, the keywords were cleaned and normalized to ensure consistency and accuracy. As a result, Virtual reality emerges as the most prominent keyword, with 158 occurrences, followed by augmented reality (150), language learning (93), virtual worlds (59), and Second Life (33). This reflects the research scope in this field. In addition, the relationship among keywords is also presented in Fig. 4. The size of each node represents the frequency of the keyword, while the link between each node indicates the co-occurrence between keywords. In this regard, according to the keywords network, Virtual reality, augmented reality, language learning, virtual worlds, and Second Life are the most prominent topics, and co-occur more frequently than any other keywords, emphasizing their importance in this research field.

4.2 Themes of Metaverse-Based Language Education Research

This section is to address the second part of RQ4: What are the key themes of metaverse-based language education research?—The researchers applied the bibliometrix package in RStudio software (Aria & Cuccurullo, 2017) to generate a diagram that illustrates the key themes within the field. As Furstenau et al. (2021) suggested, themes with higher centrality and density are considered both mature and influential, revealing their central role in this research landscape.

This diagram divides themes into four quadrants, with each quadrant representing the developmental stage of the theme accordingly.

Upper-right quadrant (Motor Themes): Themes in this quadrant signify higher centrality and density, indicating they are influential and well-established.

Lower-right quadrant (Basic Themes): Themes in this quadrant are known as basic themes, which means they form the foundation of this research field, though they have lower density.

Upper-left quadrant (Niche Themes): Themes in this quadrant are known as niche themes, which means these themes hold high impact but low centrality.

Lower-left quadrant (Emerging/Declining Themes): These themes represent emerging or declining themes.

(1) **Upper-Right Quadrant (Motor Themes) Cluster 1: Virtual Reality Environments in Language Learning**

In this cluster, keywords like virtual reality, virtual environment reflect the main focus on the impact of immersive technologies on students' language learning. Several studies have examined these themes from different perspectives. For example, Wu et al. (2023) discussed the role of virtual reality in transforming language learning. Similarly, Chien et al. (2020) found that a spherical video-based virtual reality (SVVR) environment combined with peer assessment (PA) significantly enhanced EFL students' English speaking, motivation, and critical thinking. A study by

Kaplan-Rakowski and Gruber (2024) also highlighted that high-immersion Virtual Reality (VR) is a valuable technique to improve students' reading comprehension. Moreover, ChatGPT can serve as an effective tool to create an interactive and supportive learning context, for example, providing real-time feedback and personalized guidance (Barrot, 2024). Peixoto et al. (2023) also reported that interactive immersive VR (iVR) approaches can improve students' motivation, satisfaction, and preference. These studies collectively indicate that a central role of virtual reality in fostering students' learning outcomes, including cognitive and non-cognitive learning outcomes, highlighting its potential in shaping future language learning.

(2) **Upper-Middle Quadrant (Basic Themes) Cluster 2: Augmented Reality & Mobile-Assisted Language Learning**

The upper middle quadrant of this diagram also highlights some keywords, such as "augmented reality", "mobile application", and "language learning", indicating that there are still many scholars who continue to examine the effects of Augmented Reality or mobile-based technologies on language learning. Analysis of existing literature reveals that AR is a promising tool to support language learning across different dimensions, like vocabulary, reading, cultural knowledge, and sustainable learning outcomes.

For instance, Korosidou (2024) demonstrated that AR has a positive effect on students' long-term alphabet and vocabulary learning and retention, and facilitates their motivation. Furthermore, Di Fuccio et al. (2024) further found that AR contributed significantly to students' cultural knowledge, learning progression, and workflow.

Several studies focus on the potential of augmented reality in special education, particularly for children with learning disabilities (Shaaban & Mohamed, 2024), developmental communication disability (Bryant et al., 2024). The findings revealed that AR can enhance their language skills by providing an immersive learning environment and a personalized learning experience.

Therefore, the literature collectively suggests that Augmented reality is an effective approach for language education, as it not only contributes to students' language acquisition but also facilitates students' engagement, motivation, and cultural awareness.

(3) **Lower-Right Quadrant (Niche Themes) Cluster 3: Eye-Tracking and Vocabulary Acquisition in VR**

Situated in the lower-right of this quadrant, this cluster was formed with keywords like "virtual reality", "eye-tracking", and "vocabulary acquisition", suggesting that these themes are foundational but still require further theoretical and methodological development. Several studies have focused on the implementation of these technologies to enhance students' attention focus, engagement, and overall learning effectiveness. For example, Machwate et al. (2021) integrated eye-tracking with VR technologies into a foreign language classroom. Following the intervention, findings indicated that this pedagogical approach improved students' attention focus, metacognitive regulation, and finally strengthened their vocabulary retention. In a related study, Li et al. (2022) employed VR as an audiovisual technology to improve students' vocabulary acquisition. The results demonstrated that VR not only enhanced students' vocabulary acquisition but also increased their engagement. Moreover, Wang et al. (2021) further determined Visual Prompt Scaffolding-Based Virtual Reality Approach had a positive effect on improving students' reading comprehension.

Despite these themes still being in development, the existing studies highlighted the trends of combining immersive and audiovisual technologies to support effective language learning.

(4) **Lower-Left Quadrant (Emerging/Declining Themes) Cluster 4: Emerging Immersive Environments for Vocabulary Learning**

This cluster comprises keywords such as "virtual reality", " metaverse", and "vocabulary learning", representing these themes related to the use of immersive environments for vocabulary learning. However, this cluster is positioned in the lower-left quadrant, which was known as emerging themes, meaning that this area is still in its early stage of development. Some previous studies have started to explore this area. For example, the article by Chen et al. (2024) reported a study in which students engaged with a self-regulated vocabulary learning mobile application (SRVL-MAPP) pedagogical approach, which led to improvement in students' vocabulary learning achievement and motivation. Kim Hua Tan et al. (2024) demonstrated how metaverse-based technologies can be applied in English language instruction, thereby enhancing students' communication competencies. Further contribution to students' language learning outcomes through virtual environment includes leveraging Problem-Based Learning for students' reading and writing skills, along with their motivation (AbdAlgane et al., 2024). While this area has not been fully studied, these themes have great potential for improving language learning through immersive technologies (Fig. 5).

In conclusion, these four clusters collectively revealed the evolution themes from technology-oriented applications, such as VR, AR, toward learner-centered and cognition research, such as eye-tracking and vocabulary learning. However, there remains theoretical fragmentation, as most studies pay attention to technological dimensions. It is necessary to consolidate and guide future empirical studies by integrating relevant learning theories.

4.3 Research Agenda for Metaverse-Based Language Education Research

To address research question 5, the researchers categorized the topics into three groups based on frequency: Established topics (frequency > 100), developing topics (frequency 30–100), and emerging topics (frequency < 30) (Fig. 6). The next section will explain in detail each topic.

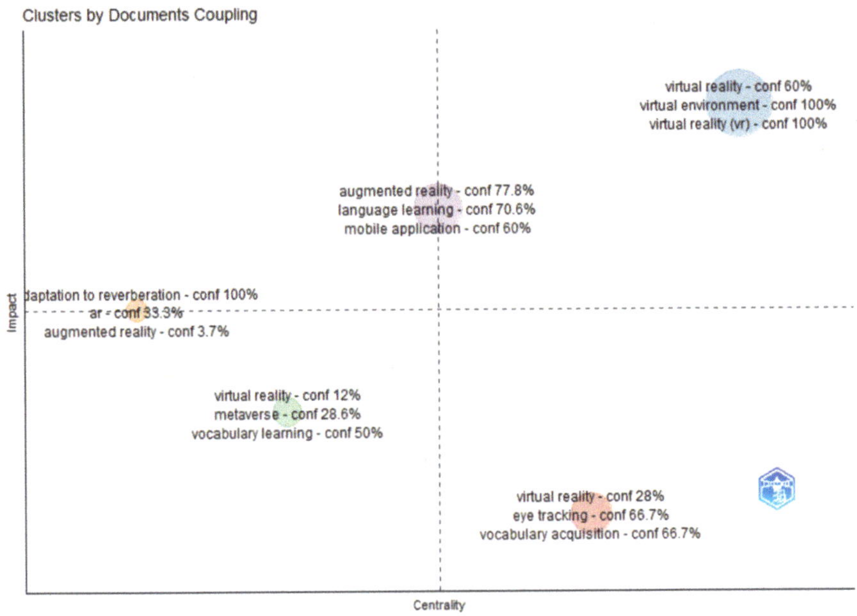

Fig. 5 Thematic mapping of metaverse-based language education

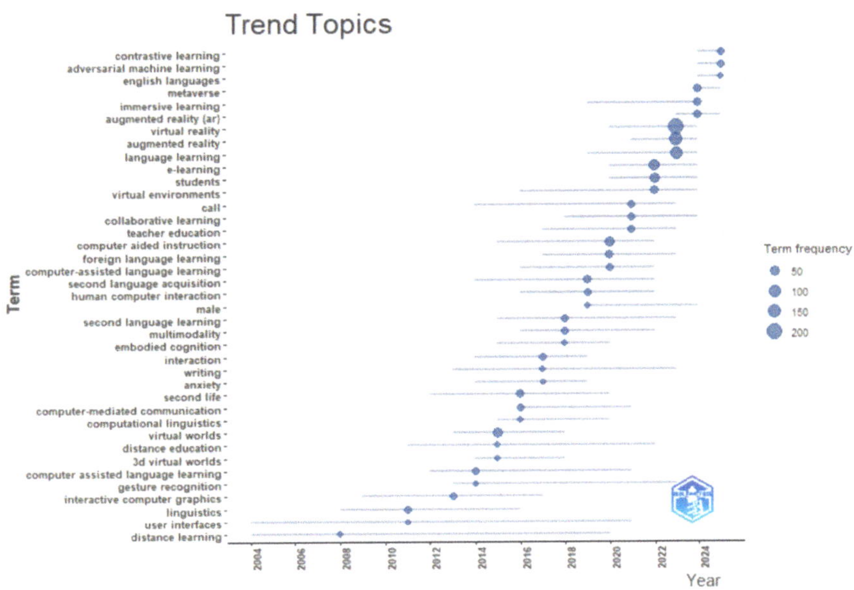

Fig. 6 Trend topics

(1) **Established Topics**

The first group is known for established topics, which include keywords like "virtual reality"(227 occurrences), "augmented reality" (146 occurrences), and "language learning"(101 occurrences), indicating these areas have been widely examined by researchers. These technologies have been proven to enhance students' language learning experience through the immersive, interactive, and personalized learning environment (Godwin-Jones, 2023; Parmaxi et al., 2024; Yadav et al., 2025).

Therefore, it may be worthwhile to integrate AI for personalized learning with VR and AR in the future. Moreover, researchers should incorporate a long-term study design (Prabakaran et al., 2025). In terms of technological barriers of VR and AR, future work is worth developing platforms accessible for students across different educational contexts to ensure educational equality (Prabakaran et al., 2025). Additionally, teachers' training programs should consider (Zhao et al., 2023). This future direction aligns with immersive learning that focuses also on personalized learning and interaction in language education.

(2) **Developing Topics**

The keywords in this group also appeared with higher frequency; the main keywords of this group are "e-learning", "computer-aided instruction", "second life", "second language acquisition", and "foreign language learning", etc. These keywords reflect the trend of integration of digital and virtual technologies into language education.

Among them, E-learning and computers played a crucial role as they provided an accessible and effective tool for foreign language instruction (Savin, 2020; Vu et al., 2019). Particularly, Second Life is a virtual world. The researchers started to incorporate it into foreign language learning, especially to improve students' intercultural communication skills (Kruk, 2022). Considering this, syllabi relevant to virtual learning environments should be carefully designed and considered in the future (Torres Martín et al., 2021). Furthermore, researchers still need to determine which intelligent technologies most effectively enhance students' learning outcomes (Zou & Thomas, 2019). Finally, comparative studies are recommended in the future, as researchers need to understand the influence of technology on language education in the world, as well as to uncover the cultural factors that moderate these effects (Chua et al., 2024).

In conclusion, these studies indicate that future work should move towards how digital and virtual technologies can improve students' language learning.

(3) **Emerging Topics**

The third group is emerging topics, which comprises the main keywords like "3d virtual worlds", "anxiety", "second language learning", "human–computer interaction", "multimodality", and "gesture recognition". This demonstrated that the researchers are beginning to pay attention to a more emotional, more immersive, and more multimodal metaverse-based language education.

The emergence of the keyword "anxiety" indicates that one of the emerging topics is students' emotional engagement. Several researchers, Han et al. (2024), Zakharova Garcia (2025), and Castro and Shelton-Strong (2024) have proposed focusing on students' emotional engagement in this complex virtual learning environment. Moreover, Ethical issues, including data privacy, network security, and digital literacy, play a vital role in ensuring the effective and safe use of metaverse-based technologies in language education (Alfiras et al., 2023; Khadivi, 2024). At the end, another promising direction is the development of an adaptive learning system in metaverse-based education. Future studies need to systematically analyze and explore how such adaptive learning systems respond to individual differences and support long-term learning effects.

Overall, future direction should focus on human-centered and students' well-being, ethical issues, and inclusive participation in metaverse-based language learning.

5 Discussion

This bibliometric analysis was divided into two main sections to provide comprehensive information about metaverse-based language education. The first section focused on performance analysis, addressing publication trends, the most influential article, and the most productive articles about metaverse-based language education research. The second section is science mapping, which includes keywords co-occurrence, themes, as well as the research agenda of this area.

Research questions from 1 to 3 correspond to performance analysis. The results highlighted that the metaverse-based language education has experienced a sharp increase in recent years, particularly from 2020–2024. This aligns with the global shift towards technology-integrated education, especially during COVID-19, which accelerated the advancement of metaverse technologies. The analysis of the most influential articles emphasized the interdisciplinary nature of this field, such as peer assessment, game-based learning, and computational language incorporated into metaverse-based language education (Alfaisal et al., 2024a, 2024b; Çelik & Baturay, 2024; Lee, 2022). Regarding the most productive countries, China and the USA were identified as the two leading contributors, demonstrating not only the remarkable development of China in recent years (Wu & An, 2024). In addition, the research output mainly concentrated on a small number of countries, emphasizing a significant problem of geographic disparity.

The aim of research question 4 was to identify the landscape of metaverse-based language education. Through keywords co-occurrence analysis, it became evident that virtual reality and augmented reality are still the main focus of this area. In addition, according to thematic mapping, VR-based language education has emerged as a motor theme (Wu et al., 2023). In contrast, other areas like augmented reality (Di Fuccio et al., 2024) or eye-tracking-based language learning (Machwate et al., 2021) are still in their initial stage of development. Furthermore, several studies have focused on students with special needs and inclusive education, demonstrating the potential of metaverse technologies in promoting access to language learning education (Shaaban & Mohamed, 2024). However, these studies often lack a systematic theoretical framework to guide their research, thus limiting the generalizability of the findings across students from different educational contexts (Porras et al., 2024). In the meantime, the application of adaptive technologies, like mobile applications, indicates a close attention to personalized learning (Barrot, 2024) in metaverse-based language education. Notably, many studies did not pay attention to ethical issues, data privacy, accessibility, and long-term effects in a real learning context (Ismail et al., 2025; Marín & Tur, 2023).

The objective of research question 5 is to formulate the research agenda for future work. The researchers identified three categories of research topics supported by different kinds of studies. In terms of established research topics, the researchers proposed integrating AI technologies to achieve personalized learning within metaverse-based language education (Yadav et al., 2025). However, despite this potential, existing studies have failed to examine its long-term effect on learning outcomes (Prabakaran et al., 2025). In addition, most research overlooks technological barriers and teachers' professional development in the teaching practice (Zhao et al., 2023). Therefore, future work should address gaps and consider the accessibility of the platform and teachers' training programs. In terms of developing topics, future work should identify the most effective intelligent technologies, optimize course design, and conduct comparative studies. Concerning emerging topics, it could be worthwhile to consider students' emotional engagement, as well as ethical issues, to ensure the effective and safe metaverse-based technologies to support language learning.

6 Conclusion

While the growing global interest in metaverse-based language education, a comprehensive overview of its publication trends, most influential articles, and most productive countries, key themes, and research agenda of this field have been underexplored. This study aims to fill in this gap by conducting a bibliometric analysis of 840 articles published from 2020 to 2024, and providing the performance analysis and science mapping of this area.

The performance analysis revealed a significant surge in research output in this area since 2020, with China and the United States emerging as leading contributors. The analysis of the most influential articles also demonstrated the nature of interdisciplinarity in this field. However, despite the promising research productivity, there is still a geographic disparity. Concerning science mapping, keywords co-occurrence analysis, and thematic mapping revealed four main clusters, from motor theme, like virtual reality-based language learning, to biographic tracking and emotional factors influencing language learning. Based on keyword analysis and thematic mapping, the researchers also present a structured research agenda for future work.

This study contributes to theory and practice in the field of metaverse-based language education. From a theoretical perspective, it presents a roadmap of the current status of metaverse technologies in education. By clarifying keyword analysis and thematic mapping, this study enables researchers and practitioners to better understand which topics should be explored in the future. From a practical perspective, educators, instructional designers may refer to our findings to effectively integrate AI technologies into metaverse-based language education, thereby improving learning outcomes. Furthermore, policymakers may use this view to consider technological barriers, ethical issues, and teachers' training programs when enacting policies.

However, this study is not without limitations. While the Scopus base was recognized for its comprehensive coverage and user-friendly features, the exclusive use may exclude the relevant publications indexed from other databases such as WOS and ERIC. This limitation may lead to selection bias in the dataset. Therefore, future studies should address this limitation by integrating multiple databases. In addition, since this study relied on a keyword-based search strategy, it potentially missed relevant studies that use different terminology. Moreover, although this study categorized clusters and provided a research agenda based on existing literature, future analysis should incorporate content analysis to deepen pedagogical insights. Finally, this study only implemented keyword co-occurrence analysis for science mapping; future work should incorporate other analyses, like co-citation analysis, citation analysis, and co-authorship analysis, to deepen the intellectual structure of this field.

In conclusion, with the rapid advancement of technology, the metaverse has become a broader research field. To align with this era, AI integration is crucial for the future development of metaverse-based language education. In this context, personalized learning supported by AI should be explored more deeply. Moreover, our analysis also highlighted the importance of students' emotions in metaverse-based education. Given this, future work should be more open-minded and consider which factors may impact students' emotions in this context. Finally, as AI-integrated metaverse-based language education continues to evolve, ethical issues, data privacy, and data security should also be addressed in the future.

References

AbdAlgane, M., Ali, R., Elkot, M. A., & Zaki Youssif, E. M. (2024). Leveraging problem-based learning via virtual environments to enhance business students' English and motivation. *International Journal of Interactive Mobile Technologies, 18*(13). https://doi.org/10.3991/ijim.v18i13.48109

Abuhassna, H., Van, N. T., Yahaya, N., Zakaria, M. A. Z. M., Awae, F., Al Zitawi, D. U. D., & Bayoumi, K. (2022). Strategies for successful blended learning—A bibliometric analysis and reviews. *International Journal of Interactive Mobile Technologies, 16*(13), 66–80. https://doi.org/10.3991/ijim.v16i13.30739

Al-kfairy, M., Ahmed, S., & Khalil, A. (2024). Factors impacting users' willingness to adopt and utilize the metaverse in education: A systematic review. *Computers in Human Behavior Reports*, 100459. https://doi.org/10.1016/j.chbr.2024.100459

Alfaisal, R., Hashim, H., & Azizan, U. H. (2024, June). Empowering the metaverse in education: ChatGPT's role in transforming learning experiences. In *International Conference on Breaking Barriers with Generative Intelligence* (pp. 13–31). Springer Nature Switzerland. https://doi.org/10.1007/978-3-031-65996-6_2

Alfaisal, R., Hashim, H., & Azizan, U. H. (2024b). Metaverse system adoption in education: A systematic literature review. *Journal of Computers in Education, 11*(1), 259–303. https://doi.org/10.1007/s40692-022-00256-6

Alfiras, M., Bojiah, J., Mohammed, M. N., Ibrahim, F. M., Ahmed, H. M., & Abdullah, O. I. (2023). Powered education based on Metaverse: Pre- and post-COVID comprehensive review [Review]. *Open Engineering, 13*(1), Article 20220476. https://doi.org/10.1515/eng-2022-0476

Almeman, K., El Ayeb, F., Berrima, M., Issaoui, B., & Morsy, H. (2025). The integration of AI and metaverse in education: A systematic literature review [Review]. *Applied Sciences (Switzerland), 15*(2), Article 863. https://doi.org/10.3390/app15020863

Aria, M., & Cuccurullo, C. (2017). Bibliometrix: An R-tool for comprehensive science mapping analysis. *Journal of Informetrics, 11*(4), 959–975. https://doi.org/10.1016/j.joi.2017.08.007

Aydın, S. (2022). The metaverse in foreign language learning: A theoretical framework. *Innovational Research in ELT, 3*(2), 12–19. https://doi.org/10.29329/irelt.2022.505.2

Barrot, J. S. (2024). ChatGPT as a language learning tool: An emerging technology report. *Technology, Knowledge and Learning, 29*(2), 1151–1156. https://doi.org/10.1007/s10758-023-09711-4

Bryant, L., Bailey, B., & Hemsley, B. (2024). Developing and evaluating an immersive augmented reality application for children with developmental communication disability: InterPlay for language learning. *International Journal of Speech-Language Pathology, 1–14*. https://doi.org/10.1080/17549507.2024.2361734

Cantone, A. A., Francese, R., Sais, R., Santosuosso, O. P., Sepe, A., Spera, S., & Vitiello, G. (2023, September). Contextualized experiential language learning in the metaverse. In *Proceedings of the 15th Biannual Conference of the Italian SIGCHI Chapter* (pp. 1–7). https://doi.org/10.1145/3605390.3605395

Castro, E., & Shelton-Strong, S. J. (2024). Exploring emotions inlanguage learning: Learners' self-awareness, personal growth, and transformation on a CLIL course. *Language Teaching Research*. https://doi.org/10.1177/13621688241267366

Çelik, F., & Baturay, M. H. (2024). The effect of metaverse on L2 vocabulary learning, retention, student engagement, presence, and community feeling. *BMC Psychology, 12*(1). https://doi.org/10.1186/s40359-024-01549-4

Chandra, S., Verma, S., Lim, W. M., Kumar, S., & Donthu, N. (2022). Personalization in personalized marketing: Trends and ways forward. *Psychology & Marketing, 39*(8), 1529–1562. https://doi.org/10.1002/mar.21670

Chen, C., Jamiat, N., & Du, S. (2024). Effect of a self-regulated vocabulary learning mobile application on EFL students' vocabulary learning achievement and motivation. *International Journal of Interactive Mobile Technologies, 18*(16). https://doi.org/10.3991/ijim.v18i16.49755

Chien, S.-Y., Hwang, G.-J., & Jong, M.S.-Y. (2020). Effects of peer assessment within the context of spherical video-based virtual reality on EFL students' English-speaking performance and learning perceptions. *Computers & Education, 146*, Article 103751. https://doi.org/10.1016/j.compedu.2019.103751

Chua, H. W., & Yu, Z. (2024). A systematic literature review of the acceptability of the use of Metaverse in education over 16 years. *Journal of Computers in Education, 11*(2), 615–665. https://doi.org/10.1007/s40692-023-00273-z

Chua, N. A., Ahmad, M. B., Ismail, I. L. M., Mutalib, N. B. A., Saputra, J., Soon, G. Y., & Leng, N. K. (2024). Technology integration in learning Mandarin Chinese as a foreign language in Malaysia and Germany. *International Journal of Advanced and Applied Sciences, 11*(9), 192–202. https://doi.org/10.21833/ijaas.2024.09.021

Darmawansah, D., Hwang, G. J., Lin, C. J., & Febiyani, F. (2025). An artificial intelligence-supported GFCA learning model to enhance L2 students' role-play performance, English speaking and interaction mindset. *Educational Technology Research and Development,* Article 100001. https://doi.org/10.1007/s11423-025-10453-6

De Felice, F., Petrillo, A., Iovine, G., Salzano, C., & Baffo, I. (2023). How does the metaverse shape education? A systematic literature review. *Applied Sciences, 13*(9), 5682. https://doi.org/10.3390/app13095682

Di Fuccio, R., Kic-Drgas, J., & Woźniak, J. (2024). Co-created augmented reality app and its impact on the effectiveness of learning a foreign language and on cultural knowledge. *Smart Learning Environments, 11*(1), https://doi.org/10.1186/s40561-024-00304-x

Donthu, N., Kumar, S., Mukherjee, D., Pandey, N., & Lim, W. M. (2021). How to conduct a bibliometric analysis: An overview and guidelines. *Journal of Business Research, 133,* 285–296. https://doi.org/10.1016/j.jbusres.2021.04.070

Fan, L., & Chiang, J. (2023). A systematic review of the application of metaverse in language education: Prominent themes, research methods, impacts, and future challenges. *Journal of Language Teaching, 3*(10), 1–14. https://doi.org/10.54475/jlt.2023.026

Furstenau, L. B., Sott, M. K., Homrich, A. J. O., Kipper, L. M., Dohan, M. S., López-Robles, J. R., Cobo, M. J., & Tortorella, G. L. (2021). An overview of 42 years of lean production: Applying bibliometric analysis to investigate strategic themes and scientific evolution structure. *Technology Analysis and Strategic Management, 33*(9), 1068–1087. https://doi.org/10.1080/09537325.2020.1865530

Godwin-Jones, R. (2023). Presence and agency in real and virtual spaces: The promise of extended reality for language learning. *Language Learning and Technology, 27*(3), 6–26. https://doi.org/10.64152/10125/73529

Gruber, A., Matt, E., & Leier, V. (2023). Transforming Foreign language education: Exploring educators' practices and perspectives in the (post-)pandemic era. *Education Sciences, 13*(6), Article 601. https://doi.org/10.3390/educsci13060601

Han, J., Liu, G., & Gao, Y. (2023). Learners in the Metaverse: A systematic review on the use of roblox in learning. *Education Sciences, 13*(3), 296. https://doi.org/10.3390/educsci13030296

Han, L., Osman, S. Z. M., & Che, J. (2024). Impact of online learning interactive experience on language learners' emotional engagement. *Eurasian Journal of Applied Linguistics, 10*(1), 115–126. https://doi.org/10.32601/ejal.10111

Hsu, T.-C. (2017). Learning English with augmented reality: Do learning styles matter? *Computers & Education, 106*, 137–149. https://doi.org/10.1016/j.compedu.2016.12.007

İri, R., & Ünal, E. (2024). Bibliometric analysis bibliometric analysis of research (1980–2023). *Ahi Evran Üniversitesi Sosyal Bilimler Enstitüsü Dergisi, 10*(2), 386–403. https://doi.org/10.31592/aeusbed.1446738

Ismail, M., Madathil, N. T., Alalawi, M., Alalawi, S., & Alrabaee, S. (2025, April). Navigating ethical dilemmas in the implementation of AI-driven educational technologies. In *2025 IEEE Global Engineering Education Conference (EDUCON)* (pp. 1–5). IEEE. https://doi.org/10.1109/EDUCON62633.2025.11016612

Kaplan-Rakowski, R., & Gruber, A. (2024). An experimental study on reading in high-immersion virtual reality. *British Journal of Educational Technology, 55*(2), 541–559. https://doi.org/10.1111/bjet.13392

Kessler, G. (2018). Technology and the future of language teaching. *Foreign Language Annals, 51*(1), 205–218. https://doi.org/10.1111/flan.12318

Khadivi, A. (2024). Investigating the applications and challenges of metaverse in education: A systematic review. *Journal of Philosophical Investigations, 18*(49), 193–218. https://doi.org/10.22034/jpiut.2024.62124.3787

Korosidou, E. (2024). The effects of augmented reality on very young learners' motivation and learning of the alphabet and vocabulary. *Digital, 4*(1), 195–214. https://doi.org/10.3390/digital4010010

Kramsch, C. (2011). The symbolic dimensions of the intercultural. *Language Teaching, 44*(3), 354–367. https://doi.org/10.1017/S0261444810000431

Kruk, M. (2022). Dynamicity of perceived willingness to communicate, motivation, boredom and anxiety in second life: The case of two advanced learners of English. *Computer Assisted Language Learning, 35*(1–2), 190–216. https://doi.org/10.1080/09588221.2019.1677722

Lee, J. (2022). Problem-based gaming via an augmented reality mobile game and a printed game in foreign language education. *Education and Information Technologies, 27*(1), 743–771. https://doi.org/10.1007/s10639-020-10391-1

Li, M., & Yu, Z. (2023). A systematic review on the metaverse-based blended English learning. *Frontiers in Psychology, 13*, 1087508. https://doi.org/10.3389/fpsyg.2022.1087508

Li, Y., Ying, S., Chen, Q., & Guan, J. (2022). An experiential learning-based virtual reality approach to foster students' vocabulary acquisition and learning engagement in English for geography. *Sustainability, 14*(22), 15359. https://doi.org/10.3390/su142215359

Lin, T.-J., & Lan, Y.-J. (2015). Language learning in virtual reality environments: Past, present, and future. *Journal of Educational Technology & Society, 18*(4), 486–497.

Liu, T. Y. (2009). A context-aware ubiquitous learning environment for language listening and speaking. *Journal of Computer Assisted Learning, 25*(6), 515–527. https://doi.org/10.1111/j.1365-2729.2009.00329.x

Machwate, S., Bendaoud, R., Henze, J., Berrada, K., & Burgos, D. (2021). Virtual exchange to develop cultural, language, and digital competencies. *Sustainability, 13*(11), 5926. https://doi.org/10.3390/su13115926

Marín, V. I., & Tur, G. (2023). Data privacy in educational technology: Findings of a scoping review. *Edutec, 83*, 7–23. https://doi.org/10.21556/edutec.2023.83.2701

Moher, D., Liberati, A., Tetzlaff, J., & Altman, D. G. (2009). Preferred reporting items for systematic reviews and meta-analyses: The PRISMA statement. *BMJ, 339*. https://doi.org/10.1136/bmj.b2535

Panda, G., Arora, M., Ghoshal, I., Garza-Reyes, J. A., & Kaswan, M. S. (2024). Application of metaverse in higher education: A systematic literature review and bibliometric analysis. *The TQM Journal* (ahead-of-print). https://doi.org/10.1108/TQM-08-2024-0279

Parmaxi, A. (2023). Virtual reality in language learning: A systematic review and implications for research and practice. *Interactive Learning Environments, 31*(1), 172–184. https://doi.org/10.1080/10494820.2020.1765392

Parmaxi, A., Berns, A., Adinolfi, L., Gruber, A., Fominykh, M., Voreopoulou, A., & Hadjistassou, S. (2024, June). Augmented reality in language learning: practical implications for researchers and practitioners. In *International conference on human-computer interaction* (pp. 138–154). Springer Nature Switzerland. https://doi.org/10.1007/978-3-031-61691-4_10

Pearson, W. S. (2024). Research topics in applied linguistics as keywords from authors and keywords from abstracts: A bibliometric study. In *A scientometrics research perspective in applied linguistics* (pp. 113–134). https://doi.org/10.1007/978-3-031-51726-6_5

Peixoto, B., Bessa, L. C. P., Gonçalves, G., Bessa, M., & Melo, M. (2023). Teaching EFL with immersive virtual reality technologies: A comparison with the conventional listening method. *IEEE Access, 11*, 21498–21507. https://doi.org/10.1109/ACCESS.2023.3249578

Porras, V. C. A., Olaya, C. I. B., & Cuervo, S. A. C. (2024). Exploring the impact of the metaverse on English language teaching: Perspectives of students from the University of Boyacá. *Journal of Infrastructure, Policy and Development, 8*(7), Article 4779. https://doi.org/10.24294/jipd.v8i7.4779

Prabakaran, N., Patrick, H. A., & Kareem, J. (2025). Enhancing English language proficiency and digital literacy through metaverse-based learning: A mixed-methods study in higher education. *Journal of Information Technology Education: Research, 24*. https://doi.org/10.28945/5484

Roy, R., Babakerkhell, M. D., Mukherjee, S., Pal, D., & Funilkul, S. (2023). Development of a framework for metaverse in education: A systematic literature review approach. *IEEE Access, 11*, 57717–57734. https://doi.org/10.1109/ACCESS.2023.3283273

Savin, N. (2020). The importance of educational resources using online platforms in pre-university education. *Scientific Bulletin of Naval Academy, 23*(2), 169–171. https://doi.org/10.21279/1454-864X-20-I2-022

Shaaban, T. S., & Mohamed, A. M. (2024). Exploring the effectiveness of augmented reality technology on reading comprehension skills among early childhood pupils with learning disabilities. *Journal of Computers in Education, 11*(2), 423–444. https://doi.org/10.1007/s40692-023-00269-9

Sylvén, L. K., & Sundqvist, P. (2012). Gaming as extramural English L2 learning and L2 proficiency among young learners. *ReCALL, 24*(3), 302–321. https://doi.org/10.1017/S095834401200016X

Tan, K. H., Naim, M. K., Wahi, W., Arham, A. F., & Yunos, N. (2024). Metaverse-based activities for enhancing communicative competencies among young learners. *International Journal of Interactive Mobile Technologies, 18*(21), 4–25. https://doi.org/10.3991/ijim.v18i21.47867

Thorne, S. L., Black, R. W., & Sykes, J. M. (2009). Second language use, socialization, and learning in Internet interest communities and online gaming. *The Modern Language Journal, 93*, 802–821. https://doi.org/10.1111/j.1540-4781.2009.00974.x

Torres Martín, C., Acal, C., El Homrani, M., & Mingorance Estrada, Á. C. (2021). Impact on the virtual learning environment due to COVID-19. *Sustainability, 13*(2), 582. https://doi.org/10.3390/su13020582

Viberg, O., & Grönlund, Å. (2013). Cross-cultural analysis of users' attitudes toward the use of mobile devices in second and foreign language learning in higher education: A case from Sweden and China. *Computers & Education, 69*, 169–180. https://doi.org/10.1016/j.compedu.2013.07.014

Vu, D. H., Nguyen, P. T., Nguyen, Q. L. H. T. T., Huynh, V. D. B., Le, Q. T. T., Doan, T. H. D., Chung, M. T., & Le, B. G. P. (2019). Success factors framework for the implementation of e-learning systems in Vietnamese universities. *Journal of Critical Reviews, 6*(4), 1–6. https://doi.org/10.22159/jcr.06.04.01

Wang, Z., Guo, Y., Wang, Y., Tu, Y.-F., & Liu, C. (2021). Technological solutions for sustainable development: Effects of a visual prompt scaffolding-based virtual reality approach on EFL learners' reading comprehension, learning attitude, motivation, and anxiety. *Sustainability, 13*(24), 13977. https://doi.org/10.3390/su132413977

Wu, J. G., Zhang, D., & Lee, S. M. (2023). Into the brave new metaverse: Envisaging future language teaching and learning. *IEEE Transactions on Learning Technologies, 17*, 44–53. https://doi.org/10.1109/TLT.2023.3259470

Wu, Y., & An, S. (2024, July). The development path and implementation challenges of integrating the metaverse into international Chinese language education. In *Proceedings of the 2nd International Conference on Educational Knowledge and Informatization* (pp. 104–110). https://doi.org/10.1145/3691720.3691738

Xie, T., Zhang, H., & Yang, Y. (2025). Effect of immersive virtual reality based upon input processing model for second language vocabulary retention. *Education and Information Technologies, 30*(9), 12365–12385. https://doi.org/10.1007/s10639-025-13333-x

Yadav, R., Nghiem, X. H., & Yadav, M. (2025). Adaptive AI in metaverse language education. In *Harnessing chatbots for effective language teaching* (pp. 49–74). https://doi.org/10.4018/979-8-3693-9974-3.ch003

Yu, Z., & Duan, P. (2024). Meta-analyses of anxiety, motivation, performance, satisfaction, and self-efficacy in virtual reality-assisted language education. *Foreign Language Annals, 57*(2), 550–580. https://doi.org/10.1111/flan.12748

Zakharova Garcia, G. (2025). The power of emotion in EFL: Discourse analysis of electronic study resources [Article]. *Journal of Vasyl Stefanyk Precarpathian National University, 12*(1), 6–14. https://doi.org/10.15330/jpnu.12.1.6-14

Zhao, X., Ren, Y., & Cheah, K. S. L. (2023). Leading virtual reality (VR) and augmented reality (AR) in education: Bibliometric and content analysis from the web of science (2018–2022). *SAGE Open, 13*(3). https://doi.org/10.1177/21582440231190821

Zou, B., & Thomas, M. (2019). *Recent Developments in Technology-Enhanced and Computer-assisted Language Learning*. IGI Global https://doi.org/10.4018/978-1-7998-1282-1

Pan Qi is a researcher in the School of Foreign Languages at Zao Zhuang University, China. Her expertise includes bibliometric analyses of immersive technologies in language education. Qi conducts comprehensive reviews of metaverse applications from virtual reality to emerging environments. She identifies major research clusters and proposes agendas for personalized learning and ethical issues. Her work contributes to theory and practice in the evolving field.

Hassan Abuhassna is a lecturer in Faulty of Social Sciences and Liberal Arts, UCSI university, Malaysia. His research focuses on educational technology and bibliometric studies in language learning. Abuhassna collaborates on analyses of metaverse integration and research trends. He addresses intellectual structures and future directions in immersive environments. His contributions support evidence-based advancements in metaverse-based pedagogy.

Index

F. Çelik and C. Yangın Ersanlı (eds.), *Metaverse-Based Language Learning and Teaching*, English Language Education 49,
https://doi.org/10.1007/978-3-032-31366-9

FSC
www.fsc.org
MIX
Papier | Fördert gute Waldnutzung
FSC® C083411

Kolibri 360 GmbH
Ferdinand-Jühlke-Straße 7
99095 Erfurt, Deutschland
produktsicherheit@kolibri360.de